PURE WORSHIP

Monographs in Baptist History

VOLUME 3

SERIES EDITOR
Michael A. G. Haykin, The Southern Baptist Theological Seminary

EDITORIAL BOARD
Matthew Barrett, The Southern Baptist Theological Seminary
Peter Beck, Charleston Southern University
Anthony L. Chute, California Baptist University
Jason G. Duesing, Southwestern Baptist Theological Seminary
Nathan A. Finn, Southeastern Baptist Theological Seminary
Crawford Gribben, Trinity College, Dublin
Gordon L. Heath, McMaster Divinity College
Barry Howson, Heritage Theological Seminary
Jason K. Lee, Southwestern Baptist Theological Seminary
Thomas J. Nettles, The Southern Baptist Theological Seminary
James A. Patterson, Union University
James M. Renihan, Institute of Reformed Baptist Studies
Jeffrey P. Straub, Central Baptist Theological Seminary
Brian R. Talbot, Broughty Ferry Baptist Church, Scotland
Malcolm B. Yarnell III, Southwestern Baptist Theological Seminary

Ours is a day in which not only the gaze of western culture but also increasingly that of Evangelicals is riveted to the present. The past seems to be nowhere in view and hence it is disparagingly dismissed as being of little value for our rapidly changing world. Such historical amnesia is fatal for any culture, but particularly so for Christian communities whose identity is profoundly bound up with their history. The goal of this new series of monographs, Studies in Baptist History, seeks to provide one of these Christian communities, that of evangelical Baptists, with reasons and resources for remembering the past. The editors are deeply convinced that Baptist history contains rich resources of theological reflection, praxis and spirituality that can help Baptists, as well as other Christians, live more Christianly in the present. The monographs in this series will therefore aim at illuminating various aspects of the Baptist tradition and in the process provide Baptists with a usable past.

Pure Worship

The Early English Baptist Distinctive

MATTHEW WARD

With a Foreword by Malcolm B. Yarnell III

◆PICKWICK *Publications* • Eugene, Oregon

PURE WORSHIP
The Early English Baptist Distinctive

Monographs in Baptist History 3

Copyright © 2014 Matthew Ward. All rights reserved. Except for brief quotations in critical publications or reviews, no part of this book may be reproduced in any manner without prior written permission from the publisher. Write: Permissions, Wipf and Stock Publishers, 199 W. 8th Ave., Suite 3, Eugene, OR 97401.

Pickwick Publications
An Imprint of Wipf and Stock Publishers
199 W. 8th Ave., Suite 3
Eugene, OR 97401

www.wipfandstock.com

ISBN 13: 978-1-62564-213-4

Cataloguing-in-Publication data:

Ward, Matthew.

    Pure worship : the early English Baptist distinctive / Matthew Ward ; foreword by Malcolm B. Yarnell III.

    xvi + 242 pp. ; 23 cm. Includes bibliographical references and index.

    Monographs in Baptist History 3

    ISBN 13: 978-1-62564-213-4

    1. Baptists—England—Liturgy—History—17th century. 2. Baptists—England—History—17th century. I. Yarnell, Malcolm B. II. Title. III. Series.

BX6276 .W37 2014

Manufactured in the U.S.A.

*To Shelly,
and to all who love God's church*

Contents

Foreword by Malcolm B. Yarnell III ix

Preface xi

List of Abbreviations xv

one   Introduction   1

two   The Liturgical World of the English Reformation   25

three   Free Worship and a New Concept of the Church   52

four   True Worship and a New Appreciation of the Scriptures   110

five   Gospel Worship and a New Purpose of the Gathering   143

six   Baptist Worship and a New Identity of the Faithful?   183

seven   Conclusion: The Importance of Pure Worship   217

Bibliography   225

Index   239

Foreword

A New Entrant in the Battle for Historic Baptist Identity

Baptist history is filled with instances of controversy between Baptists and others. It is also replete with disputes between Baptists themselves. It should be of little surprise, therefore, that the discipline of Baptist history is, true to form, also overflowing with debates between the historians of the Baptists. Moreover, the closely related discipline of Baptist theology, especially when considering the root of the Baptist identity, is no less tendentious.

Baptists engage in wars with words (though thankfully without recourse to the weapons of this world), not because they are necessarily more pugilistic than other Christians (though their forthright honesty about their disagreements may make them appear so). Rather, Baptists fight over such things as forms of worship because they have an overwhelming desire to follow their Lord Jesus Christ in the ways that He commanded them. On the positive side, Baptist congregations are motivated by love for God to worship God as God has directed them. On the negative side, Christians who belong to Baptist communities often disagree as to what exactly God ordains.

And, in the midst of these battling Baptists, their hostile historians, and their pugnacious professors of divinity, Matthew Ward introduces a new thesis, staking a position on Baptist theology regarding Baptist worship that relies heavily upon Baptist history. Ward posits that Baptist historians and theologians have overlooked the innermost issue in an important, seminal series of arguments. The Baptist distinctive is not baptism itself, for which Baptists have received their name; rather, this first

Foreword

ordinance and the subsequent dominical ordinance of communion had their forms fashioned by something yet more foundational.

"The Early English Baptist Distinctive," argues Ward, is the overarching need for "Pure Worship." The pursuit of pure worship is demonstrated historically in the Particular Baptists' quests for free worship, true worship, and gospel worship. Moreover, pure worship only receded as the central concern after a row that brought such famous fathers as William Kiffin, Hanserd Knollys, and Benjamin Keach to public polemics over hermeneutics about hymns. Oh, what a tangled web we Baptists weave!

With such a history behind them, it should have been expected that when Ward presented his thesis to three leading Southern Baptist historical theologians, he prompted some difference of opinion. His doctoral examiners were not as yet ready to embrace entirely the proposal. However, and this is most telling, they readily assented to his deep immersion in the primary sources, his wide knowledge of the secondary discussions, and his erudite and irenic presentation of his profound position.

Ward prompted the reconsideration of long-held positions during that day in the public conference room of the President of Southwestern Baptist Theological Seminary. And others who take the time to consider Ward's evidence will also reevaluate their positions, and many should be won over. While this particular theologian is not ready to cast away his own published pronouncements regarding Baptist identity in Baptist history, he is most willing to concede that Ward has a point, a very good point. Dr. Ward's thesis fits the historical evidence, and he knows that evidence far better than most historians. And that is the highest praise that one historical theologian can give another.

I highly recommend this book for scholars, pastors, and laypeople. It will inspire you to be more biblically faithful in your worship. And it will cause you to grapple with what it means to be a follower of Jesus Christ, who is present in the midst of the covenanted congregation gathered to worship Him. This could be an answer to the prayer of the Early English Particular Baptists themselves, who asked that "the Lord grant that we all may be pressing after more Purity both in the Form and Spirit of Holy-Worship; not declining to any thing that is not of Divine Institution."

Malcolm B. Yarnell III
Professor of Systematic Theology
Director, Center for Theological Research
Southwestern Baptist Theological Seminary
Fort Worth, Texas

Preface

I still smile every time I think about David Dockery's polite understatement, "Worship has not traditionally been one of the strengths of Baptist local church practice."[1] Having given a decade of my life in service of local churches as a minister with responsibilities over church gatherings, I have observed, served with, and counseled a number of well-meaning Baptists who have embodied Dockery's statement. I never cease to be amazed what Baptist churches attempt in the name of worshiping Jesus Christ (or any other churches). It seems that a careful biblical and theological consideration of the actions in God's worship is not always high on the priority list for their leaders.

Perhaps those leaders simply do not have an adequate context for their decisions. This question has been asked more than once: does the Baptist or Free Church tradition have anything unique to say about worship? For example, the current confession of faith for many Southern Baptists serves an incredibly diverse constituency with the minimalist exhortation that the Lord's Day "should include exercises of worship and spiritual devotion" with no elaboration.[2] Even I have to admit that such a statement by itself offers too little liturgical guidance. When one surveys Southern Baptist confessions of faith in conjunction with their histories and theologies, one might develop the strong impression that Baptists simply do not have further guidance to offer. Consequently, Baptist church leaders often seek guidance or models anywhere they can find it, regardless of the ecclesiological context.

That is why I was so surprised to discover the earliest generations of English Baptists not only asking complex liturgical questions but also carefully and passionately drawing conclusions of immense biblical value fully consistent with their unique ecclesiological (Free Church) perspective. Baptist pastors and laymen, with their distinct identity squarely in

1. Dockery, "Church, Worship, and the Lord's Supper," 37.

2. See *Baptist Faith and Message* 2000, Article VIII, "The Lord's Day," for text and discussion.

mind, hashed out the answers to very difficult questions of theology and ecclesiology as they intersected in worship. Their thoughtful and creative approach deserves a thorough retelling.

To any students or scholars reading this book belonging to or with experience in a non-Baptist tradition, you will likely read much that is familiar. The historical context is well established, as are many of the theological questions. What will be unique is the perspective you find. Few have attempted to give voice to a thoroughly Free Church theology of worship, fewer still a historical treatment, and none from a Baptist point of view. The Baptist tradition has not of late aquitted itself well in the ongoing worship dialog, but that must not reflect on the early English Baptists. Those early leaders made valuable contributions to the understanding of instituted corporate worship that should be celebrated and appreciated. That is one of my purposes for writing this book.

It is one thing to argue that English Baptists had a distinct theology of worship; it is a much different thing to argue that their theology of worship was in fact *the* ultimate distinctive of this group. That is the true purpose of this book—not just to convince you that pure worship was "a" distinctive of early English Baptists but "the" distinctive. I will argue that everything we find distinctive about this group, including their hermeneutic, their ecclesiology, and their soteriology, was driven by their fundamental desire to worship God purely. I am offering a significant revision of how we should understand early Baptist thought and practice.

Because this is written as an academic and historical piece, application is far beyond my scope; however, it should be quite evident throughout. These early leaders made theological insights every bit as valid today as then, and today's Baptists have forgotten them to our own impoverishment. I intend to present the historical data clearly enough that the framework for a thorough, historic Free Church theology of worship is evident. I am thoroughly convinced that the Free Church tradition has much to offer to the wider understanding of Christian worship; I hope this book establishes that and sparks a fresh discussion of Free Church worship from a Baptist perspective.

Any book with this many footnotes only comes to fruition with a very understanding family behind the author. The church building where my office is located is busy and active almost every hour of every day, and our home does not have an office, so the kitchen table became the typing table for a long, long time. There were times when that was annoying for everyone, but my family remained understanding and patient throughout.

Preface

So to my wife Shelly and our kids Micah and Sarah, thank you. The three of them kept me grounded and gave me plenty of reasons to want to finish this project well. More than anything, Shelly has shared my life and ministry throughout this journey. Few people love and care about God's church like she does.

One of those people is Malcolm Yarnell, whom I have been blessed to know almost as long as Shelly. He is a true credit to the Baptist tradition. Malcolm taught me that being in the Free Church tradition means something, and he has challenged me to identify that meaning in more and more fields. He also challenged me to take the sixteenth century a lot more seriously, but that is a story for another time. Two other men also asked me a number of challenging questions, starting with Jason Duesing but including Paige Patterson. Jason, a fellow College Station Aggie, helped me keep the big picture of my argument in mind. The real measure of success would have been to convince Paige to change the long-standing convictions he has held about the early English Baptists. I did not. But I think I presented a stronger case than he expected.

The protagonists in my book cared more than anything about making a clear presentation of the gospel of salvation in Jesus Christ. Should anyone who is not a Christian happen across this book, I pray that you will consider the heart behind their pleas and desire to learn more about this Jesus they loved so dearly. He is worth every second.

Abbreviations

BHH	*Baptist History and Heritage*
BCP [1559]	*The Boke of Common Praier, and Administration of the Sacramentes, and other Rites and Ceremonies in the Churche of Englande*. London: Richard Grafton, 1559.
BCP [1641]	*The Booke of Common Prayer, now used in the Church of England, Vindicated*. London: n.p., 1641.
BQ	*Baptist Quarterly*
Broadmead	Underhill, Edward Bean, ed. *The Records of a Church of Christ, Meeting at Broadmead, Bristol. 1640–1687*. London: J. Haddon, 1847.
Crosby	Crosby, Thomas. *The History of the English Baptists*. 4 Vols. London: John Robinson, 1739–40.
Directory [1645]	*A Directory for the publick Worship of God*. London: n.p., 1645.
Fenstanton	Underhill, Edward Bean, ed. *Records of the Churches of Christ, Gathered at Fenstanton, Warboys, and Hexham. 1644–1720*. London: Haddon, Brothers, and Co. 1854.
Gangraena	Edwards, Thomas. *The First and Second Part of Gangraena: or A Catalogue and Discovery of many of the Errors, Heresies, Blasphemies and pernacious Practices of the Sectaries of this time*. London: T. R. and E. M., 1646.
JEH	*Journal of Ecclesiastical History*
London [1644]	*The Confession of Faith, Of those Churches which are commonly (though falsly) called Anabaptists*. London: n.p., 1644.
London [1646]	*A Confession of Faith Of seven Congregations or Churches of Christ in London, which are commonly*

Abbreviations

	(but uniustly) called Anabaptists. London: Matthew Simmons, 1646.
London [1651]	*A Confession of Faith, Of the several Congregations or Churches of Christ in London, which are commonly (though unjustly) called Anabaptists*. London: M[atthew] S[immons], 1651.
London [1677]	*A Confession of Faith. Put forth by the Elders and Brethren Of many Congregations of Christians (baptized upon Profession of their Faith) in London and the Country*. London: Benjamin Harris, 1677.
London [1688]	*A Confession of Faith, Put forth by the Elders and Brethren Of many Congregations of Christians, (Baptized upon Profession of their Faith) in London and the Country*. London: n.p., 1688.
Narrative [1689]	*A Narrative of the Proceedings of the General Assembly Of divers Pastors, Messengers and Ministering-Brethren of the Baptized Churches, met together in London*. London: n.p., 1689.
Narrative [1692]	*A Narrative of the Proceedings of the General Assembly, Consisting Of Elders, Ministers and Messengers, met together in London, from several Parts of England and Wales*. London: n.p., 1692.
ODNB	*Oxford Dictionary of National Biography*
Savoy [1659]	*A declaration of the faith and order owned and practised in the Congregational Churches in England*. London: John Field, 1659.
RE	*Review and Expositor*
Westminster [1646]	*The humble Advice of the Assembly of Divines, Now by Authority of Parliament sitting at Westminster*. London: n.p., 1646.

one

Introduction

With the words "worship," "the," "Baptist," and "distinctive" in its title, this book must be asking for trouble. "Worship," in addition to being rejected as a theologically and historically robust topic of study in some circles, stirs up intense and sometimes quarrelsome feelings. "The" simply puts people on the defensive by connoting finality or superiority. Just about everyone has drawn some sort of conclusion about "Baptists," and few want to hear anything else about those Baptists and their "distinctives." But please bear with this book's presentation, for it will offer a benevolent approach to a trendy matter of surprising historic significance. As more Christian traditions, including Baptists, seek new (and old) resources for local church worship, it might be refreshing to learn that Baptists once had a great deal to say about its foundational principles and practices.

The book's overall argument culminates in a Restoration declaration, "But the Lord grant that we all may be pressing after more Purity both in the Form and Spirit of Holy-Worship; not declining to any thing that is not of Divine Institution."[1] Innocent as that request may sound, it was part of a hugely destructive debate among London Baptists about corporate worship that at least one layman wanted to end "for the preservation

---

1. Kiffin et al., *Serious Answer to a Late Book*, 63. Based on the tone and content, it is likely that Robert Steed (Hanserd Knollys's co-pastor) was the primary author of the treatise.

of the Peace and Purity of the Baptized Churches."[2] In other words, the purity and unity of their Baptist movement was tied to the purity of their churches' worship. Individual church actions in worship could not be overlooked any more than doctrinal declarations in a sermon. Most importantly, this layman understood that a church's identity and its worship were inseparable.

That such an idea, particularly the intrinsic relationship between worship and a church's foundation, might be foreign to some readers is an obstacle this book seeks to overcome. An important group of early Baptists, the primary subjects of this book, so prioritized the pure worship of God that they shaped their entire tradition around it. Their conclusions about worship were unique, ultimately setting them apart from many surrounding Christians and even at odds with one another. Worship was their central distinctive, more so than concerns of polity, hermeneutics, or even baptism, for each of those concerns was birthed or driven by a quest for pure worship. Baptists have long been known for their driving commitment to key principles or "distinctives"; it is perhaps telling that worship is not longer recognized as one of them.

The Winding Quest for a Baptist Distinctive

Many Baptists today care about their identity—what they prioritize and what makes them unique.[3] Baptist history is one of controversy upon controversy with respect to their distinct identity as various groups have competed for associative supremacy, claiming to represent the true Baptist way.[4] Alexander Campbell drew away thousands of Baptists by claiming to be the true restorationist of his generation. J. R. Graves nearly redefined Baptist identity through "old landmarks," ultimately costing W. H. Whitsitt his position at Southern Seminary for arguing that English Baptists

---

2. Marlow, *Clear Confutation of Mr. Richard Allen*, 32.

3. Or, at least, a few Baptists in positions of leadership do the majority of the caring, while vast numbers of Baptist church members remain ignorant of the issue or the supposed stakes, leading Wayne Ward to observe twenty years ago, "Our failure to reach and even indoctrinate new converts, as well as more mature Christians, in the foundational soteriology and ecclesiology which characterize Baptist theological heritage is coming back to haunt us now." Ward, "The Worship of the Early Church," 69. True or not, such a claim assumes that there is a distinct Baptist approach to the church worth indoctrinating.

4. Patterson called Baptists "the San Andreas fault of Christendom." Patterson, *Anatomy of a Reformation*, 1,

Introduction

had not always practiced baptism by immersion. Cities and counties rehashed old prejudices as they trumpeted the superiority and antiquity of the traditions that came to be known as Charleston and Sandy Creek.[5] As questions of biblical orthodoxy began to dominate denominational talks in the middle part of the last century, Baptist leaders and historians argued amongst themselves into which theological lineage they should trace their roots.[6] When it became evident that a conservative faction would claim key victories that would enable them to direct the Southern Baptist Convention, their opponents claimed that their tactics and beliefs ran contrary to the traditional Baptist identity, the outcome of which has been numerous splits and secessions.[7] Even more recently, Baptist leaders have lined up on both sides of the debate over Reformed theology, in each case appealing to a traditional Baptist identity in their support.[8]

There are countless challenges in any study of this nature. One should already be evident: so far, this introduction has used the terms "distinctive," "identity," "way," "tradition," and "principle" almost interchangeably, though each has a unique meaning. The word "distinctive" is particularly problematic because technically it does not exist as it is being used (as a noun); there might be "distinctive Baptists," but not "Baptist distinctives." The connotation is clear enough, and the word has already embedded itself in this debate.[9] In common usage, it seems to mean "that which distinguishes Baptists from other Christian traditions." This defini-

---

5. This uneasy alliance between city and country created tensions that would exacerbate each of the subsequent controversies. See Patterson, *Anatomy of a Reformation*; and Brewer, "Embracing God's Word in Worship," 13–22. Hustad described the severe differences in the two traditions as they related to worship before suggesting that Baptists should find unity by turning to a Genevan tradition. Hustad, "Baptist Worship Forms," 31–42.

6. See Elliot, *"Genesis Controversy."*

7. Baptist historian Bill Leonard explained that the birth of the Cooperative Baptist Fellowship was tied specifically to questions about "the shape and future of Baptist identity." Leonard, *Challenge of Being Baptist*, xi. Other readable resources describing this period include Ammerman, *Baptist Battles*; and Hankins, *Uneasy in Babylon*.

8. For example, James Renihan wrote in bold letters that Edward Terrill, elder in the Broadmead Church, Bristol, "knew" he was Reformed in order to defend Renihan's interpretation of Baptist history. See Smith, "1677/89 BCF Assistant." That Calvinism was singled out in Executive Committee President Frank Page's report during the 2013 Southern Baptist Convention is adequate proof that no one should overlook this issue.

9. Hammett, *Biblical Foundations for Baptist Churches*, is an ecclesiology based on the observation that Baptists were losing their "distinctives." A more obvious example would be Stan Norman's pair of books, *More Than Just a Name* and *Baptist Way*, in which "way," "identity," and "distinctive" were given similar connotations.

tion of a distinctive immediately points to a second challenge to this quest: that a traditional Baptist identity exists and that it is distinct from other Christian traditions. Acknowledging "a" Baptist identity creates further problems because it assumes that there is some kind of characteristic that unites all of the different groups who claim to be Baptist (or baptist), and that they will agree on those characteristics. The previous paragraph perhaps established the wistfulness of such an assumption.[10] As a result, the word "distinctive" will take on a unique connotation in these pages.[11] Finally, the idea of "distinction" tends to put different groups on the defensive in a world that is getting ever smaller. To be "distinct" from someone else implies a type of superiority, and indeed some Baptists have used their "distinctive identity" in such a condescending way.[12] At no point will "distinct" ever mean "superior" in this book. One of the beliefs the early Baptists championed was the concept of a kingdom of priests (1 Pet 2:4–10; Rev 1:4–7) in which all Christians stood together before God the Father, all fallen, all forgiven, and yet given different gifts and put in different circumstances. When these chapters consider that which made Baptists unique, it is only to tell the story of part of God's people, believing that their struggles and conclusions are worth identifying and remembering.[13] Explaining the arguments for or against certain beliefs is not meant as a value judgment of those who held them.

---

10. This understanding of "a" tradition also creates animosity when two parties disagree on its characteristics; one of them must be wrong. For example, compare the two books mentioned by Norman, representing a conservative theology, with the more moderate offerings by Leonard, *Challenge of Being Baptist* and *Baptist Questions, Baptist Answers*. Both authors were equally passionate for and convinced of their accuracy with respect to a Baptist identity. Illustrating the fine line that must be walked, the Peace Committee of 1987 repeatedly used the phrase "Baptists generally." In a recent book on Baptist hermeneutics, one contributor suggested, "It is not authentically Baptist to fight over terms like inerrancy and infallibility," presuming such a statement to be authentically Baptist in the first place. Birch, "Baptists and Biblical Interpretation," 171. One way or another, these authors assumed that authentic Baptists exist; that every Baptist would not agree with their qualification should give pause.

11. John Owen, an important Independent leader who will play a large role in this book as a dialogue partner for the early Baptists, attempted something similar when he redefined the word "schism" to take pressure off of the Baptists and Independents; in essence, he argued that "schism" only applied to an action within a church.

12. Dare and Woodman, *"Plainly Revealed" Word of God?*, reacts to this perception.

13. Jeter once wrote about distinctives that they should be used to build up one's own sect, not tear another's down; all truths may not be equally precious to God's church, but they have significant value to those who hold them. This book seeks to honor that benevolent stance. See Jeter, *Baptist Principles Reset*, 12, 128.

Introduction

To help set the stage for any reader who may not be familiar with Baptist history or theology, consider these illustrations. Baptists in America have claimed a number of distinctives over the years, including believers' baptism by immersion, regenerate church membership, soul competency, biblical inerrancy, and modified Calvinism.[14] Others could easily have been chosen, including religious liberty and the missionary mindset. And Baptists will disagree strongly as to exactly what each of these examples could or should mean (discussions of Baptist distinctives become hazardous quickly). Further, a number of other Christian groups hold to one or all of these beliefs, so "distinctive" rather entails a distinct combination or tenacity with which Baptists hold such beliefs. Discussions of a particular distinctive often follow one of these paths abbreviated below.

The name "Baptist" generally encourages one to think about baptism, namely believers' baptism by immersion. Those joining a Baptist church from a tradition with a different understanding of baptism often have to be "re-baptized" as a term of joining.[15] Baptism itself is a commitment (a symbol or a seal) reserved for those who have knowingly professed to follow Jesus Christ. This view of baptism creates a formal distinction between Baptists and many other Christians, though very few authors actually start their list of Baptist distinctives with baptism.[16] Instead, the priority

---

14. The following Southern Baptist resources variously identified congregationalism, voluntarism, commemorationalism, freedom of conscience or religious liberty, separation of church and state, scriptural authority, and close communion. Middleditch, *Baptist Church, the Christian's Home*, put congregationalism as second only to regenerate church membership. Pendleton, *Three Reasons Why I Am a Baptist*, gave two reasons as congregationalism and commemorationalism/close communion. Jenkens, *Baptist Doctrines*, prioritized the authority of scripture for Baptists. Burrows, *What Baptists Believe*, saw congregationalism, voluntarism, and commemorationalism as three of the four primary distinctives. Dargan, *Doctrines of Our Faith*, started with freedom of conscience. Carroll, *Baptists and Their Doctrines*, prioritized the authority of the New Testament. More recent authors have tended to modify the terms based on current usage. For example, Leonard in *Challenge of Being Baptist* prioritized congregationalism and conversionism, which in the past was subsumed under baptism. Norman in *Baptist Way* added the Lordship of Jesus Christ as the second most important Baptist distinctive, while the authors of *Whosoever Will* considered it to be the highest such principle.

15. From very early, however, Baptists did not consider their practice "re-baptism." "To obviate a Cavil, which may be made, the Reader may understand that under the term [*Unbaptized*] we comprehend all persons that either were never Baptized at all, or such as have been (as they call it) *Christned* or Baptized (more properly *Sprinkled*) in their Infancy." Kiffin, *Sober Discourse*, 9.

16. Pendleton, *Three Reasons Why I Am a Baptist*, for example, included baptism as one of his three reasons without establishing priority. Whitley, *Witness of History to*

of believers' baptism by immersion often comes from an argument from history. A number of Baptist historians have said not that baptism is a primary distinctive today but that it was so to the early English Baptists.[17]

Baptists often point to their regenerate church membership as that which distinguishes them from many other Christians. Related to believers' baptism by immersion, Baptists believe that only actual followers of Jesus Christ (however that might be determined) should be members of a church and that the church is responsible for holding its members accountable to walk worthy of their calling. Many Baptists reflect this distinctive in their rejection of all hierarchy either within a church or among churches, with congregationalism being the ecclesiastical model. It has direct connections with the doctrine of the priesthood of all believers and the practice of church discipline. This particular belief, because it has so many factors, heads a number of lists of Baptist distinctives. The challenge behind this principle has been an inconsistent dedication thereto.[18]

E. Y. Mullins made the very frank admission that religion should be seen primarily as a personal relationship between a child and Father God, so when he wondered, "What is [the Baptists] distinctive contribution to the religious life and thought of mankind?" he stepped away from the more traditional answers and advocated a catch-all category called "soul competency." Its biblical application is the right of private interpretation, its moral application is soul freedom, ecclesial is regenerate church membership, political is the separation of church and state, and social is the social gospel. Thus Mullins attempted to create a comprehensive distinctive, an approach which heavily influenced Baptist thought at the turn of the previous century. Some have reduced this concept to the freedom of conscience, but Mullins clearly had much more in mind in coining the

---

Baptist Principles, was one of few to put baptism first on his list, though in a similar book in 1914, he put baptism much lower.

17. One of the most influential and controversial pronouncements along these lines was Whitsitt's aforementioned belief that baptism was the *sine qua non* of Baptist identity, leading him to proclaim that Baptists did not exist before 1641. Other historians have reduced the central teaching of the First London Confession of 1644 to baptism, reinforcing this idea. See, for example, Garrett, "Restitution and Dissent Among Early English Baptists: Part I," 203 (as an illustration); and Nelson, "Reflecting on Baptist Origins," 33–46 (as an example).

18. Both Jeter and Middleditch considered regenerate (or spiritual) church membership to be the primary Baptist distinctive, as did Wamble, "Early English Baptist Sectarianism," 60. Charles Jenkens, E. C. Dargan, Edgar Folk, and W. T. Whitley also included this early in their lists. But see also Hammett, *Biblical Foundations*, 99–107.

Introduction

term.¹⁹ Dissatisfaction with it has arisen from the extreme emphasis on the individual at the potential expense of the church and the Bible.

Baptists have always been people of the Book, committed to following Christ in obedience to His words in Scripture. But in a critical society, that commitment has been stretched to include a wide range of paradigms. Among the conservative approaches, biblical inerrancy became a watchterm in the mid-twentieth century and the rallying cry for the Evangelical Movement, though no fewer than six different views of inerrancy have regularly been identified.²⁰ This principle became intimately tied up with Baptist identity during what is often called the conservative resurgence (or takeover) of the Southern Baptist Convention, during which one group claimed inerrancy a vital Baptist distinctive, and the other a disruption to cooperation and unity.²¹ A belief closely related to inerrancy, biblical authority, has generated similar posturing and problems—what parts of the Bible are authoritative, and for whom, and in what sense?²²

---

19. Mullins, *Axioms of Religion*, 44–58. After this book was published, a number of similar books began emphasizing more individualistic principles. Folk, *Baptist Principles*, prioritized the right of private interpretation; Jones, *Restatement of Baptist Principles*, soul liberty; Kirtley, *Baptist Distinctive and Objective*, soul liberty; Whitley, *Witness of History to Baptist Principles* (1914 edition), soul responsibility. Carroll, *Baptists and Their Doctrines*, listed soul responsibility the number two doctrine; Dargan, *Doctrines of Our Faith*, freedom of conscience; Nowlin, *What Baptists Stand For*, soul competency.

20. Hart's wonderfully entertaining description of this development concluded that inerrancy was a "slim hook" that never could have united the amorphous evangelicalism because no one could agree on its meaning. Hart, *Deconstructing Evangelicalism*, 151. Dockery classified inerrancy as naïve, absolute, balanced, limited, functional, and nonexistent. Dockery, *Doctrine of the Bible*, 86–88.

21. Leonard, speaking from a moderate vantage, called inerrancy "central to the effort of conservatives to gain control of the convention from 'moderates.'" Leonard, *Baptists in America*, 137. Elsewhere, he summarized, "Some go so far as to insist that one cannot be a Baptist without affirming that particular view [inerrancy] of the biblical texts. Without it, they believe, all other doctrines grounded in Scripture are untrustworthy. Other Baptists refuse to affirm such a strenuous view of the nature of Scripture, not because they deny biblical authority but because they hesitate to bind the texts to one theory of interpretation." Leonard, *Baptist Questions, Baptist Answers*, 80. Leonard affirmed the Bible for Baptist identity, but he used the much looser term "Biblicism" with respect to a Baptist distinctive. Leonard, *Challenge of Being Baptist*, 18. See Wooddell's effort to describe a Baptist understanding of inerrancy in *Baptist Faith and Message 2000*, 1–9.

22. Norman, *Baptist Way*; and Hammett, *Biblical Foundations for Baptist Churches*, considered biblical authority the primary driver for a Baptist identity, and they both developed a nuanced understanding of that authority that mirrors developments explained in chapter 4.

Finally, theological system has become the focus of a wide-ranging debate about Baptist identity with the ascendancy of Calvinist theology after many decades of adhering to a more Arminian system. This has been a particularly interesting debate because it has so many historical implications. Baptists prioritizing Calvinism and Arminianism both point to different groups of early Baptists in support of their beliefs, the former to the Particular Baptists associated with the First London Confession, and the latter to the General Baptists loosely connected with John Smyth and Thomas Helwys. Baptists desiring not to be tied to either group have injected other historically meaningful options.[23]

Each of these concepts represents an aspect of that which is important to different Baptists: their separation (believers' baptism by immersion), their operation (regenerate church membership), their responsibility (soul competency), their authority (biblical inerrancy), and their perspective (theological system). This book offers an alternative, but *not* to argue that Baptists *should* hold some specific distinctive. Rather, it will simply make the case that a group of Baptists known as the early English Particular Baptists *did* do so—a distinctive that has not retained its historic significance. It is a secondary benefit that their conclusions in this field have immense value for Baptist churches today. Recently, Mark Bell offered a wide sweep of early English Baptists and concluded that they were distinguished by a unique form of apocalypticism.[24] I will follow a similar, if narrower, path to a very different conclusion: pure worship was the early English Baptist distinctive.

---

23. Yarnell, "Neither Calvinists nor Arminians but Baptists," offered such an alternative. Leonard gleefully identified the "schizophrenia" of a tradition that somehow embraces both Calvinists and Arminians. See Leonard, *Challenge of Being Baptist*, 61ff.

24. Bell, *Apocalypse How?* Bell referred to many of the same sources as I do, drawing different conclusions. I do not deny that Baptists held a unique eschatology but will argue that, at least for the early Particular Baptists, worship was primary. Perhaps the distinction could be made that politically-minded Baptists prioritized millenialism where church-minded Baptists did worship. These kinds of historical revisits have gained recent popularity. For example, Renihan used several of the sources referenced in this book to argue for an English Separatist origin of the Baptists and that their priority was the ordinance of Baptism. Renihan, "'Truly Reformed in a Great Measure,'" 24–32. Pitts likewise argued that baptism was the "unquestionable foundation" of the Baptists and that their distinctiveness was found in the regenerate church, although he seemed to misunderstand the relationship between the Independents and their seed. Pitts, "Arguing Regenerate Church Membership." None of these addressed worship.

"Great Matters": Free Worship, True Worship, Gospel Worship[25]

What does it mean that pure worship was the early English Baptist distinctive? Early Separatists approached the church in three categories: ministry, worship, and government; John Canne even built his important *A Necessitie of Separation* around them.[26] By this they meant the offices, the actions, and the structure of the church. Baptism and discipline, as actions, were considered subsets of worship. However, calling worship the Baptist distinctive does not mean that those Baptists devalued ministry or government (or baptism or discipline), or that every Baptist equally focused on worship. Indeed, some might read the sources and come to the opposite conclusion. For example, in 1550 Thomas Cranmer wrote that the chief error of the Anabaptists and related sects was believing with John Knox, "Whatsoever is not commanded in the scripture, is against the scripture and utterly unlawful and ungodly."[27] That seems to indicate hermeneutics as their chief distinctive. For another example, in 1650 Nathaniel Stephens similarly identified the chief bone of contention with the Baptists, "That there was no word of command for the Baptisme of Infants in the New Testament. I found that this principally moved them to renounce the old, and to take up a new Baptisme; to leave the old, and to joyn themselves to a new Church."[28] That seems to indicate baptism as their chief distinctive. One of the major purposes of this book is to put such statements in their historical context, which will cast a different light on meanings that otherwise seem obvious. In the case of these two examples, in 1550, Cranmer's context was the instituted worship of the church in general. And by 1650, although some Baptists had probably taken to disputing about baptism in isolation, the Baptists at the focus of this book recognized it as a specific element of instituted worship. Calling pure worship the early English

25. Burroughs, *Gospel-Worship*, 45. Burroughs was the Independent pastor of two of the most significant churches in London, Stepney and Cripple-gate. He preached a series of sermons on worship in the mid 1640s during the Westminster Assembly that were published posthumously by a group including Thomas Goodwin and Philip Nye, going through multiple printings from 1648.

26. Canne, *Necessitie of Separation*, first printed in 1634. Canne claimed to have compiled nonconformist thoughts on the church and used them to prove against Ames and Bradshaw that separation was fully principled. Praisegod Barbone used this pattern in his arguments against the Baptists. See, for example, Barbone, *Reply to R. B.*, 59. Not all authors used the terms exactly as Canne did.

27. MacCulloch, *Thomas Cranmer*, 526.

28. Betteridge, "Early Baptists in Leicestershire and Rutland, Part 1," 272.

Baptist distinctive means that all of their important beliefs were intimately shaped by their beliefs about worship.

In other words, worship was the immediate concern that sparked and ordered the subsequent development of their beliefs. The early English Baptists did not backtrack from worship to a conviction that the Bible must be authoritative, but their commitment to worship led them to ask unique questions and draw unique conclusions about the Bible. Similar observations can be made about the church, baptism, ministry, and even their own identity as a tradition. This will be seen in what they held in common with other English Christians about worship and where they disagreed, bringing them into and out of cooperation with various other Englishmen. In some cases, the priority of worship was rather evident, as Edward Terrill recorded of Broadmead Church, Bristol, in 1640,

> And in those halcyon days of prosperity, liberty, and peace, it pleased the Lord to break forth more primitive light and purity in reformation of worship, to bring the church to a more exact keeping to the holy scripture; so that some of the members began to question what rule they had for sprinkling of children.[29]

William Kiffin acknowledged that as a young man he knew he should separate from the established church for its false worship but was too weak to take such a bold step; later, after gaining the courage to do so, he gave three reasons: coercive worship, limited participation in worship, and the church tax.[30] Thomas Patient, Kiffin's early co-pastor, reflected that the spark which caused him to leave the Church of England (and only after leaving to begin to question infant baptism) was her government and liturgy: "I was resolved, God willing, to examine all Religion, as well in worship, and the order of Gods house."[31] However, most cases are less

---

29. *Broadmead*, 39. An earlier passage was even more explicit: the Broadmead Church began with a simple covenant between local Christians; under the later influence of John Canne, pastor of an English Separatist church in Amsterdam, they continued a stepwise program of reformation—"then they stepped further in separation, and would not so much as hear any minister that did read common prayer. Thus the Lord led them by degrees, and brought them out of popish darkness into his marvellous light of the gospel." Ibid., 23, 18–23. However, Hayden pointed out that Terrill did not actually join the church until 1658, so these early details may have been inaccurate. Hayden said Canne, who was not a Baptist, probably did not come to Bristol until some time after his return to England from Amsterdam in 1645/6. Hayden, "Broadmead, Bristol in the Seventeenth Century," 349–52.

30. *Remarkable Passages in the Life of William Kiffin*, ed. Orme, 13–14; Kiffin, *Briefe Remonstrance*, 8ff.

31. Patient, *Doctrine of Baptism*, The Epistle to the Christian Reader. Patient was pastoring in Dublin by this time.

Introduction

obvious, else how could so many Baptist historians overlook such a supposedly key distinctive?

To be sure, some historians have noted this importance, though sometimes indirectly. For example, E. B. Underhill defended his chosen primary Baptist characteristic, freedom of conscience, in exactly the opposite manner proposed:

> Its practical assertion brought them [the early Baptists] into collision with every form of human invention in the worship of God. Faith, God's gift, must not be subjected to man's device, nor enchained by the legislative enactments of parliaments or kings. To worship God aright, the highest function of humanity, the spirit must be set free; true worship can only come from a willing heart.[32]

Similarly, Murray Tolmie wrote about the early Separatists (which included Baptists) that they were willing to overlook their internal differences in order to achieve "the fundamental right of conscience: to worship the way it saw best."[33] These historians might seem to say that worship was a derivative of the freedom of conscience, but in reality the reverse is true. They observed that worship was the basis of the prized freedom of conscience (as powerful a principle as it is, freedom of conscience alone cannot account for all of the developments made in Baptist thought). But they are lonely voices. Even B. R. White, who recognized faith, discipline, and worship as the basic elements of Separatism, still minimized worship with respect to his preferred emphasis of discipline.[34]

---

32. *Broadmead*, xliv.

33. Tolmie, *Triumph of the Saints*, 1. It must be acknowledged that the freedoms of conscience and worship have not always been connected by Baptist historians, likely adding to the neglect of a historical Baptist theology of worship. For example, Torbet highlighted liberty of conscience as a Baptist fundamental without ever mentioning freedom of worship. Torbet, *History of the Baptists*, 30ff. Somewhat inbetween would be McBeth who also highlighted freedom of conscience but at least acknowledged that such desire extended to their own form of worship. McBeth, *Baptist Heritage*, 41ff.

34. White, *English Separatist Tradition*, 24. White did not use that triad of terms, but implied it saying, "[The separatists] had abandoned the worship of their parish churches and were now organized independently of them with their own prayer, preaching, and sacraments; they rejected episcopal authority but administered their own discipline; finally, they made their overriding appeal to the authority of Scripture." But "their most urgent desire was to restore the practice of discipline" (ibid., 24, 32). The triad, "faith, discipline, and worship," played a prominent role in the primary literature as, for example, Tombes, *Short Catechism about Baptism*, 17. Smyth and Ainsworth used "ministry, worship, and government." See Smyth, *Paralleles, Censures, Observations*, 14, 23. Minimizing worship seems common among historians, if

Other traditions have been quicker to embrace the importance of worship. Independent leader Jeremiah Burroughs called the acts of worship "the greatest things that do concern you here in this world."[35] Anglican Samuel Parker issued the accusation in 1670 that the "foundation of all Puritanism" was that "nothing ought to be established in the worship of God but what is authorized by some precept or example in the word of God, which is the complete and adequate rule of worship."[36] Horton Davies concluded, "Puritanism in England was, therefore, of necessity a liturgical movement."[37] Slayden Yarbrough recognized the importance of worship to the Separatist Henry Barrow.[38] And at least some Presbyterian historians have not forgotten that the dual purpose of the Westminster Assembly was the complete reformation of church government and worship,

---

unintentional. Briggs, "The Influence of Calvinism on Seventeenth-Century English Baptists," discussed worship only with respect to the ceremony of baptism; Weaver, *In Search of the New Testament Church*, looked at elements of early Baptist worship without ever actually investigating worship itself. The clearest example might be Brackney's *Genetic History of Baptist Thought* in which he entitled a chapter "Singing the Faith" but simply used the chapter to review the theology in Baptist hymns (starting with Benjamin Keach). At no point did he actually discuss worship. Even Garrett's majestic *Baptist Theology* did not address the matters at hand except for a summary of Benjamin Keach's involvement in the hymn-singing controversy.

35. Burroughs, *Gospel-Worship*, 45.

36. Owen, *Truth and Innocence Vindicated*, in *Works*, 13:462. Parker, a High Churchman, had printed this accusation in "Discourse of Ecclesiastical Polity." Rather than deny it, Owen responded by further expanding their differences: "1. That whatever the Scripture hath indeed prescribed and appointed to be done and observed in the worship of God and the government of the church, that is indeed to be done and observed . . . 2. That nothing in conjunction with, nothing as an addition or supplement unto, what is so appointed ought to be admitted, if it be contrary either to the general rules or particular perceptive instructions of the Scripture . . . 3. That nothing ought to be joined with or added unto what in the Scripture is prescribed and appointed in these things without some cogent reason, making such conjunction or addition necessary . . . 4. That if any thing or things in this kind shall be found necessary to be added and prescribed, then that and those alone be so which are most consonant unto the general rules of the Scripture given us for our guidance in the worship of God, and the nature of those institutions themselves wherewith they are conjoined or whereunto they are added" (ibid., 464). In addition to being a helpful introduction to an important concept often called the "regulative principle," Owen's response also illustrated the overlap between worship and other doctrines.

37. Davies, *Worship of the English Puritans*, 8. Puritans wanted to purify English worship from unbiblical action. Whereas Luther thought scripture was necessary for salvation but not church government or worship, Calvin thought it was for all three. Most Puritans followed Calvin in this respect. Ibid., 1–24.

38. Yarbrough, "English Separatist Influence on the Baptist Tradition of Church-State Issues," 14–23.

though few realize that their efforts in worship were of the greater immediate consequence.[39]

A more fundamental question must be answered at this point: what is worship? Worship is a difficult subject to discuss because it means something different to everyone and causes intensely personal reactions; indeed, chapter 6 will argue that that is the primary reason Baptists began to deemphasize worship in their associations in the 1700s. The first two chapters will establish the historical context for the thesis: what did worship mean to the English people, and what did it look like? They will also clarify exactly what is meant by "early English Baptists." The following three chapters will develop the overall topic of "pure worship" under the heads of "free worship," "true worship," and "gospel worship," because those have the most historical significance for these Baptists and their partners in dialogue, establishing the ways in which the Baptists truly were distinct in their thought. The final chapter will explain why worship lost its significance for Baptists as a whole.

Unlike today, English authors of the seventeenth century were remarkably consistent in their use of the term "worship." Cambridge Puritan William Bradshaw established the basic framework, writing around 1604, "Divine Worship is any action or service that is immediately and directly performed unto God himself, whether the true God or a false, whether commanded by Divine Authority, imposed by humane, or assumed upon our own heads and pleasures."[40] This divine worship, which was given different names, was a combination of the external and internal: "External worship is an expressing and setting forth of the internal by outward signs

---

39. The next chapter will note the argument that the Westminster Puritans adopted Presbyterianism as much for political as theological reasons; the most significant changes affecting the people coming out of the Assembly were those related to public worship. But consider these diverse perspectives: Hetherington, *History of the Westminster Assembly of Divines*, focused mainly on the political motives behind presbyterianism and the *Directory*; *History of the Westminster Assembly of Divines* thought that their attention to worship was driven by a desire to prevent confusion and disorder; Carruthers, *Everyday Work of Westminster Assembly*, managed to ignore the *Directory* entirely; Mitchell, *Westminster Assembly*, on the other hand, recognized the divergent views represented on ceremony and liturgy and greatly appreciated the accomplishment of the *Directory*; Muller and Ward, *Scripture and Worship*, likewise appreciated the divisive work connected to worship; Chapell, *Christ-Centered Worship*, spoke of the possibilities of Westminster for worship.

40. Bradshaw, *Several Treatises of Worship and Ceremonies*, 1. Bradshaw originally published these treatises in 1604–1605 arguing against the lawfulness of imposed ceremonies in worship; Thomas Gataker compiled and republished them in 1660 during the Restoration.

and rites," which were called ceremonies. Ceremonies (including sacraments) made manifest a hidden devotion; they might be natural, such as bowing and praying, or instituted, such as baptism and the Lord's Supper. By "religion," then, was simply meant instituted outward or public worship, regardless of *who* instituted it.[41] Separatist teacher Henry Ainsworth added the nuance that "the worship of God generally, comprehendeth the performing of all duties required in the first table of the Law: specially and properly, to worship is to bow downe & supplicate unto God" while recognizing a distinction between spiritual and formal worship.[42] Independent leader and pastor Jeremiah Burroughs introduced the term "Gospel worship" in part to distinguish between the "divine worship" contained in the established written liturgies (the *Book of Common Prayer* and to a lesser extent the *Directory for Public Worship*) and the worship God required. He focused on the actions of worship, chiefly hearing the word, receiving the sacrament, and prayer.[43] His peers John Owen and Henry Lawrence likewise saw the scope of argument to be that of "the due observance of his outward institutions," or "instituted worship only," "since the ordinance lyes in a ceremony." Only this worship was "solemn and stated for the church, the whole church, at all times and seasons, according to the rules

---

41. Ibid., 2–6. "So that by *Religion*, in this position is meant the outward (especially publick) worship of God; *Religion* being but for *Worship*, because the fear of God to serve him precisely according to his Word, is, of all the actions of men, especially to be manifest in worshipping God, who will be sanctified in all them that come near him, if they offer strange fire, *Lev.* 10. 3. *Religion* (then) being put for *outward Worship*, the Position is granted. For indeed the outward worship of God, doth consist only of Ceremonies, that is, outward demonstrations of inward Worship" (ibid., n.p.). At the end of the century, Benjamin Keach called "the foundation of all Religion" "that Sacred Homage and Worship which is due to [God]." Keach, *God Acknowledged*, 33. Even the exiled separatist pastor Henoch Clapham, who restricted the sacraments to baptism, the Lord's Supper, and the laying on of hands at baptism, saw the sacraments as "A Ceremonie instituted by The Lord, bringing with it to the faithfull receiver som celestial or spiritual blessinge signified therby." Clapham, *Theological Axioms*, not paginated.

42. Ainsworth, *Defence of the Holy Scriptures, Worship, and Ministerie*, 6. Ainsworth wrote this book specifically against Smyth, *Differences of the Churches of the Seperation*.

43. Burroughs, *Gospel-Worship*, 161. Burroughs also preached series on Gospel-conversation, Gospel-remission, and Gospel-fear. Divine worship and divine service were synonyms; Fifth-Monarchy Baptist Vavasor Powell complained "it is so much Idolized, called *Divine Service*, as I heard one lately say, that brought a Bible to a Bookbinders shop to bee new bound, when the Book-binder said he could hardly bind it and that we would see a new Bible for a little more money; The answer was, *That that Bible was worth twenty New ones*, and the only reason was, because the Book of *Common-Prayer* was in it." Powell, *Common-Prayer-Book no Divine Service*, 15.

of his appointment."⁴⁴ The mark of a true church ("the clear definition of the Church of the living God"), namely the right administration of the sacraments, meant the church's worship.⁴⁵

The group of Baptists who will be specified in the next section latched on to these starting points. In his great exposition of church worship, William Kiffin leaned on Burroughs in restricting his argument to instituted worship, which he described as "lying in nothing else but the right and Orderly Administration of Ceremonies."⁴⁶ Hanserd Knollys drew a strict interconnection between the "pure worship of God" and the "holy Ordinances of the Gospel," as did Henry Jessey, who said, "Formes or Ordinances, are wayes and meanes of divine worship, or Christs appointment."⁴⁷ John Tombes defined worship as "the honour and service that is done unto a God" in the context of "religious service we performe" in an immediate sense.⁴⁸ This basic semantic might partially explain why Baptist historians

44. Owen, *Truth and Innocence Vindicated*, in *Works*, 13:447, 468; [Henry Lawrence], *Of Baptisme*, 106. Lawrence, Cromwell's council president, is credited with this book by virtue of his later treatises on baptism—a ceremony rooted in its mode. Owen distinguished instituted from private worship in order to respect the individual's right of access to God through Jesus Christ and also acknowledge the rule of Scripture in the life of the church. He offered three explanations in his defense: "1. That this inbred light of reason guides unto nothing at all in or about the worship of God, but what is more fully, clearly, and directly taught and declared in the Scripture . . . 2. As there can be no opposition nor contradiction between the light of nature and inspired vocal or scriptural revelation, because they are both from God, so if in any instance there should appear and such thing unto us, neither faith nor reason can rest in that which is pretended to be natural light, but must betake themselves for their resolution unto express revelation . . . 3. Our inquiry in our present contest is solely about *instituted worship*, which we believe to depend on supernatural revelation" (Owen, *Truth and Innocence Vindicated*, in *Works*, 13:466–67). Baptists followed this reasoning.

45. Grantham, *Christianismus Primitivus*, 2:2ff. The entire purpose of the second book, which identified the proper external form of a true church, was to define "*the practical way of Gods worship.*" Ibid., 2:2. In a common confusion of terminology, Brackney noted the focus of this second book on Christian "externals" without realizing that Grantham meant instituted worship. Brackney, *Genetic History*, 114.

46. Kiffin, *Sober Discourse*, 117. This book's argument, as well as a defense of calling it an exposition of worship, will be clarified in chapter 3. Thomas Grantham, a General Baptist who will serve as a common foil for the primary group of authors in this paper, also mirrored Burroughs in saying that "the work of Christian exhortation, praising the Lord, and the celebration of his divine Supper, doth as it were comprize the whole body of Christian Worship." Grantham, *Seventh-day-Sabbath Ceased*, 4. He identified religion with public worship; see Grantham, *St. Paul's Catechism*, 12.

47. Knollys, *Exposition Of the Revelation*, 189; Jessey, *Storehouse of Provision*, 9. The terms "ordinance" and "worship" often had the same field of meaning, as chapter 4 will explain.

48. Tombes, *Jehovah Jireh*, 3. There is some debate whether or not Tombes should

have undervalued worship in their histories. For example, Henry Jessey's *Miscellanea Sacra* rarely used the word "worship," but rather focused on the "new administrations" of the new covenant, namely the ordinances. But when it is remembered Jessey used the concepts of the ordinances and the church's worship in parallel, his treatise actually said a great deal about worship.[49] Indeed, Particular Baptists concerned themselves greatly with their tradition's worship. What was pure worship? How were its actions determined? Who participated in it? To what extent could one person or group prescribe actions of worship to another? What happened when two churches disagreed over those actions? The process of working out the answers to these and other such questions shaped and distinguished the early Particular Baptists from all other English Christians.

As stated above, I will explore the early English Baptist concepts of worship under three headings. "Free worship" represents the precious belief that pure worship could not be coerced or prescribed, a belief with wide-ranging consequences. If worship must be freely given, then only Christians could worship. John Tombes realized,

> Right worshippers worship God from a right principle. Two principles of our worship are necessary that our worship be right. First, the Spirit of God; no man can worship the Lord in truth, unless the Spirit of God dwell and act in him, 1 *Cor.* 12. 3. *No man can say that Jesus is the Lord but by the Holy Ghost.* Secondly, a right faith, without which a man cannot worship truly, for the doctrine of our Lord Jesus is the doctrine which is according to godlinesse, 1 *Tim.* 6. 3.[50]

---

be considered a Baptist, namely with respect to his willingness to recognize the established church. Though an outlier in many ways, Tombes had significant contact with early Baptists, so his opinion will be valued.

49. For example, in this book Jessey defined the purpose of the church as "Communion with [God], and with one another, in all his Holy Ordinances." Jessey, *Miscellanea Sacra*, 130, cf. 59. But in an earlier publication he had similarly defined that purpose as "a gathering of these out from the world and *joyning of them together* to worship the Lord in truth, so far as they *know*, or shall know; and edifie themselves." Jessey, *Storehouse of Provision*, 102. It is possible that Jessey and others intentionally shifted from the language of "worship" to that of "ordinance" in order to distance themselves from Anglicans. The impact on historians, and hence those who read their histories, can be summarized in Torbet who recognized the early Baptist emphasis on discipline, gospel, and ordinance but focused on believers' baptism. Torbet addressed many of the matters in this book and never used the word "worship." Torbet, *History of the Baptists*, 40–57.

50. Tombes, *Jehovah Jireh*, 5. This was actually the fifth of six requisites for being a "right worshipper," the others being to worship only the true God Jehovah, to worship

Introduction

The Baptists took the critical step of applying this belief to the church, wondering with whom they could join in worship, at which point they would be justified in separating from worship with which they disagreed, and whether or not baptism should be considered an act of worship. "True worship" was the ideal to which all English dissenters aspired, in which "divine revelation is the sole rule of divine religious worship."[51] Hanserd Knollys lamented after the Restoration about "the *Congregations* of Saints, & *Churches* of several perswasions, *in this Age*, how unlike they are to the Churches of God recorded in the Scripture, with respect unto Ministry, Gifts, and Discipline or Government, besides what is amiss in the Worship of God."[52] For the Baptists, the answer was to run to the refuge of God's Word for all church action. William Kiffin insisted,

> 1. That God hath Prescribed a particular way and method in which he will be Worshiped.
>
> 2. That he is so tender and nice therein, that the least Variation from his own Stated Order will not be allowed by him, which appears by the punishment of such as Transgressed, and the praises given to such as kept his Ordinances and they were Delivered unto them, mentioned at large before.
>
> 3. That to swerve from the Lords Institutions, and Invert his Order, has a direct Tendency to Destroy all Modes of Worship, and consequently all the publick and solemn Exercise of Religion, in as much as the same Reason by which one Ordinance may be changed, or Discontinued, will equally prove the change or Discontinuance of any, yea of all at long Run.[53]

But the Baptists disagreed with their Protestant brethren as to how God's prescriptions should be interpreted and applied—New Testament versus Old Testament, literal versus allegorical—and when they explored the extremes to which the Scriptures could be taken in worship, they discovered that freedom had limits. "Gospel worship" represents the most important principle the early Baptists associated with their church gatherings: a clear and simple presentation and embodiment of the gospel of Jesus Christ. This led them to push even further the questions asked by the Puritans.

---

only through the true Mediator Jesus Christ, to worship only by the true rule (God's own prescription and appointment), to worship only for the end of God's glory, and to worship only in spirit and truth. Ibid., 2–5.

51. Owen, *Truth and Innocence Vindicated*, in *Works*, 13:465.
52. Knollys, *Apocalyptical Mysteries*, To the Reader.
53. Kiffin, *Sober Discourse*, 57–58.

Pure Worship

What was the purpose of their gatherings, or their preaching? Did set forms of worship enhance or inhibit the only transaction that truly mattered—the salvation of a soul? John Tombes considered,

> Hee that shall goe as far as *Hierusalem* to visit Christs Sepulchre, that shall sprinkle himselfe with holy water, keepe reliques of Saints, observe old customes of former Christians, abstaine from eating flesh, if he could keepe all the traditions of men, not faile in any point of ceremony, and thereby thinke to please God as if hee did him honour, thereby shall not onely misse of his end, but also in stead thereof provoke the wrath of God against himself through his superstition.[54]

In this book, "worship" will refer to the instituted worship of a particular church, or the administration of ceremonies therein for the purpose of corporate worship. That is why I will regularly use the word "liturgical" (lest that become a cause for concern), for liturgy simply refers to the form of public worship and not necessarily its *prescription*. The early Baptists sought the pure worship that God desired, hoping their obedience would overcome their conceit, knowing, "No Religion nor Ordinance of God is valued by some Men but what suits with their own affected Principles and Notions."[55] They did so in the context of a dramatically changing religious landscape in England, mindful of the progress that had already been made in religious reform, and believing that God wanted them to take the next steps. The next chapter will describe the progress of reformation specifically as it related to instituted worship.

"From Our Own Writings": Scope and Limits[56]

"Baptist" represented a widespread group of loosely organized dissenters practicing believers' baptism. This book will focus on one group of Baptists centered in London and united in their agreement over limited, or

---

54. Tombes, *Jehovah Jireh*, 4.
55. Keach, *Counterfeit Christian*, 22.
56. Kiffin issued an apology in which he pleaded, "These things we have herein recited, the rather because that such judgement as shall be made by any concerning us, may be fairly and duly taken and calculated from our own writings, and not from the aspersions unjustly cast upon us by such who have not only rendred many guilty for the offence sake of some one person, but also called others after the same name given to us, with whom we have had or held no correspondency or agreement" (Kiffin et al., *Humble Apology*, 18). Signees included Henry Denne, Thomas Lambe, and John Spilsbury.

"particular," atonement. They exerted a wide influence in England due to their advanced sense of orthodoxy, cooperation, and evangelism. After the publication of their confession of faith in 1644, these London Particular Baptists possessed an enduring self-identity that sustained them through decades of persecution.[57] But even before that, their convictions about the church and salvation had begun bringing them together. Henry Jacob, an English clergyman who had contact with separatists but was unwilling to deny the validity of the Anglican Church or its ceremonies, nonetheless desired to protect the purity of the Lord's Supper and maintained a "semi-separate" congregation in London in the early 1600s. Jacob's church both fulfilled a popular desire for Christian worship and became a training ground for a generation of "tub-preachers."[58] John Lathrop succeeded him as pastor during whose tenure the congregation began asking a number of questions brought up by the early separatists, particularly with respect to Anglican ceremonies and infant baptism. Lathrop and his successor Henry Jessey (1637) refused to separate from the Church of England, thus separate-leaning church members began leaving them in the 1630s. One group called John Spilsbury as its pastor (or joined a church he had previously gathered), a man committed to believers' baptism and as early as 1638 adopted the practice of immersion.[59] Another group ultimately

---

57. Tolmie said that this group had "an impact out of all proportion to their numbers." Tolmie, *Triumph of the Saints*, 27. See also White, "English Particular Baptists and the Great Rebellion, 1640–1660," 16–29. Tombes explained, "And that the Anabaptists have been so cast out and rendered odious as they have been hath been the reason why they have been forced to become a Sect (which I do not justifie) and by reason thereof, factious spirits have joyned with them, and perverted them with other errours, which perhaps had not happened, had they been more tenderly and considerately handled at first." Tombes, *Apology or Plea for the Two Treatises*, 32. It was probably on this note that Jessey lamented, "If one that is in the *Presbyterian* way, or in the way of the *Independants*, or *Anabaptists*, so tearmed: If one, or two, or divers of them be *Hypocrites*, or *proud*, or *deceitfull*, or *cruell*, &c. Do not thence say, These are your *Presbyterians* . . ." (Jessey, *Storehouse of Provision*, To the Reader).

58. Tolmie, *Triumph of the Saints*, 14. He thought that the church demonstrated the explosive potential of Separatism (and semi-separatism) in that it cut through social barriers as well as institutional ones. Semi-separate meant they kept communion with the Anglican Church but met separately.

59. White surveyed an important document supposedly passed from William Kiffin to Richard Adams to Benjamin Stinton to Thomas Crosby. He concluded that the secessions in 1633–1638 did not have to be related to infant baptism, although they could have been; rather, the seceders believed that English parish churches were not true churches. White, "Baptist Beginnings and the Kiffin Manuscript," 27–37. He recognized that "outright rejection of the Church of England as false at once brought the baptism she had administered into question," a belief going back to Barrow. Ibid., 35.

called William Kiffin as its pastor and became notable for its stance on closed-communion. Jessey's church decided to split amicably in 1640 with one group being led by Praisegod Barbone and remaining connected with the establishment and infant baptism. Jessey's group, having held a "sober conference" on the matter in 1640, experienced two more secessions of members who adopted believers' baptism by immersion. The first, around 1641, resulted in three churches: a short-lived congregation led by Richard Blunt, a congregation led by Thomas Kilcop that was joined by Benjamin Cox, and a congregation led by Thomas Shepard. The second, around 1644, called Hanserd Knollys as its pastor. Knollys eventually baptized Jessey in 1645, but Jessey decided that such action was an individual's decision, and his church remained open-membership. The churches led by Spilsbury, Kiffin, Kilcop, and Shepard were four of the seven to sign the First London Confession, and Knollys's church joined them in 1646.[60] A number of these men had extensive connections with the established church. Cox graduated from Christ Church, Oxford; Jessey and Knollys graduated from Christ College, Cambridge (as did Francis Johnson, Francis Cornwell, and Henry Denne); Cox and Knollys both left livings in the Church of England.[61]

The London Particular Baptists had a widespread influence in England, and the actions and practices of the churches with which they had contact will also be used to provide a glimpse into how they applied their principles in worship. For example, B. R. White went to great lengths to explain the importance of the London churches in a nationwide strategy of church planting and associating superintended particularly by William Kiffin. Kiffin had extensive contact with the Irish Baptist churches, the first

---

He also insisted that Jacob's church was only semi-separate, leading to tension with the members who leaned toward full separation. See also White, "Who Really Wrote the 'Kiffin Manuscript'?," 3–10. Duesing concluded that believers' baptism had become the divisive issue sometime between 1633 and 1638. Duesing, "Counted Worthy," 123–29.

60. See White, "Baptist Beginnings and the Kiffin Manuscript," 27–37; Duesing, "Counted Worthy," 141ff. Wooley believed that Kiffin joined Lathrop's church in 1634 and formed his own church out of Spilsbury's in 1640. Wooley, "Editorial," 2. Kiffin noted the influence of Burroughs in his joining a semi-separatist congregation and was comfortable allowing baptism to be an individual decision. However, when Knollys reopened the issue in 1644, Kiffin took a harder stance and some left Jessey's church to join him. Alarmed, Jessey sought the advice of Goodwin, Nye, Burroughs, Simpson, and Barbone, who counseled him to recognize Kiffin's church. Tolmie, *Triumph of the Saints*, 42–56; Duesing, "Counted Worthy," 156–58.

61. See Owen, *Records of an Old Association*, 151; and Nutter, *Story of the Cambridge Baptists*, 8–20. Wright had Jessey graduating from St. John's College, Cambridge. *ODNB*, s.v. "Jessey, Henry," 1.

Introduction

Baptists in Bristol, Daniel King in the Midlands, and he (and Jessey) steered the Dorchester Association away from a Fifth-Monarchist position. Kiffin and Spilsbury worked with Thomas Tillam in Northumberland as well as the Abingdon Association.[62] Hanserd Knollys maintained a relationship with Tillam at Hexham, exchanging multiple letters with him. Knollys also visited Suffolk, and even (while his church shared Jessey's building in Swan Alley, Coleman Street) joined Tombes and Jessey in a 1653 circular appealing for unity among a number of Baptist churches in the countryside.[63] Henry Jessey, who had helped start an Independent church in Wales, maintained relationships with Tombes's network of churches practicing believers' baptism in the west and even baptized Broadmead's pastor, helping them and the nearby churches during a Quaker upsurgance in 1654–5.[64] Benjamin Cox appeared at multiple meetings of the Midlands Association and the Abingdon Association, as did Kiffin and Edward Harrison in person or print.[65]

However, the Particular Baptists were not the only Baptists in London (or even on Coleman Street). Two men have already been mentioned as having extensive connections with Particular Baptists, Thomas Lambe and Edward Barber, who had begun baptizing by dipping before any Particular Baptists. Their church meeting at Bell Alley, Coleman Street (later to be known as a General Baptist church), boasted connections with

62. See White, "William Kiffin," 91–103; White, "Henry Jessey," 98–110. White further hinted that Jessey and Kiffin may have remained kindred spirits partially because their personal wealth separated them from the majority of the Baptists. Bell noted that London was the hub of all Particular Baptist organization in England. Bell, *Apocalypse How?*, 129.

63. *Broadmead*, 334–51; Klaiber, *Story of the Suffolk Baptists*, 204. A similar 1653 circular related to the Fifth Monarchy movement also signed by Jessey and Tombes was recorded in Anderson, "Fifth Monarchist Appeal and the Response of an Independent Church at Canterbury, 1653," 72–80; also White, "Organisation of the Particular Baptists, 1644–1660," 214.

64. *ODNB*, s.v. "Jessey, Henry;" Duesing, "Counted Worthy," 111ff., 136ff. Duesing attributed an enduring, widespread influence to Jessey. Jessey and Tombes even sent joint letters to New England. See Anderson, "Letters of Henry Jessey and John Tombes to the Churches of New England, 1645," 30–40.

65. White, *Association Records*, 33ff., 43ff., 95ff., 131ff., 168ff. Another Baptist, Thomas Collier, heavily influenced the Western Association of Particular Baptists. Collier directly wrote against both the First and Second London Confessions and was well known to the London Particular Baptists, and his perspective identified Baptist challenges. *ODNB*, s.v. "Collier, Thomas." White noted multiple connections between Collier and London. White, "The Organisation of the Particular Baptists," 222. Bell believed that Collier, though unorthodox and opposed to particular atonement, was deeply committed to the Particular Baptist movement. Bell, *Apocalypse How?*, 145.

Francis Cornwell, Henry Denne, Samuel Oates, and Benjamin Cox, and also maintained an evangelistic presence across England.[66] Important to later developments in this book, John Griffith broke away from Lambe's church in 1652 over a disagreement about the laying on of hands in baptism (and another General Baptist church started this same year by William Rider in favor of laying on of hands would be noteworthy for performing the first dissenting ordination in London—for Benjamin Keach—in 1668).[67] These Baptists offered a valuable perspective with respect to worship in that they occasionally promoted different conclusions than did Particular Baptists.

There are a few more men of note to our purposes. One, a baptizer named John Tombes, was contemporary with the early London Particular Baptists and had extensive contact with them. Oxford trained, he began to doubt infant baptism and asked the Westminster Assembly to debate the matter. When they refused, he sought counsel from London Particular Baptists, including Jessey, and became the most famous baptizing opponent of Westminster. Tombes represented an interesting intersection of beliefs: a believers' Baptist who desired a relationship with the established church. His voluminous and scholarly publications affected Baptist

---

66. Coleman Street was a densely populated parish and a hotbed of separatist activity. Coffey, *John Goodwin and the Puritan Revolution*, 47, 59. Winter argued that the General Baptists cooperated with one another but no one else. Winter, "The Lord's Supper: Admission and Exclusion among the Baptists of the Seventeenth Century," 267–68. This perspective certainly contributed to the idea that the General Baptists were a self-conscious, independent denomination. However, the connections between the two groups of London Baptists indicate that the line was not so clear. Wright, "Baptist Alignments and the Restoration of Immersion, 1638–44 Part 1," 261–80, and idem, "Part 2," 346–69, focused on a 1641 meeting at Whitechapel as proof of their overlap. Nicholson and others saw the General Baptist office of Messenger primarily as an evangelistic or church planting office. Particular Baptists had a similar office in the 1650s, but General Baptists maintained it in their confessions throughout the century. Nicholson, "Office of 'Messenger' amongst British Baptists in the Seventeenth and Eighteenth Centuries," 206–25.

67. See Whitley, *Baptists of London*, 101–11. Samuel Oates was notorious for being accused of murder in Essex when a woman he baptized died of chill. See Klaiber, *Story of the Suffolk Baptists*, 19. Payne noted that Francis Cornwell promoted the laying on of hands as early as 1646, and his church tolerated him until he later insisted there be separation between those in favor and opposed. Payne, "Baptists and the Laying on of Hands," 203–15. Tolmie believed that Griffith was Cornwell's most important convert. Tolmie, *Triumph of the Saints*, 78ff. Wright believed that the controversy over laying on of hands was more about forming churches than anything liturgical. Wright, *Early English Baptists*, 12.

Introduction

thought in ways described below.⁶⁸ Other men were co-workers with early London Particular Baptists. In 1656, Spilsbury was called by the church at Wapping, where John Norcott succeeded him (and then Hercules Collins, who had close relationships with the next generation of leaders). Benjamin Cox joined Kilcop's church in 1646; Edward Harrison offered them a meetinghouse in Petty France in 1663, and that church ordained Nehemiah Cox and William Collins in 1676. William Kiffin, who led the church at Devonshire Square until his death in 1701, served variously with Thomas Paul, Thomas Hardcastle, and Richard Adams. Hanserd Knollys, whose church wandered around Wapping, Tower Street, Broken Wharf, and George Yard until his death in 1692, was joined and eventually succeeded by Robert Steed. Knollys and Kiffin were also instrumental in discipling a man named Benjamin Keach who had been a General Baptist.⁶⁹

Be aware that this book's heavy emphasis on the writings of these key leaders is a limitation, however necessary. Worship was an experience shared by the entire church; it was the one regular event in which a church member participated in the life and function of the church. In other words, worship was not a subject about which to be written but an event to be enjoyed. It was the actual point of contact between real people and the debates recounted in this book. These leaders made valuable and powerful contributions to Baptist belief and practice in worship, but they cannot speak absolutely for the masses. Baptist meetings were not theological symposiums but gatherings of ironmongers and butchers and cobblers, often poor ones at that, regularly in groups of less than twenty.⁷⁰

---

68. *ODNB*, s.v. "Tombes, John," 1–4; Tombes, *Apology or Plea for the Two Treatises*; Klaiber, "Baptists at Bewdly," 116–24; Duesing, "Counted Worthy," 162–63. Though he fostered a number of Baptist churches across England, Tombes was ultimately vilified by Baptists and Presbyterians alike. See Tombes, *Addition to the Apology*, 19–21, for an example of his contact with Particular Baptists.

69. See Whitley, *Baptists of London*, 101–10. White also noted the difficulty of establishing a clear timeline for some leaders in their churches. White, "The Organisation of the Particular Baptists," 217.

70. Kiffin acknowledged, "True it is, that our Churches since the first, have not been filled with many of them that have the Riches of this World." Kiffin et al., *Serious Answer*, 17. Betteridge reported the following descriptions of small Baptist churches. In Frolesworth: "An anabaptisticall meeting for several yeares held at house of Thomas Townsend of this pish kept by the same psons as in Leire do every fortnight in number 10 or 15 of the meaner sort." In Leire: "One Conventicle of Anabaptists of the poorer sort of people about 20 in number John Kitchin of Lutterworth Ironmonger being theire teacher they usually meet on Sundayes at the dwelling house of Elisha Lord husbandman." In Ashby Parva: "One Conventicle of Anabaptists consisting of the poorer sort of people about twenty in number Tho: Morris husbandman being theire teacher

Most of them simply wanted to obey God with a clear conscience (as many Baptists today want to be "a simple Bible believer"). They may never have participated in a printed theological debate, especially in rural areas, but they participated in worship every week. These leaders gave their principles a voice, else no one would have followed them, but they can never claim full representation for all early English Baptists.[71]

---

they usually meete on Sunday at the dwelling house of Roger Norman an excommunicate person." Betteridge, "Early Baptists in Leicestershire and Rutland, Part 3," 361.

71. Ellis acknowledged this in his essay, "Gathering around the Word," 101. However, then as today, there must be some point of contact between Baptist layman and Baptist theologian. Marshall rejected the First London Confession because he did not think it spoke for the common Anabaptist, most of whom he believed held continental Anabaptist doctrines. Tolmie, *Triumph of the Saints*, 64. But if that were true, then the leaders would have been inexplicably out of touch with their church members. There was too much at stake for church members to risk persecution and imprisonment unless they held a deeply shared interest with their church leaders.

two

The Liturgical World of the English Reformation

The Tudor Church and Revolutions in Worship

To demonstrate that pure worship was the early English Baptist distinctive, the perspectives on worship of the London Particular Baptists as defined in the previous section can be compared with that of three other groups. The most obvious group would be those Protestants who interacted with them (whether approving or disapproving), specifically with respect to worship. Not only did their perceptions offer potential insight into Baptist practices and ideas, but they also showed where the Baptists took the same influences and priorities to unique conclusions about the purposes and actions of the church's worship. But two other perspectives were equally important for shaping and directing the Baptists' beliefs of worship, if very much in the background, namely that of the Church of England, especially as represented in London, and that of the early English Separatists. The London Particular Baptists did not develop their convictions in a vacuum. Many of them emerged from the Church of England, and not a few of their early leaders had been trained as Anglican clergymen. Many of them took inspiration from the earlier Separatists. All of them lived in a society whose identity was intimately tied to the rituals and ceremonies of their religious life, though that had begun to change in the seventeenth century. The liturgical context of the English Reformation may be less familiar to the reader, so this chapter will summarize the perspectives of the established church and the early Separatists with respect to worship, divided for convenience into the eras of the Tudors and the Stuarts. English worship was instrumental in English society, and these eras saw the birth of many complaints that Baptists would consider as they forged their separate identity in the 1640s and beyond.

National Worship, National Identity

However one chooses to understand the process of reformation that began in England under Henry VIII, the word "complex" applies.[1] As Western Europe slowly convulsed under the political and religious implications of Luther's doctrine of justification, England took a path unlike any of her neighbors. Diarmaid MacCulloch believed the West had been based on two pillars: "a devotional pattern centred on the power of the mass and the power of the clergy who performed it" and "the unity provided by the Pope."[2] If correct, that would very elegantly explain England's uniqueness. When Luther overthrew the mass and rewrote the liturgy, he toppled both of those pillars, for the church's ceremonies were the single point of contact between most people and the teachings of the church. Luther believed the Reformation would tap into a dissatisfaction many commoners had with the church's ceremonies, ceremonies that were controlled by written liturgies, steeped in centuries of mystery, and performed in a language that few understood.[3] But he miscalculated its impact, for the German Mass of 1524 appeased neither those who wished to overthrow Roman supersti-

---

1. Even historians as disparate as Dickens and Haigh (who considered Dickens a Whig interpreter) agreed on this descriptor. See Dickens, *English Reformation*, 325; and Haigh, *English Reformation Revised*, 19.

2. MacCulloch, *Later Reformation in England*, 5.

3. The Mass, ordered by the Missal and augmented by the Processional, may have been the most infamous but was not the only one. Priests also celebrated the Divine Office, a series of daily prayer services ordered by the Breviary (Matins in the night, Laud at daybreak, Prime in early morning, Terce at 9:00, Sext at noon, None at 3:00, Vespers in the evening, and Compline at bedtime). They carried a Manual, or Sacerdotal, for the occasional services of marriage, baptism, and extreme unction. Finally, bishops carried a Pontifical for their own occasional services of ordination and confirmation. Adding to the dissatisfaction, many bishops made minor modifications to these liturgies. In England alone at the time of the Reformation, there were at least two hundred different Missals in use with the five major ones being the Salisbury (Sarum), Hereford, Bangor, York, and Lincoln.

The Liturgical World of the English Reformation

tion in their worship nor those who realized they preferred the traditional ceremonies of their heritage. The commoners' experience of the German Reformation was too often violent, as the Peasants' War demonstrated.

On the other hand, when Henry VIII declared himself supreme head of the English church in 1536, he toppled the pillar of the Pope but kept the pillar of the ritual or liturgical identity, which was undeniably rooted in Roman Catholicism. Henry was doctrinally a Catholic with respect to the ceremonies, but he built his independent, national church with the help of reform-minded Thomas Cromwell and Thomas Cranmer.[4] This unique convergence of evangelical and royalist impulses, combined with the conservative sentiment of many Englishmen, set the table for the sensational events that would identify the English Reformation. Henry himself was strongly attached to the traditional forms of worship; he believed in the Mass and transubstantiation and declared in 1536 that the clergy should instruct the people as to the true meaning of all of the ceremonies.[5] Consequently, Henry limited the extent of the liturgical reform allowed during his lifetime to the removal of all traces of the Pope from the liturgy and permission to offer prayers in English for England during certain processions.[6] But his court put into place the mechanisms by which future liturgical change would be inevitable: Cromwell was able to

---

4. MacCulloch thought that this confluence of factors, namely that Henry was "a doctrinal Catholic who nevertheless left the future of his realm in the hands of Protestants," more than anything made England's Reformation unique. MacCulloch, *Later Reformation in England*, 6.

5. See Brightmann and Mackenzie, "History of the Book of Common Prayer," 140ff. Duffy believed that Henry's defense of elevation, procession, creeping to the cross, Candlemas, churching women, and chrisoms (the white robe given to the infant at baptism) was a tremendous setback to the reformers. Duffy, *Stripping of the Altars*, 411, also 421ff.

6. This attachment prevented any kind of alliance with Protestant Germany, especially problematic for Cromwell and his Lutheran tendencies. They had negotiated the Thirteen Articles in 1537 based on the Augsburg Confession, but Henry could not agree to it. In it, the Germans had insisted that ceremonies "are in themselves not worship, but only expressions of 'the fear of God, faith, love, and obedience,' which are the true worship; and if they do not conduce to true worship, or are contrary to the Word of God, or involve sin, or obscure the glory and benefits of Christ, they ought to be abolished." Henry disagreed. See Cranmer's personal documents cited in Brightmann and Mackenzie, "History of the Book of Common Prayer," 146. Upon his death, Henry requested that "the said dean and canons [of St. George Chapel], and their successors forever, shall find two priests, to say masses at the said alter, to be made where we have before appointed our tomb to be made and stand, and also, after our decease, keep yearly four solemn obits for us within the said college of Windsor." Rust, *First of The Puritans*, 28. Lord Somerset struck down this request posthumously.

sever the English Church from the Pope and subject her to the king by declaring Britain an empire under an emperor, Cranmer argued the divine sanction of royal authority, and Henry located in himself the power of the common priesthood so embedded in the Reformation. Though Cranmer never allowed him the authority to establish doctrine (and Henry distrusted any limitation of his power), this established the precedent of the English monarch violating the traditional boundary between clergy and laity in ruling England's church.[7]

In the second place, Henry left the training of his son in the hands of committed Reformers. When Edward VI inherited the throne in 1547, Cranmer called him a second Josiah who would see God truly worshiped in England. That first year, Edward's uncle, the Lord Protector Somerset (the first ruling "Protestant" in England), saw that English was introduced into the Mass. He also passed a Chantries Act that, in addition to providing the crown with significant income, heavily damaged rural cohesion by removing many houses of worship.[8] By far the most important liturgical events of Edward's reign would be the publication of two Prayer Books, one in 1549 and a second in 1552. In beautiful prose, Thomas Cranmer offered what he thought was a cautious, careful compromise between all of the religious currents flowing in England in the first *Book of Common Prayer* in 1549. He appreciated, better than the continental Reformers who found his pace too slow, that the liturgy and ritual of the church was the "principal reservoir" of the identity of the English people, or their "traditional religion," and thus made only subtle changes to their worship.[9] He condensed the Divine Office to two services, Matins and Evensong, focused on the reading of scripture and the Psalter, and removed key actions that he believed led to the adoration of the elements in the Mass, the

---

7. See Yarnell, *Royal Priesthood in English Reformation*, chapters 4 and 5; and Dickens, *English Reformation*, 117ff., 168.

8. Dickens, *English Reformation*, 202, 215. Duffy thought that the greater impact of this act was removing the associated religious guilds (readers, singers, and lay pastors) that provided most of the opportunity for lay involvement in the liturgy. Duffy, *Stripping of the Altars*, 454ff. See also Brightmann and Mackenzie, "History of the Book of Common Prayer," 151.

9. Duffy, *Stripping of the Altars*, 2, 3. He convincingly noted, "The teaching of late medieval Christianity were graphically represented within the liturgy, endlessly reiterated in sermons, rhymed in verse treatises and saints' lives, enacted in the Corpus Christi and Miracle plays which absorbed so much lay energy and expenditure, and carved and painted on the walls, screens, bench-ends, and windows of the parish churches" (ibid., 3). See also Dickens, *English Reformation*, 218; and MacCulloch, *Later Reformation in England*, 14.

procession and elevation. But even this was too much for conservative Englishmen who wanted to keep their traditional forms. Some revolted, but others realized that Cranmer's language was so ambiguous that they could maintain their Catholic identity and still use the official Prayer Book. It was this observation, not a desire for further reform (although he likely always intended to modify the first book), that led Cranmer to supervise a more determined break from England's Catholic past in a second Prayer Book, heavily influenced by Martin Bucer and Peter Vermigli, and a much stricter Act of Uniformity that accompanied it.[10] The new Prayer Book was most notable for reducing the Mass to a Communion, moving the signing of the cross in baptism such that it no longer functioned as an exorcism, and drastically reducing the vestments.[11]

Edward died in 1553. In a dramatic foreshadowing of the future, while Cranmer was burying him according to the new English rite, Edward's sister Mary and her court did so according to the Requiem Mass.[12] Before the year was out, Queen Mary issued an Act of Repeal undoing every liturgical reform under Edward. As did Henry and Cranmer, she knew the importance of ritual structure and worship to her people and her reign.[13] While many Englishmen may have in fact welcomed the return of Catholic forms of worship, there can be no doubt that her more extreme actions, including burning Protestants at the stake and marrying into Hapsburg Spain, circumvented any hope of endearing herself or her Roman Catholicism to the majority.[14] Therefore when Elizabeth I ascended to the throne in 1558, she faced the daunting challenge of reuniting a nation that now knew how diverse its opinions on worship were, understanding that uniform liturgical worship would be the key to national unity. She also faced a sudden influx of ideas from the continent, particularly Geneva and Zurich, with the returning the Marian exiles. She simultaneously had to battle a conservative or Catholic presence (her decision to reintroduce

---

10. See Smyth, *Cranmer & the Reformation under Edward VI*, 233ff.; Duffy, *Stripping of the Altars*, 467ff.; and Dickens, *English Reformation*, 233.

11. For example, compare the invitations of the priests: "The body of our Lord Jesus Christ, which was given for thee, preserve thy body and soul unto everlasting life" (1549), and "Take and eat this in remembrance that Christ died for thee, and feed on him in thy heart by faith with thanksgiving" (1552). Among other things, the second Prayer Book replaced the word Mass with Holy Communion, Altar with Lord's Table, Corporal with vessel, Vestment with cope, and Chalice with cup.

12. Brightmann and Mackenzie, "History of the Book of Common Prayer," 178ff.

13. See Duffy, *Stripping of the Altars*, 5.

14. See in particular Haigh, *English Reformation Revised*.

Edward's second Prayer Book with minor changes in 1559 passed the House of Lords by only three votes) and a growing "Puritan" sentiment (a measure that would eliminate the sign of the cross in baptism, the use of organs, and kneeling at communion in 1562 failed the House of Commons by only one vote). Though Elizabeth was no Catholic, she preferred the ceremonialism that captivated her father; her injunctions tended to be conservative, such as allowing hymns to be sung in the Office and reintroducing vestments, particularly the surplice. Her reign would be marked by conflict with the new Puritanism, particularly with respect to the Prayer Book.[15]

"Puritan" is a vague term for one could find "Puritans" inside and outside the Anglican Church prescribing every theory of church government and located in every social class. Dickens and Davies thought of Puritans as those who desired to worship God by purified forms, emphasizing the Bible and moral living.[16] Obviously such Christians were always a part of English Church, but the name "Puritan" came to be applied to a distinct religious party in England, of which some would become Separatists, perhaps in 1566 or 1567. In 1566, Archbishop Parker (without the Queen's signature) forced through an *Advertisement* demanding uniformity to the "rites and manners in the ministration of God's holy word, in open prayer and ministration of sacraments, as also to be of one decent behaviour in their outward apparel." Hetherington believed that was the year that Puritan patience gave way to active resistance and that the first secret "Puritan" churches appeared.[17] William Bradshaw offered a more detailed description of English Puritanism around 1604: the primary Puritan principle was the desire to worship God by the perfect rule of His Word and no invention of man. Following that, Puritans believed in the

---

15. See Brightmann and Mackenzie, "History of the Book of Common Prayer," 180ff.; Phillips, *Background of the Prayer Book*, 32; and Cardwell, *History of Conferences*, 40–41.

16. Dickens, *English Reformation*, 313, 319; Davies, *Worship of the English Puritans*, 8ff. White similarly emphasized the Puritan marks of a church: right preaching, right administration of the sacraments, and right discipline. White, *English Separatist Tradition*, 35.

17. *The Advertisements*, in Gee and Hardy, eds., *Documents Illustrative of English Church History*; Hetherington, *History of Westminster Assembly*, 36–38. Somewhat ironically, Pope Pius V issued a decree in 1566 that forbade attendance in Anglican services. MacCulloch thought the first overtly "Puritan" church appeared in 1567. MacCulloch, *Later Reformation in England*, 35. See also White, *English Separatist Tradition*, 33.

equality of every visible church, the vitality of the pastorate as a preaching and teaching office, and the importance of proper church discipline.[18]

It should come as no surprise that many of Elizabeth's conflicts with Puritans were on the subject of worship. In some ways, she was betrayed by the "slackness and slovenliness" of her ministers, whose poor observance aggravated many serious churchmen.[19] But it seems clear that the Puritans wanted nothing short of a new English Church regardless of the qualities of the old. In the late 1560s, Puritan ministers began organizing "prophesyings," voluntary clerical worship services involving prayer and a sequence of short sermons based on a given subject, which the Marian exiles had observed in Zurich under Heinrich Bullinger.[20] In 1576, Edmund Grindal, Archbishop of Canterbury, officially employed prophesyings as a means of training the clergy, at which point Elizabeth intervened. She knew that she needed a strong clerical hierarchy to match the growing power of the secular hierarchy, and she knew that powerful preaching was an invaluable tool to influence the people, but she believed such gatherings would be likely to stir dissent. She decided that a few loyal bishops would

---

18. Bradshaw, *Several Treatises of Worship and Ceremonies*, 35–50. Morgan traced Puritan ideas of elected church officers (pastor, teacher, elder, deacon), no clerical hierarchy, and a regenerate church membership to 1588. Morgan, *Visible Saints*, 11–12. The four primary parties in English religion were termed "Prelatical, Presbyterian, Independent, Anabaptist." Kiffin, *Sober Discourse*, 2. The term Puritan often (but not always) related to Presbyterian. The terms dissenter and separatist generally referred to an Independent or Anabaptist. Hill thought the political meaning was such that Presbyterian referred to a conservative Parliamentarian and Independent referred to someone in favor of religious toleration. Hill, *Century of Revolution*, 165.

19. Phillips, *Background of the Prayer Book*, 47. He blamed the Prayer Book's failure on the priests. An anonymous document published in 1565 complained, "Some say the service and prayers in the chancel, others in the body of the church: some say the same in a seat made in the church, some in the pulpit with their faces to the people; some keep precisely to the order of the book, others intermeddle psalms in metre; some say in a surplice, others without a surplice" (Brightmann and Mackenzie, "History of the Book of Common Prayer," 184). The surplice was of particular interest to the Puritans because the people revered it, creating an impossible barrier to the pure worship of God.

20. These services, which included a series of prayers and psalms and sermons on a given theme (as they interpreted 1 Corinthians 14 to enjoin), became the basis for several variations of Puritan worship. John a Lasco, superintendent of foreign churches (Strangers' Churches) in England, began using them in the 1550s, and John Knox followed suit in Scotland in the 1560s. Hetherington noted their use in Northampton 1571 to the jealousy of the bishops. Hetherington, *History of Westminster Assembly*, 41. White felt that Puritanism would always result in Separatism once patience was exhausted. White, *English Separatist Tradition*, 33. See also Leuenberger, *Archbishop Cranmer's Immortal Bequest*, 133.

better serve her purposes for a unified England than many diversely educated Puritans, and the state-controlled universities produced a strong but predictable preaching ministry.[21]

The heart of Elizabeth's struggle was one for national identity. Her overarching policy was to unite as many subjects as possible in uniform liturgical worship, to suppress all variant forms of worship, and to claim absolute supremacy.[22] The Queen was painfully mindful of the instability created by the seismic liturgical shifts under her three predecessors—Paul Rust quipped, "Church-going never fully recovered from the shock"[23]— and concluded that diversity in worship could only weaken England. The majority of loyal Englishmen clearly agreed. Murray Tolmie argued, "Separatism remained an unpopular alternative with the mass of puritans" precisely because they were unwilling to abandon "the uniform and universal national church in principle," especially as they defined themselves against Catholic Spain.[24] This attitude carried well into the seventeenth century. Common worship bred common beliefs and a common identity: to be English was to worship with England's church; to disobey the queen in a thing indifferent was schismatic.[25] Furthermore, and perhaps even

---

21. Although Elizabeth's logic may have been sound, her execution was disastrous. She replaced Grindal with John Whitgift in 1583. Extremely anti-Puritanical (conservative in the sense of "conformist"), Whitgift unwittingly generated sympathy for Separatist principles by feeding accusations of incompetence in the established church. In 1581, Cambridge-educated schoolmaster Robert Browne officially separated from the Church of England and formed the first Separatist congregation (albeit in Middleburgh, Netherlands). The cry of his short-lived church was "Reformation without Tarying for Anie," and he was soon followed by fellow Cambridge graduate John Greenwood and supporter Henry Barrow who established and defended Separate congregations in London before their executions in 1593. In 1585, Presbyterian Puritan Thomas Cartwright was caught possessing a directory with a detailed description of synods and presbyteries surpassing five hundred clergy—a veritable church within a church. See Dickens, *English Reformation*, 294ff.; Yarnell, *Royal Priesthood*, conclusion; and Mitchell, *Westminster Assembly*, 42ff.

22. Brightmann and Mackenzie, "History of the Book of Common Prayer," 180.

23. Rust, *First of the Puritans*, 81. In disclosure, Rust was a Roman Catholic who saw the subsequent discord in English society as proof of the inferiority of Protestantism.

24. Tolmie, *Triumph of the Saints*, 37. He beautifully captured the experience of those who did saying, "These persons went out from hearing Common Prayer, not knowing whither they went" (ibid., 29). Wright less-beautifully called it the "separatist oblivion." Wright, *Early English Baptists*, 50. Social historian Wrightson believed the use of the catechism to teach honor to parents, good neighborliness, and submission to the governing authorities to be a "barefaced" manipulation of this innate English patriotism, but he failed to admit the possibility that their religion had legitimate significance. Wrightson, *English Society*, 68.

25. Bradshaw, *Several Treatises of Worship and Ceremonies*, 32.

more importantly to the masses of Englishmen, to separate from England's church was to cut one's self off from weddings, baptisms, burials, and civil summons.[26] When the early Baptists chose to break with common worship, they put themselves into a firestorm of accusation; however, they did not believe they disobeyed the (by that time) king in anything indifferent, nor that they were schismatic. In doing so, they followed a well-trod path of earlier Puritans and Separatists.[27]

A Separate Church, A Separate Identity

Whether one agrees with A. G. Dickens that the English Reformation was an inexorable progression towards a peculiarly Anglican form of Protestantism carried along by a generally accepted ideology or with Christopher Haigh that the English people actually preferred their traditional symbols and rituals in their churches and that the Reformation proceeded by a fortunate series of unrelated events, the appearance and continued existence and growth of a party of separating English Christians was quite

---

26. See L. F., *Speedy Remedie against Spirituall Incontinencie*. No one has ever identified "L. F." Canne listed a number of reasons he had heard from those unwilling to separate, including, "The Law of the Land is, that all should come to heare this service, and therefore they will be punished which refuse to doe so . . . We shalbe charged with sedition, schisme, heresie, abstinancie, &c. if we goe not to it . . . We shall quite loose the love of our friends, if we refuse to joyne with them in this worship . . . But our feare is, if we should separate our selves from this false worship, that we shall not be able to beare the troubles, which will follow thereupon" (Canne, *Necessitie of Separation*, 123–24).

27. The debate over things indifferent was intimately tied to the Prayer Book. In 1559, reductionist Protestants appealed against Marian Catholics to Elizabeth to simplify the so-called things indifferent. "By 'ceremonies and rites of the church,' we understand those ceremonies and rites, which neither expressly, neither by necessary deduction or consequence, are commanded or forbidden in the Scriptures, but are things of their own nature indifferent. As for example, the form and manner of prayers before and after baptism, and at the administration of the sacrament, public prayer, number of holydays, times of fasting, and such like." They explained that these ceremonies would fall into abuse, "First, if they be taken as [necessary] things pertaining to the worshipping of God. Next, if they grow to an inordinate number. Thirdly, if they teach nothing, nor no man can have understanding of them. And to conclude, if they be invented for lucre's sake, to get money" (Cardwell, *History of Conferences*, 72–73, 78). The first two reasons would resonate with Baptists for more than a century. However, the arguments used against Baptists and Puritans in defense of Anglican worship—even when that worship was moderated by a formerly Catholic priest and attended by openly profane men—would also be taking shape during this time. See, for example, Some, *Godly Treatise containing and deciding certaine questions*, published in 1588.

remarkable. In either case, those Puritans who began to separate from Elizabeth's church travelled a road very different from their countrymen. For the sake of space, the voice of the dissenters will be heard through a famous family of Separate or semi-Separate (meaning they functioned autonomously but did not declare for separation) churches, those led by John Smyth, Thomas Helwys, Francis Johnson, Henry Ainsworth, and Henry Jacob, that directly or indirectly influenced the London Particular Baptists.[28]

Francis Johnson declared his cause for separation to be "Ministerie, Worship, and Government Ecclesiasticall."[29] Anglican worship was substantially unchanged from Cranmer's second Prayer Book that Elizabeth had reinstated in 1559 to Johnson's day and beyond.[30] When one visited an Anglican house of worship for communion, he or she would have enjoyed a remarkably consistent experience throughout his life and largely throughout the country. After the people took their places, the priest stood in between them and a cloth-covered table, read a Collect and the Ten Commandments. Following each commandment the congregation asked forgiveness for their transgressions. The celebrant then read more Collects, a passage from an Epistle and a Gospel, the Nicene Creed, verses

---

28. John Smyth was a member of Francis Johnson's Independent presbyterian congregation in London (which he formed with Greenwood and Barrow) before becoming the leader of a Separatist congregation in Gainsborough. Under persecution, part of his church emigrated to America (the "Pilgrim Fathers") by route of Scrooby Manor, and he himself emigrated to Amsterdam with the patronage of Thomas Helwys. Part of Johnson's church had also emigrated to Amsterdam while Johnson was in prison, and Smyth came into conflict with their new teacher Henry Ainsworth. Smyth and Helwys adopted Baptist principles, and Helwys returned to London upon Smyth's death only to be executed. Henry Jacob was the leader of a Puritan congregation in London that would go on to give birth to the English Particular Baptists, but at the turn of the century he strove to convince Johnson to return from Separatism to Puritanism. Having seen that Separatism inevitably led to Smyth's de-churching position, he was rather torn in his sympathies.

29. Cited in Jacob, *Defence of the Churches and Ministry of Englande*, 70, who replied to Johnson's argument for separation with a careful defense of England's worship. Worship played a central role in the exchange. John Canne summarized their context as "the outward worship, used in the assemblies of England, the summe whereof (as the *Nonconformists* say) is contained in their communion booke, and hence the same is called divine service, (as for *preaching*, it is held to be no part thereof)." Canne, *Necessitie of Separation*, 72.

30. MacCulloch described, "The liturgy, already more elaborate and more reminiscent of older liturgical forms than any other Protestant service-book, took no account of developments in Protestant thinking after the early 1550s" (MacCulloch, *Later Reformation in England*, 32).

The Liturgical World of the English Reformation

of exhortation or a Homily, and a prayer for the king, church, clergy, and the people. Next, he read a general confession, the absolution, the Sursum Corda, the Sanctus, the Prayer of Humble Access, and the words of consecration followed by the Communion of the people. The service concluded with the Our Father, a prayer of thanksgiving, the Gloria in Excelsis, and the minister's blessing.[31]

Because they rejected the *Book of Common Prayer*, Separatist worship would have been very dissimilar. A critical difference came down to an approach to the Bible: most Puritans and Separatists believed that only those things commanded in Scripture should be included in worship; most Catholics and Anglicans believed that only those things forbidden in Scripture should not be included in worship (the so-called regulative and normative principles).[32] Unfortunately, there are very few early descriptions of Separatist worship. An early Barrowist group clearly emulated the prophesyings:

> In the summer time they met together in the fields a mile or more about London. There they sit down upon a bank and divers of them expound out of the bible so long as they are there assembled. In the winter time they assemble themselves by 5 of the clock in the morning to that house where they made their Conventicle for that Sabbath day men and women together. There they continue in their kind of prayer and exposition of Scripture all that day. They dine together, after dinner making collection to pay for their diet and what money is left some of

---

31. *BCP* [1559], chapter 12. In cathedral churches, communion was celebrated weekly; in parish churches at least monthly. Hutton, *English Church*, 103.

32. Johnson wrote, "All parts of divine worship and service imposed onely by the will and pleasure of man upon the communicants in divine service, & that of necessity to be done, is will-worship" (*Twelve generall arguments, proving that the Ceremonies imposed . . . are unlawfull* [1605]; cited in Bradshaw, *Unreasonablenesse of the separation*, 106). Edward Coke, a lawyer and judge in Norwich, observed, "The last sort of recusants, though troublesome, yet in my conscience the least dangerous, are those which do with too much violence contend against some ceremonies used in the church; with whose indirect proceedings, in mine own knowledge, his majesty is not a little grieved. But I will hope (as his highness doth) that in time they will grow wise enough to leave their foolishness, and consider that ceremonies not against the analogy of faith, nor hindering faith's devotion, are no such bugbears as should scare them from the exercises of divine duties, nor cause them to disturb the peace of our church, whose government is more consonant to Scripture than all the best reformed churches at this day in the world" (cited in Cardwell, *History of Conferences*, 125). The use of the terms "regulative principle" and "normative principle" will be critiqued in chapter 4. Note that I use them out of convention, not precision; they are not terribly helpful terms.

them carrieth it to the prisons where any of their sect be committed. In their prayer one speaketh and the rest do groan or sob or sigh, as if they would ring out tears. . . . Their prayer is extemporal. In their conventicles they use not the Lord's Prayer, nor of any form of set prayer.[33]

A famous letter from Hugh and Anne Bromhead similarly described worship in John Smyth's church:

> We begin with a prayer; after read some one or two chapters of the Bible, give the sense thereof, and confer upon the same: that done, we lay aside our books, and after a solemn prayer made by the first speaker, he propoundeth some text out of the Scripture, and prophesieth out of the same by the space of one hour or three quarters of an hour. After him the third, the fourth, the fifth, etc. as the time will give leave. Then the first speaker concludeth with prayer as he began with prayer, with an exhortation to contribution to the poor, which collection being made, is also concluded with prayer. This morning exercise beginneth at eight of the clock and continueth unto twelve of the clock. The like course and exercise is observed in the afternoon from two of the clock unto five or six of the clock. Last of all, the execution of the government of the Church is handled.[34]

---

33. This came from a letter dated 1588, recorded in Payne, "Free Church Tradition and Worship," 55. Barrow himself spent that entire year in Fleet Prison. Underhill connected this letter with a conventicle that had recently stopped baptizing children. *Broadmead*, lxxii. Interestingly, Payne argued for a stronger Lutheran than Zwinglian influence on Baptist worship, specifically noting the vernacular, the centrality of the sermon, and the passion for worship. Perhaps he did not know about prophesyings. When Morgan described early Separatist worship, he stressed "spontaneity." He said, "Following the regular sermon of the minister, they set aside a time for 'prophecying,' that is, little extempore sermons or speeches by members of the congregation. These in turn were followed by a period for questions from the congregation about any points in which the sermon or prophecying had left them in doubt. They frowned on all set forms of prayers and liturgies, including the Lord's Prayer, which they regarded simply as a perfect example of a prayer, not as a set form of words to be repeated" (Morgan, *Visible Saints*, 27–28).

34. White, *English Separatist Tradition*, 126–27. Although it is beyond the scope of this book, Smyth held a unique but highly developed understanding of instituted worship, believing that worship was purely spiritual and thus could not be aided by any manmade appliance ("we lay aside our books"). This became a huge bone of contention with Ainsworth, who thought that the only difference between their churches had been Smyth's exclusive use of the Greek New Testament in worship compared with Ainsworth's willingness to use translations. Armed with this new variable, he accused Smyth of removing the matter of worship (the Scriptures) from his worship. See Smyth, *Differences of the Churches of the Seperation*, and Ainsworth's response, *A*

Thomas Helwys continued that path, writing in his confession, "That the church ought to assemble on every first day of the week: to pray, prophesy, praise God, break bread and perform all the other duties of spiritual communion which pertain to divine worship, the mutual edification of the members and the preservation of true religion."[35] The church at Fenstanton under the influence of John Denne maintained a simple service of prayer, exhortation, and business.[36] Any visitor to such a church "service" would have been taken aback, which is why some Puritans attempted to maintain their relationship with the comfortable English liturgy even as they stepped further into reformation.

There is no shortage of Separatist thoughts about worship, especially the abuses within the Anglican liturgy, and English Baptists as late as Benjamin Keach continued to refer to these early documents in their writings. Puritans and Separatists equally abhorred two elements of established worship: superstition and human precepts. Francis Johnson called the Anglicans "Samaritans" for worshipping through a manmade mediator (the liturgy) that which they did not know, a charge Henry Jacob could only half-heartedly deny by appealing to the general acceptance of their rule of worship.[37] Henry Ainsworth excoriated the Crown for expelling the Pope but keeping his "Prelacy and Ministry, his Lawes, Traditions and Canons, his Worship & service," and the greatest sin of replacing Christ's own liturgy of the New Testament with a human invention—the very definition of Antichrist. The woeful priests were so trapped in their ceremonies that they could not even begin to justify them biblically, leaving Ainsworth's group alone to "discerne betwixt the true worship of God & the Antichristian leitourgie."[38] Part and parcel with this accusation was the

---

Defence of the Holy Scriptures. Wright noted that the Bromheads' letter came from the Smyth church's post-rebaptism era. Wright, *Early English Baptists*, 33.

35. Rich, "Thomas Helwys' First Confession of Faith," 239.

36. See *Fenstanton*, gathered from a number of entries. McKibbens attempted to create an "order of worship" for all separatists based on these few sources. McKibbens, "Our Baptist Heritage in Worship," 53–69. McBeth included a short section on early Baptist worship that began with the Bromhead letter. He used the words "spontaneous" and "unpredictable" to describe it. McBeth, *Baptist Heritage*, 91–95.

37. Johnson attacked everything from the liturgy to the calendar to the prayers for the dead. Cited in Jacob, *Defence of the Churches and Ministry of Englande*, 17–18, 26–28, 35–38, 48. Jacob only defended preaching, prayer, and sacraments; the other elements he listed under possible corruptions that did not invalidate the rest of the worship. Jacob believed a church was incomplete without a pastor and needed to follow the pastor's direction. Duesing, "Henry Jacob," 289–93. This latent hierarchy explained at least one affinity he had with the established church.

38. Ainsworth and Johnson, *Confession of faith* (1607), 17, 7. This document was

indictment of their rules of enforcement, which violated the fundamental concept of a "voluntarie profession of the faith of Christ, in the fellowship of the Gospell."[39]

It is perhaps telling that Thomas Cranmer had shared their loathing of superstition. He looked with horror on the attitudes of the people:

> What made the people to run from their seats to the alter, and from altar to altar, and from sacring to sacring, peeping, tooting, and gazing at that thing which the priest held up in his hands, if they thought not to honor the thing which they saw? What moved the priests to lift up the sacrament so high over their heads? Or the people to say to the priests, "Hold up! Hold up!" or one man to say to another, "Stoop down before"; or to say, "This day I have seen my Maker"; and "I cannot be quiet except I see my Maker once a day"?[40]

Indeed, the second Prayer Book was designed to stamp out such superstition. However, he kept human precepts in worship—in fact, he built English worship on the principle that the Bible was not the sole source of worship practices: "If this saying be true, take away the whole Book of Service."[41] As a result, the superstition inherent in the people's traditional religion "slowly, falteringly, much reduced in scope, depth, and coherence[,] re-formed itself around the rituals and words of the prayer-book."[42]

---

almost identical with their earlier confession, *True Confession of the Faith* (1596). They argued that "the Lord is to be worshipped and called upon in spirit & truth, according to that forme of praier given by the Lord Jesus, Mat. 6. & after the Leitourgie of his own Testament, not by any other framed or imposed by men, much lesse by one translated from the Popish leitourgie, as the Book of common praier &c." Ibid., 71. Later, Ainsworth goaded the nonseparating Puritan Richard Bernard for his *The Separatists Schisme* saying, "[Let] him in his next book, proove that the Apocrypha scriptures and homily books, which they read in Gods worship are his *true Word*; that the sacraments which the unpreaching [priests] minister to their profane parishioners by their popish leitourgie, are true sacraments; let him approve by Gods word the observation of all their holy dayes, fasting dayes, with their prescript peculiar service; breifly, let him shew warrant for his service book, the making & use therof with al the popish contents therin" (Ainsworth, *Counterpoyson*, 194). Smyth credited Ainsworth with calling all Anglican churches false ("Idols") on account of their false worship. Smyth, *Paralleles, Censures, Observations*, 11, 103.

39. Ainsworth and Johnson, *Confession of faith*, 67–68.

40. Cited in Rust, *First of the Puritans*, 75–76.

41. Cranmer to Convocation, in Smyth, *Cranmer & the Reformation under Edward VI*, 264.

42. Duffy, *Stripping of the Altars*, 589. Duffy did not use the word "superstition," and it would be fair to note Haigh's caveat, "One man's superstition is another's spirituality"

The Liturgical World of the English Reformation

The Puritans, especially the Separatists, seethed about this outcome of Anglican worship. The final decades before the English Particular Baptists declared their separation saw a great polarization of these beliefs that ultimately erupted into Civil War.

THE STUART CHURCH AND A PURITAN REVOLUTION

A. G. Dickens thought that Anglicanism originated in a concept called *adiaphora*, or "things indifferent" in worship, a concept that will be central to chapter 4. England was unique for celebrating a spirit of compromise and a middle way between extremes, something Cranmer exemplified in his Prayer Books.[43] But England's middle way thrived only when those extremes were suppressed.[44] When the Puritans and Separatists declared that they would only worship God according to the rule of Scripture and the example of the apostles (and thus not the rule of the king), Cranmer loathed them, especially the Radicals. He rejected the apostolic church as incomplete and the Papal church as corrupt, leaving only the Constantinian church and the rule of the crown.[45] Mary and Elizabeth perpetuated the clerical hierarchy and their own royal priesthood, leaving no place for freedom of worship for the Puritans. While Elizabeth reigned in England, James VI did so in Scotland, where he struggled with a stronger party of Presbyterian Puritans. Therefore, when James united the thrones of England, Scotland, and Ireland as James I in 1603, he was not favorably disposed toward the desires of the English Puritans. When some such Puritans intercepted him on his way to London (to claim the throne!) with a petition to reduce the "burden of human rites and ceremonies" in English worship, his response was anything but enthusiastic.[46] As a

---

(Haigh, *English Reformation Revised*, 3). Dickens and MacCulloch regularly used the word "superstition."

43. Dickens, *English Reformation*, 180.

44. "[I]t is contended that there can be no peace in any churches or states whilst this principle [freedom of worship] is admitted." Owen, *Truth and Innocence Vindicated*, in *Works*, 13:463. Owen, of course, disagreed with that contention insofar as it suited him.

45. See MacCulloch, *Thomas Cranmer*, 280ff.

46. The document was called the "Millenary Petition" because 1,000 Puritan ministers supposedly signed it. Most of the document referred to religious ceremony. Specifically, they asked "that the cross in Baptism, interrogatories ministered to infants, confirmations, as superfluous, may be taken away: baptism not to be ministered by women, and so explained: the cap and surplice not urged: that examination may

gracious new sovereign, he agreed to a conference at Hampton Court in 1604, but he soon dismissed the Puritans saying, "If this be all the party hath to say, I will make them conform, or else I will harry them out of the land, or else do worse, hang them."[47] The failed Gunpowder Plot of 1605 only increased James's demands for conformity.[48] Both James and his son Charles I were coarse, holding their divine right over the church with the mantra, "No bishop, no King" (or its more cynical consequence, "the dependency of the Church upon the crown is the chiefest support of regal authority").[49] But James also brought scandal and financial failure, exacerbated by catastrophic harvest failures and regular outbreaks of the bubonic plague. During James's kingship, Puritanism took on a political character that it would keep through the Restoration; those who did not leave for the New World found themselves backed into the proverbial corner.

Charles I took the throne in 1625, and with the counsel of the Duke of Buckingham immediately entered into costly failures involving Spain and France and the Thirty Years War (which featured his reluctance to support the mainland Protestants), even dismissing an irate Parliament. Charles leaned towards Arminianism in his personal beliefs, significant because Puritans, especially Scottish Presbyterians, were aligning themselves more and more with a form of Calvinism. Charles inflamed this difference by appointing William Laud Archbishop of Canterbury in 1633.

---

go before the Communion: that it be ministered with a sermon: that divers terms of priests and absolution and some other used, with the ring in marriage, and other such like in the book, may be corrected: the longsomeness of service abridged: church-songs and music moderated to better edification: that the Lord's Day be not profaned: the rest upon holidays not so strictly urged: that there may be a uniformity of doctrine prescribed: no popish opinion to be any more taught or defended: no ministers charged to teach their people to bow at the name of Jesus: that the canonical Scriptures only to be read in the Church" (Cardwell, *History of Conferences*, 131–32).

47. Mitchell, *Westminster Assembly*, 70, although that last phrase may be apocryphal; see Clark, *History of English Nonconformity*, 1:246. The only Puritan gain from this conference was the commissioning of a new "authorized" translation of Scripture which was completed in 1611. See also Phillips, *Background of the Prayer Book*, 35ff. Hill thought that James smelled the Presbyterian system he was only too glad to leave behind. Hill, *Century of Revolution*, 80.

48. However, Wright and others valuably pointed out that enforcement was haphazard at best; for a time after 1604, "Offensive liturgical practices were often quietly omitted, in services dominated by the sermon, delivered by a minister who dressed plainly, in a building furnished in like manner" (Wright, *Early English Baptists*, 48). This leniency allowed pockets of dissatisfaction to grow, which would eventually lead to harsher crackdowns.

49. Charles I to Charles II, cited in Hill, *Century of Revolution*, 80.

The Liturgical World of the English Reformation

In some ways Arminian and in some ways simply anti-Calvinist (Peter Lake suggested the term "Laudian"), Laud promoted a vision of the church rooted in "the ceremonial and liturgical aspects of the beauty of holiness."[50] For Laud, the ceremonies of worship were so central to true religion that salvation depended on absolute conformity to the *Book of Common Prayer* (Laud used Elizabeth's version, which confusingly mixed Arminian and Calvinist elements of the 1549 and 1552 editions; Puritans already viewed it as vastly different from any continental, Reformed liturgy).[51] He employed the feared High Commission and Star Chamber to root out all Puritan dissent, likely inciting further radicalism. Their ambition proved their undoing, though, when Charles ordered Laud to enforce uniformity in Scotland in 1637.

The Scottish Calvinist Presbyterians had long been stirred up against James. In 1606, Presbyterian leaders had submitted a protest against all forms of prelacy. James responded by banishing John Welsh (John Knox's son-in-law), Andrew Melville, and others involved. By 1618, the leadership turnover was so complete that James was able to push the Five Articles of Perth through Scottish Parliament, which included kneeling at communion, celebrating Easter, Pentecost, and Christmas, observing Episcopal confirmation, and allowing private baptism and private Lord's Suppers—not just Romish ceremonies, but antipredestinarian ones with sacramental overtones. Public unrest, which both James and Charles ignored, ignited rebellion on July 23, 1637. Before the Dean of Edinburgh was to say the first English service as decreed by Laud, an old woman named Jenny Geddes stood up and hurled her stool at him, causing a full-scale riot; the English liturgy was never used in Scotland.[52] In 1638, the

---

50. Lake, "Laudian Style," 165.

51. Ibid., 167. MacCulloch noted that the very different theologies of the 1549 and 1552 books would be a problem for Laud and his opponents. MacCulloch, *Thomas Cranmer*, 625ff. Laud, however, was known to modify the liturgies without royal sanction. Tyacke argued that Laud was more interested in sacramentalism than Arminianism. Tyacke, "Archbishop Laud," 51–70.

52. This year also saw the publication of the most important book written on this particular subject. Gillespie, *A dispute against the English-popish ceremonies*. Gillespie and his arguments would go on to have a tremendous impact on the Westminster Assembly as they considered their own liturgical decisions. Gillespie also explained exactly why the practice of kneeling at the Lord's Supper offended so many: "The question about the idolatry of kneeling between them and us stands in this: Whether kneeling, at the instant of receiving the sacrament, before the consecrated bread and wine, purposely placed in our sight in the act of kneeling as signs standing in Christ's stead, before which we, the receivers, are to exhibit outwardly religious adoration, be formally idolatry or not? No man can pick a quarrel at the stating of the question

Scots drew up a National Covenant rejecting prelacy and English worship, drawing Charles into a war. Lacking funds and support, Charles had to recall Parliament to ask for money. Infuriated by their opposition to him, Charles quickly dismissed them, only to have to recall them again (the Short and Long Parliaments) in humiliation. Parliament began insisting on changes in the Church of England and her liturgy, noting a drift into Romism (the appearance of unauthorized candles and curtains in many churches) and superstition, to the point that Charles decided his battle was not against Scotland, but Parliament and the English Puritans.[53]

---

thus; for, 1. We dispute only about kneeling at the instant of receiving the sacramental elements, as all know. 2. No man denies inward adoration in the act of receiving, for in our minds we then adore by the inward graces of faith, love, thankfulness, etc., by the holy and heavenly exercise whereof we glorify God; so that he controversy is about outward adoration. 3. No man will deny that the consecrated elements are purposely placed in our sight when we kneel, except he say, that they are in that action only accidentally present before us no otherwise than the table-cloth or the walls of the church are. 4. That the sacramental elements are in our sight (when we kneel) as signs standing in Christ's stead, it is most undeniable" (ibid., 205). He concluded that the practice was idolatrous.

53. A conference took place at Savoy in 1641 in which English Puritans including Daniel Featley, Edmund Calamy, and Edward Reynolds demanded equal footing with the Prelates, led by Irish Archbishop James Ussher (note that they did not offer to extend this privilege to any other parties), in deciding England's form of worship. They declared to the king, "We are satisfied in our judgments concerning the lawfulness of a liturgy or form of worship, provided it be for matter agreeable to the word of God, and suited to the nature of the several ordinances and necessities of the church; neither too tedious, nor composed of too short prayers or responsals, not dissonant from the liturgies of other reformed churches, nor too rigorously imposed, nor the minister confined thereunto, but that he may also make use of his gifts of prayer and exhortation. Forasmuch as the Book of Common Prayer is in some things justly offensive, and needs amendment, we most humbly pray, that some learned, godly, and moderate divines of both persuasions may be employed to compile such a form as is before described, as much as may be in Scripture words; or at least to revise and reform the old, together with an addition of other various forms in Scripture phrase, to be used at the minister's choice. Concerning ceremonies; we hold ourselves obliged in every part of divine worship to do all things decently and in order and to edification; and are willing to be determined by authority in such things as, being merely circumstantial or common to human actions and societies, are to be ordered by the light of nature and human prudence. As to divers ceremonies formerly retained in the Church of England, we do in all humility offer to your majesty the following considerations: that the worship of God is in itself pure and perfect and decent without any such ceremonies: that it is then most pure and acceptable, when it has least of human mixtures: that these ceremonies have been imposed and advanced by some, so as to draw near to the significancy and moral efficacy of sacraments: that they have been rejected by many of the reformed churches abroad, and have been ever the subject of contention and endless disputes in this church: and therefore being in their own nature indifferent and mutable, they ought to be changed, lest in time they should be apprehended

Civil war, sometimes called the "Puritan Revolution," broke out in 1642. Hill noted that although there is a tendency to emphasize its social and political causes, the religious background to the war must not be missed. In other words, the term "Puritan Revolution" might be misleading, but it is not entirely inaccurate.[54] During these years, the Puritans consolidated their authority in Parliament. They believed that there could be no uniformity in worship until there was one form of government (dismissing episcopacy as an option, leaving Scottish Presbyterianism as the preferred option, and then the only option after the Solemn League and Covenant in 1643), and there could be no uniformity of confession until there was uniformity of worship. George Gillespie had warned Scotland in 1637, "If once you yield to these English ceremonies, think not that thereafter you can keep yourselves back from any greater evils, or grosser corruptions which they draw after them."[55] People began to petition Parliament for a national synod to abritrate the local differences they observed in church practice.[56] The Westminster Assembly met for the first time on July 1, 1643, and continued to meet through 1649. It consisted of some Prelates, who never actually joined the Assembly lacking the King's permission; some Independents, including Thomas Goodwin and Philip Nye; some Scots, including George Gillespie and Robert Baillie; but mostly Puritans who would become Presbyterians. In four years, it produced four important documents: *The Directory for the Publick Worship of God* (1645), *The Form of Presbyterial Church Government* (1645), *The Westmin-*

---

as necessary as the substantials of worship themselves. May it therefore please your majesty graciously to grant, that kneeling at the Lord's supper, and such holidays as are but of human institution, may not be imposed on such as scruple them: that the use of the surplice, and cross in baptism, and bowing at the name of Jesus may be abolished: and forasmuch as erecting altars and bowing towards them, and such like, having no foundation in the law of the land, have been introduced and imposed, we humbly beseech your majesty, that such innovations may not be used or imposed for the future" (Cardwell, *History of Conferences*, 252–53).

54. Hill, *Century of Revolution*, 75ff. Fincham thought there was no doubt as to the centrality of religion in the war. Fincham, *Early Stuart Church*, 22.

55. Gillespie, *Dispute Against the English Popish Ceremonies*, xliii. Klaiber posited that the main reason Parliament adopted Presbyterianism was to gain the support of Scotland against the King. Klaiber, *Story of the Suffolk Baptists*, 17.

56. The letter, *Humble Remonstrance In The Behalfe of the Protestants of this Kingdome* (1643), would seem to downplay the importance of worship in that it called for reform in "doctrine and discipline." But worship was clearly subsumed under one of those heads, for much of the letter dealt with "diversity touching the Liturgie, or Book of Common Prayer," asking the question, "who shalbe judges of these differences?" *Humble Remonstrance*, 1, 3.

ster *Confession of Faith* (1646), and a *Larger* and *Shorter Catechism* (1647). On December 2, 1643, the Assembly appointed a subcommittee chaired by Stephen Marshall, considered the best preacher in England, to replace the English liturgy with a simplified directory that would guide a minister through public worship without squelching his spiritual gifts. One history described their experience, "In regards to the forms of public worship, it was found much easier to agree in pulling down than building up."[57] After a year of debate about how the English service should be changed, Parliament approved the new *Directory*, started printing it in March of 1645, and took the dramatic step of ordering all Prayer Books destroyed. The haste with which churches returned to the Prayer Book after the Restoration indicated how little the people regarded their order.[58]

A number of liturgical currents flowed into Westminster, critical because these were quite literally the formative years for the London Particular Baptists. Gillespie had declared, "To say the truth, a church is in so far true or hypocritical as it mixes or mixes not human inventions with God's holy worship."[59] Smectymnuus, a Westminsterian pseudonym, soon called for the end of all imposed liturgies, appealing, "If it be objected, that this will breed divisions and disturbances in Churches, unlesse there be a uniformity [in worship], and that there are many unable. It hath not bred any disturbance in other reformed Churches."[60] An anonymous author

---

57. *History of Westminster Assembly*, 92. The description continued, "The different habits and customs of the Scotch and English gave rise to protracted debates on questions of little intrinsic importance, but necessary to be settled, upon the plan which all approved, of having complete uniformity in the modes of worship." Ibid. That wording effectively illustrates how historians have minimized the subject. The committee included Thomas Young, the Independent Thomas Goodwin, and Scots Robert Baillie and George Gillespie. The highlight of the *Directory* was its section on preaching: "But in this formulary, drawn up in the heyday of Puritanism, we have from the hand of one of the greatest masters, and revised by the ablest of the school, a summary of their thought and experience on a subject which they had made peculiarly their own, and on which if on any they may claim to give counsel still" (Mitchell, *Westminster Assembly*, 240). Marshall clearly prioritized fervent preaching over any potentially indifferent ceremony. ODNB, s.v. "Marshall, Stephen," 3. Conventional wisdom says Marshall based his method on that of William Perkins and Richard Sibbes; however, the Anglican Edward Wetenhall thought that William Ames was the "great Father" of this preaching method. Wetenhall, *Of Gifts and Offices*, 677.

58. See MacCulloch, *Thomas Cranmer*, 626ff.; and Maltby, *Prayer Book and People in Elizabethan and Early Stuart England*, 228–36; as well as the summary of her argument in "'By this Book,'" 115–37. Clark argued that this rejection and reversion was the ultimate victory of Laudianism. Clark, *History of English Nonconformity*, 275ff.

59. Gillespie, *Dispute Against the English Popish Ceremonies*, xxxv.

60. Smectymnuus, *Answer to a Booke Entituled, Humble Remonstrance*, 13.

The Liturgical World of the English Reformation

took that attitude a step further, calling not only national worship but also a national church a false savior because such a church inevitably brought in some sort of human corruption into God's worship.[61] During the thick of Westminster, the influential Independent preacher Jeremiah Burroughs (who also sat at Westminster) preached his great series *Gospel-Worship* in which he warned that no one had the right to change God's worship, not even Aaron's sons—the greater the human status, the more dangerous the fall—"For there is nothing wherein the Prerogative of God doth more appear than in Worship."[62]

At the same time, a battle emerged with the new sectaries, the Anabaptists, a movement hated by Presbyterian and Prelate alike. They did not require education or ordination for their preachers, did not believe the government had authority over their churches, and questioned the validity of any established ceremonies.[63] Royalist "water poet" John Taylor

---

"Smectymnuus" was the pseudonym chosen by Stephen Marshall, Edmund Calamy, Thomas Young, Mathew Newcomen, and William Spurstowe, all of whom sat as Presbyterian Divines at Westminster. Much of the book was an attack on Episcopacy, but its basis was the liturgy. While they attacked the ceremonies and the fact that such ceremonies enabled a non-preaching ministry (a favorite whipping-post), they primarily argued, "That which makes many refuse to be present at our Church service, is not only the Liturgie it selfe, but the imposing of it upon Ministers. And we finde no way to recover our people to a stinted prayer, but by leaving it free to use or not to use" (ibid.). This became a huge stumbling block for Westminster because they knew that the only way they could end the false English worship was to impose a new form of worship, but they did not want to be seen as new Prelates.

61. "I know that much is saide and done in many places in behalfe of uniformity, a Nationall Church and Covenant; which things indeed *carry a great shew of wisdome in wil-worship*, as the Apostle saith, *Col.* 3. 23. were it not that one Saviour told us, *That in vaine they worship him, teaching for doctrines, the commandements of men, Matth.* 15. 9. But wherefore such labouring in vaine, and striving against the streame to obtaine a superficies, and false lustre of a Nationall Church" (*Liberty of Conscience* [1643], 27).

62. Burroughs was speaking of the incident of "strange fire" involving Nadab and Abihu in Leviticus 10. Burroughs, *Gospel-Worship*, 11ff. L. F., also an Independent, believed that only the "separated, independent, spirituall particular politicke bodies or Corporation Churches" possessed the true church and worship, not the papists, prelatists, presbyterians, or anabaptists. L. F., *Speedy Remedie*, 55.

63. For example, the nonseparating (at that time) preacher John Goodwin confronted the layman Samuel Howe by asserting no unlearned man could preach. Howe countered with the well-received sermon, *Vindication of the Cobler* (1640). Infuriated, Goodwin closed the printers to Howe, who had to have his *Sufficiencie of the Spirits Teaching* (1640) published abroad. See Coffey, *John Goodwin and the Puritan Revolution*, 60–61. Kiffin was so impressed with *Sufficiencie* that he issued a reprint in 1683. Bakewell, a Puritan, wrote *Confutation of the Anabaptists, And All Others Who Affect Not Civill Government* (1644), arguing against "the *Brownists*, who call themselves *Independent*; there bee many Sects of them, since *Browne* first broached that *Schisme*:

launched the campaign in 1641 with *Swarme of Sectaries, Religions Enemies*, and *The Brownists Synagogue*, indiscriminately taking the offensive against all Separatists, especially the baptizers.[64] Aided by a brief collapse of government control over the press in 1640, Samuel Howe (who may have still been a Separatist but was connected with Baptists) responded with *A Vindication of the Cobler* and Edward Barber with *A Small Treatise of Dipping*. But wider political events conspired against them as the Independents in Westminster, alarmed by the rapid increase of sectarianism, disavowed the separatists in hopes of preserving their own freedoms. The Presbyterians were only too happy to use that to push through their own agenda. Presbyterian preacher Edward Bowls summarized their portrayal of the parties:

> The condition of England may be thus represented, for the body of it: It consists of *Papists, Protestants, viz.* the King, Prelates, Courtiers, and Cavaliers, the dissoluter Gentry, the superstitious Clergy, the profane and ignorant people, the only Protestants now accounted of, all the rest are but Anabaptists and Brownists; and a third party of *Puritanes*, that is, Lovers of the Protestant Religion, with the desire of Reformation, friends to the Parliament, and native Liberty of the Subject.[65]

It was during this time that key leaders of the group to be known as the London Particular Baptists led seven like-minded baptizing churches to take control of their own image, distancing themselves from the sectarian

---

some follow *Smith*, some *Iohnson*, some *Robinson*, some *Ainsworth*, but they all dash one against another, and all excommunicate themselves from the Church of Christ" (ibid., To the Reader).

64. In *Swarme of Sectaries* (1641), Taylor attacked preaching coblers, tinkers, pedlers, weavers, sowgelders, and chymney-sweepers, particularly Samuel Howe (drawing the ire of an ironmonger named Henry Walker). In *Religions Enemies* (1641), he lumped together Anabaptists, Brownists, Papists, Familists, and Atheists into a heretical sack. In *Brownists Synagogue* (1641), he attacked different gatherings of proto-Baptists (the particular churches mentioned did not appear in later Baptist circles) for their disorderly and irreverent behavior in worship, but noted the sect's rapid growth in London. He wrote, "Downfall those Beetle-brains, who have expounded / False Doctrine in their Tubs, and truth confounded, / The glorious peace we had by them lies wounded, / No men in thoughts so bad ever abounded: / That I could wish they were all hang'd or drownded, / We might say ther's an end of a Right Round-head" (Taylor, *Swarme of Sectaries*, 6). "Round-head" was a derogatory term applied to Separatists and Baptists out of Leviticus 19:27. It is important to note that such propagandists routinely and deliberately misrepresented or confused the different London sects.

65. Bowls, *Mysterie of Iniquitie*, 25. Baillie admitted that the Presbyterians used the Independents achieve liturgical reform. See Shaw, *History of English Church*, 337.

swarm and identifying themselves as reasonable, orthodox Christians. They issued a confession of faith in 1644 in which they vehemently denied being (continental) Anabaptists, Anarchists, or Arminians. They did not ask that all England agree with their beliefs, only that they be granted the freedom to worship according to their own light of the Scriptures.[66] The Presbyterians simply turned the spotlight on them all the brighter with the most famous entries in this pamphlet war: the sensational *Dippers dipt* in 1644 by Westminster Divine Daniel Featley and *Gangraena* in 1646 by heresiographer Thomas Edwards (Edward Barber included Thomas Bakewell in his discussions of those two).[67] Many baptizers responded. Thomas Collier called for Westminster's end saying, "I know no rule in the Booke of God for such an Assembly; therefore they cannot expect a Blessing."[68] John Tombes argued that the Baptists did not deserve to be called a sect.[69]

66. *London* [1644], [1646], and [1651] are all known as the First London Confession. Wright argued vehemently that the "Particular Baptist" tradition did not exist before this first confession in October 1644. Wright, *Early English Baptists*, 110. The concept of "light" was related to God illuminating truth in stages. Cox granted, "Although we know that in some things we are yet very dark, and in all things as yet we know in part, and doe therefore waite upon God for further light; yet we beleeve that we ought in our practise to obey, and serve, and glorifie God in the use of that light which he hath given us" (Cox, *Appendix to a Confession of Faith*, 11).

67. Featley, *Dippers dipt*. Edwards, not a member of Westminster, showed less restraint in his writings, which also included *Reasons Against the Independent Government of Particular Congregations* (1641) against religious tolerance and *Antapologia* (1644) against the Independents at Westminster. In addition to being scandalous, *Gangraena* often comes across petty and whining that the Baptists did not wait their turn, so to speak, like the Presbyterians. See also Barber, *Certain Queries*, 15–16. The difference between 1644 and 1646 was that by 1646 the Presbyterians had cast aside the Independents, which is one of the reasons the London Particulars issued a second edition of their confession as a means of rebuilding bridges.

68. Collier, *Certaine Queries*, 27. Admittedly, Collier seemed to plagiarize his argument from Roger Williams, "What Precept or Pattern hath the Lord Jesus left you in his last Will and Testament for your *Synod*, or Assembly of *Divines*, by vertue of which you may expect his *presence* and *assistance*?" (Williams, *Queries of highest Consideration*, 1). Williams had passed into being a Seeker by this time.

69. "I thinke the Reformed Churches have been to blame, and so may be our present Reformers, that they have never yeelded to reforme it in a regular way; and if *Anabaptists have never sought it afore me*, it hath been it's likely, because they saw mens spirits so bent against them, that they thought it in vaine, yea they have beene rather forced to conceale themselves, it having been accounted criminall, justly deserving excommunication, deprivation, and sometimes death, so much as to question it" (Tombes, *Apology or Plea for the Two Treatises*, 32). He later expanded his argument, "Let reason be heard; why should men be any more called a *Sect*, for denying that it is of Divine appointment, that a Synod of many Churches should have power to excommunicate, then others called *Presbyterians* for holding it? why should Antipaedobaptists

Edward Barber propounded *Certain Queries* to the churches in London about rules that had been imposed upon them, accusing the Presbyterians of hypocrisy.[70] William Kiffin attempted to respond judiciously to the accusations and aspersions cast by the Westminster Divines and also the common conformists.[71] But it soon became evident that religious toleration would not be forthcoming, or even offered; London's leaders believed, "It is much to be doubted, lest the power of the Magistrate, should not onely bee weakned, but even utterly overthrown, considering the principles and practices of *Independents*, together with their compliance with other Sectaries, sufficiently known to be Anti-Magistraticall."[72]

---

be called a *Sect* for denying that Infants are appointed by Christ to be Baptized rather than Paedobaptists for affirming it? If for their Tenet they are called a *Sect*, surely they that so plainly turne aside from the expresse institution, Mat. 28. 19, 20. Mark 16. 5, 16. which almost all Expositors, and not a few Paedobaptists even in their writings for Paedobaptisme do acknowledge to appoint onely the Baptizing of Disciples made by Preaching, and from the manifest Practice of the Apostles, are more worthy the Name of *a Sect, or Sectaries*; if for non-Communion with others of a contrary judgement I wish each man would lay his hand on his heart, and examine whether he hath not been the maker of the breach" (Tombes, *Antidote*, 20).

70. Barber, *Certain Queries*. His third query was, "Whether any thing may be brought into the worship of God, for matter or form, that is not exprest in the Gospell, or the Epistle of the Apostles, seeing the Jewes were required so strict obedience under the Law" (ibid., 1). His thirty-first query was particularly compelling, "Whether those Priests or Ministers that are so forward for pulling downe of stone and wooden crosses, pictures, surplices, common prayer book, and to stand for the liberty of the Subject, yet hold the Ordination received by the authority from Rome, with church state, tithes and baptisme, or rather Infants sprinkling, also prohibiting the libertie of conscience, and the very institutions of christ, are not guilty of that who, which christ pronounceth to the Scribes Pharisees, and hipocrites" (ibid., 8).

71. In Kiffin, *Briefe Remonstrance*, 3, Kiffin recorded these queries: "By what warrant of the Word of God doe you seperate from our Congregations, where the Word and Sacraments are purely dispensed? . . . By what Scripture Warrant doe you take upon you to erect new framed Congregations, seperated to the disturbance of the great Worke of Reformation now in hand? . . . What warrant have you either to be a member, much lesse Minister of any such separate Congregation? . . . What warrant have you to admit into your seperate Congregations sillie seduced Servants, Children or People?" The asker was upset that his daughter and servant had recently joined Kiffin's church. A counterresponse by Ricraft, *Looking glasse for the Anabaptists*, identified Kiffin as the Baptist grand ringleader.

72. *Letter of the Ministers of the City of London*, 5. The letter also submitted, "All these mischiefes in the Church will have their proportionable influence upon the Common-Wealth. The Kingdome will be wofully weakned by scandals and Division, so that the enemies of it both Domesticall and Foreign will be encouraged to plot and practice against it" (ibid., 4).

The Liturgical World of the English Reformation

In a way, the Presbyterian fears were well founded; a number of baptizers were caught up with the Diggers, Levellers, and Fifth Monarchists—radical groups seeking full equality across English society. Some adherents were a part of the New Model Army under their successful and charismatic lieutenant general Oliver Cromwell under whose leadership they routed the Royalist forces in 1645.[73] Upset by Parliament's unwillingness to pay their wages and willingness to replace one form of autocracy with another, Levellers including John Lilburne began agitating for more dramatic changes in government. Common soldiers became preachers, marching tunes became the basis for a nonconformist hymnody, and a generation developed its understanding of worship completely isolated from liturgical history. Ultimately, Charles I was executed in 1649 by order of Parliament, starting yet another war between the three kingdoms. Cromwell eventually united them by force, dissolved the stubborn Long (Rump) Parliament, and installed the Barebones Parliament in 1653 with the task of finding a religious settlement. Their failure led to Cromwell being appointed Lord Protector, a position he held until his death in 1658. As Protector, Cromwell pursued freedom of worship, appointing "triers" to determine the qualifications of each preacher independent of affiliation. Even the devout Anglican Edward Wetenhall conceded that this Puritan influence had resulted in more sermons of higher quality (though he still preferred the Homilies).[74] But sectarianism also continued at an ever-increasing rate. The lingering weariness of instability led England to invite Charles I's son to reclaim the throne after Cromwell died and return to the older, familiar forms of worship, making the failure of the Presbyterians and Independents complete.[75]

---

73. The records of the Baptist church at Warboys in 1647 mentioned as a result of these movements that "several churches were so shaken that most of our Christian assemblies were neglected or broken up." *Fenstanton*, 270. Mark Bell argued in particular that the Baptists and Levellers shared an important desire for religious liberty, but that their informal alliance was always unstable, ending around 1647. Bell, *Apocalypse How?*, 99, 102, 119.

74. Wetenhall, *Of Gifts and Offices*, 757–58.

75. One complaint noted by Richard Baxter was that Puritan sermons were too intellectual and the catechism was too complicated. The people did not want moral meddling, only simple rituals, and so they rejected the Puritan program. At the same time, society was still in upheaval, not only from the war but also from population explosion and relocation. There came a need for a delicate balance between identification and differentiation; with so much changing, religion was almost universally placed in the former category. See Wrightson, *English Society*, 70ff., 222ff.; Hill, *Century of Revolution*, 170ff. Regardless of its actual continuity with England's past, the Church of England held clear sway with the vast majority of the people until further intellectual

Charles II was in favor of religious tolerance (he sympathized with Roman Catholicism at least in part due to his Catholic spouse).[76] Before his coronation in 1661, he issued the Declaration of Breda offering a general indulgence and religious freedom, and he even heard the Puritans' request to ban the *Book of Common Prayer* at the Savoy Conference of 1661.[77] Unfortunately for them, the Savoy reforms were catholicizing (for example, separating catechism as a special service before confirmation and making the sign of the cross at baptism and laying on of hands at confirmation even more central to the rites). Ironically, Charles turned their appeal for freedom against them, noting that he too had freedom to decide what he should do (and the prerogative of the royal priesthood). With reservation, but knowing public sentiment was strongly against the Puritans, he approved Parliament to pass an Act of Uniformity for Public Prayers and the Administration of the Sacraments in 1662 ordering that the *Book of Common Prayer* again become the rule for all worship in England. Twenty percent of the clergy, less than 2,000 ministers, were unwilling to sign the Act and thus ejected from their livings. Further restricting the actions of the nonconformists, Parliament passed a Conventicle Act in 1664 prohibiting any assembly of more than five people unless according to the Prayer Book and a Five Mile Act in 1665 prohibiting any banished preacher from coming within five miles of his previous parish. During this time, London also experienced the tragedies of the Great Plague of 1665 and the Great Fire of 1666.[78]

While the Restoration and subsequent persecution generally marks the end of the era under immediate consideration, some of the early English Baptists survived through the Glorious Revolution of 1689 to see their freedom to worship finally granted. Hanserd Knollys even calculated 1688 as the end of the Great Tribulation.[79] They discovered that toleration

---

and philosophical novelties challenged its position in the late 1600s.

76. Leuenberger, *Archbishop Cranmer's Immortal Bequest*, 144.

77. It was at this conference that Richard Baxter produced his ill-advised Savoy Liturgy.

78. Owen calculated that between Charles II and his son James II, 70,000 persons were fined a total of 12 million pounds. They also ordered countless imprisonments, including eleven years for Vavasor Powell (who eventually died in the Fleet), eight years for Francis Bampfield (who died in Newgate), three years for Abraham Cheare (who died in exile), ten imprisonments for Thomas Grantham, fourteen years for John Griffith, and twenty years for Joseph Wright. Owen, *Records of an Old Association*, 31–32. Matthews identified at most 1,760 ejections from these acts. *Introduction to Calamy Revised*, 6–11.

79. Knollys, *Exposition Of the Revelation*, 130.

brought a completely new set of challenges with respect to worship, which will be explored in chapter 6.

This chapter has established the importance of a liturgical identity to this era of England. The early London Particular Baptists emerged in a society that still saw itself as a product of its worship, and those Baptists deeply cared about their own expression of the same. It is inconceivable that worship could not have had a foundational effect on their theology and practice. The next three chapters will investigate the way worship influenced three specific doctrines: their doctrine of the church, their doctrine of the Scriptures, and their doctrine of the gathering. The central factor that most distinguished those early Baptists from other English Christians in these doctrines was their perspective of worship, which took them in unique theological directions.

three

Free Worship and a New Concept of the Church

Dedicated unto Worship: A New Identity as a Result of Pure Worship[1]

Congregational polity in a hierarchical society generated no shortage of persecution for early Baptists in England. But the unique Particular Baptist practice of congregationalism was heavily influenced by their perspective of worship. Most importantly, their belief in the true New Testament church as a worshipping community led them to conclude that such a church must be independent and regenerate as well as emphasize a one-class priesthood of all believers, which was in many ways a liturgical doctrine. However, their unique ecclesiology created a number of serious challenges for their movement sometimes exacerbated by their theology of worship. The Baptists appreciated England's desire for uniformity and knew that worship was central to that agenda. But their conclusions about worship were strong enough to drive them not only to separate from the established church on the basis of its false worship but also to accept nonuniformity amongst themselves to protect their freedom of worship. Unfortunately, that nonuniformity led to most of their early schisms. Of

---

1. See Kiffin, *Sober Discourse,* To the Christian Reader.

Free Worship and a New Concept of the Church

those, this particular chapter will focus on the open-communion debate, arguing that both sides saw it as a liturgical question.

Competing Definitions of the Church and Her Purpose

The dominant understanding of the church in England began with the Thirty-Nine Articles, and all nonconformists interacted with its definition.[2] Article XIX ("Of the Church") declared, "The visible Church of Christe, is a congregation of faythfull men, in the which the pure worde of God is preached, and the Sacramentes be duely ministred, accordyng to Christes ordinaunce in all those thynges that of necessitie are requisite to the same." Article XX ("Of the authority of the Church") gave the church "power to decree Rites or Ceremonies," but not "to ordayne any thyng that is contrarie to Gods worde written."[3] All English Protestants started with these two marks of the church, right preaching and right sacraments.[4] In these articles, England combined the Reformed view of marks of the church with the Catholic view of authority, albeit with the king in place of the pope. These beliefs would be the stepping-off points for the Baptists. The latter relates to the regulative principle and will be discussed in the next chapter. The former has to do with the identity of a true church and will be the focus of this chapter.

Subtle but important modifications to this definition floated around Separatist circles. Some Brownists added the idea of true separation—separation from unbelievers and from those who ruled not according to the laws of Christ. Johnson and Ainsworth added to that a voluntary mutual covenant and profession of faith.[5] Both opposed the parish system

---

2. *Articles agreed on by the Archbyshoppes.*

3. Article XXXIV went on to explain, "Every particuler or nationall Churche, hath aucthoritie to ordaine, chaunge, and abolishe ceremonies or rites of the Churche ordyened onlye by mans aucthoritie, so that all thinges be done to edifiyng" (ibid.). In 1641, John Taylor defined "faythfull" as "all the faithfull people of God that have even been created, or that are to be to the end of the world, of what Nation, condition, or sex soever they be, if they make a conscience, to be obedient to Gods Lawes, and with gladnes embrace the Gospel of *Jesus Christ* in whose faith if they live here." Taylor, *Religions Enemies*, 3.

4. Featley emphasized that all Reformed English confessions started with this document to define a true visible church; Featley, *Dippers dipt*, 4. Ussher, an influential bishop, added the verification of a true church to be its faith and worship. Ussher, *Body of Divinity*, 359ff. The first edition appeared in 1645.

5. See the Brownist confession recorded in *Broadmead*, xl, and Ainsworth and Johnson, *Confession of faith*, 52ff. Morgan, *Visible Saints*, argued that these ideas

used in England with its compulsory membership and tithes (which was simply keeping with the Reformed understanding that God's covenant with Israel had been transferred to the church, such that the entire nation was God's people). Most Separatists realized that there must be a "separation" between the sheep and the goats although some quite intentionally included their seed in their churches, delineating Independents from Baptists. They also modified the purpose of the church. Whereas a parochial system necessarily emphasized social and civic functions, these Separatists believed that they "gathered in the name of Christ, whom they truly worship, and readily obey" as a peculiar congregation, "wherein, as members of one body wherof Christ is the only head, they are to worship and serve God according to his word, remembering to keep holy the Lords day."[6] Finally, Henry Jacob added the component that each church had autonomy "to exercise Ecclesiasticall government and all Gods other spirituall ordinances (the meanes of salvation) in & for it selfe immediatly from Christ."[7] A church did not derive its power or its right to perform ceremonies from a higher ecclesial structure but from Christ Himself who was the immediate King of all.

By the 1640s, some additional thoughts had entered into dissenting mindsets. Jeremiah Burroughs connected the Christian's separation from the world with the priesthood of all believers: all those who desired to minister to God in Christ must be set apart from the sinful world.[8] L. F. highlighted the role of the covenant with God for the church, but rooted it in worship: "the *true Church* is a company of discernible Christians, entred into a *Covenant of God* to be his *Sabbath assembling Corporation*, for his *worship*, and their own *salvation*."[9] Roger Williams realized that Peter

---

gained traction in Puritan circles first in America; while that may be true, the Separatists in England well outpaced them by virtue of the societal differences.

6. *Broadmead*, xl; Ainsworth and Johnson, *Confession of faith*, 52.

7. Jacob, *Divine Beginning and Institution of Christs true Visible or Ministeriall Church*, not paginated. However, Jacob also argued adamantly that there was no single form of church government prescribed in the New Testament. Consequently, those who rejected Episcopalianism were only being destructive. Tolmie thought that the kingship of Jesus was the most important contribution of the Independents. Tolmie, *Triumph of the Saints*, 85.

8. Burroughs, *Gospel-Worship*, 40–41; "[N]ow there is no Beleever, but Jesus Christ hath separated him or her from the rest of the world to be neer unto God" (ibid.).

9. L. F., *Speedy Remedie*, 7. Later in his treatise he gave a full description of a church, noteworthy for its emphasis of worship. He said that (1) the true church must be based on the ground of true worship: in spirit; (2) it must be particular because they must know who is in it; (3) it must be visible because their worship must be seen by the

Free Worship and a New Concept of the Church

connected his image of "living stones" with the spiritual temple, concluding that the church must consist of true Christians who alone could offer spiritual worship.[10] And Thomas Goodwin heavily emphasized the goal of unity, even for Independent churches "in a Congregationall way." Although he may have had political motives for doing so (being a member of the Westminster Assembly), he exhorted that any cause of division—including worship—brought scandal and reproach on their cause. He also pointed to the eschatological union of all churches in belief and practice as proof of a pure church.[11]

The London Particular Baptists did not ignore such matters of worship as they developed their own ecclesiology. They walked in the same circles, read the same treatises, and attended the same debates as these dissenters.[12] While baptism may have been central to the First London Confession, by no means did Baptists birth that doctrine in a vacuum.

---

world; (4) it must be constituted, not loosely placed together; (5) it must be free from humane inventions; (6) it must be independent; (7) it must be spiritual; (8) it must be a corporation having real civil powers; (9) it must consist of discernible saints; (10) it includes their seed; (11) it must be small enough to meet together in one place. Ibid., 61ff. Because L. F.'s identity and influence is unknown, this particular work only serves as an illustration of contemporary belief.

10. Williams, *Queries of Highest Consideration*, 3–4. He summarized, "This matter, the One of you confesse and practice, the Other questions and mingles Sheep and Goats together, contrary to the spirituall nature of the Lord Jesus, and his true Pattern; contrary to the nature of God, who is a Spirit, and will be Worshipped by Spirituall Worshippers" (ibid., 4).

11. For Goodwin, this meant during the millennial reign of Christ on earth. He wrote passionately, "Dissentions in any one Congregation are evill; and for one Church to dissent from another is a grievous evill. Blessed will the Time be, when all dissentions shall bee taken away; and when there shall bee a perfect Union of all, and not any distinction of *Calvinists* or *Lutherans*, or the like" (Goodwin, *A Glimpse of Sions Glory*, 28). Goodwin believed that doctrine, not worship, was the primary cause of schism. William Kiffin wrote the forward to the book, demonstrating the interconnection between these dissenters.

12. In 1690, after freedom and indulgence had been granted, the Baptists still acknowledged their debt to the early Separatists in this matter. In one book, Kiffin and Keach wrote in the foreword, "And since that [early Reformation], God has been pleased to raise up many Learned Men, namely Dr. *Ames*, Mr. *Ainsworth*, and Dr. *Owen*, with others, who have Learnedly, and with much clearness and strength of Argument made it appear, that a true Gospel visible Church, is to consist only of such as are Saints by Profession, and who give up themselves to the Lord, and one to another by Solemn Agreement, to practise the Ordinances of *Christ*" (Cary, *Solemn Call*, To the Reader). Cary is admittedly a minor and late character in the matter at hand, but this particular book received the explicit approval of William Kiffin, Benjamin Keach, Richard Adams, and Robert Steed. It represented an interesting reflection on the Glorious Revolution.

Many if not most of the early Baptists grew up worshipping according to the *Book of Common Prayer*. Some of them probably had it memorized.[13] When they thought of the church, they thought of its gatherings; when they thought of baptism, they thought of a ceremony. Some Anglicans and Presbyterians would write esoteric discourses on baptism totally isolated from the life of the church, but not the early London Particular Baptists.[14] The New Testament church existed in particular form for visible function. While it is true that Baptists spilled much ink on the subject of baptism, that is mainly because it was such a visible repudiation of paedobaptism and such a tangible representation of their radical beliefs. But even before they jointly published their beliefs to the world, their thoughts about worship were illuminating a new ecclesiology.

Baptist Ideas Take Shape

When Praisegod Barbone assumed leadership over part of Jessey's congregation in 1640, he quickly stood at odds with the rest of the family tree, both by defending infant baptism and attacking believers' baptism. Between 1641 and 1643, he engaged in printed debates with Thomas Kilcop, Edward Barber, and John Spilsbury, likely in addition to many verbal exchanges.[15] Kilcop, Barber, and Spilsbury responded to Barbone differently, but all of their reasonings had liturgical roots. Kilcop issued the most basic argument against Barbone: infant baptism should be rejected because it

---

13. Cox specifically said of qualified pastors that they must be "converted from unbeliefe and false-worship," likely referring to the Prayer Book. Cox, *Appendix to a Confession of Faith*, 10.

14. Hussey, *Answer To Mr.* Tombes; Marshall, *Defence of Infant-Baptism*; and Hammond, *Baptizing of Infants Reviewed and Defended* are examples of thus. All were written against John Tombes, and all were entirely theoretical. Hussey was an Anglican clergyman in Kent, Marshall has already been noted as the Presbyterian chairman over the *Directory*, and Hammond was an Oxford-educated Royalist. Independents were not immune to this charge; Homes, *Vindication of Baptizing Beleevers Infants*, was a painfully dry treatise against Tombes from a non-Calvinist perspective.

15. The Kiffin Manuscript established a rough timeline for these debates. In 1640, Richard Blunt pressed Jessey to consider the mode of baptism; the following year Blunt travelled to the Netherlands to confirm the practice of believers' baptism by immersion. In 1642, Blunt and Samuel Blakelock founded the first church on that principle, drawing members from Jessey's church. Barbone reacted strongly to this particular turn of events. See Duesing, "Counted Worthy," 141–58; and Wright, *Early English Baptists*, 81–89. Wright believed that Edward Barber was the only one to defend the actions of Blunt and Blakelocke, though that assumes a later date for Kilcop's undated *Short Treatise of Baptisme*.

is not found in the Word of God but is a tradition of men. This was the exact argument used against all such ceremonies in public worship (the basis of which will be explored in the next chapter). Barber took a much broader approach; he saw sprinkling as proof of the corruption of baptism, a ceremony that required a right subject, right element, right words, and right mode. As Antichrist changed all other church ordinances, "So hath he destroyed that true Apostolicall institution."[16]

Barbone's debate with Spilsbury (as well as that with a Baptist named R. B.[17]) echoed that with Barber—at its heart it was a battle about baptismal succession—but it hinged on an argument about the proper form of a ceremony. Barbone believed that true baptism required a continuous succession, but the Baptists based their succession either on the Dutch, who did not practice total immersion, or on John Smyth, whose shocking se-baptism had neither biblical precedent nor extraordinary commission. If the former, the Baptists would have to admit that baptism's validity lay not in the form of the ceremony but the doctrine behind it (else a failure to immerse the crown of the head would nullify an entire baptism). If the latter, then their baptism was simply not biblical. Either scenario, Barbone believed, turned the Baptists on their heads:

> But touching the Baptisme of Children or Infants, if it were an error as some suppose, and would have it; doth it then follow that it is a nullitie, and so voyd, because an error is in it? if it were so, then is their Baptisme, their Church, and all their actions, nullities and voyd, having error attending them, as they will confesse and must doe.[18]

---

16. Barber, *Small Treatise of Baptisme*, 28. This was the famous work in which Barber declared himself blessed that God would "raise up mee, a poore Tradesman, to devulge this glorious Truth, to the worlds censuring." Ibid., Preface. Note that the Kiffin Manuscript said that Richard Blunt was convinced of dipping in 1640, which would have been very close to this time. White, "Baptist Beginnings and the Kiffin Manuscript," 31.

17. Barbone, *Discourse Tending to Prove*, first appeared in 1642; R. B. (identified on the cover as R. Barrow) replied with *A briefe answer to A discourse, lately written*; Barbone countered with *A Reply to R. B.* Most sources identify R. B. as an Irish Baptist colonel Robert Barrow, but Wright says it was probably misprinted on the cover and should have remained R. B., for Richard Blunt. Wright, *Early English Baptists*, 206–8.

18. Essentially, Barbone argued that even though the established church may be corrupt, its ceremonies including baptism were still valid. If the Baptists were right and Anglican baptism were invalid, then Christ would be a "Widower," and "all the reformed Churches & [separated] Churches, & also of all other Christians either Reformed, or yet in defection" would be condemned, "An opinion so rare and singular, so high and presumptuous as I suppose all persons godly wise will abhorre the verie

If form were not the essence of the ceremony, then sprinkling should be a valid mode and infants a valid subject. Barbone concluded that worship belonged to the non-essential "form and administration" of the church, which was transient and determined by men; the essential "manner and relation" of the church abided only in Christ and could not be destroyed by men. This issue became so important to Baptists that it will be treated in its own section at the end of this chapter.[19]

Spilsbury countered with the underappreciated claim that the Baptists derived their succession solely from the Scriptures; any claim to temporal succession must go through Rome, but "the Scriptures [have] the same authoritie in the Church now as the Apostles had then, the same Spirit being present now to reveale them, as then to write them, 1 Cor. 5. 4, 5. 2 *Tim.* 3. 15, 16."[20] But in the context of his debate with Barbone, Spilsbury then had to make an astounding admission:

> *But some will say, that the Word speaks of no church before Baptisme.* For answer to this, I must distinguish in Baptisme between the truth in the doctrine of Baptisme, and the outward administration of the same. In the first sense Baptisme is one branch of the covenant, as a truth to be revealed, and by faith to be received, as an essentiall truth, together with other truths, for the constituting of the church, and no church according to the other of Christs new Testament, either without it, or before it.
>
> But for the last, namely, the outward administration of Baptisme, that ever follows the Saints joining in fellowship, by

---

thinking of it." "Widower" seemed to be a favorite retort of Barbone, as he used it multiple times both in *A Discourse Tending to prove* and *A Reply to R. B.* Barber specifically noted Barbone's use of this term and rejected it because the church always had existence in heaven. Barber, *Small Treatise of Baptism,* 27. The extended quote comes from Barbone, *Reply to R. B.,* 31; but see also ibid., 19; and idem, *Discourse Tending to Prove,* 19ff. Later in that treatise, he wondered how God could maintain Israel through her great "Apostacie" but not the church to whom He gave the greater promises. He concluded that succession belonged to the established church.

19. Barbone, *Discourse Tending to Prove,* 20. Bunyan took up this argument in his battle with Kiffin over open-communion, saying that "a failure in such a circumstance as Water doth not unchristian us." Bunyan's immediate influence may have been Jessey, but Jessey and Barbone clearly discussed the matter. Bunyan perhaps went too far in his analysis of administration, arguing that in that sense baptism was like eating—it was an individual's choice. Bunyan, *Confession of my Faith,* 94. Bunyan's declaration drew testy responses from John Denne (Henry Denne's son), Thomas Paul, and William Kiffin.

20. Spilsbury, *Treatise Concerning Baptism,* 40. See also the response in Barbone, *Defence Baptizing Infants,* 38ff. The next chapter will develop his understanding of the Bible in more detail.

> mutuall faith & agreement in the doctrine, wherein consists the stating of the Church in her conjoining in covenant, which ever goes before the administration of Baptisme, and gives power and authoritie for the same. So that in the first sense, the Church is not before Baptisme; but in the last sense, the church is before Baptisme.[21]

He did not believe that a mistake in form invalidated a baptism, but he also believed the Scriptures taught believers' baptism by immersion. Therefore he countered that the essentials of baptism, including the administrator, mode, and subject, truly belonged to Doctrine of Baptism, but the physical administration of baptism—the ceremony—belonged to the *church* as part of its covenant. Baptism would be necessary, "for that Church where Baptisme is the true ordinance of God in the administration of it, is by the rule of the Gospel a true Church," but dependent on the church's covenant.[22] Baptism was nonnegotiable, but its use in worship might be. In other words, Spilsbury recognized that the Baptists' debate with Barbone went beyond cleaner doctrinal into muddier ceremonial categories and the Baptists would have to acknowledge theological subtleties if they were to protect themselves from public self-incrimination.

Stephen Wright realized that the doctrine of the church in the First London Confession was a compromise between Kilcop (and Kiffin) who thought baptism should be the form of the church and Spilsbury who had just concluded that baptism could not be the form of the church, but Wright missed the liturgical scenario behind it.[23] Everything in their first confession dealing with the church and her ceremonies was rather vague, tacit proof that they were still negotiating. Their doctrine of the church combined everything about which they could agree: "a company of visible Saints, called & separated from the world, by the word and Spirit of God, to the visible profession of the faith of the Gospel, being baptized into that

---

21. Spilsbury, *Treatise Concerning Baptisme*, 41. Barbone countered that a church could not initiate baptism apart from an extraordinary commission; baptism necessarily came before Scripture. Furthermore, Spilsbury's admission meant that he denied the succession of the church—that "he rather chuseth to asperse Christ of unfaithfulness in his promise, then by acknowledgement to give him the glory of it." Barbone, *Defence of Baptizing Infants*, 47ff., 60ff.

22. Spilsbury, *Treatise Concerning Baptisme*, 32. Barbone replied, "Let J. S. if he can, shew when Baptisme became such a corner-stone in the foundation of that building" (Barbone, *Defence of Baptizing Infants*, 6).

23. Wright, "Baptist Alignments Part 2," 359ff. In his revision, he emphasized Kiffin's desire for orderly practice and Spilsbury's concern that he had not been baptized before baptizing his church members. Wright, *Early English Baptists*, 108.

faith, and joyned to the Lord, and each other, by mutuall agreement, in the practical injoyment of the Ordinances, commanded by Christ their head and King."[24] They copied their doctrine of worship from Ainsworth and Johnson's *Confession*, noting that Christ "finished & removed al those Rites, Shadowes, and Ceremonies," and "makes his people a spirituall House, an holy Priesthood, to offer up spirituall sacrifice acceptable to God through him; neither doth the Father accept, or Christ offer to the Father any other worship or worshippers."[25] They thought that this confession provided a sufficiently broad basis for cooperation for the time being, but conditions would not remain such that they could rely on vague statements to bind them together. For the rest of a generation they would work through the implications of these definitions: the relationships between baptism, covenant, ordinance, holiness, and church.

A Cause and Commitment to Separate

The First London Confession did not answer the most basic question, however. What did the early Baptists think was the purpose of their churches? Why did they form churches? None of them answered that question directly, though "to preach the Word and enjoy the Ordinances" seems appropriate. But they knew why they formed *new* churches, and those reasons sufficiently clarify the answer. Two of the three reasons Kiffin gave for separating from the Church of England were the manner of their worship: there was no freedom of worship, and there was limited participation on the part of the congregants. In his argument, he claimed the obligation to separate from congregations "as doe not dispense the

---

24. *London* [1644], Article XXXIII. Though generic, this statement accurately depicted how the London Baptists formed their churches. Knollys said they preached from house to house, "And whosoever (poor as well as rich, bond as well as free, servants as well as Masters) did make a profession of their Faith in Jesus Christ, and would be baptized with water into the Name of the Father, Sonne, and Holy Spirit; were admitted Members of the Church." But he added, "This hath been the practice of some Churches of God in this City, without urging or making any particular covenant with Members upon admittance" (Knollys, *Moderate Answer*, 20). Edwards corroborated that story, adding that the London Baptists would also send preachers out into the counties to repeat the process there, specifically mentioning Lambe and Kiffin. *Gangraena*, 1:57/2. *Gangraena* part 1 reset its numbering at page 67; those pages will be indicated by "/2."

25. *London* [1644], Article XVII. The Baptists used the updated language in *The Confession of faith* (1607), Article XIV, rather than *A True Confession of the Faith* (1596).

Free Worship and a New Concept of the Church

Word and Sacraments purely," elaborating that "if wee cannot keep faith and a good Conscience, in obeying all the Commands of Christ, so long as we assemble our selves with you, then are wee necessitated to seperate our selves from you,"[26] focusing on the commands for the church, particularly in worship. He desired freedom to worship as he believed the Bible commanded, fully engaged in such worship as a priest of God.

One could view Kiffin's claim from the perspective of John Tombes who argued that a "defect in outward order and ordinances" was not a sufficient cause for separation, but only an evil "in Faith, Worship, or Discipline, as is not consistent with Christianity, or the state of a visible Church, or is intolerable oppression, maintained with obstinacy, after endeavors to cure them."[27] In that case, one might conclude that Kiffin's real concern behind obeying "all the commands" was proper church discipline as opposed to worship. But there are three immediate reasons to reject that perspective: when the early London Particular Baptists spoke of such obedience in this context, they routinely emphasized the commands for instituted worship; when they spoke of holiness, it was not with respect to their discipline but to Christ and His commands for the church; finally, discipline simply cannot account for all of the implications they drew from the emphasis on pure worship.[28] Discipline itself was the outgrowth of a

---

26. Kiffin, *Briefe Remonstrance*, 5, 8. Featley recorded a similar accusation from Kiffin in Featley, *Dippers dipt,* 4.

27. Tombes, *A Short Catechism About Baptism*, 17. The Baptists often wrote of their agreement with the established church's doctrine. This particular statement is noteworthy because, as the rest of the chapter will explain, Tombes had been unwilling to separate fully from the established church in the 1640s and join with the Baptists. Dowley, for one, thought discipline was indeed the Baptists' primary concern. Dowley, "Baptists and Discipline in the 17th Century," 157–66.

28. Grantham, for example, included discipline as a subset of the proper external form of a church, which he considered the church's worship. Grantham, *Christianismus Primitivus*, 2.2ff. This is not even to mention that Tombes rejected any test for church membership beyond a public profession; he worried about being "over-rigid about admission of members." Tombes, *Antipaedobaptism*, 259–60. Perhaps the clearest explanation of this position came from Thomas Paul in his reaction to John Bunyan's defense of open communion, much of which will be discussed later in this chapter. Bunyan had argued that behavioral holiness ("faith, experience, and conversation") was sufficient for him to have church fellowship with someone, for "that which manifesteth a person to be a visible Saint, must be conformity to the word of Faith and Holyness," meaning Abraham's faith and not water baptism. Paul countered that if one should emphasize any commands with respect to obedience in church membership, it should be those instituted by Christ for His church, not Moses: "if *Moses* Law in his Moral precepts, be the onely bounds of a Christians Holiness or Sanctification, under the Gospel, for what end, then are all those Gospel-Commands, especially in instituted

commitment to a holy priesthood and a regenerate church, both of which were outgrowths of a commitment to pure worship. Proper discipline absolutely would have led some people to abandon the established church. But the existence of Puritan conventicles proved that one could remain faithful to national worship and meet additionally for teaching and discipline. Something else must have contributed to the Baptist separation and desire to proselytize others to join them, namely that their discipline be maintained in order that their worship be made pure. That driving factor was their weekly experience of (in their minds) unbiblical worship. Tolmie noted that the Broadmead church began with five Puritans listening to the Puritan preacher and then leaving before the Prayer Book ceremonies began; they were not the only five in all of England.[29]

This reason for their separation would indicate that the Baptists believed, as did John Owen and John Canne, that pure worship was a fundamental element of the church's assembly and purpose, a visible mark of their community and identity.[30] Later reflections from this early gen-

---

Worship, they are in your cense of little use to us: obedience to them doth not add to our Holiness, therefore a breach of them, by that rule, must be no part of our sin." Bunyan, as this chapter will explain, had to take the dramatic step of severing baptism from Christ's commands for His church: "As to those Commands that respect God's Instituted Worship in a Church, as a Church, I have told you that Baptism is none of them." See Bunyan, *Confession of my Faith*, 78, 86; Paul, *Some Serious Reflections*, 6; Bunyan, *Differences in Judgment about Water-Baptism*, 15. This was not an argument about discipline, but worship. Note that Kiffin wrote the foreword to Paul's *Serious Reflections*.

29. Wetenhall noted a similar phenomenon with the followers of Cartwright, who waited until after the prayer service was complete and then came in to hear him preach. Wetenhall, *Of Gifts and Offices*, 155–57. A conventicle, according to Archbishop Laud, was "ten or twelve or more or less meet together, to pray, read, preach, expound." Tolmie, *Triumph of the Saints*, 30, 29. Note that the records of Broadmead Church seem to talk about nothing but examples of church discipline. In his *Briefe Remonstrance*, Kiffin considered his main complaint with respect to the church's discipline was its suffering profane people communion with them (mixed communion). That was as much a consequence of infant baptism as any understanding of church discipline. Both scenarios still had a worship focus.

30. Canne wrote that all nonconformists believed, "The Lord in scripture, hath laid it as a straight charge upon all the faithfull, to *separate* themselves from Idolaters, and to be as unlike to them as may be, specially in their religious observations and ceremonies. The second commaundement proves this effectually, for these is absolutely forbidden *all participation in any feigned service*, whether it be to the true God or any other" (Canne, *Necessitie of Separation*, 83). Owen's earlier thoughts on this matter have already been included, but it is important to note that at the end of his life he was still identifying true churches relative to their public worship, "for whereas the Lord Christ hath instituted sundry solemn ordinances of divine worship to be observed jointly by his disciples, unto his honour and their edification, this could not be done

Free Worship and a New Concept of the Church

eration of Baptists validated such development along those lines. Hanserd Knollys wrote in 1674,

> A true visible Constituted Church of Christ under the Gospel is a Congregation of Saints, 1 *Cor.* 1. 2. Called out of the World, *Rom.* 1. 7. Separated from Idolaters and Idol Temples, 2 *Cor.* 6. 16, 17. from the unbelieving Jews and their Synagogues and all legal observations of holy dayes, Sabbath dayes, and Mosaical Rites, Ceremonies and shadows, *Act.* 19. 9. *Col.* 2. 16, 17. and assembled together in one place, 1 *Cor.* 14. 23. On the Lords Day the first day of the Week, *Acts* 20. 7. to worship God visibly by the spirit and in the truth, *Joh.* 4. 23, 24. In the holy Ordinances of God, 1 *Cor.* 11. 2. according to the faith and order of the Gospel, *Col.* 2. 5.[31]

In 1681, he reiterated his conviction, powerfully connecting the purpose of the church with the purpose of Christ saying, "That the Chief Work of Jesus Christ in his *first* Coming into the World was to save sinners; to build up his own House, *the Church of the Living God*; and to institute all Gospel-Ordinances *necessary* for his Disciples to worship God in Spirit and in Truth."[32] That same year, William Kiffin based his foray into the open-communion debate with Bunyan on the conviction,

> By being Baptised into the Name of the Father, and of the Son, and of the Holy Ghost, we are Sacredly Initiated, and Consecrated, or Dedicated unto the Service and Worship of the Father, Son, and Holy Ghost; this we take upon us in our Baptism:

---

but in such societies, communities, or assemblies of them to that purpose." He appealed that he would willingly hold communion with any church as long as he would not be compelled to act in any way he considered sinful. Out of respect for his life-long struggle for the Independent model, it is also appropriate to acknowledge his very elegant conclusion that the purpose of the church was "our edification in faith, love, and obedience." Owen, *Discourse concerning Evangelical Love*, in *Works*, 15:86, 87, 99.

31. Knollys, *Parable of the Kingdom*, 5–6. Knollys, as will become evident, seemed to reflect more on this true nature of the church than his peers, and his stature was such that his conclusions must have resonated with more than a few common Baptists. Even after his death in 1691, Thomas Whinnell still invoked his name reverently. Whinnell, *Sober Reply*, 64. Not entirely tangential, it should be noted that Knollys brought Benjamin Keach into the Particular Baptist fold around the time he began publishing these views on the church. Keach later shared Knollys's love for the book of Revelation and its image of the church, something that may not be coincidental.

32. Knollys, *World that Now is*, 2. This statement, in fact, summarized the primary argument of the book and was the crux of his entire understanding of John's revelation. Garrett, relying on Bustin, *Paradox and Perseverance*, missed this. Garrett, *Baptist Theology*, 64.

herein lies the Foundation of all our Faith and Profession with that ingagement of ourselves unto God, which Constitutes our Christianity.[33]

The two could not have been clearer about their commitment to pure worship and its connection with the purpose of a true church.

The Second London Confession of 1677 seems to be a red herring in determining Particular Baptist emphases. Perhaps worship has been overlooked in Baptist studies because its Article XXII, "Of Religious Worship," was almost an exact copy of the Westminster Confession (as was the Savoy Declaration) and its Article XXVI, "Of the Church," though still heavily dependent on Westminster and Savoy, contained the most significant deviations therefrom. In other words, one might conclude that Baptists focused on the church and not the church's worship. Such would be a gross misunderstanding of the situation and the confession. This group of Baptists did not disagree about the basic elements of instituted worship. The confession came about to demonstrate the Baptists' affinity with other nonconformists ("we have no itch to clogge Religion with new words"), by which time included the Presbyterians, after almost twenty years of intense persecution with no end in sight. Prayer, preaching, reading the Scriptures, praise, baptism, and the Lord's Supper were not in dispute as the basic parts of God's worship.[34] But the *administration* of God's worship in a particular church was. Thus was informed the most significant (and overlooked) change in Article XXII: following the Independents rather than the Presbyterians in moving the descriptor "to be performed in obedience to him, with understanding, faith, reverence, [and godly fear]" from the referent only of preaching and hearing to apply to every part of religious worship.[35] Thus was also informed a distinct Baptist emphasis on the purpose of the church, the work of the pastor, and the duty of church

---

33. Kiffin, *Sober Discourse,* To the Christian Reader. Kiffin repeated this statement three times. Very late in the book, he acknowledged the statement as a quote from John Owen. Ibid., 100.

34. *London* [1677], To the Reader. These statements are hedged by "basic" because the Baptists were willing to divide over other elements of worship. Winter, "Calvinist and Zwinglian Views of the Lord's Supper among the Baptists of the 17th Century," 323–29, argued that most Baptists held a Zwinglian view of the Supper (except for perhaps Keach and Collins who drifted towards real presence), so that traditional source of disagreement among the Reformers would not be a major focus of this instance of debate.

35. Compare *Westminster* [1646], chap. 21, "Of Religious Worship, and the Sabbath Day," with *Savoy* [1659], and *London* [1677], chap. 22, "Of Religious Worship, and the Sabbath-Day." Westminster did not include "and godly fear."

members. Jesus called His followers "to walk together in particular societies, or Churches, for their mutual edification; and the due performance of that publick worship, which he requireth of them in the World," giving them "all that power and authority, which is any way needed, for their carrying on that order in worship, and discipline, which he hath instituted for them to observe; with commands, and rules." The officers were "appointed by *Christ* to be chosen and set apart by the Church (so called and gathered) for the peculiar Administration of Ordinances, and Execution of Power, or Duty, which he intrusts them with," whereas the members were "bound to joyn themselves to particular *Churches*, when and where they have opportunity so to do; so all that are admitted unto the priviledges of a *Church*, are also under the Censures and Government thereof, according to the Rule of *Christ*."[36] The Baptists' original contributions had to do with the administration of the church. Every individual church had complete authority, under the appointment of her pastors, to administer all ordinances of worship, and every church member had the privilege and responsibility to enjoy those ordinances. The outward holiness of a church member, certainly of importance to the Baptists, concerned them inasmuch as that member submitted himself to proper church order, not as a Puritan obsession with visible sainthood for a test of salvation. A more detailed analysis of Baptist ecclesiology with respect to worship will explain this distinction.

"The Church His Holy Spouse": Ecclesiology as a Function of Pure Worship[37]

The Second London Confession highlighted a number of important ecclesiological beliefs for the Baptists: the freedom and authority of each individual church under Christ, the ability of each church member to participate in the ordinances of worship, and the requirement that only true worshipers be admitted into church membership. They believed that the church was a worshiping community, though in a purer sense than the Anglicans.[38] Each of these beliefs had a specific connection with instituted

---

36. *London* [1677], chap. 26, "Of the Church."

37. "It is a high contempt and injury to Christ, as he is Husband of the Church his holy Spouse, to force upon him an naturall wife" (Spilsbury, *Treatise Concerning Baptisme*, 25).

38. Woodhouse thought the Anglicans believed the church was a worshiping community in the same sense as the Eastern Orthodox: the purity of the customs and

worship, and the liturgical context clearly influenced their doctrinal development. As they will be here, these concepts are often discussed under the identifiers religious liberty, congregationalism, and regenerate church membership, though modern connotations should not be read into these terms.

Religious Liberty: A Free Church for Free Worship

In 1643, Leonard Busher made an appeal to the Westminster Assembly that had been woven into the fabric of English Separatism from the very beginning: do not impose a "Rule or Pattern of Fayth an Religion;" "seeing there are many Assemblyes of Christians, and each thinke (as you doe) theyr owne Fayth and Religion to be best, you may set orders therein for your selves, upon condition that you tolerate others."[39] He understood that the Westminster Divines thought they were simply cataloging apostolic beliefs and practices, but he also disagreed with their conclusions. He granted that Westminster could establish a set of rules for any church that willingly submitted to them but denied that they could impose their rules on any other church.[40]

---

traditions were far more important than the purity of the worshipers. Woodhouse, *Doctrine of the Church in Anglican Theology*, 154ff.

39. "But I exhort you herein, to follow the Apostles Doctryne, and order (they as Master buylders) have set downe, for a Pattern and Rule for every man to follow and practise: so that you, nor any whosoever have Authority (though of high degree, or learned) to set downe an other order, Rule or Pattern of Fayth and Religion, for all men to follow and practise, seeing that is done already by Christ and his Apostles, which we all ought to follow and practise, but none other order on payne of the curse. Gal 1. 8. 2. Tim. 1. 13. Luk. 9. 49. notwithstanding" (Busher, *An Exhortation Unto the Learned Divines assembled At Westminster*, 4). Busher was associated with the early separation of Smyth and Helwys, though he remained in exile in Amsterdam. See McBeth, *Early English Literature on Religious Liberty*, 39–47. This particular work was the occasion for the Independents' *An Apologeticall Narration* which stood aloof from Busher's appeal for unlimited toleration but still gave more freedom than the Presbyterians would allow. But Busher was by no means the only appellant to Westminster in this matter. Walwyn, who was later scolded by Kiffin for his involvement with the Levellers, also wrote to Westminster specifically in defense of the Baptists against imposed worship. See Walwyn, *Compassionate Samaritane*.

40. Many of the so-called tracts on religious liberty actually came from the Restoration and not the war era as dissenters predicted and then experienced that liberty removed. Vavasor Powell, a Fifth-Monarchy Baptist well respected by the Particular Baptists, warned that the *Book of Common Prayer* was mutually exclusive with freedom of public worship. Powell, *Common-Prayer-Book no Divine Service*, 10. A group of General Baptists from London and the surrounding areas issued an excellent appeal

Free Worship and a New Concept of the Church

Chapter 2 of this book established the conflicted ideals of Reformation England: England wanted to be free from Roman authority, but England's rulers also wanted to maintain control over her church for all of the reasons given, namely uniformity in national identity (primarily in worship) and control over dissent. The Presbyterians inherited that perspective when they realized control over Parliament; for these conservative Parliamentarians, "religious toleration was anathema."[41] Presbyterian polemicist Thomas Bakewell, who was not a member of Westminster, believed that civil authority could not *determine* Christ's laws, but it could *enforce* those laws; all of society was responsible for obeying Christ's laws as determined by the appropriate religious authority, in that case Westminster.[42] A major concern for Westminster's legislation (as it was for the Anglican Convocation) was England's instituted worship. Scot George Gillespie built a careful argument defending a church's right to impose indifferent matters in church worship, that "neither does the authority of the church bind, except the thing be lawful and expedient, nor does the

---

for the free liberty of conscience in matters of "Religion, or Worship." *Brief Confession or Declaration of Faith* (1659), 10. Sturgion, another Fifth-Monarchy Baptist, reminded Charles II that his Declaration of Breda granted freedom to "Worship God according to the Light" and from punishment for separating from the "Publick service of worship." Sturgion, *Plea for Tolleration,* 5. He argued, "Be pleased, *Royal Sir,* to consider, that such imposing of the Magistrates, is contrary to the Nature of the Gospel; because it is one of the Glories of Christian Religion, that it was so pious, Excellent, Powerful, and Perswasive, that it came in upon its own Piety and Wisdom" (ibid., 9). Grantham offered a clever poem summarizing the magistrate's opinion about the Baptists: "It seems my Union thou approvest not, / This savours of Sedition, or some Plat. / The Land shall never quiet be, untel / Rulers, by their Edicts, all sorts compel / To Uniformity, in things Religious; / And therefore thy Opinion is Prodigious" (Grantham, *The Prisoner against the Prelate*, 24). Alternatively, Tombes chose to defend the new King's right to govern ecclesiastical matters, especially with respect to worship. It is possible that he had abandoned Baptist principles out of self-preservation in the Restoration or that he was trying to paint the Baptists in a positive light. He also may have fallen into the same trap as the Presbyterians. He wrote, "Nevertheless Princes may require those under their Dominions, to worship God in Christ, according to the plain direction of the Scriptures of the new Testament," assuming that such direction was "plain." Tombes, *Serious Consideration of the Oath of the Kings Supremacy*, 26.

41. Hill, *Century of Revolution*, 166. "The idea of a single state Church was so deeply embedded in most men's thought that freedom to choose one's religion seemed in itself subversive" (ibid.). He also thought that Independents took up toleration as a political necessity, not from conviction or theological conclusion. Thomas Edwards believed that England's toleration had created a unique mess and blamed the authorities for the experienced ills of sectarianism. *Gangraena*, The Epistle Dedicatory.

42. Bakewell, *Confutation of the Anabaptists,* 3. One historian called Westminster's opposition to religious liberty the "chief blot" against them. *A History of Westminster Assembly,* 169ff.

lawfulness and expediency of the thing bind, except the church ordain it; but both these jointly do bind."[43] Daniel Featley left nothing uncertain when he declared (to Kiffin), "Men may be compelled by the civil Magistrate to the true worship of God."[44]

The First London Confession (published before Westminster's) devoted six articles to the idea of religious liberty, primarily with respect to the civil magistrate, demonstrating how important the subject was to them. While they acknowledged the magistrate's right to enact civil laws, they countered that "we should suffer never so much from them in not actively submitting to some Ecclesiasticall Lawes, which might be conceived by them to be their duties to establish, which we for the present could not see, nor our consciences could submit unto."[45] Some might assume that the Baptists were primarily concerned with the inevitable announcement of an English Presbyterian system with respect to these "Ecclesiasticall Lawes." Though the Baptists did disagree with Presbyterianism, they were not solely opposed to it as a system of polity, but moreso as a system of enforcement. They appealed to Westminster that "long we formerly have groaned under by the tyranny and oppression of the Prelatical Hierarchy, which God through mercy hath made this present King and Parliament wonderful honorable, as an instrument in his hand, to throw down," hoping that it would not replace one hierarchical government with another (Presbyterians openly touted their system's ability to crush heresy or dissent), demonstrating that they were more worried about the oppression

---

43. Gillespie, *Dispute Against the English Popish Ceremonies*, 17. He assumed that the religious authority would be sensitive to social and cultural differences between churches.

44. Featley, *Dippers dipt*, 5–6; cf. Bakewell, *Answer, or confutation of the Anabaptists*, 41. Both drew justification from the practice of Israel as recorded in 1 Kings and 2 Chronicles. This made Westminster's impressive defense of the liberty of conscience seem terribly hypocritical: "God alone is Lord of the Conscience, and hath left it free from the Doctrines and Commandments of men, which are, in any thing, contrary to his Word; or beside it, if matters of Faith, or Worship" (*Westminster* [1646], chap. 20, "Of Christian Liberty, and Liberty of Conscience"). But the wording was quite consistent with their belief. The individual conscience was free from the doctrines and commandments of men, but bound to the doctrines and commandments of God. Westminster simply undertook to determine which was which. Interestingly, the Second London Confession copied this statement verbatim from Westminster. John Owen, on the other hand, defended the magistrate's right to impose worship by claiming it was a moral duty for all men. Owen, *Two Questions Concerning the Power of the Supreme Magistrate*, in *Works*, 13:510.

45. *London* [1644], Article XLIX. While they asked for mercy, they also willingly submitted themselves to whatsoever punishment the magistrate commanded for opposition.

Free Worship and a New Concept of the Church

than the polity.⁴⁶ They committed themselves "to obey God rather then men," concluding, "And if any take this that we have said, to be heresy, then do we with the Apostle freely confess, that after the way which they call heresy, worship we the God of our Fathers, believing all things which are written in the Law and in the Prophets and Apostles."⁴⁷ Their whole way of "doing church" was their act of worship, their act of service, one for which they would not apologize. And they would not suffer any authority other than Christ to tell them how to worship.⁴⁸

---

46. Ibid., Article L. Edwards waxed eloquent about the power of Presbyterianism in *Gangraena*, 1:54/2, 1:102, et al. Hetherington, *History of Westminster Assembly*, 131, echoed his fawning. Knollys did consider polity on biblical grounds, saying that "if by Dependent hee also intendeth a Presbyterian-Government, which hath a Dependence upon a supream Judicature of a Common-councell of Presbyters, and who must in matters Ecclesiasticall be subject unto the Decrees, Sentences, Constitutions, and Commandments of a Common-councell, Colledge or Consistorie of Classicall, Provinciall, or Synodicall Presbyters; Then I do conceive the Doctor hath not proved, (nor will he ever be able to prove) That the Presbyterian-Government-Dependent is Gods Ordinance." Knollys, *Moderate Answer*, 2. When Bastwick replied in 1646, he labeled Knollys as one of the three leaders of the Independents.

47. *London* [1644], Article LI, LII[I].

48. This as much as anything angered the Presbyterians against them, for to refuse to submit to Westminster's prescription was to accuse it of heresy. Featley listed six errors of the Baptists: that none are rightly baptized but those who are dipt, that no children ought to be baptized, that there ought to be no set form of Liturgy or prayer by the Book but only by the Spirit, that there ought to be no distinction by the Word of God between the Clergy and the Laity, but that all who are gifted may preach the Word and administer the Sacraments, that it is not lawful to take an oath at all, and that no Christian may with a good conscience execute the Office of a civil Magistrate. Featley, *Dippers dipt*, 32 (Featley clearly conflated a number of Baptist sects). It has already been mentioned that Westminster replaced the strict and comprehensive *Book of Common Prayer* with a more general *Directory for Public Worship* (and in doing so claimed that it was not imposing a liturgy), but even that was too much for the Baptists. During the Interregnum, Caryl, a member of Westminster, rebuked Baptist churches for intending "by the use of those Ordinances to stand and walk by it self, as divided and separate from other Congregations professing the same Faith and obedience towards Christ," even though all the *Directory* imposed was the use of prayer, preaching, and reading Scripture. Caryl, *Moderator*, 44ff. Presbyterian Cragge singled out the tolerance apparent in the *Directory* as the real culprit behind the divisions in England for not squelching the dissenters; he warned, "Liberty in Religion is like free conversing without restraint, or watch in time of pestilence, one house easily infects a whole City" (*Publick Dispute Betwixt John Tombs, John Cragge, Henry Vaughan, Touching Infant-Baptism* [1654], The Epistle Dedicatory). The author was not a Baptist, for he identified the initial infection thus: "The fitness of the engin for devastation, and ruinating all former Churches, under colour of first baptisms nullity, gathering of new ones (after their own mould) out of the old ruins, by re-baptizing" (ibid.).

Historians have overlooked these Baptists' arguments for religious liberty because they were more implicitly than explicitly tied up in the doctrines that will be explained throughout this book.[49] But their arguments were real, powerful, and intimately connected to worship. Knollys preached that Christ alone, no man or manmade thing, gave power to His church in worship—"we are nothing, having nothing, can do nothing without Christ."[50] Spilsbury added that Christ was the sole Mediator of the New Covenant, the sole gardener who could engraft new branches onto His vine, the benefits of which were "communion with the Church of Christ in the outward worship of God and the use of Christs Ordinances."[51] Their conclusion was simple, yet elegant: the *form* of worship in a church was meaningless unless it was joined with the *power* of Christ in the Spirit, but that power was reserved for the "true branches." Only true believers could truly worship—all other worship was vain[52]—which undercut the very reason given for imposed national liturgies: the poor common people and their immature ministers who needed help to worship. Anglican and Presbyterian alike ridiculed the Baptists, "which in seven years can scarce learn the Mysterie of the lowest profession, think half seven years enough (gain'd from their worldly imployments) to understand the Mysterie of Divinity, and thereupon meddle with Controversies, which they have no more capacity to pry upon, than a Batt to look up into the third Heaven."[53] But the Particular Baptists knew that they had the Spirit and the Word; they needed nothing else to worship God aright. Indeed, anything imposed upon them in worship interfered with their communion with God and was the greatest sin, as chapter 4 will explain.

Pure worship must be free worship because salvation could not be coerced, although the clearest statements of this belief did not come until

---

49. For example, Underhill, *Tracts on Liberty of Conscience*, and McBeth, *Early Baptist Literature on Religious Liberty*, really addressed the main protagonists of this paper only tangentially. The sometimes-mentioned *Humble Apology* signed by Kiffin and others was more about proving their loyalty to the King than arguing for religious liberty.

50. Knollys, *Christ Exalted* (1645), 6ff. Interestingly, Knollys was unable to finish preaching this sermon in Debenham because the constable stirred up the crowd, and it literally stoned Knollys out of the pulpit.

51. Spilsbury, *Gods Ordinance, The Saints Priviledge*, 72.

52. See Knollys, *Parable of the Kingdom*, 46.

53. *Publick Dispute*, The Epistle Dedicatory. Powell, *Common-Prayer-Book no Divine Service*, 14; and Owen, *Discourse Concerning Liturgies*, in *Works*, 15:17, acknowledged this reason. Owen considered it the first argument for liturgies, the second being national uniformity in worship.

the very end of the time period in question. Hercules Collins's imaginary Baptist conversant said to a conformist, "If you sought God's Glory and my Salvation, then you would not threaten me with punishment, and make that a motive to fit me up to come to Church," and Benjamin Keach ultimately declared that non-believers absolutely could not worship.[54] Because pure worship was intimately connected with the nature and purpose of the church, free worship demanded a free church.[55]

Congregationalism: One Class of Holy Priests

If the previous section be at all convincing, then it follows that only one ecclesiastical system could apply to the concept of a free church, namely congregationalism. Indeed, Kiffin wrote, "*Christ* hath given this Power to his Church, not to a *Hierarchy*, neither to a Nationall *Presbytery*, but to a company of Saints in a Congregationall way."[56] When William Twisse and the Westminster Assembly called on the dissenters to cease from forming new churches, claiming "that it belongs to Christian Magistrates in

---

54. Collins, *Some Reasons for Separation*, 20; Keach, *Christ Alone the way to Heaven*, 65. Collins succeeded John Norcot as the pastor of John Spilsbury's church in Wapping. He knew Kiffin and Keach well and was a messenger at all of the General Assemblies of the London Particular Baptists.

55. Owen produced equally compelling arguments for religious liberty. First, if a magistrate had the power to institute new ordinances, he had the power to create a new religion (ordinances were only significant according to the meaning given them). Creating a new religion destroyed the religious liberty of those adhering to the old who rejected the new. Second, while compulsion might bring men to a form of agreement, such an agreement was not built on the "foundation of faith towards God" and thus invalid in the matters of true worship. See Owen, *Truth and Innocence Vindicated*, in *Works*, 13:451, and Owen, *Vindication of the Animadversions on "Fiat Lux,"* in *Works*, 14:280. But the clearest statement of this doctrine was actually made *to* the Baptists by Bishop who wrote, "The worship of God is of another nature then Force: Force is carnal, that is spiritual. And a carnal thing cannot effect a spiritual end," and, "How *unnatural* a thing is it then to force a *man* to worship *God*, or to make him to suffer for not *worshipping* by that which is not *spirit*?" (Bishop, *An Illumination to Open the Eyes of the Papists*, 30, 47).

56. Goodwin, *Glimpse of Sions Glory*, The Epistle to the Reader (by Kiffin). There was one additional argument the Baptists used: the one golden candlestick of Zechariah 4 (one national church) versus the several candlesticks of Revelation (many congregational churches). See Knollys, *Exposition Of the Revelation*, 150. But even this had a liturgical connection, for Knollys explained that the churches were candles "*First*, from the purity of the Worship of God administred in the Churches of Saints, *John* 4. 23, 24. according to Christs Institutions, 1 *Cor.* 11. 1, 2. *Secondly*, From the Holiness of the Ministers and Members in the Churches of God" (ibid., 9). See also Knollys, *Apocalyptical Mysteries*, and even Cary, *A Solemn Call*.

an especiall manner to be authorizers of, and Ministers of the Gospel to be Leaders in, such Reformation," Baptists ignored him.[57] But that is not the only way worship influenced the Baptist commitment to congregationalism, for congregationalism not only applies to a hierarchy between churches but also within a church. Both the Anglicans and the Presbyterians were committed to what can only be called a two-class system of membership (or a multi-class system, as in the case of the Laudians[58]) in which the clergy were distinct from the laity, symbolized by the rail surrounding the Communion table. Featley responded to Kiffin's challenge by saying that "the distinction of Clergy and Laity" was as implicit in the Scriptures as Trinity and Sacrament, and that even deacons "were not meer Lay-men" but full of the Holy Spirit.[59] Independents believed that only duties distinguished pastors from people, but they still required that an ordinary church member "must have a warrant by an immediate call from God" before being allowed to teach or preach in a church. Each required a "lawful call" in addition to personal gifts in order for a man to be "set apart" to ministry. Owen explained that all Christians were called priests "inasmuch as they are members of Christ, not ministers of the gospel," and John Bewick, a rector at Stanhope, denied that the apostles' extraordinary calling in any way applied to the ordinary tradesmen in England.[60]

The reason for this distinction was the minister's responsibility in worship. Baptists mocked Catholic clergy "that a Priest can make a whole

---

57. Twisse et al. *Certaine Considerations*, 2. Marshall actually wrote the draft. *ODNB*, s.v. "Marshall, Stephen," 6. He claimed that even if the dissenters did not get everything they wanted, they would have the peace of knowing that they did not cause further division. Interestingly, Tombes heeded this request, which is one of the reasons why he stayed at arm's length from the Particular Baptists. He realized that his antipaedobaptism would cost him his living, but he still could not justify gathering a separated church or joining such a church. See Tombes, *Apology*, 10, and Tombes, *Addition to the Apology*, 21. A Scot took Tombes to task for sympathizing with the Baptists yet being unwilling to join with them in church membership. Baillie, *Disswasive From The Errors of the Time*, 81.

58. Lake, "Laudian Style," 177.

59. Both Anglicans and Presbyterians identified the Old Testament Levitical system as their proof. Featley also appealed to the spiritual gifts of apostle, prophet, and teacher and the authority of a presbytery. Featley, *Dippers dipt*, 8, 12–13, 18. Kingsley thought that their lay ministry was the chief cause of derision for the early Baptists. Kingsley, "Opposition to Early Baptists," 23–26.

60. See Owen, *Duty of Pastors and People Distinguished*, in *Works*, 13:29, 19, 21. Also I. B. [John Bewick], *Antidote Against Lay-Preaching*, 4, 26ff. Bewick argued, "Preaching or dispensing of the word is a peculiar calling distinct from other callings" (ibid., 4).

Free Worship and a New Concept of the Church

Christ of a Wafer Cake, by uttering a few words," but Presbyterians argued for the same importance of clerical duty:

> For the workes of their administration towards the Church are all the Ordinances of God belonging to the publick worship in the word and prayer, whereunto the Sacraments, the Government and the Discipline are subordinate, that therein by the Word and Prayer the Saints may have communion with God through the Spirit.[61]

They took the administration of the public worship of God so seriously that only a man trained and set apart for the task could endeavor to help a congregation perform it. Ideally, I have already demonstrated that Baptists took the public worship of God very seriously as well; the difference was that Baptists took the privileges of salvation equally seriously. The First London Confession declared that Christ alone was Prophet, Priest, and King of His church, the result of which was that Christ "removed all those Rites, Shadowes, and Ceremonies" and made his people "a spirituall House, an holy Priesthood, to offer up spirituall sacrifice acceptable to God through him."[62] As a royal priesthood, a holy nation, and a peculiar people, God's saints therefore had "authoritie to restore the solemne worship of God appointed in his Word for the time of the Gospel." God's people were priests not merely as members of Christ but truly as ministers of the gospel. All believers, or "visible Saints," were "inrolled amongst his houshold servants, to be under his heavenly conduct and government," and all such servants were called "to present their bodies and soules, and to bring their gifts God hath given" in edification of their local church.[63] God gave each church power to appoint qualified officers only for the order and well being of the church, and the power of excommunication remained with the church, not an officer.[64]

---

61. Keach, *Antichrist Stormed*, 72; Caryl, *Moderator*, 109. Even Owen declared "that the people are neither able nor fit to judge for themselves" the matters of worship and doctrine. Owen, *Discourse concerning Evangelical Love*, in *Works*, 15:127.

62. Spilsbury, *Gods Ordinance*, 35; London [1644], Articles X, XIII, XVII. Crosby celebrated this priestly equality. Crosby, 3:295.

63. *London* [1644], Articles XXXIII–XXXV. These ideas had been floating around England for some time. While most Englishmen considered a priesthood under the king (with or without a distinction between the clergy and laity), Yarnell noted that Tyndale promoted a vision of no clerical distinctions, even for the king. Yarnell, *Royal Priesthood*, chapter 5.

64. *London* [1644], Articles XXXVI–XLII. Knollys confirmed that a church had authority over its elders. Knollys, *Moderate Answer*, 7. The one possible influence of the Presbyterian two-class system came with their assertion that only a preaching disciple

Pure Worship

Wright believed this conviction developed out of their rejection of liturgical formality; there could be no hard division of labor amongst officers because that was a function of such formality. Thus the authority of the church could not rest on the officers at all: "It was founded mainly upon the direct collective inspiration to be found in the preaching, prophecy and prayer of all the members, and from its source, the immediate presence amongst them of the risen Christ."[65] But there were even greater consequences of this conviction. Baptist polity was unique precisely because they believed that every church member was a worshiper of Jesus; there could be no hierarchy because all believers were priests unto God on a level plane. They rejected the Laudian claim that the church's physical and liturgical structures—not its congregation—gave it identity. They also rejected Westminster's claim that they needed help with their "Ordering of the publique Worship of God, and Government of his Church" because they also were full of the Holy Spirit.[66] Sometimes this led to sensational results, as with the Diggers and Levellers and other radicals in the New Model Army. Sometimes this led to a spectacle, as Thomas Edwards charged repeatedly in *Gangraena* with all of the contempt he could drip onto a printed page. For example, Edward Barber's church on Bishopgate Street shared a love feast together and then laid hands on one another. Thomas Lambe's church in Bell Alley on Coleman Street was characterized by "such a confusion and noise, as if it were at a Play; and some will be speaking here, some there: young youths and boys come thither, and make a noise while they are at their Exercises, and them of the Church will go to make them quiet, and then they fight one with another." Henry

---

could lawfully baptize, but this seems more a response to charges of disorder than a commitment to the principle. This led to a dilemma for the Baptists: they believed that every church had the authority to elect and ordain its own ministers, but they were under intense pressure to provide some kind of standard education or training. A number of their early ministers were educated in Anglican schools, but by 1662 all dissenters were banned from Cambridge and Oxford. Edward Wetenhall pitied the poor nonconformists, "These men, being (as above supposed) of upright and honest hearts, truly conscientious and fearing God, are not to be inveighed against, because they are in some regard adverse; nor to be laught at, because they have not judged more maturely: (As things went twenty or thirty years ago [during the Civil War], considering how many were then in the very *Crisis* of their Education, it is not to be wondered that the Age abounds with men of such sentiments in Religion)" (Wetenhall, *Of Gifts and Offices*, 2–3). It was not until 1679 and Edward Terrill's endowment of what would become Bristol Baptist College that Baptists really began to take control of their own education. See Clements, "Significance of 1679," 2–6.

65. Wright, *Early English Baptists*, 32.
66. *Westminster* [1646], chap. 31, "Of Synods and Councels."

Denne was baptized by a Mechanick and then commissioned by Lambe's church to go out and preach: "He Preaches and Prays, and after he hath done, he calls to know if any be not satisfied; and then they stand up that will, and object, and then he Answers. Others of the Brethren that will, meer Mechanicks, one, two, or more sometimes, do Exercise after him." William Kiffin was the uneducated servant of John Lilburne who gathered children and servants without parental consent; Kiffin and his co-pastor Thomas Patient even anointed a sick woman with oil; Hanserd Knollys forced his way into pulpits in Suffolk against the will of the minister and now preached at Finsbury Fields. Every description was calculated to create revulsion on the part of his reasonable Puritan readers.[67]

William Kiffin knew that such criticism damaged the Baptists' reputations, and he desired greater respectability not only through their statement of beliefs but also through the order of their worship. This as much as anything led to the division between the London Particular Baptists and other Baptists, especially after Barber's church adopted the debatable practice of laying hands on believers at baptism.[68] But they remained committed to congregationalism over against a priestly class. When Thomas Hardcastle, the Baptist minister at Broadmead who considered John Owen his dear friend and William Kiffin his trusted advisor, was in prison in 1671, he wrote to his church members to assume the responsibility of preaching (with no pastoral oversight).[69] William Kiffin republished Samuel Howe's famous treatise, *Sufficiencie of the Spirits Teaching, without humane-learning: or A treatise, tending to proue humane-learning to be no help to the spirituall understanding of the Word of God*, in 1683. Benjamin Keach took great offense against John Child's accusation sometime before 1684, "Take two or three [Baptist] Mechanicks in a Town, and put to these

---

67. *Gangraena*, 1:6–45/2. On April 25, 1645, Parliament outlawed unlicensed preaching; the billposter specifically went to the "rude multitude" in Bell Alley. Less than a month later, Parliament went after Knollys for similar disorders. See Carruthers, *Everyday Work*, 99.

68. See Wright, "Baptist Alignments Part 2," although Wright thought Kiffin was more interested in an orderly form of church planting. Interestingly for one who otherwise spoke little about worship, Wright noted the ceremonial stress of a priestly role of the pastor in the laying on of hands. This also would have isolated the Bell Alley church from Particular Baptists. Wright, "Edward Barber and His Friends Part 1," 364.

69. *Broadmead*, 267. However, it is important to note that after Hardcastle died in 1678, the church did not "break bread" until they had called the next pastor. It seems that every church had a limit as to how far they would accept the duties or privileges of their priesthood. Ibid., 396. McBeth's characterization of this congregational responsibility as "audience participation" was most unfortunate. McBeth, "Baptist Beginnings," 39.

so many Priests and Jesuits to dispute, and what fearful baffling work will they make with these poor Mechanicks or Lay-Preachers."[70]

The Baptists' convictions about worship with respect to the priesthood eventually created significant challenges on this very matter. John Owen taught, "The main exercise of spiritual gifts, on which their growth and improvement doth depend, lies in the administration of gospel ordinances; that is, the work of the ministry, for which they are bestowed," something with which the Baptists could agree. But Owen restricted such growth to the men called to administer those ordinances.[71] On this matter, the London Particular Baptists seemed torn between their impulses and their desire for respectability, for they restricted the administration of baptism and the Lord's Supper to men called and gifted for the task. However, they believed that each church was able to identify and appoint those men. In other words, their priestly class (which was not a separate class) was drawn from and bound to the full congregation of priests and so was unlike the rest of England's. Writing about this matter, the Baptist church in Fenstanton declared "That it shall be lawful for any person to improve their gifts in the presence of the congregation" and also "That it shall be lawful only for such as are approved by the congregation, to

---

70. *English Spira*, 38. This was a truly bizarre exchange, mentioned because the accuser still demeaned the Baptists as uneducated fussbudgets even in the 1680s. John Child was a Baptist preacher for twenty years before changing his mind and turning on them (the quote contrasted the Baptists with the influential and persuasive Anglicans). He then hanged himself in 1684. This publication argued that he hung himself in despair for that decision, confessing his errors to Baptist preachers Hercules Collins and Benjamin Keach before succumbing to his grief. The supposed recantation played a key role in Keach's conclusion. The title hearkens to Francis Spira, an infamous Italian Protestant who also supposedly killed himself in despair for abandoning Protestantism in 1548, whose story was injected into the English subconsciousness by Nathaniel Bacon in 1638. To be fair, Tolmie hinted at a tacit reason why some churches may have eliminated the priestly class: money. Many churches were too poor to support a minister, leading to itinerant and tent-making ministries. This, coupled with the congregation's power to call and release (hire and fire), may have contributed to the pastor being seen as less priestly. Tolmie, *Triumph of the Saints*, 21. However, most of the early Baptist leaders were tradesmen: Eaton was a button-maker, Howe and Spilsbury were cobblers, Barbone was a leather-seller, and so on. Being so common, it was probably seen as a function rather than a cause of this one-class priesthood.

71. Owen, *Discourse Concerning Liturgies*, in *Works*, 15:53, 49ff. I have already described a central argument of the Independents and Presbyterians at Westminster against the *Book of Common Prayer* as how it prevented ministers from exercising their gifts in worship. Even Powell argued against reinstating the Prayer Book in that "the Ministers of Christ, and his Gospel, ought to be so gifted as not to need it." Powell, *Common-Prayer-Book no Divine Service*, 2.

preach publicly to the world."[72] But on a related note, a most enlightening accusation came from Thomas Bakewell, "Independent people exclude women and children from having any voice in their Churches, yet they deny a representative church gathered out of many particular Churches."[73] Indeed, it seems that many Baptist churches had (perhaps) created a two-class system of membership despite their convictions; chapter 6 will note that this issue blew up during the hymn-singing controversy and even contributed to Baptist defections to Quakerism.

But there was another way in which churches had multiple classes of members: infants. John Tombes, the first Divine to defect to Baptist principles and the one to write by far the most against the Presbyterians, recognized that Richard Baxter's church actually had three classes of members: those who had saving faith, those who professed it, and those whose parents professed it for them.[74] The first two did not bother Baptists because most of them believed that they must accept a man's profession of faith on its face,[75] but the latter flew in the face of everything they believed about true members of the worshipping church. The argument was simple: "if it were true [that infants are church members], it would follow infants are capable of the Kingdom and the blessing, which is the greater, therefore they are capable of the Lords Supper, Ordination to the Ministry, Church-discipline, which are the less," but Presbyterians did not admit infants to ordinances, tacitly acknowledging that infants were incapable of worship (most of them baptized infants while asleep).[76]

---

72. *Fenstanton*, 98.

73. Bakewell, *Confutation of the Anabaptists,* not paginated.

74. Tombes, *Felo de Se,* 34. Granted, Baxter was one of those who believed that "Presbyterian" referred more to "Puritan" than to any commitment to an ecclesiastical polity. He himself was comfortable with elements of episcopacy. *ODNB,* s.v. "Baxter, Richard," 12.

75. See, for example, Goodwin, *Quaere, Concerning the Church-Covenant,* 4; *London* [1644], Article XXXIII; Cox, Knollys, and Kiffin, *Declaration Concerning The Publike Dispute,* 20; Kiffin, *Briefe Remonstrance,* 13; Spilsbury, *Gods Ordinance,* 25; and so on.

76. Tombes, *Plea for Anti-Paedobaptists,* 35. He continued, "Though into the Kingdom of Heaven infants be admitted by God who knows who are his without any visible expression, yet into the visible Church persons are not admitted without visible testimony of their faith, of which sort were all added to the Church." See also Grantham, *Quaeries Examined,* 4–5, 42–43. However, Tombes and all of the Baptists practicing open-communion inevitably had multiple classes of members; for some it was the difference between those they would admit to the Lord's Supper and those they would admit to leadership, for others it was creating a class of "hearers" by which they could avoid the debate over the Lord's Supper. Denying the place of a test for church

Thomas Grantham perceptively asked "whether the difference between the *Baptists*, and *Paedobaptists* be not chiefly (if not only) about imposing Ceremonies upon Infants?"[77] Grantham did not appreciate the depth of their differences, but his question was valid. One of the chief differences between Baptists and Presbyterians was purely liturgical.

In summary, the Baptists' commitment to the church as a worshipping congregation led them to challenge the ecclesiological beliefs and practices of the rest of England, including both the relationship between the clergy and the laity and between an infant and the church. It would be several decades before the Baptists really acknowledged the radical end of the former, namely the ability of a woman to exercise her spiritual gifts in church, as chapters 5 and 6 will explain. But they realized very quickly that the latter would have cataclysmic implications for their theology and their relationship with the rest of Reformation England.

A Pure Church: A Spiritual Bride and Paedobaptism

All of these considerations came to a head with respect to the concept of a regenerate church, or a church in which every member made a personal profession of faith in Christ. Hanserd Knollys clearly identified his priorities for the church:

> 1. That our Lord Jesus Christ in building up his own House, *the Church of God*, ordained and appointed a preceeding Ministry, to be workers together with him in building his House, *Heb.* 3. 4. 1 *Cor.* 3. 9, 10, 11. *We are labourers together with God—Ye are God's Building*, &c. 2. That the Churches of God under the Gospel, are not *National*, but *Political*, and *Congregational*. 3. That a particular visible true Constituted Gospel Church of God doth consist of fit Matter, and due Form. Jesus Christ the Chief Corner Stone, is a lively Stone, and the Materials of the Church ought to be living Stones, 1 *Pet.* 2. 4, 5. Sanctified Believers, 1 *Cor.* 1. 2, 6. And Christ himself was Baptized with Water,

---

membership, Tombes said, "I confess such triall is requisite in admitting into special function, or intimate society; but not to communion in worship" (Tombes, *Apology*, 94).

77. Grantham, *Queries Examined*, 9. Collins similarly complained, "Can it be shewed that ever our Lord Instituted Gospel Ordinances for Infants?" (Collins, *Antidote Proved A Counterfeit*, 8). Early discussions among Baptists about the so-called age of accountability largely revolved around the age at which a child could meaningfully participate in the ordinances and duties of the church. See Tombes, *Apology*, 64.

> and with the holy Spirit; every one in his Visible Churches of Saints, ought to be Baptized with Water, and with the holy Spirit. 2. Those sanctified Believers ought to be *fitly* framed together, and *orderly* compacted, joined and built together, an *habitation* of God through the Spirit, *Eph.* 2. 19, 20, 21, 22. & *chap* 4. 15, 16. which is the Form of the House of God, the Church of the Living God, 1 *Tim.* 3. *v.* 15.[78]

On the one hand, this certainly annoyed the parochial Anglicans and Presbyterians.[79] But the conclusion that upset everyone, including Independents, was spelled out by John Spilsbury who said, "It is a high contempt and injury to Christ, as he is Husband of the Church his holy Spouse, to force upon him an naturall wife, himselfe being spirituall, and desires the like associate, as such a Church is founded upon the natural birth, namely, Infants."[80] If the church must be able to worship in Spirit and Truth, and infants could not worship, then infants could not be in the church (or be baptized). Only Baptists restricted the fit matter of a true church to be a sanctified believer in which the Spirit dwelt.

This belief struck a nerve in England. Anglicans had inherited a type of covenant theology based on the nation of Israel, and Presbyterians and Independents employed a covenant theology based on the family: "It's not a slight thing to consider, how that ever since the Fall this hath been an usual method of God in administration of the Covenant, and priviledges

---

78. Knollys, *World that Now is,* 45–46.

79. The early Baptists followed the Separatists in the pragmatic arguments against the parish system, arguing that a national church would become a natural church, and a natural church would always fall away from God's holy rules; "It is a practice that overthrows, and destroys the body of Christ, or holy temple of God; for in time it will come to consist of naturall, and so a nation, and so a nationall Generation, & carnal members, amongst whom if any godly be, they will be brought in bondage, and become subjects of scorn & contempt, and the power of government rest in the hands of the wicked" (Spilsbury, *Treatise Concerning Baptisme,* 25). Kilcop identified mixed membership as the source of all church problems. Kilcop, *Short Treatise of Baptisme,* 8. Importantly, Keach would later turn this argument against certain preachers "whose great Business 'tis to bring Men into visible Profession, and make them Members of Churches, whose Preaching tends more to bring Persons to Baptism, and to subject to external Ordinances, than to shew them the necessity of Regeneration, Faith, or a changed Heart" because the disorders they faced in their churches and their associations could have been prevented "were there not many false and deceitful, carnal and hypocritical Professors." Keach, *Counterfeit Christian,* 54, 50. Note that even though Keach published these sermons in May 1691, he actually preached them in August 1690, before the major events of chapter 6. He does not seem to be taking any shots specifically at his anti-hymn-singing church members with these comments.

80. Spilsbury, *Treatise Concerning Baptisme,* 25

of grace, to make it run through families and houshoulds of Believers, as the special veins." The idea that a visible church was a subset of the invisible church was laughable to them.[81] They acknowledged that only the elect could be saved, but all (who were baptized into the covenant) were still entitled to the benefits of the covenant.[82] More importantly, rejecting covenant theology was seen as rejecting Calvinism, a charge that harassed Particular Baptists for a long time. This also opened all Baptists to the charge of making their children "Bastards" or "illegitimate" because they were not "holy" in a Calvinistic sense, which proved to be a very effective tool in public debate.[83]

John Spilsbury guarded against this by redefining the covenant in its most basic terms. London Particular Baptists understood the biblical images of chosen generation, royal priesthood, and holy nation to mean that only the elect were God's people; nonetheless, Spilsbury defined the

---

81. Sidenham, *Christian Sober and Plain Exercitation*, 105–6. He continued, "Hence families, as they were the first natural societies, so they were the first Churches, the Covenant and the priviledges of it was among them" (ibid.). Hall conceded, "Did we certainly and infallibly know which [infants] were Reprobates, we ought not to baptize them: but in the judgement of Charity (which believeth all things, and hopeth all things, which may with reason and a good conscience be believed and hoped) we must judge the best of every one, till by their wicked conversation they shall shew the contrary. There is a twofold being in Covenant; *vel quoad jus faederis, vel quoad faederis beneficia* [one has either the right to or the benefits of the covenant]. Only the Elect enjoy the internal benefit of the Covenant, such as Pardon of sin, Justification, Sanctification, Salvation, &c. A Reprobate born in the Church, may have right to the external Seal of the Covenant (though he want the inward Grace) nor may we exclude any but such as by their open impiety do exclude themselves" (Hall, *Font Guarded*, 104). Circumcision was assumed to be parallel with baptism.

82. Tombes conceded Marshall's argument that elect infants were members of the *invisible* church, but challenged him to prove the same for Christ's visible church. Tombes, *Examen of the Sermon Of Mr.* Stephen Marshall, 166–67. When Marshall realized that Tombes was connecting the visible and invisible churches, he was incredulous. Tombes, *Apology or Plea for the Two Treatises*, 71. Collier, the very controversial western Baptist, gave the pithiest reply, "We are not to Administer Ordinances from Gods election, but from faiths manifestation" (Collier, *Certaine Queries*, 17). Contrasting the two personalities, Hall loved Tombes but despised Collier: "Collier is your name, and Collying is with you" (Hall, *Font Guarded*, 121).

83. See, for example, Barbone, *Discourse Tending to Prove*, 27. He argued that no one could know someone's election, so none should be kept out of the church. Barbone, *Defence of Baptizing Infants*, 2. Tombes and Baxter had an extensive debate over the meaning of 1 Corinthians 7:14, with Tombes arguing that in no way did the holiness applied to children in that passage mean the same as the holiness of believers set apart to the service of God in a regenerate church. See Tombes, *Antidote Against the Venome of a Passage*. See also White, "Thomas Collier and Gangraena Edwards," 99–101, for thoughts on Calvinism in this context.

Free Worship and a New Concept of the Church

"covenant of grace" as an agreement between God and a man "as Gods giving of man life and peace, and all things in Jesus Christ, and that he will be his God, upon whom he shall relie." Those who entered into this covenant of grace were then organized by Christ "into an orderly body among themselves; wherein the Saints are the matter, and the covenant the forme" on four principles: the word of God, Confession of faith, the mutual consent of the saints, and the uniting power of the Spirit of Christ.[84] For most Baptists, the confession necessarily included the profession of faith in public baptism—"this is the pledge of our entrance into Covenant with God, and of our giving up our selves unto him in the solemn Bond of Religion."[85]

Benjamin Cox added a liturgical argument to this discovery of saint, covenant, and church. Baptism was a ceremony: it had an administrator, a subject, a mode, an order, and a verbal invocation. In its most basic biblical form it consisted both of the administration of water *and* the profession of faith—all sides agreed about this (although they disagreed about the amount of water). Cox drew an obvious liturgical conclusion: "this necessarily excludes Infants, who can make no such profession." He then attacked the paedobaptist's liturgical solution saying, "The supply of this want of profession, by the profession of those that have been called Sureties, doth now appear to all wise men, to be as ridiculous and absurd as Paedo-rantisme (now falsely called, Infant-Baptisme)."[86] All of this was to be presented in a scheduled debate with Edmund Calamy together with six arguments against baptism: only believers were to be baptized, Christ did not teach infant baptism, infant baptism was will-worship, infant baptism denied Christ to come in the flesh (by the nature of the ceremony), the seed of Abraham according to the flesh should not be baptized, and infant baptism was not according to the Rule of the Word. Cox and the

---

84. Spilsbury, *Treatise Concerning Baptisme*, 8–9, 42. See also Tombes, *Apology or Plea for the Two Treatises*, 129.

85. Kiffin, *Sober Discourse*, To the Christian Reader. Tombes added about infants that "the entring into Covenant with God, which is the act of the baptized, and cannot be done ordinarily by an infant, who is onely passive, and makes no promise at Baptisme; and therefore cannot be rightly said to enter into Covenant with God." Tombes, *Apology or Plea for the Two Treatises*, 47.

86. Cox, Knollys, Kiffin, *Declaration*, 20. Sureties were also sometimes called "gossips," "pro-parents" or "godparents." This is one of very few instances, with Barber's thirty-first query, in which an author clearly said that infant baptism was no baptism at all.

others clearly considered the liturgical element of infant baptism a significant point of contention and a viable course of public debate.[87]

While their antagonists accused them of removing infants from the covenant (Baptists believed that infants were never in the covenant), London Particular Baptists emphasized the heart of the matter, namely the need for salvation. Spilsbury, for his part, appealed to this most basic truth,

> And this is the Gospel, which is called the *Word of Reconciliation*, the *Gospel of the Kingdome*; which holds forth Christ to be King, Priest, and Prophet, and the onely way unto the Father; and brings persons to be of the houshold of God. Which houshold is that composed order, and instituted state of Christs Church of the new Testament, with the subjects in that order and state, according to the same Testament; of which Testament Christ is the Mediator, who hath confirmed the same by his own bloud, and sanctified all things therein contained.[88]

He reminded his audience of the benefits for those in the covenant, namely a vital relationship with God in Christ: "Withhold not your selves then from worshipping God, and enjoying the appointed priviledges of sons. Feare not, but believe: for you being Christs, all things are yours; and have you not then a right to his Ordinances?"[89] Spilsbury took the privilege of worship—of which infants were not capable (not according to the accepted sense of "worship")—very seriously. This emphasis reinforced the Baptists' commitment to a pure church and it also drove them to seek a pure model, not only for polity but also for worship.[90]

---

87. Ibid., 1ff. Cox, Knollys, and Kiffin had agreed to a six-hour debate with Edmund Calamy which the mayor prohibited for fear of public disturbance.

88. Spilsbury, *Gods Ordinance*, 22.

89. Ibid., 38. Subsequent sections will explain how some Baptists took this privilege so seriously that they were willing to isolate themselves over it (certainly not Spilsbury's intention).

90. Near the end of his life, Kiffin endorsed one of the clearest statements on the content of this section: "*Therefore if any Man be in Christ he is a new Creature: Old things are past away, all things are become New*: A new Church State, and new Ordinances, a new Seed, and a new way of Introduction, unto the Participation of the Priviledge of Church-membership under the Gospel Dispensation. Now nothing but a *New Creature* will serve the turn; for God expects that they that Worship him now, do *Worship Him in Spirit and in Truth*; The *Priviledge* of being admitted into God's House, and to stand before His Presence in the Actual Celebration of Gospel Ordinances, being now Entailed only upon the Spiritual Seed, even such who *as lively Stones are built up a Spiritual House, a Holy Priesthood to offer up Spiritual Sacrifices acceptable to God, by Jesus Christ.* 1. Pet. 2. 3. 4. Or such at least as make a visible Profession thereof" (Cary, *Solemn Call*, 15).

A Way of Worship That Was Never Known Before: The Apostolic Church as a Model of Pure Worship[91]

Although Garrett concluded that Separatists were primarily concerned with dissent, it seems rather clear that they were very interested in restoration. Indeed, John Owen declared the foundation of "dissent" to be "restoration": "Their design of reducing themselves in worship and conversation to the primitive pattern, they openly avow; nor dare any directly condemn that design, nor can they be convinced of insincerity in what they profess."[92] White argued that the radical Puritans going back to the 1570s always believed the apostolic church to be an "achievable model" (though in a different way than the Quakers).[93] Samuel Howe exhorted that the true church must be truly based on the Scriptures, and John Spilsbury made it clear that the scriptural church was the apostolic church, not only in structure and doctrine but also especially in worship. God intended the apostle's model for the entire age: "They were the layers of the foundation, and the ministeriall institutes of the whole state and order of Christs Church to be observed of all to the end of the world."[94] On the one hand, this enabled the Baptists to bypass centuries of formal worship; on the other hand, this created endless tension between those churches that could not agree on the apostolic model. This section will explore that model from the perspective of worship and introduce the discord it caused.

A True Church for Pure Worship

Spilsbury knew that the Antichrist would be able to twist the Scriptures into his own form of worship "with ordinances suitable thereunto" were

---

91. See Spilsbury, *Gods Ordinance*, 2.

92. Owen, *Truth and Innocence Vindicated*, in *Works*, 13:503; cf. Garrett, "Restitution and Dissent Part I." Collins agreed that the apostolic model covered "all things practicable, not only following them in matters of Faith respecting Salvation, but in those Ordinances of the Gospel which respect Church Constitution." Collins, *Some Reasons for Separation*, 12.

93. White, *English Separatist Tradition*, 53. The goal of the Reformation was "to reduce all things and actions to the true and ancient and primitive pattern of God's word." Ibid., 73.

94. Howe, *Sufficiency of the Spirits Teaching*, 36–37; Spilsbury, *Gods Ordinance*, 3.

the church not wary of his plan.[95] Essentially, Particular Baptists agreed with Gillespie that this would demarcate a true church from a false church: a true church would not mix human error in their instituted worship. The difficulty was in knowing where that line was drawn, therefore the church should be especially mindful of the examples left by the apostles.[96] Even at the end of the century, Benjamin Keach argued that Christ's true sheep would follow the flock of the primitive church and "*contend for that Faith which was once delivered to the Saints*, and keep the Ordinances as they were at first given forth; they are for no mixture in Doctrine nor Discipline."[97] He still believed that a pure church was marked by pure ordinances: "Thou hast thy Institutions, / and *Ordinances pure*; / Thou hast thy *Churches*; tell me when, / and where I may be *sure!*"[98]

London Particular Baptists regularly sought the expression of the "pure" church in Acts. Benjamin Cox defined the church saying, "Beleevers baptized ought to agree and joyn together in a constant profession of the same doctrine of the Gospel, and in professed obedience thereunto, and also in fellowship, and in breaking of bread, and in prayer, *Acts* 2. 42. And a company of baptized beleevers so agreeing and joining together, are a Church or Congregation of Christ, *Acts* 2. 47."[99] In the Acts 2 model, Hanserd Knollys emphasized covenant and gathering:

---

95. Spilsbury was specifically speaking about infant baptism and the Roman Catholic Church. Spilsbury, *Treatise Concerning Baptisme*, 35.

96. When Spilsbury used a version of this argument against him, a flustered Barbone responded, "Observe, he hath got the word *true* to helpe him along; that Church, saith he, by the rules of the Gospel is a true Church; what rule or rules he meaneth is hard to guesse, he setteth downe no place of Scripture" (Barbone, *Defence of Baptizing Infants*, 6–7).

97. Keach, *Golden Mine Opened*, 119.

98. Keach, *Feast of Fat Things*, 69.

99. Cox, *Appendix to a Confession of Faith*, 10. Tombes appealed to this same passage saying, "Therefore we seek out the true Church of Christ: its image is here painted to the life, and verily it begins for the doctrine, which is as it were the soul of the Church, neither doth he name any doctrine, but of the Apostles, that is to say, which the Son of God had delivered by their hands, therefore wheresoever the pure voice of the Gospel sounds, where men remain in the profession of it, where they exercise themselves to profit in the ordinary hearing of it, there undoubtedly is the Church. Wherefore *Luke* mentions these four things not without just ground, when he would describe the duly constituted state of the Church, and its convenient that we should endeavour to attain to this order, if we desire to be a true Church in the sight of God and Angels, and not onely to boast of the vain name thereof before men. And *vers*. 47. it is said that the Lord added daily to the Church such as should be saved. It describeth them that there added to the Church, viz. that they were such as should be saved, or as *Beza* yieldeth to another reading [and so Grotius and many others] such as saved

> they giving up themselves *professedly first* to the LORD, and *then* one to another, *mutually* and *solemnly* with one accord engaging themselves to come together in ONE Congregation, and to Assemble themselves together in some *one* Place every *first* Day of the week, to worship God *publickly* in all his holy Ordinances, with their *mutual* professed Subjection unto the Laws of God's House.[100]

William Kiffin applied the Acts 2 model to believers' baptism saying, "First they Preached; and such as were Converted, were Baptized; such as were Baptized, walkt in Church-Fellowship, *&c.* Breaking of Bread and Prayers."[101]

These Baptists also looked at churches outside of Acts 2 to corroborate their model. Knollys observed in the church at Ephesus "a few baptized Believers, who were separated from the profane Idolatrous Gentiles and their Idol Temples; also from the formal superstitious Jews and their Synagogues, by the Ministers of Christ, and congregated together to Worship God in Spirit and in Truth *visibly*, walking in all the Commandments and Ordinances of God *blamelesly*, according to the Order of the Gospel," and found in Sardis "the soundness of *Doctrine*, purity of Gospel-*Administrations* in the Worship of God, and the strictness of *Discipline* in this Church, did give her a Name and a Praise among other Churches."[102] A clear pattern could be seen in all of Knollys's analyses: in the apostolic churches, Knollys found pure worship and pure discipline, and he desired it. He was not alone; the General Assembly of Particular Baptists in 1689 lauded those churches,

> Forasmuch as they did nothing in those purest Primitive Times in the sacred Worship of God, either as to time or form, but by a Divine Warrant from the Holy Apostles, who were instructed by our Lord Jesus, and were guided in all those Affairs by his faithful and infallible Holy Spirit.[103]

Indeed, the watchterm was "primitive purity," and Baptists prized it highly.

---

themselves from that untoward Generation" (Tombes, *Felo de Se*, 32–33).

100. Knollys, *World that Now is*, 49.

101. Kiffin, *Sober Discourse*, 29. The model was "not only Commanded, but Practised."

102. Knollys, *Exposition Of the Revelation*, 18, 42.

103. *Narrative* [1689], 17. Keach elaborated, "Because that was in truth the time of the Churches greatest Glory, Perfection and Beauty, and very soon after the Apostles fell asleep, the Church, though she grew older, yet she decayed, and Corruptions crept in" (Keach, *Gold Refin'd*, 75).

Exactly what they found is a far more complex question, and most of chapter 4 will be devoted to it. Knollys set the parameter "that the whole Worship of God, and all the sacred Ordinances of the Lord be Administred according to the Gospel Institutions, Commandments, and Examples of Christ and his holy Apostles."[104] This sent Particular Baptists on a hazardous search for all of the biblical ordinances of worship, not only those commanded by Christ but also those observed by the apostles. They observed prayer in worship but encountered the belief that the Lord's Prayer was not a model but a set form. They knew that Christ and the apostles sang a psalm at His last supper but did not know how to apply it to their own churches. They read Paul's command that women be silent in churches but wanted women to give an account of their salvation nonetheless. They noted the laying on of hands in baptism but feared it was an apostolic privilege. About all they could agree on was the centrality of the sermon, that all things should be done for edification, and there should be no man-made liturgies.[105]

The Jerusalem church represented a unique glimpse into some Baptists' goals. Thomas Grantham believed that "all Churches, in all Ages and Nations, are indispensibly bound to follow this Church, in the Observation of all things whatsoever Christ commanded them."[106] Hanserd Knollys chose to look instead at the eschatological Jerusalem, or "the Heavenly State of the Church of God on Earth, restored to its Apostalical institutions, and Primitive purity," as opposed to "an earthly State of a false Church with respect unto corrupt Doctrine, superstitious Worship, and tyrannical Discipline, after the Inventions and precepts of Men."[107]

---

104. Knollys, *Exposition Of the Revelation*, 123–24.

105. John Owen derided a Catholic opponent, "For him who hath affirmed that it is likely they used forms of prayer and homilies composed for them by St Peter, I suppose he must fetch his evidence out of the same authors that he used who affirmed that Jesus Christ himself went up and down singing mass!" (Owen, *Discourse Concerning Liturgies*, in *Works*, 15:16).

106. Grantham, *Hear the Church*, 2. Indeed, that was the primary argument of his book.

107. Knollys, *Apocalyptical Mysteries*, 3 (he repeated this definition on 31), and 9. He emphasized the true church with respect to "soundness of Doctrine, purity of Worship, and power of Discipline." Ibid. Later in life, he worded it as "its Apostolical Constitution, and Primitive purity of Worship, and spiritual Gifts, and unto Christ's Ecclesiastical Government." Knollys, *Exposition Of the Revelation*, 150. Keach later echoed him about the time when the Spirit would be poured out on all people such that "all the Saints and Protestants Churches may be United into one Body and Communion, according to that holy Primitive and Apostolical pattern and purity." Keach, *Antichrist Stormed*, 144.

Free Worship and a New Concept of the Church

This perspective had an interesting effect on Knollys, namely the belief that there was only one right form of worship because there was only one eschatological church. He yearned, "In this holy City the heavenly New-Jerusalem, shall the pure Worship of God be celebrated, and his Sacred Ordinances shall be administred according to his Divine Institutions," believing that his church should strive for that worship.[108] Knollys pursued that conviction to an extreme end, namely that there should only be one church in every city broken into distinct companies small enough to meet together. Each company would employ the same divine model of worship and thus be "of one heart, and of one soul."[109]

---

108. Knollys, *World that Now is*, 8. Knollys, like most of his peers, held an eschatology that we would probably label "postmillennial," so when he imagined this setting he imagined it happening on earth; his quote continued, "and his Spiritual Gifts shall again be given unto his Saints for the Glory of his holy Name, and for the Conversion of the Nations." Ibid. Knollys, Keach, and Thomas Goodwin all believed that 1688 was the end of the Great Tribulation and London was John's Great City. See Knollys, *Exposition Of the Revelation*, 130; and Keach, *Antichrist Stormed*, 231. But see also the caveat in Garrett, *Baptist Theology*, 64–65.

109. "So that the Apostles had their own *distinct* Companies, Societies, or Congregations in Jerusalem [*Act.* 4. 13, 19, 23. *And* Peter *and* John *being let go, they went to their own Company.*] Yet they all being of one heart, and of one soul, were but one Church, and are so denominated, *Act.* 15. 4" (Knollys, *World that Now is*, 44–45). Knollys further believed that there should be a bishop over such companies as long as they gave "their Consent, Suffrage and Assistance." Ibid., 69, 61. He developed that idea even further with respect to the seven churches of Revelation, concluding "That each Church contained and comprehended, the whole number of them that believed in Jesus Christ, confessed the Faith of the Gospel, and walked in the Order and Ordinances of the Lord in one City and Suburbs thereof; and had the Denomination of that City, and was called the Church of God in that City. Search these Scriptures, *Act.* 8. 1. and 11. 22. also, 1 *Cor.* 1. 2. and 14. 34. likewise, *Phil.* 1. 1, 5. and 1 *Thess.* 1. 1. *Rev.* 2. 1, 8, 12, 18. and Chap. 3. 1, 7, 14" (Knollys, *Exposition Of the Revelation*, 8ff.). This was not a late development in Knollys's thought, for he argued for this system as early as 1645. See Knollys, *Moderate Answer*, 11ff. Interestingly, Grantham also promoted this idea, as did Jessey. See Grantham, *Second Part of the Apology*, 84; and Jessey, *Storehouse of Provision*, 199–200. Even Kiffin conceded, "[We] and should still be Planted together by Baptism, not into this or that particular Church, but into that one Church of Christ, which is distributed into several parts and particular Societies" (Kiffin, *Sober Discourse*, 138). Kiffin was actually answering a question about the nature of baptism, but his answer revealed sympathy to the idea of a closely united church. Tolmie dismissed this perspective as a safeguard to show magnanimity to the Independents. Tolmie, *Triumph of the Saints*, 115ff. Wright thought the Particular Baptists emphasized the one-church model in an attempt to convince the Presbyterians that they could maintain control of their members and were thus worthy of toleration. Wright, *Early English Baptists*, 136. Neither realized how enduring this conviction was for Knollys, long after any political motive would have been necessary.

These possibilities raised two very important issues for the Baptists. They understood the value of a united identity cultivated in a united worship; after all, that was the world in which they lived. They were not immune to the pull of stability in uniformity or its sense of arrival, that they would have discovered the apostolic pattern for worship. But they also felt the tension between such uniformity and the freedom they demanded. Nowhere was this more evident than in their worship practices.

The Tension between Freedom and Uniformity

Stephen Brachlow noted that the radical Puritans were aware of a delicate balance between autonomy and uniformity during Elizabeth's reign. They placed a high value on the individual local church, but realized that there might be a need for accountability between churches. A number of them proposed a kind of Presbyterian system in which church leaders would gather to settle disputes and answer questions, but in which the decisions could not be binding on a local church. Brachlow noted in particular that these early Puritans did not have much opportunity to develop their beliefs in practice (and when they did, their beliefs sometimes changed; Henry Ainsworth, for example, stepped back from his commitment to such cooperation when a sister congregation disagreed with one of his teachings). Unfortunately, Brachlow did not address the most visible and personal way in which this balance was manifested: the local church's worship.[110]

Liturgists often use a phrase, *Lex Orandi, Lex Credendi*,[111] to defend the importance of liturgies by saying that the rule of prayer is the rule of belief. However one chooses to interpret that famous Latin phrase, two things cannot be denied: the content of one's worship does shape one's belief, and similarities in worship will bring people together. William Bradshaw used his perceptive statement, "The more one Church differeth from another in Rites and Ceremonies, the more it useth to differ in substance of Doctrine," to introduce the high stakes of early separatism; he

---

110. Brachlow, *Communion of Saints*, 203–29.

111. The actual statement from which this phrase was taken was *legem credendi lex statuat supplicandi*, which meant, "let the law of that which must be prayed establish the law of that which must be believed." Prosper of Aquitaine was not arguing that liturgies establish truth, as is often assumed, but rather that the apostolic prayers handed down in those liturgies could clarify theological questions (in his case that of predestination). Setting aside the fact that the prayers he mentioned were not actually apostolic, his point was that *apostolic* liturgies could establish truth. Prosper, *Responsianes ad Capitula objectionum Vincentianarum*; PL 51:209–10.

Free Worship and a New Concept of the Church

went on to say "and the more one Church draweth nearer unto another in Ceremonies, the more it draweth near unto it in substance of Doctrine."[112] Most of the English authorities appreciated the power of worship to unite their people and spread their teachings. Westminster considered such uniformity "almost indispensable."[113] Edmund Bonner, a catholicizing bishop under the Tudors, was attributed the harrowing quote, "If they sup of our Broth, we will make them eat of our Meat."[114] He was speaking of Cranmer's decision to retain so much of the Roman Mass, knowing that as long as England continued worshipping in old forms, they would never drift far away from Rome.

That the early London Particular Baptists appreciated and desired a common identity is surprisingly obvious. The First London Confession included the important article,

> And although the particular Congregations be distinct and several Bodies, every one a compact and knit City in itself: yet are they all to walk by one and the same Rule, and by all means convenient to have the counsel and help one of another in all needful affairs of the Church, as members of one body in the common faith under Christ their only head.[115]

This idea of one "Rule" was very important to these Baptists. The first article declared that because there was one God and one Faith, there must be "one Rule of holiness and obedience for all Saints, at all times, in all places to be observed." The confession went on to state that there was one gospel through which man could know the only true God, and "The Rule of this Knowledge, Faith, and Obedience, concerning the worship and service of God, and all other Christian duties, is not man's inventions, opinions, devices, laws, constitutions, or traditions unwritten whatsoever, but only the

---

112. Bradshaw, *Several Treatises of Worship and Ceremonies*, 8.

113. See Hetherington, *History of Westminster Assembly*, 276ff., although he seemed to consider liturgy more a doctrinal tool than an expression of devotion.

114. Cited in Cook, *Some Considerations*, 7. I have not been able to corroborate this quote. John Canne remembered a similar sentiment from a bishop and "his hope that the maintenance of them [the Roman ceremonies maintained in the Prayer Book] against the puritans, would make England the sooner returne to Rome in the rest." Canne, *Necessitie of Separation*, 79.

115. *London* [1644], Article XLVII, copied almost verbatim from *True Confession* [1596], Article 38. Fiddes read this article as planting an implicit seed for an inclusive voluntary society—early ecumenism. While that benevolent potential certainly existed, I must insist that early Particular Baptist inclusivity was absolutely exclusive to those who agreed with their understanding of the "Rule." See Fiddes, *Tracks and Traces*, 44–45.

word of God contained in the Canonical Scriptures."[116] Essentially, articles VI and VII put this "Rule" in apposition with the gospel, not only the good news of salvation but also the good news that God has given man a rule for life and worship. This article preceded their article on the Scriptures, explaining that God's "Rule" preceded and was thusly recorded in the Word. That Word was now the only inviolable source for the Rule—one Word, one Rule, and all congregations were bound to live by it.[117]

Something fundamental had changed by the time the Baptists gathered for a new confession of faith a generation later. The Second London Confession continued to speak of a rule for saving knowledge, faith, and obedience, but it was the rule given to believers to reveal God's will for their behavior. There was no more Rule for the church, only "rules, for the due and right exerting, and executing of that power [for their carrying on that order in worship, and discipline, which he hath instituted for them to observe]." The rule of Christ controlled "the Censures and Government thereof," but only with the approbation of the individual. Christians were called "to maintain an holy fellowship and communion in the worship of God, and in performing such other spiritual services, as tend to their mutual edification," but the only "rule" was that the individual should not withhold his communion from other Christians.[118] Hanserd Knollys, as the previous section explained, called on the churches to unite under the primitive purity of the apostolic pattern, but only Benjamin Keach truly joined him. Keach prayed for such an outpouring of the Spirit "as to convict all Gods Children who they are that are in the true order of the Gospel; so that all the Saints and Protestant Churches may be United into one Body and Communion, according to that holy Primitive and Apostolical pattern and purity."[119] They were the only two of this group of Baptists who found such an identity possible or even desirable.

A number of causes would have led to this change of view, not the least of which would have been the course of Westminster's *Directory*. Joseph Caryl had suggested,

---

116. *London* [1644], Article I, VII. Bell thought that the primary "rule" in question was the doctrine of baptism. Bell, *Apocalypse How?*, 77.

117. Kiffin referred to the importance of the Rule in his *Humble Remonstrance* and as late as his *Sober Discourse*, as did Spilsbury in *A Treatise Concerning Baptisme*.

118. *London* [1677], Article I, XXVI, XXVII. However, the Assembly of 1689 declared they would help churches "in the right understanding of that perfect Rule which our Lord Jesus, the only Bishop of our Souls, hath already prescribed." *Narrative* [1689], 10.

119. Keach, *Antichrist Stormed*, 144.

Free Worship and a New Concept of the Church

> That although it is not in the power of any men to prescribe unto, or impose upon, the Churches and ministry of Jesus Christ, any set forms of publick worship, otherwise then Christ hath ordained: yet that the Ministers of the Gospel may and ought without prejudice to their libertie in Christ, agree amongst themselves, to observe some rules of uniformitie in their publick wayes.[120]

As has already been mentioned, the *Directory* was an abject failure. On the one hand, it attempted to give structure without rubric, so those who followed it supplied their own rubrics (often from what they remembered of the *Book of Common Prayer* leading to a very Anglicanized service), and the rest simply ignored it.[121] On the other hand, it demanded an unreasonable discipline on the part of the disinterested commoner.[122] Hanserd Knollys, who desired the pure worship of God administered according to His divine institutions, stumbled into both of these challenges by envisioning only one pattern of worship. He said unequivocally that "there must be a Conformity unto the Revealed Will of God in his Word, especially in the External part of the Instituted worship of God in the Gospel," and "there ought to be a Uniformity among all the Churches of God in every Nation, in every City and in every Village. All that worship God in one place, are to Worship him in one way, with one accord and with one shoulder."[123] But who would determine it, who would enforce it, and what would be done when one church believed it found a different apostolic pattern?

One solution, intimately tied with the concept of open-communion, was to leave the topic alone. John Bunyan exhorted that a church not be measured by its outward circumstances or practices, "Especially when there are in the hearts of the Godly; different perswasions about it: then it becometh them in the wisedom of God, to take more care for their peace

---

120. Caryl, *Moderator*, 44.

121. John Goodwin felt that their experience with the *Directory* would drive the people to ask for their bishops and liturgy, the outcome of which would be open mutinying. He was half-right. See Woodhouse, ed., *Puritanism and Liberty*, 186.

122. Dickens thought that the Puritans failed most significantly in their unrealistic expectations of "that large proportion of the English people who were willing to worship in church but not to embrace so intense and so disciplined a religious life." He concluded, "A national church cannot become a club for religious athletes" (Dickens, *English Reformation*, 320). Haigh generally agreed, "But the men and women of Reformation England were, Catholic or Protestant, generally confused ordinary mortals, not saints and martyrs" (Haigh, *English Reformation Revised*, 14).

123. Knollys, *Parable of the Kingdom*, 42, 43.

and unity; then to widen or make large their uncomfortable differences."[124] He said that divisions were carnal, but the church should be spiritual; worship was spiritual, but ceremonies were carnal, therefore churches should not divide over ceremonies. Another solution was to retreat into tighter sectarianism. Thomas Grantham unwittingly represented that view saying,

> The Complaint is both great and just, that Christians are so divided amongst themselves, to find where to fix for his own comfortable Society. And this Calamity is much aggravated by the backwardness of each Party to offer any thing to accommodate these Differences, each expecting rather that their Opposites should wholly conform to their Sentiments, [than] relinquish their own.[125]

Grantham seemed to think that it should be a small matter that a church modify its practical (as opposed to doctrinal) beliefs. But Murray Tolmie best explained Grantham's naivety in observing that "the search for an exclusive and universally binding model of a true Christian church placed upon the tiny separatist congregations a burden impossible to bear" because "the very smallest detail of church order and worship became a heavy responsibility."[126] Consequently, the sectaries had to divide over every detail of worship about which they could not agree, and that list was long.[127]

---

124. Bunyan, *Confession of my Faith*, 99. Bunyan was admittedly talking about the ceremony of baptism and not worship *per se*, but the next section will explain that he did not consider baptism an act of worship. Jessey had earlier written about baptism "that instead of being the means of uniting as the Spirit doth, that it hath not only rent his seamless Coat, but divided his Body which he hath purchased with his own blood, and opposed that great design of Father, Son, and Spirit, in uniting poor Saints, thereby pulling in pieces what the Spirit hath put together." Cited in Bunyan, *Differences in Judgment*, 113. Jessey's original document included in its entirety in *Differences* is lost, and Bunyan claimed he had already written his *Differences* before he discovered Jessey's work. Perhaps importantly, Bell thought that individual wealth played a background role in the debates between Bunyan and Kiffin. Bell, *Apocalypse How?*, 132.

125. Grantham, *Friendly Epistle to the Bishops and Ministers of the Church of England*, 3. Grantham wrote this letter on behalf of a group of Baptist pastors, and it became quickly evident that his purpose was to convince the rest of England to conform to their sentiments rather than "relinquish their own."

126. Tolmie, *Triumph of the Saints*, 2.

127. The more subjective elements of personality and character cannot be ignored in any discussion of divisions. Unfortunately, such a discussion becomes equally (and dangerously) subjective. Richard Baxter's powerful testimony will serve as a window into the possibilities: "If all the bishops had been of the same spirit as archbishop Usher, all the Independents like Jeremiah Burroughs, and all the Presbyterians like

Free Worship and a New Concept of the Church

London Particular Baptists had already established the connection between a free church and free worship. They had also established a connection between a true church and pure worship. It simply took them several decades to realize that they could not reconcile these connections. They earnestly hoped and believed that the apostolic pattern would be such that the mind of Christ would guide them together to follow it, but experience dictated otherwise. It cannot be overstated what was lost to those early Baptists. In the beginning, they had genuine aspirations for a single Baptist communion in the city of London.[128] In the end, they were left only with a vague appeal to unity:

> 15. In cases of difficulties or differences, either in point of Doctrine, or Administration; wherein either the Churches in general are concerned, or any one Church in their peace, union, and edification; or any member, or members of any Church are injured, in or by any proceedings in censures not agreeable to truth, and order: it is according to the mind of Christ, that many Churches holding communion together, do by their messengers meet to consider, and give their advice in, or about that matter in difference, to be reported to all the Churches concerned; howbeit these messengers assembled, are not entrusted with any Church-power properly so called; or with any jurisdiction over the Churches themselves, to exercise any censures either over any Churches, or Persons: or to impose their determination on the Churches, or Officers.[129]

The cause of that failure was differences in judgment about worship. Those differences, then as now, prevented anything beyond nominal unity. They also unmasked a much more significant concern for these Particular Baptists. Most of them believed that the Church of England was a false church

---

Stephen Marshall, the divisions of the church would soon have been healed" (*A History of Westminster Assembly*, 345). Of course, the reality was that non-centrist persons did (and always will) exist and could not be ignored simply because they made discussion messy or inconvenient.

128. "Wee doe therefore here subscribe it, some of each body in the name, and by the appointment of seven Congregations, who though wee be distinct in respect of our particular bodies, for conveniency sake, being as many as can well meete together in one place, yet are all one in Communion, holding Jesus Christ to be our head and Lord" (*London* [1644], To the Christian Reader). Even Fiddes sold this declaration short of its intention; he saw in it a desire for visible unity when in actuality these Baptists sought true organic unity: one church in London sharing one system of belief and worship. Cf. Fiddes, *Tracks and Traces*, 198–200.

129. *London* [1677], Article XXVI.

due to her false worship; not a few of them had similar thoughts about one another for the same reason. This was the important question that they could not answer: how gross an error in worship was necessary to declare a church a false church?

"Either the Church of God or Not": The Essence of a Church as a Consequence of Pure Worship[130]

All parties in England believed that a true church was marked by the pure Word and Sacraments. Separatists believed that the Church of England suffered from a defect in those marks; therefore, it was not a true church, and they were justified in separating from it. William Kiffin even admitted that if it could be proven the established church purely dispensed the Word and Sacraments, he sinned in his separation.[131] But what exactly did that mean? The tenor of the discussion changed when Puritans ascended to power and Baptists continued to remain separate. Now they were challenged to explain themselves clearly. A circular letter asked, "It is true, by reason of different lights and different sights among Brethren, there may be dissenting in opinion; yet why should there be any separating from Church-communion?"[132] Westminster specifically called for a moratorium on separation until they could clarify all the elements of their reformation.[133] Baptists had to establish for themselves and those to whom they evangelized exactly why they were justified in maintaining their separate churches. More importantly, they had to publish exactly what they thought about the established churches. Not surprisingly, worship played a central role.

The Form of the Church: Faith, Baptism, or Covenant

I have already hinted at some of the fundamental disagreements amongst Baptists about the nature of the church. In order to explain that from which they believed they separated, they had to know that to which they

---

130. See Barbone, *Reply to R. B.*, 12.
131. Kiffin, *Briefe Remonstrance*, 5; Featley, *Dippers dipt*, 3–4.
132. *Letter of the Ministers of the City of London*, 1.
133. Twisse, *Certaine Considerations*, 2ff.

aspired. Two concepts shaped the Baptists' belief about the church: matter and form. All agreed that the matter was a believer, a saint, a person "professing faith in the righteousness of Jesus Christ." All basically agreed that the form was the frame of the church, or "that by which these are united and knit up together in one fellowship."[134] All variously defined that form to be a profession of faith, baptism, or a covenant, and their argument generally took one of the following forms. Those supporting baptism as the form of the church noted that the only thing lacking for a believer to become a member of a Baptist church was believers' baptism, and that baptism "did immediately qualifie them for Church fellowship." They did not need a verbal covenant because the bond they shared in the Spirit was far greater.[135] Those favoring a covenant observed that a church existed and ceased to exist by the will of the congregants; the order of their church was defined by their covenant, just as God knit together His people by a covenant, to which baptism was the entrance or seal. If baptism were the form of a church, then an individual would have to be rebaptized every time he moved, and churches could only be started by unbaptized people.[136] The third group made a very basic appeal: that which qualified someone for membership in the universal church qualified him for membership in a particular church. Baptisms and covenants had no standing with salvation; therefore, they could not be the form of a church. Only faith, or the profession of it, could be the foundation-principle for a true church.[137]

---

134. Spilsbury, *Treatise Concerning Baptisme*, 41. See also Lambe, *Confutation of Infants Baptisme*, 35ff. Jessey offered the most generic description, "Where is *matter* and *forme*, there is a true Church; the *Matter* of a true Church, to be Saints visibly; the *Forme*, a gathering of these out from the world and *joyning of them together* to worship the Lord in truth" (Jessey, *Storehouse of Provision*, 102).

135. Goodwin, *Quaere*, 5. See also Norcot, Kiffin, and Claridge, *Baptism Discovered Plainly & Faithfully*.

136. Lambe, *Confutation of Infants Baptisme*; Spilsbury, *Treatise Concerning Baptisme*. Note that, coming from opposite perspectives, Spilsbury and Jessey ultimately concluded that the first baptizer in an area did not have to be baptized. Spilsbury, *Gods Ordinance*, 10; Jessey, *Storehouse of Provision*, 39.

137. Barbone, *Defence of Baptizing Infants*; Bunyan, *Differences in Judgment*. Collins gave a long list of "Primitive Churches" he believed founded thus: "Church at *Jerusalem, Samaria, Cesaria, Philippi, Coloss, Corinth, Rome, Galatia, Ephesus*, &c. [Heb. 6. 1, 2. Acts 2. 41. Chap. 8. 12. Chap. 16. 14. Coloss. 2. 10. Acts 18. 8. Rom. 6. 4. Gal. 3. 26. Acts 19. 1, 2, 3. Ephes. 4. 4.]" (Collins, *Believers Baptism from Heaven*, 23). There was further confusion whether or not believers' baptism itself was the *necessary* profession of faith. As an added twist, Fiddes thought that the idea of covenant was implicit in these professions. Fiddes, *Tracks and Traces*, 26–31.

All of the discussions to this point in the chapter came into play in this debate. Praisegod Barbone submitted to the Baptists that all Reformed churches agreed that the true matter of a church was a baptized believer, and they only admitted such to their membership.[138] But William Kiffin believed that the practice of Christ and His apostles was to baptize someone who had professed faith in Christ "and that being thus baptized upon profession of Faith, they are then added to the Church, 2 Act. 41,"[139] meaning that infant baptism did not qualify. Most outsiders unflatteringly referred to their baptism as a wall of division, for the "seven Anabaptist Churches" were "for no admitting of any of the Independents or Separatists who will not receive a new baptisme."[140] John Spilsbury agreed that "the ordinance of baptisme instituted by Christ is so essentiall to the constitution of the Church under the new Testament, that none can be true in her constitution without it," but protected the church from a mistake in baptism's administration by declaring the attendant covenant to be the form.[141] John Tombes interpreted the First London Confession to mean "rather to import that Baptisme is necessary to the right order of a Christian Church, then to the being of a Church," and he accused the outsiders

---

138. Barbone, *Reply to R. B.*, 63.

139. Kiffin, *Briefe Remonstrance*, 13. Lambe agreed, although he felt the word "constitution" was more appropriate than "form." He did not deny that a covenant helped to define a church but believed that baptism took priority. Against the argument that a church ceased to exist when the membership agreed to dissolve their covenant, he argued that a church *never* ceased to exist except with physical death. Lambe, *A Confutation of Infants Baptism*, 38ff. Goodwin believed that the apostolic pattern was quite explicit about baptism and said nothing about covenant. Goodwin, *Quaere*, 4ff.

140. Baillie, *Disswasive From the Errors of the Time*, 81. Interestingly, the immediate cause of Baillie's outburst was John Tombes's unwillingness to join one of those seven churches even though Tombes met with them and they were all willing to baptize him. He rightly understood that Tombes believed one could be in the universal church and not a particular church. But Tombes was more worried about another condition, "But that baptizing of infants, and taking as Church-members all born in a so called Christian Nation hath been the true cause of horrible perverting and profaning the rule of Christ about baptism, and hath so corrupted the Church of God, that instead of his house it hath been made a den of theeves, is too manifest by experience" (Tombes, *Antipaedobaptism*, 260). He would rather lean toward open membership than overemphasize baptism. On the other end of the spectrum, years later, Kiffin responded to another accusation of "wall of division" that although he did not like the term, it accurately reflected what he practiced with respect to church fellowship. Kiffin, *Sober Discourse*, 19.

141. Spilsbury, *Treatise Concerning Baptisme*, 32.

Free Worship and a New Concept of the Church

of minimizing the importance of baptism not for biblical reasons but because they realized its relationship with Separatism.[142]

The words "true" and "right" erupted into the great scandal of this conviction, for such implied that every other church was "false" or "wrong." Those who seriously considered the Baptists' position took the same offense: "'Tis no little sin to unchristen all Christendom, as *Anabaptists* do in the pride of their hearts, separating from all Reformed Churches, as no Churches, because unbaptized."[143] Praisegod Barbone, who nonetheless desired to meet separately from the established church, believed the Baptists could not support such a grand charge. Instead, he differentiated between the "being" and "well-being" of a church ("there being difference, as before, betwixt a thing and the corruption that attends it"), otherwise corrupt members would invalidate a church. He put the being of a church in God's hands; proper baptism was for the well-being of a church, but men by their actions could not destroy God's church.[144] Bunyan would later agree, saying of the ordinances, "I count them not the fundamentals of our Christianity; not grounds or rule to communion with Saints: servants they are, and our mystical Ministers, to teach and instruct us."[145] Bunyan and Barbone, as well as Jessey and Tombes, all acknowledged the validity of believers' baptism, but none were willing by such belief to declare all churches not of its practice false. Not surprisingly, each of the four men had roots in the established church, as did their church members. They knew firsthand the character of those who had not reached the Baptist

---

142. Tombes, *Apology or Plea for the Two Treatises*, 65–66. Note that Tombes rejected any thought of baptism being the form of a church, however, "considering the many errours and ill consequences that would follow thereupon." But Marshall and Geree, to name two, made the grosser error by minimizing baptism. Ibid., 66–71. The first person to publish in favor of dipping as the true mode of baptism was a paedobaptist, Daniel Rogers, in 1635 or 1636. See Burrage, *Early English Dissenters*, 331; also Wright, *Early English Baptists*, 67. It is unknown if Rogers eventually embraced believers' baptism, as did Jessey, or changed his mind completely when he realized the full end of the immersion practice.

143. Hall, *Font Guarded*, To my beloved and approved Friends.

144. Barbone, *Defence of Baptizing Infants*, 4, 7, 10, 36, 37. Knollys followed this language, saying, "The Well-Being of a *particular* Church of Saints, doth *principally* consist in three things, viz. Oneness, Order, and Government," which by Order he meant "in the Administration of God's Sacred Ordinances, in the Admission of Members, in the Ordination of Church-Officers, and in withdrawing from every Brother that walketh *Disorderly*." Knollys, *World that Now is*, 50, 52.

145. Bunyan, *Confession of my Faith*, 65.

position and they believed them true Christians. Therefore, they differentiated between a false church and a defective church.[146]

At its heart this scandal was a debate about worship. A true church would worship truly because false worship was of the Antichrist. Worship, it will be remembered, was the "right and Orderly Administration of Ceremonies," and by that Kiffin was clear he meant the ordinances.[147] Christ instituted or gave significance to certain ceremonies for the church to use in His worship, and those were by definition ordinances. Thomas Grantham was bold enough to say that every church not practicing true baptism essentially corrupted each of its subsequent church actions.[148] Six-Principle Baptists, discussed in the next chapters, pushed the argument to its end: "Churches rightly constituted do not transgress against the Doctrine of Christ, but continue in it."[149] Any church that violated any part of God's Word proved by its action not to be a true church at all. Consequently, the debate over the form of the church came down to two primary questions: what was the essential relationship between a church and her ordinances, and at what point was a corruption therein justifiable of separation?

The Relationship between the Church and the Ordinances

John Owen captured the stakes of this debate saying,

> Some are utterly regardless of [instituted worship], supposing that if they attend, after their manner, unto moral obedience, that neither God nor themselves are much concerned in this manner of his worship. Others think the disposal and ordering of it to be so left unto men, that, as to the manner of its performance, they may do with it as it seems right in their own eyes;

---

146. Baillie, who believed that infant baptism was true baptism, interpreted Tombes's stance to mean that he would have church fellowship with an unbaptized person; even Barbone did not believe that unbaptized persons could constitute a church. See Baillie, *Disswasive From The Errors of the Time*, 81; Barbone, *Reply to R. B.*, 56. As to their personal convictions, see Bunyan, *Differences in Judgment*, 41; Barbone, *Reply to R. B.*, 21–23; Jessey, *Storehouse of Provision*, 75; and Tombes, *Felo de Se*, 15–16. Duesing argued that Jessey's willingness to make baptism a personal conviction should not disqualify him from being considered a Baptist; the same argument would apply to Tombes. Duesing, "Counted Worthy," 170–71, 211ff.

147. Kiffin, *Sober Discourse*, 117.

148. Grantham, *Paedo-Baptists Apology for the Baptized Churches*, 1–2.

149. Griffith, *Searchers for Schism Search'd*, 43.

Free Worship and a New Concept of the Church

and some follow them therein, as willingly walking after their commandments, without any respect unto the will or authority of God. But the whole Scripture gives us utterly another account of this matter. The *honour* of God in this world, the *trial* of our faith and obedience, the *order* and beauty of the church, the *exaltation* of Christ in our professed subjection to him, and the saving of our souls in the ways of his appointment, are therein laid upon the due and right observance of his instituted worship; and they who are negligent about these things, whatever they pretend, have no real respect unto any thing that is called religion.[150]

If the Baptists seemed obsessed with the right administration of the ordinances, that is because they were. At root, they wanted to know at what point an error in a church's ordinances discredited her as a true church. While that might seem severe today, Baptists were surrounded by churches practicing variant ordinances. Infant baptism was the main offender but hardly the only one. Baptists were receiving church members from other churches, called upon to cooperate with them in church matters, sharing facilities and sometimes even services with them. In extreme cases of persecution, especially in communities away from London, churches of different traditions had to work together to survive.[151] They could not ignore the qualifications for a true church regardless where it led them. Nowhere was this more evident than in the famous debate between John Bunyan and William Kiffin over open-communion.[152]

Henry Jessey had earlier set up this issue as a matter of worship. He did not oppose believers' baptism by immersion. In 1649, Robert S., a member of the Independent church sharing Jessey's building, expressed his conviction for believers' baptism. The entire church, and Jessey as well, approved of his reasoning and contrition, and four adults were soon

---

150. Owen, *Brief Instruction in the Worship of God*, in *Works*, 15:471–72.

151. Terrill recorded an era in Bristol between 1672 and 1675 in which his church, a Baptist church, an Independent church, and a Presbyterian church routinely alternated locations so that the same congregation did not get raided every week. By 1675, all of their pastors were in prison, so the churches tried to establish a joint weekly meeting; they investigated their differences and proposed to ignore them. The Presbyterians decided not to participate. *Broadmead*, 241ff. Broadmead was an open-communion church.

152. The literary outline was as follows: Bunyan published *A Confession of my Faith* in 1672, replied to in the next year by Denne, *Truth outweighing error*, and Paul, *Some serious reflections* (foreword by Kiffin). Bunyan immediately countered with *Differences in Judgment*, and it was almost a decade until Kiffin published *A Sober Discourse*.

Pure Worship

baptized. From that account, it appears that Jessey simply wanted adults to come to the conviction of believers' baptism on their own, without any compulsion. Indeed, when he looked at Peter's sermon in Acts 2, he saw a clear preparation for the doctrine of baptism. Not until after the converts "professed themselves to be one body with them in Christian Worship" did Peter explain that circumcision was nothing and that they must submit to baptism. When they desired to worship truly, they were ready to learn about baptism. Baptists were wrong for excluding Christians from their churches based on their ignorance of baptism; the Bible clearly said that Christians were disciples *before* they were baptized, not after (as some Baptists tried to argue). If the Baptists pursued that criterion for communion, there could be no end to the debates resulting in separation.[153]

John Bunyan followed a similar train of thought in his confession of faith explaining with whom he could hold church fellowship, by which he meant "in the things of the Kingdom of Christ, or that which is commonly called Church communion."[154] Bunyan declared that he could hold such communion with all visible saints, determined solely by their faith, experience, and conversation, and not their baptism. At the same time, he would not have communion with an openly profane person. His mantra was, "*God hath received him, Christ hath received him*, therefore do you receive him."[155] In no way did Bunyan defend the Church of England; rather, he argued that he did not have to baptize a Christian coming out of it to join

---

153. Jessey, *Storehouse of Provision*, 127–45, 176ff., 183ff.; see also Tolmie, *Triumph of the Saints*, 59. It is certainly possible that Robert S. was Robert Steed. Steed died in 1703 and little is known about his early life. By 1663, he was pastoring the Baptist church in Dartmouth.

154. Bunyan, *Confession of my Faith*, 48. The two terms, roughly equivalent with membership today, were used because the Lord's Supper was seen as the most intimate act of the church. Bunyan held the first pastor of the Bedford church, John Gifford, in high esteem, especially Gifford's priority of "Faith in Christ, and Holiness of life, without respect to this or that circumstance." This was why Bunyan so highly promoted "brotherhood" and thus open-communion. See Hussey, "Christian Conduct in Bunyan and Baxter," 80–82; and Nuttall, "Church Life in Bunyan's Bedfordshire," 307. Interestingly, Benjamin Cox's son, Nehemiah, was censured in his position as pastor of a Bedford sub-congregation in 1674 and soon left for the closed-communion church at Petty France. It is probable that these events were related.

155. Bunyan, *Confession of my Faith*, 92. He judged fitness by "the word of faith and good works." Ibid., 79. He spoke most magnanimously, "I hold therefore to what I said at first; That if there be any Saints in the Antichristian Church, my heart, and the door of our Congregation is open to receive them, into closest fellowship with us." (But at the same time he believed, "Mixed communion polluteth the ordinances of God." Ibid., 132, 48.) In this he went beyond Barbone, who did not think is was possible to know who was a child of God and so did not worry about it.

Free Worship and a New Concept of the Church

his church at Bedford. And that was the crux of his argument: a Christian was a Christian independent of his baptism; "It [baptism] therefore gives thee neither right to, nor being of membership at all." With respect to the Baptists' interpretation of the churches in Acts, he noted, "For herein lyes the mistake, To think that because in time past, Baptism was administred upon conversion, *that therefore it is the initiating, and entring ordinance* into Church-communion: when by the word no such thing is testifyed of it." Neither the Ethiopian eunuch nor Cornelius or Lydia was baptized into any specific church. Though Bunyan had "reverent esteem" for baptism and the Lord's Supper, he did not believe God made them the fundamentals of Christianity, but servants and instructors. He even countered with the powerful attack, "Tis possible to commit Idolatry, even with Gods own appointments."[156]

Bunyan's "theologically surprising"[157] position was a twofold liturgical argument. In the first place, he was conjuring the Baptists' own loathing of book-worship, for the biggest idol in England was the *Book of Common Prayer*, and the cruelest accusation he could make echoed the sentiment, "the ceremonies are idols to Formalists."[158] Essentially, he believed that the Baptists were setting up the ceremony of baptism above Christ's gift of salvation, the very definition of idolatry. In the second place, he was redefining baptism as an act of worship. This became clear after Thomas Paul's response in which Paul perceptively (but not graciously) noted that Bunyan's opinion made "all those Gospel-Commands, especially those in in-

---

156. Ibid., 76, 70, 74–75, 65. Note that Barbone had earlier accused the Baptists of making baptism an idol. Barbone, *Discourse Tending to Prove*, 7. In his argument, Bunyan was simply (if unknowingly) following Jessey who had written that the open-communion position did not admit profane persons into the church, and especially not into the Supper, but simply acknowledged that baptism was not a sufficient ground to refuse such communion. See Jessey, *Storehouse of Provision*, 43, 98ff.

157. Brackney, *Genetic History*, 112. Brackney posited several reasons for Bunyan's divergence, none of them liturgical.

158. Gillespie, *Dispute Against the English Popish Ceremonies*, 198. Nonconformists thought of the Prayer Book as an extension of Rome. Those who called the Prayer Book an idol included Smectymnuus, *Answer to a Booke*, 12; Canne, *Necessitie of Separation*, 82; and Powell, *Common-Prayer-Book no Divine Service*, 14. The Mass was also considered an idol in Knollys, *Exposition Of the Revelation*, 101; and L. F., *Speedy Remedie*, 31. More generally, all book-worship was considered idolatry in Ainsworth, *Arrow Against Idolatrie*, 2; Tombes, *Jehovah Jireh*, 3; and Tombes, *Supplement to the Serious Consideration of the Oath of the Kings Supremacy*, 26. The rejection of book-worship or formal worship was a standard accusation against the separatists, as in *Gangraena*, 1:28ff. Keach and Knollys continued to use the term "idol" with respect to formal worship even after Kiffin's controversy with Bunyan.

stituted Worship" worthless, of no importance whether they were obeyed or breached.[159] Bunyan's Puritan sentiments would allow no countenance of a breach in worship—"must I therefore be judged to be a Man without Conscience to the Worship of Jesus Christ?"—so he proceeded to remove baptism from worship: "It is none of those Laws, neither any part of them, that the Church, as a Church, should shew her Obedience by. For albeit that Baptism be given by Christ our Lord to the Church, yet not for them to worship him by as a Church."[160] Instead, Bunyan made baptism an act of individual worship, that his faith "might be strengthened in the death and resurrection of Christ."[161] This severed baptism from most discussions about the church and removed it from any form of argument related to worship.

William Kiffin would have no part of Bunyan's opinions, and he responded with one of the greatest Baptist treatises ever written about worship. He made it very clear, "I have no other design, but the preserving the Ordinances of Christ, in their purity and Order as they are left unto us in the holy *Scriptures* of Truth; and to warn the Churches *To keep close to the Rule*, least they being found not to Worship the Lord according to his prescrib'd Order he make a *Breach* among them."[162] The Baptists could

---

159. Paul, *Some Serious Reflections*, 6. Interestingly, Paul accepted Bunyan's conclusion about baptism as not an initiating ordinance; "It's consent *ON* all hands, and nothing else, that makes them Members of this or that perticular Church, and not Faith and Baptism" (ibid., 4). Kiffin would go on to agree with him. Even more interestingly, Bunyan responded, "Consent, simply without Faith, makes no man a Member of the Church of God; because then would a Church not cease to be a Church, whoever they received among them" (Bunyan, *Differences in Judgment*, 12). Though tearing down a straw-man (that consent and faith were mutually exclusive), Bunyan clearly accused Baptists of treating baptism in a Catholic sense.

160. Bunyan, *Differences in Judgment*, 48, 13. He later added, "There are some of the Ordinances that, be they neglected, the being of a Church, as to her visible Gospel-Constitution, is taken quite away; but Baptism is none of them," meaning the Lord's Supper. Ibid., 87, cf. 52. There is no doubt he was deeply offended by Paul's charge; "What? Because I will not suffer Water to carry away the Epistles from the Christians; and because I will not let Water-baptism be the Rule, the Door, the Bolt, the Bar, the Wall of Division between the Righteous, & the Righteous; must I therefore be judged to be a Man without Conscience to the Worship of Jesus Christ? The Lord deliver me from Superstitious, and Idolatrous thoughts about any the Ordinances of Christ, and of God" (ibid, 48).

161. Bunyan, *Confession of my Faith*, 76. Haykin and Robinson caught this distinction, especially as against the Lord's Supper, and even noted the accusation of will-worship, but they seemed to lose the arguments in an overly rigid view of the regulative principle. See Haykin and Robinson, "Particular Baptist Debates about Communion and Hymn-Singing," 289–94.

162. Kiffin, *Sober Discourse*, To the Christian Reader. I must respectfully disagree

not be idolaters because they were following Christ's institutions; Christ did not set up idols. The will-worshiper, the one who worshiped according to the will of men, was Bunyan. Kiffin believed that believers' baptism by immersion before church membership was a clear ordinance laid down by Christ and the apostles, the foundation of their faith and covenant. To break this rule of worship "has a direct Tendency to Destroy all Modes of Worship, and consequently all the publick and solemn Exercise of Religion, in as much as the same Reason by which one Ordinance may be changed, or Discontinued, will equally prove the change or Discontinuance of any, yea of all at long Run."[163] If Baptists backed down on baptism, they would have no way to stand against all of the other inventions of worship they saw in the world around them.

Kiffin countered Bunyan with two meaningful liturgical arguments. One was to preserve the integrity of baptism: "For if Unbaptized Persons may be admitted to all Church Priviledges, does not such a practice plainly suppose that it is unnecessary?"[164] But to admit that was to accuse Christ of issuing an unnecessary command, and there was no question that Christ commanded His disciples to baptize the nations. Baptists desired to remove the ceremonial accretions of the established church, not the ordinances of Christ. The second was the use of the regulative principle of worship, a concept that will be the focus of the next chapter. In the immediate context, it meant "that where a *Rule* and *express Law* is prescribed

---

with Garrett who thought that Kiffin's primary purpose was to defend close communion against Bunyan. Kiffin's concern was far greater than that. But even Garrett's description of the treatise identified the topics of "Gospel Order" and the normative principle without realizing their connection with instituted worship. Garrett, *Baptist Theology*, 66–67.

163. Ibid., 57–58. He continued, "And if the first Churches might not be Constituted without this Ordinance of Baptism, neither may those that succeed them, because the same Reason that made Baptism necessary to them, makes it also necessary to us. For Gospel Order setled by Apostolical Authority and Direction, as this was, hath not lost any of its native worth and efficacy, or obliging Vertue, by any Disuse or Discontinuance occasioned by any, but ought to be the same to us now, as it was to them in the beginning of such Order; especially considering the day wherein we live, many indeavouring to bring in their own Inventions into the Worship of God, which should make all Christians be more careful and Zealous to Cleave to the Institutions of Jesus Christ, as they were first Delivered by the holy Penmen, and the Practice of the Primitive Christians" (ibid., 58–59). Collins later added to this perspective, "Those who lay too much stress upon Circumstantials, 'tis doubtless their Evil: But can any lay more stress upon it, than our Saviour, who though unspotted, yet would not live without it, and calls it *Righteousness*?" (Collins, *Believers Baptism from Heaven*, 45).

164. Kiffin, *Sober Discourse*, 13.

to men, that very *Prescription*, is an express prohibition of the contrary."[165] Christians were bound to obey every command of Christ in worship of which this command about baptism *was* one. It was an act of worship by the church; therefore, churches not in its use were false worshipers.[166]

Just Causes of Separation: Corruption in Doctrine and Worship

But was that reason enough to separate from a church? Could the Devonshire Square and Bedford churches recognize each other in communion? To some extent everyone agreed on the answer in principle. All Reformed churches had separated from Rome based on corrupt worship, in full agreement "not onely in forsaking *Babylon* and comming out of the Church in deepe defection: But also of their Congregating together and worshipping of God purely according to his word."[167] But when churches further separated from the first Reformed churches for the same reason, they were told that any potential, subsequent defection was not deep enough for such separation. Anglicans believed that all churches were imperfect but were sustained by the Holy Spirit; "schism" was separation from any true church, however imperfect.[168] Immanuel Knutton appealed

---

165. Ibid., 28–29.

166. In the appendix to the 1688 edition of their confession, the Baptists made the argument against infant baptism based on its treatment as instituted worship; "As for those our Christian-Brethren, who do ground their Arguments for Infants Baptism, upon a presumed Foederal Holiness, or Church-Membership; we conceive they are deficient in this, that albeit this Covenant-Holiness and Membership should be as is supposed, in reference unto the Infants of Believers; yet no Command for Infant-Baptism does immediately and directly result from such a quality, or relation. All Instituted Worship receives its Sanction from the Precept, and is thereby governed in all the necessary circumstances thereof. So it was in the Covenant that God made with *Abraham* and his Seed" (*London* [1688], 114–15). Poe recognized this as a battle between church and individual worship but thought it secondary to the doctrinal battle over believers' baptism. Poe, "John Bunyan's Controversy with the Baptists," 25–35.

167. Barbone, *Reply to R. B.*, 63. Jessey similarly said, "Its true, that in the Mysticall *Babylon*, all Ordinances generally were lost, and grossely defiled; and Images were in their stead, Mattens, Beads, and books were all the prayer and generally. The Scriptures were in an unknowne Tongue. Regeneration was counted to be by sprinkling an Infant. Altars, Crosses, Crucifixes, Surplesses, in stead of Gods Ordinances. Now must we tarry in this *Babylonish* way, till such a mighty glorious Angell come? Or must we reforme as farre as we see?" He later concluded that "there the Saints are called to forsake such a Church-State, & to seek to enjoy all purely else-where." Jessey, *Storehouse of Provision*, 16, 159.

168. Anglicans justified Henry's separation (not schism) by saying Rome was not a

to Baptists not to abandon the church due to defects in discipline because "Jesus Christ leaves us not for our defects and weakenesses, but continues with us, and I hope will doe for ever."[169] At what point was the line drawn between the church and the corruption that attended it, or how deep did the defection have to be to justify separation? Most of the early nonconformists believed that they must separate from all false worship "for there is absolutely forbidden *all participation in any feigned service*, whether it be to the true God or any other." They appealed to a powerful mantra: "the sitter is accessary to the sin of the kneeler."[170] But Wright noted that even they fell along a wide spectrum of attitudes, from non-separating Puritans to the "bitter, ingrained and unyielding . . . friendless isolation" of Thomas Helwys.[171]

The London Particular Baptists had a great struggle to find solidarity, especially after the Presbyterian ascendancy. In a great irony of "counter-reformation," John Owen appealed to the authority of the established church's leaders as a reason why the Baptists should not separate. He

---

true church. Truth may have been more important than unity to Anglicans, but their view of truth was broad. Woodhouse, *Doctrine of the Church*, 171–72.

169. Knutton, *Seven Questions about the Controviersie*, 23. A Puritan, he later added the more useful argument against separation, "Because the Separatists themselves, had their first illumination in our Church, by the word taught amongst us" (ibid., 26). The title page summarized the seven questions proposed to the Baptists: "1. Whether is the Church of England as it now stands a true church? 2. Whether the Church of England be a right nationall church? 3. Whether are the ministers in the Church of England sent of God, and so are true ministers or not? 4. Whether is the baptisme of infants a true and lawfull baptisme or no? 5. Whether it be lawfull to be rebaptized or not? 6. Whether it is lawfull to separate from all the publike ordinances and Christian assemblies in our English church, because there are some defects in discipline, and in other things amongst us? 7. Whether is it necessarie to demolish our churches (steeple-houses as the Separatists call them,) and to build them in other places, because they were built by idolators for idolatrous worship, were abused with images, and dedicated to saints?"

170. Canne, *Necessitie of Separation*, 83, 98 (quoted from Ames and used against Ames's unwillingness to separate). He said, "For the *Nonconformists* doe grant the thing: *We may not* (say they) *have any religious communion, or partake in divine worship, with idolaters in their false idolatrous worship* (no not in body be present at idolatrous service,) but we must absteine from all participation of idolatrie" (ibid., 91). Barber similarly argued, "The cause of propounding these Queries is, that notwithstanding, being ready to submit to His Majesty, and State, as Masters of our flesh, so farre as concernes our Estates, Libertie and lives; And walking conscionable in the way and worship of God; according to Christs institution, and the primitive practice, To whose Word, as our onely Law giver, we ought to have recourse" (Barber, *Certain Queries*, 15).

171. Wright, *Early English Baptists*, 50.

scolded them for being "like the ambitious sons of Levi" and disregarding Christ's body and ministers. Even John Tombes and Henry Jessey argued that differences in judgment about baptism was not a sufficient reason to leave a church, though both agreed in principle that believers' baptism was necessary for right order. Tombes believed that such a road was fraught with "superstitious perplexities" that would only beget more schism. Jessey thought that the Independents (though "weak") had the matter and form of a true church, and he sympathized with their offense over the Particular Baptists' distance.[172] Particular Baptists had to set a clear line for the reasons of their separation, what it meant that the word and ordinances were not dispensed purely.

Essentially, the London Particular Baptists agreed with Separatists that they were separating from false worship, discipline, and government.[173] John Spilsbury described a Separatist as "being content to part with all things that he may enjoy Christ in his Word and Ordinances."[174] The First London Confession did not directly address their separation apart from the obvious observation that their articles of faith did not fully match those of the established churches. However, it did mention that no Christian should separate from a church "rightly gathered, established, and still proceeding in Christian communion, and obedience of the Gospel of Christ."[175] Such a comment heavily implied the centrality of baptism and discipline to their separation. Indeed, to the query of why he separated from a church dispensing the pure Word and Sacraments, Kiffin replied that that church's infant baptism and practice of discipline were in fact not pure (remember that Kiffin connected discipline with a regenerate church). To the query of his warrant for establishing new churches during an ongoing (Puritan) reformation, he replied first that they were saving themselves from a corrupt generation and superstitious worship,

---

172. Owen, *Duty of Pastors and People Distinguished*, in *Works*, 13:45; Barbone, *Defence of Baptizing Infants*, 57; Tombes, *Apology or Plea for the Two Treatises*, 53–54; and Jessey, *Storehouse of Provision*, 102–3. Note that Owen later changed the definition of schism when it became apparent that he would be on the schismatic side. He argued that schism only dealt with causeless differences within a church; being forced out by virtue of an ecclesiological conviction was not schism. Owen, *Of Schism: The True Nature of It Discovered and Considered* (1657), in *Works*, 13:108–9.

173. See Jacob, *Defence of the Churches and Ministery of Englande*, 70; Ainsworth, *A Defence of the Holy Scriptures*; L. F., *Speedy Remedie*, 67; the late-century Independent Isaac Chauncy still emphasized the Anglicans as being "polluted in Doctrine, Worship, Manners, both as to the Ministry and People." Chauncy, *Ecclesiasticum*, 42.

174. Spilsbury, *Gods Ordinance*, To the Christian Reader.

175. *London* [1644], Article XL.

Free Worship and a New Concept of the Church

and second that the said reformation did not impress, "for what great thing is it to change *Episcopacie* into *Presbytery*, and a Book of *Common Prayer* into a *Directory* . . . I pray you consider, is there not the same power, the same priests, the same People, the same Worship, and in the same manner still continued[?]"[176] Consequently, as an instituted ordinance of God's worship for the church of Christ, Particular Baptists agreed amongst themselves that baptism was indeed a sufficient cause for separation.

The most effective counterargument seemed to come from Barbone, who argued that every action of men contained some error being tainted by sin—even the Particular Baptists—yet they would never nullify their own churches. "But if an error doe not make a nullitie, as it is most sure it doth not, no though the error should be great, then may the Baptisme in and under the defection, be and remain Gods Ordinance, notwithstanding all the error or errors that attend it, or are in it."[177] This argument seemed to impress Henry Jessey and John Tombes (and even John Spilsbury, as noted earlier[178]), who regularly counseled grace and patience. Jessey travelled about England encouraging churches to union and cooperation despite potential differences, and he even maintained a group in London "of some eminent men of each denomination, in order to maintain peace and union among those christians that differed not fundamentally." He specifically counseled churches not to divide over baptism, laying on of hands, or singing—matters of worship that did cause divisions for Baptists—although he acknowledged such separation as a last resort.[179] Likewise, Tombes was

---

176. Kiffin, *Briefe Remonstrance*, 6–7.

177. Barbone, *Discourse Tending to Prove*, 11. Jessey would later agree that if a baptism were valid only with respect to circumstances of its administration, no one could ever be absolutely certain of his own baptism. Jessey, *Storehouse of Provision*, 96ff.

178. Spilsbury still desired unity but only with patience, asking all parties to test themselves against the Scriptures that God might change hearts "to bring all his people into one unitie of faith, and uniforme order of truth, that God may have glory, the Gospel honour, the Saints comfort." Spilsbury, *Treatise Concerning Baptisme*, 37.

179. Crosby, *History of the English Baptists*, 1:312. See also Jessey's letter to the church at Hexham in 1653; *Fenstanton*, 347. Jessey applied the pattern of discipline to a church as a whole, "But if the Church, after conviction of the offence, shall still obstinately persist in it, and grow (as is usuall in such cases) to defend the evill of their way, by running into a greater evill; or take it offensively at my hand, that I doe not goe along with them, in allowing the offence: or be unwilling to receive my testimony in other necessary truths: In *such cases*, I may withdraw my selfe wholly from Communion with them, [Having first thus proceeded, with the advice of other Churches.]" (Jessey, *Storehouse of Provision*, 50).

unable to separate fully from the Presbyterian establishment even though he had spectacular disagreements with them about infant baptism.[180]

While Barbone may have convinced Spilsbury to proceed with grace, he certainly did not convince Spilsbury to change his mind. Spilsbury offered the clearest defense and explanation of the Baptist's separation with respect to this particular topic. He noted that one of the primary arguments used against them (especially by Barbone) was the idea of succession, that the efficacy of an ordinance was derived from its position in a long chain stretching back to the apostles. Spilsbury noted that such a succession necessarily stretched through Rome, a church all parties agreed was corrupt. Barbone, of course, argued that Rome's corruption did not stretch to her ordinances; there was no essential connection between them. Spilsbury disagreed:

> if they meane by defection, the outward forme of worship, and government Ecclesiasticall, I thinke they doe, then all the power and authoritie that ever hath carried out any administration, or constituted ordinance, hath taken its beeing thence, and depends upon the same; and if so, then the power and ordainer, and the ordinance so ordained, must be both of one and the same stamp, as I have already proved, if the one be Antichrists, the other must be also Antichristian.

Corrupt ordinances spilled out of a corrupt church even as they perpetuated the corruption. There was no essential distinction between a church and her ordinances; to look for such a church was to look for "a man in the Moone."[181] In bold terms, this meant that a church was her worship. The two could not be separated. Every error in worship was potential grounds for separation.

In conclusion, this chapter has reinforced that the early Particular Baptists thought deeply about government and discipline and baptism.

---

180. Tombes referred to these disagreements throughout his works. Carruthers offered the explanation that Parliament prevented the Assembly from dealing directly with any private publications, which is why they resorted to caustic sermons and pamphlets on the subject instead of public debate with Tombes. Carruthers, *Everyday Work of Westminster Assembly*, 102–4.

181. Spilsbury, *Treatise Concerning Baptisme*, 39. Kiffin's early co-pastor and signatory of the First London Confession, Patient, wrote in 1654 (after he had left Devonshire Square) that to receive a member based on infant baptism was to "receive that Church and Ministry, from which he had his supposed baptism, and must certainly own all those Churches which that ministry stood in fellowship with." Patient, *Doctrine of Baptism*, 172. Kiffin did not seem to be quite as absolute as Spilsbury and Patient in this matter.

Free Worship and a New Concept of the Church

But their thoughts were intimately shaped by their commitment to pure worship. Pure worship was expected of all true Christians, and it could not be coerced. Therefore, a true church must be a free church, and only one polity allowed such freedom. But congregationalism also answered another consequence of the Baptists' commitment to the priesthood of all believers, removing the class structure of membership. Clergy were not elevated above laity, neither were infants admitted at some lower tier. All church members were expected to engage in the worship of God together (although the treatment of women as a second class provided a hint of problems to come). To build their true church, Baptists sought a model church, a church of primitive purity, which they found in the Scriptures. But their joy and zeal of reconstituting around a true apostolic identity in a truly unified church was hampered by the tension innate in the search for that identity. The one thing they could agree on was that the apostolic identity was found in the Scriptures, not in church tradition.[182] Their use of the Scriptures drew from a long-standing Separatist tradition, but it also took them far afield from the other English Protestants.[183] The next chapter will investigate exactly how the London Particular Baptists related pure worship with their understanding of God's Word.

---

182. This is not to say that all Baptists rejected all such tradition. Collins gladly called the Nicene, Athanasian, and Apostles' Creeds "necessary truths." Collins, *Orthodox Catechism*, 8. His catechism was itself a recension of the continental Reformed Heidelberg Catechism.

183. For example, both Coffey and Spurr pointed out that Puritans (including Presbyterians and Independents, demonstrated in their alliance against the Baptists in 1641) were willing to use the *Book of Common Prayer* as long as they had some "latitude" in its use. Coffey, *John Goodwin and the Puritan Revolution*, 80; and Spurr, *English Puritanism*, 134. It is hard to imagine any of the Particular Baptist leaders ever saying something like that under any conditions.

four

True Worship and a New Appreciation of the Scriptures

"The Tryall of the Holy and Pure Word of God": The New Testament as the Sole Warrant for the Church's Practice[1]

Worship had a profound interaction with the London Particular Baptists' developing doctrine of the Scriptures. The Scriptures were not only a record of the gospel of Jesus Christ in the sense of telling men how they must be saved but also a record of the good news that God had established a way in which He might have an ongoing relationship with men in this life. Specifically, they told men how to approach God in the pinnacle of all existence: worship. These Baptists saw the Scriptures as more than a source for doctrine or a manual for polity, but the "Foundation and Rule of our Faith and Worship."[2] The Scriptures revealed first

---

1. Spilsbury, *Treatise Concerning Baptisme*, 37. He concluded about baptism, "but to lay the chaine of succession of truth this way, namely, through the Popedome of *Rome* as all such must doe that hold a personall succession, or a Church, and ordinances to consist in the same, from the Apostles untill now; what will such doe, and where will their succession of truth lie?" Ibid.

2. *London* [1688], "An Appendix," 109.

True Worship and a New Appreciation of the Scriptures

how man could enter into a relationship with God through Jesus Christ and second how he could maintain that relationship by God's own prescription. They would only worship God by His own rules, terrified of the possibility of approaching Him with "strange fire." This perspective has been called the "regulative principle" (as associated with the Reformed tradition and as opposed to the "normative principle" associated with the Lutheran and Anglican traditions). I will use that phrase to describe the Baptist perspective on worship and Scripture but only with great reluctance because it creates an artificial dependence on the Calvinist tradition. They were independently working out the implications of their desire for pure worship (as was the rest of England). Most importantly, as chapter 6 will highlight, they used this principle inconsistently because the questions they asked became increasingly complex. What was the relationship between Israel and the church, between Moses and Christ, between the Law and the Gospel in terms of worship? Were apostolic examples as authoritative as divine commands? Should such examples be treated literally or symbolically? Were worship commands given to all Christians in all times? Could these commands be enforced? Particular Baptists answered these questions in a way that separated them from the rest of England and even from each other.

It has already been mentioned that Cranmer rejected the regulative principle, rooting all of Anglicanism in the idea that the church had the authority to decree ceremonies not found in Scripture. The famous contest between John Whitgift and Thomas Cartwright took up that very issue with Whitgift playing the role of the loyal Anglican.[3] William Bradshaw warned that God must not be worshiped falsely, but he also argued that ceremonies simply were "outward demonstrations" of what really mattered, "inward worship." He concluded, "Ceremonies [not explicitly found in Scripture] are lawful, when they are warranted by lawful Doctrine."[4] But William Ainsworth threw down the proverbial gauntlet when he declared, "And that the Lord is to be worshipped and called upon in spirit & truth, according to that forme of praier given by the Lord Jesus, Mat. 6. & after the Leitourgie of his own Testament, not by any other framed or imposed by men, much lesse by one translated from the Popish leitourgie, as the

---

3. Smyth, *Cranmer & the Reformation under Edward VI*, 264; Cartwright, *Replye to an Answere Made of M. Doctor Whitgifte*; and the rest of that literary chain.

4. Bradshaw, *Several Treatises of Worship and Ceremonies*, not paginated. Baptists approached the separation of the inward and the outward in a number of ways; the next chapter will address those thoughts in more detail.

Book of common praier &c."[5] He made the same argument as Bradshaw, that the magistrate had the right to establish laws for Christian doctrine, worship, and ministry, but insisted that the magistrate's authority did not extend beyond the explicit word of Scripture into the so-called things indifferent such as traditional rites and ceremonies.

Scottish Presbyterian George Gillespie issued one of the most important words on this subject in 1637. The Anglican Church had taken the position that ceremonies could be imposed on the people as long as they were necessary, expedient, lawful, or indifferent, a position often called the normative principle. Gillespie countered that the church could establish rites to serve the public order and edification, but the authority to do so was not found in the church but in the Scriptures. The church's rules were binding only insofar as that which they prescribed was lawful (in context, he actually meant not unlawful, somewhat muddying his argument) and expedient. Once the church ruled a rite necessary, it could no longer be considered indifferent. However, he left open the possibility that the church could decree a thing indifferent as long as it was lawful and expedient so to do, such as what time the church's services might begin. Westminster used Gillespie's argument to overturn the authority of the Anglican Church but still maintain its own.[6]

John Spilsbury knew that Westminster's position was incompatible with the Particulars Baptists' convictions. They did not need any kind of succession or human authority for their actions; it equally did not matter

---

5. Ainsworth and Johnson, *Confession of faith*, 71.

6. Gillespie walked a fine line: "Now, for making the matter more plain, we must consider that the constitutions of the church are either lawful or unlawful. If unlawful, they bind not at all: if lawful, they are either concerning things necessary (as Acts 15:28), and then the necessity of the things bind, whether the church ordains them or not; or else concerning things indifferent, as when the church ordains, that in great towns there shall be sermon on such a day of the week, and public prayers every day at such an hour. Here it is not the bare authority of the church that binds without respect to the lawfulness or expediency of the things itself which is ordained (else we were bound to do everything which the church ordains, were it never so unlawful, for *quod competit alicui qua tali, competit omni tali* [*what is suitable for someone as such, is suitable for all such*]; we behold the authority of the church making laws, as well in unlawful ordinances as in lawful), nor yet is it the lawfulness or expediency of the thing itself, without respect to the ordinance of the church (for possibly other times and diets were as lawful, and expedient too, for such exercises, as those ordained by the church), but it is the authority of the church prescribing a thing lawful or expedient. In such a case, then neither does the authority of the church bind, except the thing be lawful and expedient, nor does the lawfulness and expediency of the thing bind, except the church ordain it; but both these jointly do bind" (Gillespie, *Dispute Against the English Popish Ceremonies*, 17).

True Worship and a New Appreciation of the Scriptures

to them if a corrupt church had observed their practices. God superseded men:

> And the Rule by which all must be tryed, though an Angel from heaven, and the Apostles themselves, as *Gal.* 1. 8, 9. So that the holy Scripture is the onely place where any ordinance of God in the case aforesaid is to be found, they being the fountain-head, containing all the instituted Rules of both of Church and ordinances, so that, when, or wheresoever any of these are wanting in their constitution, and cannot be found in their outward orderly forme, wee are to go directly unto its institution, and recover the same againe from thence, as *Cant.* 1. 7. *Isa.* 8. 19, 20. *Rom.* 10. 6, 7, 8.[7]

This aligned well with another early Particular Baptist conviction, the role of the Holy Spirit in discerning truth. Whereas most traditions believed that a pastor must be extensively trained to understand and interpret the Bible, these Baptists realized that theological institutions inherently propagated that tradition's truth or error, as their own experiences proved. Kiffin latched on to Howe's provocative claim that all a true church needed was the true Word and true salvation, which yielded the Spirit to interpret the Word. The learning the Apostle Paul demanded of a pastor was "the teaching of the Spirit, whereby the man is made sound in the Faith, for that learning onely will make men low in their own eyes."[8]

The enormity of Spilsbury's claim must not be undersold. Barbone was just as shocked by it as he was Smyth's se-baptism and called it "the sum of the matter" between them. To Barbone, this claim marginalized and potentially invalidated every church before them (making Christ a "widower"). That belief alone, being unsubstantiated by Scripture, nullified Spilsbury's entire case. Spilsbury had to counter that he was not speaking about other churches at all, but only the authority of Scripture. This led to Barbone's more important charge, that such an approach made the Baptists no better than Papists, for claiming the power to make a church was no different than claiming the power to make a Christ in the Mass. Both had scriptural referent without scriptural warrant, and Barbone was unwilling to grant Scripture the power to institute; that power was given to the apostles alone: "The Scripture (with the Spirit of life in them) act

---

7. Spilsbury, *Treatise Concerning Baptisme*, 38. He wrote on the matter in 1643 and 1646; all of the London Particular Baptist leaders were concerned about the proceedings and determinations of Westminster.

8. Howe, *Sufficiencie of the Spirits Teaching*, 10, 36, 37.

nothing, but onely direct and furnish men how to act according to the will of God."[9] Scripture said nothing about instituting a new church, only continuing the apostles' church.[10] To this charge Spilsbury replied with an profound Trinitarian statement clarifying the exact nature of Scripture: God had left the church three helps, "his Spirit for their guide, his Word for their rule, and himself for their warrant."[11] Never again would the Particular Baptists have to appeal to any human authority.

But this debate between Spilsbury and Barbone revealed an important dilemma that remained. When Barbone argued that Christ's church remained "stable and firm, abiding to perpetuity," he drew its line all the way back to Israel. He argued that God's everlasting covenant with man, though recorded in Scripture, was above Scripture, "so it is a distinct thing from either of the Testaments, old or new." Consequently, there was a direct line connecting Israel and the Church, a standard Reformed conclusion. Daniel Featley argued that same year, "Whatsoever the Prophets or Saints of God practised in the substantial worship of God under the Law, may and ought to be a president [precedent] for us." For paedobaptists, a great significance and a great blot against the Baptists was the line between circumcision and baptism.[12] Defending the claim that baptism was a sign of a new covenant having nothing to do with the old, Spilsbury said vaguely, "Hereby it is manifest, that the authoritie of the new Testament, is equall with, if not above the authoritie of the old Testament, to command obedience."[13]

Indeed, the earliest Baptist statements about the Scriptures were all somewhat vague. The First London Confession simply declared that the

---

9. Barbone, *Defence of Baptizing Infants*, 28; see also 19ff.

10. Ibid., 30, 41.

11. Spilsbury, *Gods Ordinance*, 12. He would apply this as well to pastors whose "authority comes from Christ, and no man's ordination." Ibid., 8.

12. Barbone, *Discourse Tending to Prove*, 17, 20; Barbone, *Defence of Baptizing Infants*, 1; Featley, *Dippers dipt*, 86. Barbone actually used this argument to prove that a human defection such as the corruption in Rome could not invalidate God's eternal promises to His church. Another Presbyterian, Geree, said clearly, "Baptism is instituted in the place of Circumcision, not by any thought of ours, but the designment of God" (Geree, *Vindiciae Paedo-Baptismi*, 34).

13. Spilsbury, *Gods Ordinance*, 24. Illustrating a rare alternative position, on at least one occasion, Presbyterian Cragge was astounded that John Tombes would appeal only to divine arguments, not human tradition, believing that the church indeed had the authority to overrule Scripture. Cragge's partner Henry Vaughan quickly distanced himself from Cragge's statement, saying Cragge was talking about the authority to impose circumstances of ceremonies. *Publick Dispute*, 9, 13, 21.

True Worship and a New Appreciation of the Scriptures

"Canonicall Scriptures" contained the rule of the worship and service of God, as opposed to men's inventions or traditions, and, "In this written Word God hath plainly revealed whatsoever he hath thought needfull for us to know." Later, however, it declared that the church should only consider the offices and ordinances appointed by Christ in His New Testament, of which baptism was one.[14] In his 1646 *Appendix*, Benjamin Cox possibly may have been responding to a concern about their minimizing the Old Testament when he noted, "Though we be not now sent to the Law as it was in the hand of *Moses*, to be commanded thereby, yet Christ in his Gospel teacheth and commandeth us to walk in the same way of righteousness and holyness that God by *Moses* did command the Israelites."[15] John Spilsbury's *Heart Bleedings*, appended to the 1651 edition, explained that Moses and Joshua were types of Christ, just as physical Israel was a shadow of spiritual Israel and the written Law pointed to the spiritual gospel. It asserted, "That the Scriptures which doe declare this great mysterie of Jesus Christ and his *Gospel*, be the holy Scriptures, and the infallible Word of God."[16]

The London Particular Baptists were left in a somewhat open position: the Scriptures were authoritative for the church, most particularly the parts dealing with the gospel of Jesus Christ. But how exactly should they handle the not-entirely-abrogated Old Testament? One approach, used by Thomas Grantham and followed at various times by Particular Baptists, was to spiritualize it. Grantham argued,

> So then it is clear, that *some part of our time, some part of our substance*, and *some place* must be set apart for the Worship of God, *&c.* And what part that must be, either Christ and right reason, or the Law of *Moses* must inform us; If *Moses's* Law, then the *Seventh day* of every week, the *Temple of Jerusalem*, and *Tythes* must be assigned: But if Christ and right reason, then the time is, *whenever you can*; the place is, *wherever you can*; and for substance, *what you can, or what is necessary*.[17]

---

14. *London* [1644], Article VII, VIII, XXXVI–XL. The content of these articles did not substantially change between 1644 and 1651.

15. Cox, *Appendix to a Confession of Faith*, 7. He specifically listed both tables of the Ten Commandments, citing Matthew 22:37–40 and Romans 13:8–10. Additionally, Henry Jessey published annual "Scripture Almanacks" during this time which leaned very heavily on the Old Testament.

16. *London* [1651], 21.

17. Grantham, *Seventh-day-Sabbath Ceased*, 3.

Interestingly, this specific quote was how Grantham countered the scriptural argument made by other Baptists in defense of the seventh-day Sabbath. Grantham knew that the Papists accused them "if we must only argue out of Scripture, and be our own Interpreters of it, there can be no end of arguing." He could only respond that the same Spirit that reminded the apostles of all truth would inform all Christians of that same truth.[18] Another approach, explained throughout the rest of this chapter, was to focus on the New Testament with respect to God's church. The Second London Confession explained that God gave the Israelites typical ordinances for their worship that prefigured Christ; when "Jesus Christ the true *Messiah* and only Lawgiver who was furnished with power from the Father, for that end" came, He had them "abrogated and taken away."[19] Benjamin Keach added that although the Israelites were made holy by their participation in the Old Testament ceremonies, there was now "a new Church-state, new Ordinances, a new Seed, and new way of Introduction unto the Participation of the Priviledge of Church-membership now under this new and more glorious Dispensation."[20]

The overriding purpose for such a commitment was to follow God's "particular way and method in which he will be Worshiped." With the Separatists, these Baptists sought the liturgy of Christ's New Testament as it was followed during the primitive purity of the apostolic church.[21] Such a liturgy was not the sensory experience of the Roman or Anglican churches, but the order of Christ's ordinances prescribed for God's wor-

---

18. Grantham, *Baptist against the Papist*, 20–21. Jessey called this the "mystical" sense of the Scriptures and cited Jesus' understanding of the Sabbath as proof of its existence, which could be allegorical or metaphorical. However, one always looked for a literal meaning first. Jessey, *Miscellanea Sacra*, 16ff., 33ff.

19. London [1677], Article XIX. Cary later posited that moral institutions in the Old Testament (such as the Sabbath) were still obligatory. Otherwise, Old Testament types and figures required an express New Testament command to be enjoining on Christians. Cary, *Solemn Call*, 12, 71.

20. Keach, *Gold Refin'd*, 117.

21. Kiffin, *Sober Discourse*, 57. One Separatist document, circulated in 1643, went so far as to say that such a liturgy would be binding on all Christians: "If the whole manner of Gods worship were revealed unto us, or any State or Church, and that such a Church or State could be certain to be in the present possession, and practice of the whole truth, without any mixture of superstition and Idolatry, then would there be far more colour and ground for erecting an Inquisition Office, or Spirituall Court to bring a Nation, a Countrey, or all Christendome unto a uniformity both of Discipline and Doctrine" (*Liberty of Conscience*, 48). It would be invaluable to know if any Baptists agreed with this claim. Davies thought Calvin originated the idea of a New Testament liturgy. Davies, *Worship of the English Puritans*, 49.

True Worship and a New Appreciation of the Scriptures

ship. To be clear, "ordinance" meant more than baptism and the Lord's Supper. Praisegod Barbone applied "ordinance" to everything ordained by Christ in worship and church government;[22] Baptists challenged much of what he said but never that. The First London Confession only explicitly listed baptism as an ordinance, but it did say that the saints were entitled to enjoy the "ordinances" in their churches. In 1645, Hanserd Knollys stated prayer, preaching, and conference as the ordinances; in 1654, Thomas Patient identified prayer, hearing, baptism, the Lord's Supper, thanksgiving, almsgiving, and maintenance as such. Over time, the list expanded further. The Second London Confession, which followed Westminster (and thus avoided the language of "ordinance"[23]) identified prayer, reading Scripture, preaching and hearing the Word of God, teaching and admonishing one another in psalms, hymns, and spiritual songs, baptism and the Lord's Supper as the "parts" of God's worship, with baptism and the Lord's Supper being the two ordinances. But there was no doubt that the Baptists meant "ordinance" with respect to those parts. In 1681, Knollys listed the "Gospel-Ordinances, in which his Churches of Saints must worship God in Spirit, and in Truth," as prayer, reading Scripture, expounding Scripture, preaching the gospel, baptism, the Lord's Supper, and singing. A decade later, Joseph Wright added to that list collection and discipline as "the permanent standing Ordinances of the Church of Christ."[24]

---

22. Barbone, *Reply to R. B.*, 59.

23. Fiddes correctly noted that Baptists did not use "ordinance" in opposition to "sacrament." Fiddes, *Tracks and Traces*, 158–60. For example, Cox said of baptism, "And where this obedience is in faith performed, there *Christ* makes this his Ordinance a means of unspeakable benefit to the believing soul, *Acts* 2. 38" (Cox, *Appendix to a Confession of Faith*, 9). "Benefit" did not mean "sacramental grace."

24. *London* [1644], Article XXXIII, XXXIX; *London* [1677], Article XXII; cf. *Westminster* [1646], Article XXI, Section V. The 1644 confession also listed the civil magistrate as an ordinance. Also compare Knollys, *Christ Exalted*, 2; Patient, *Doctrine of Baptism*, 171; with Knollys, *World that Now is*, 70–76; and Wright, *Folly Detected*. For example, Knollys defined the circumstances of singing: "The manner of Singing Psalms, Hymns, and Spiritual Songs, is to Sing in Meeter and Measure, with audible Voice, as our English manner is." He specifically differentiated between prayer and singing as "two distinct Ordinances under the Gospel, 1 *Cor.* 14. 14, 15. and two distinct parts of the Worship of God." Knollys, *Exposition Of the Revelation*, 76. Keach remained more open-ended, listing "Prayer, Preaching, Baptism, the Lord's Supper, and every other Duty and Ordinance." Keach, *Breach Repaired in God's Worship*, 147. Showing consistency, he later identified, "Prayer, the Word of God, and Preaching, with Baptism, and the Lord's Supper, &c." Keach, *Laying on of Hands upon Baptized Believers*, 19. These lists of ordinances were also used disputationally. Collier declared the list of ordinances to include baptism, prayer, praise (singing), preaching, the Lord's Supper, assembling, admonition, discipline, community of goods, and holiness. He

Importantly, the Baptists attempted to define the ordinances both by the ceremony and the circumstances that attended it. This allowed them to argue that baptism required a proper subject *and* mode. Unfortunately, this led them into a number of inconsistencies, as this chapter will explain. John Geree, for one, argued against them, "I conceive there's a great difference between an Ordinance it self, and some particular Circumstance, or Subject, to which that Ordinance is to be applied." He appealed to the specific example of excommunication; though biblical, they were not given exact instructions how to do it.[25] Henry Jessey realized the precarious position in which this left the Baptists and warned that if they were willing to die on the circumstances of baptism (if indeed subject and mode were circumstances), they must either declare baptism more important than the other ordinances or apply the same treatment to every ordinance, including the laying on of hands, singing, washing of feet, and anointing with oil—disputed ordinances which were the source of great consternation for the Baptists. Otherwise, they should show the same patience in baptism with which they were shown in these others.[26]

---

then spent many pages explaining why the laying on of hands was *not* an ordinance. Collier, *Right Constitution and True Subjects Of the Visible Church of Christ*, 9–18, 70–86. There were yet further options considered. Jessey considered fasting an ordinance, but noted that it was distinct from the instituted ceremonies. Jessey, *Miscellanea Sacra*, 3. The *Orthodox Creed*, written in 1679 but never adopted by a Baptist group, also listed fasting, or "publick Humiliation" as an ordinance. Monck et al., *An Orthodox Creed*, 127–82. Perhaps surprisingly, footwashing did not receive much attention from the Baptists. The frontispiece of *The Anabaptists Anatomiz'd* contained a cell of Baptists washing feet. Tombes commented about the cell that neither he nor those he ministered with did so, although he thought it could be justified from John 13. The Western Association decided it was not an ordinance. White, *Association Records*, 60. Collins, *Marrow of Gospel-History,* 34–35, mentioned it without calling it an ordinance.

25. Geree, *Vindiciae Paedo-Baptismi*, 4. This allowed him to expand that the errors connected with infant baptism had nothing to do with the ceremony, but it was the fault of the church in its subsequent doctrine and discipline; for example, even unregenerate adults could be baptized—more severe an error than baptizing a non-elect infant. Ibid., 58–59.

26. He wondered who among them was so faultless as "must not confess the Change of Times doth necessitate some Variation, if not Alteration either in the matter or manner of things according to Primitive Practice, yet owned for true Churches, and received as visible Saints, though ignorant either wholly or in great measure, in laying on of hands, singing, washing of feet, and anointing with oyl, in the Gifts of the Spirit, which is the *Urim* and *Thummim* of the Gospel? and it cannot be proved that the Churches were so ignorant in the Primitive times, nor yet that such were received into Fellowship; yet now herein it is thought meet there should be bearing, and why not in Baptism, especially in such as own it for an Ordinance, though in some things miss it, and do yet shew their love unto it, and unto the Lord, and unto his Law therein, that

"The Ways of His Own Appointment": The Regulative Principle and Right Hermeneutics[27]

The heart of the matter was the extent to which the New Testament was "the sole Canon and rule of all matters of *Religion*, and the worship & service of God whatsoever." William Bradshaw identified the parameters of this authority as every ecclesiastical action: "all outward means instituted and set apart to express and set forth the Inward worship of God" and "all typical rites and figures ordained to shadow forth in the solemn worship and service of God." The implication was profound: those who had the power to invent forms of worship had "power to make and invent a Religion and Worship of their own." Ceremonies and their circumstances were no minor concern but the very identity of the Christian religion. But Bradshaw added two important Puritan gray areas, namely that every action in worship should be commanded in the word "either expresly, *or* by necessary consequent," and that "to forbid any thing indifferent, is to forbid no evil."[28] The Baptists in word rejected the ideas of the necessary consequent and the thing indifferent, but the development of their appreciation of the Scriptures hinged greatly on their disagreements therein. Indeed, the subject of worship illuminated areas of Baptist thought, especially the extent to which they understood the Scriptures literally, unlike any other.

God Stands Upon Little Things: Will-Worship as Sin

It has already been noted that Jeremiah Burroughs was very influential among the early English Baptists; Kiffin identified him as a pivotal figure in his conversion to Independency. Kiffin also cited an important sermon series Burroughs preached about worship in either 1645 or 1646.

---

they should be willing to die for it rather than to deny it." Cited in Bunyan, *Differences in Judgment*, 116–17.

27. See Owen, *Brief Instruction in the Worship of God*, in *Works*, 15.447.

28. Bradshaw, *Several Treatises of Worship and Ceremonies*, 10, 35, 36; emphasis added. He used the scandalous illustration, "Those that have power upon their own will and pleasure to bring into Gods Service some indifferent thing, may bring in any indifferent thing: those that may bring in without special warrant from God, pyping into his service, might as well bring in dancing also: those that have authority to joyn to the Sacrament of Baptism the sign of the Cross, have authority also (no doubt) to joyn to the Sacrament of the Supper, Flesh, Broth, Butter or Cheese, and worse matters than those, if they will" (ibid., 10).

Burroughs made the statement, "In the matters of Worship, God stands upon little things."[29] He was making the point that "we must all be Willing worshipers, but not Wil-worshipers; We must come freely to worship God; but we must not worship God according to our own wils."[30] Burroughs did not coin the term "will-worship," it came from the Authorized translation of Colossians 2:23, Paul's warning about a "shew of wisedome in will-worship," but the term would be a lightning rod for the proper application of the regulative principle of Scripture.[31] Tombes exposited the passage to mean, "It is vaine to worship or to thinke to please God by the doctrines which are Commandements of men: for God is not pleased with mans devices, what is devised by man comes from a corrupt and foolish heart, and such a corrupt fountaine must needs send forth but puddle water."[32]

Tombes noted that all such will-worship began as a defensible rite, perhaps even a thing indifferent having the pretence of order, before the passage of time resulted in its binding the consciences of those obliged to observe it. Godly men may have proposed it initially, and soon enough it would become the tradition of wise and pious men. But their descendents would be forced to maintain it, and Tombes concluded dramatically, "Many a pound is given in Legacies and Contributions, is extorted by Courts, for maintaining vestments, organs, processions, windowes, buildings, and other things unnecessary, when the poore want, painefull Preachers live on small stipend, the Common-wealth is brought to straights: For superstition is costly."[33] William Kiffin took a much more

---

29. Burroughs, *Gospel-Worship*, 11; quoted in Kiffin, *Sober Discourse*, 50; and even Collins, *Believers Baptism from Heaven*, 10 (without credit).

30. Burroughs, *Gospel-Worship*, 10. Much earlier, Johnson had said, "All parts of divine worship and service imposed onely by the will and pleasure of man upon the communicants in divine service, & that of necessity to be done, is will-worship" (this was part of Johnson's *Twelve Arguments* cited in Bradshaw, *Unreasonablenesse of the separation*, 106).

31. See Tombes, *Fermentum Pharisaeorum*, 4.

32. He gave the illustration, "For as children doe count many things wise which understanding men doe laugh at: so carnall hearts of men esteeme as wise among men doe count many things to be wise, as duckings, bowings, washings, whippings, creepings, pilgrimages, and such like gestures, usages, and rites invented by men to express humility, devotion and reverence to God, which the Almighty, who is a most holy Spirit, contemnes as childish, apish, theatrical and ridiculous" (ibid.).

33. Ibid., 6, 11. Somewhat humorously, Featley, who had been an Anglican, wrote that same year a defense of organs because Westminster had decreed an end to their use; he declared that they might not be necessary for worship "but very lawfull, and of good use both in the Kings Chappell, Cathedral Churches, Colledges, and elsewhere." [Featley], *Gentle Lash*, 11.

True Worship and a New Appreciation of the Scriptures

cynical stance against such inventions in worship (admittedly after several more decades of ministry):

> Mans Nature is very prone to be medling with things beyond his Commission, which has prov'd the very pest and bane of Christianity; for notwithstanding that dreadful prohibition, *Rev.* 22. 18, 19. of *adding to,* or *taking from* his word, is not *Europe* full of pernicious Additions and Subtractions in the Worship of God, which are imposed as Magisterially as it enstampt with a Divine Character, though in themselves no other than (as Christ himself calls them) the *Traditions of men: Matth.* 15. 3. It is a superlative and desperate piece of audacity for men to presume to mend any thing in the Worship of God; for it supposes the All-wise Law giver capable of error, and the attempter wiser than his Maker.[34]

He could not have made a stronger argument. An invention in worship was not an exercise in a thing indifferent but a flagrant declaration that God had somehow failed to decree proper worship of Himself. Keach called it a result of "depraved Judgment and Self-Interest," and Cary said its only purpose could be "either to slacken and abate something that is *Excessive,* or to supply something that is *Deficient*" as if God's revelation could be deficient. Knollys looked both at Wormwood and the plague of blood in Revelation as an allegory for "the Inventions and Traditions of Men being mixed with the holy Ordinances of God."[35]

The power of the accusation of will-worship was made clear in two debates over infant baptism. In 1645, Benjamin Cox and the rest had prepared the following syllogism for Edmund Calamy, "That religious worship, for which there is no command nor example in the Scripture of truth, is Will-worship, and unlawful. But your Infant baptisme is a religious worship, for which there is no command, nor any example, written in the Scripture of truth; Ergo, Your Infant baptisme is Will-worship, and

---

34. Kiffin, *Sober Discourse,* Preface. Owen had earlier said something similar, "But such is the corrupt nature of man, that there is scarce any thing whereabout men have been more apt to contend with God from the foundation of the world. That their will and wisdom may have a share (some at least) in the ordering of his worship, is that which of all things they seem to desire" (Owen, *Discourse Concerning Liturgies,* in *Works,* 15:40). Cary said directly, "Men Love to have something of their own in God's Worship. They are not content with what the Infinite Wise God commands them; but will Presumptiously be adding something of their own thereto" (Cary, *Solemn Call,* 91).

35. Keach, *Gold Refin'd,* 149; Cary, *Solemn Call,* 90; Knollys, *Exposition Of the Revelation,* 101, 103.

unlawfull." Calamy had earlier taken recourse to the claim of "necessary consequences," a defense Cox found unacceptable because in principle it "ushers in all Popish Innovations; as Prelacy, Common-prayer-book, Ceremonies, &c. and therefore is unsound, absurd, and sinfull." The Baptists were not satisfied with any other response.[36] In 1649, while Richard Baxter and John Tombes were having their very public debate about baptism, some of Tombes's neighbors asked him about their own infant baptism. Tombes simply explained "that my exception against Pedo-baptism is, that it is will-worship for want of divine institution." This argument apparently so impressed the neighbors that "the only way to satisfie them was to prove a divine institution of Paedo-baptism." Tombes suggested to Baxter that if he would write to the neighbors "a few Syllogisms," they might be duly satisfied.[37]

Just as John Bunyan was snubbed by the charge that he minimized true worship, Presbyterians took mortal offense at the possibility that they might be worshipping God improperly. Thomas Hall reflected on this charge, "Then all the Reformed Churches of Christ in the world are Will-worshippers, and none know the mind of Christ so well as the tender conscienced harmless Anabaptists, (as some call them) they, they only are the Saints and true worshippers of God; all the world besides is deceived."[38] Considering the Baptists were thought of as tub-preachers and mechanics, well-educated Presbyterians probably found the entire scenario completely impudent. It could only mean that those Baptists understood Scripture better than they did.

---

36. Cox, Knollys, and Kiffin, *Declaration*, 10, 11. He later expanded the definition of will-worship to include "every administration and application of an Ordinance of Christ, otherwise then according to the Rule of the Word." Ibid., 18.

37. Baxter and Tombes had maintained a voluminous debate going back to 1649 with Baxter's first printing of *Plain Scripture proof*. Baxter wanted a public disputation while Tombes would rather exchange letters. Over time, Baxter appended those letters and sermons to subsequent editions. This particular letter was published in 1652 in an appendix titled, "Letters That passed between Mr. Baxter and Mr. Tombes Concerning the Dispute." Baxter, *Plain Scripture proof* (1653), 410–11. Baxter found Tombes's request a bit cheeky.

38. Hall, *Font Guarded*, 95. He counter-claimed, "All Will-worship must be avoided. But restraining Baptism only to Adults, is Will-worship, as I have proved *Arg.* 18." Frankly, his argument was underwhelming, for he simply noted that though Romans 6:4 and Colossians 2:12 indeed spoke of adults, they did not technically prohibit infants from baptism.

Determining What Was Indifferent: Liturgies, Examples, and Traditions

The regulative principle was not simply a forum in which to throw around accusations of will-worship; it was a proving ground for very divergent interpretations of Scripture. Particular Baptists genuinely wanted to know what God had commanded in worship, and what God had left (if anything) to their discretion. They knew they had drawn different conclusions about worship than their counterparts, especially with respect to baptism, and they put great effort into understanding their own methods and justifications. A second major area related to Scripture in worship was the "thing indifferent" (or *adiaphoron*), a circumstance of worship itself neither good nor evil, such as the length of a prayer or the size of a communion table. Dickens believed that all of Anglicanism was founded on this concept.[39] The established churches regularly appealed to the thing being indifferent when they defended the circumstances of their imposed worship, and such arguments regularly took center stage in liturgical disputes. Unfortunately, all sides—Baptists not excepting—treated the arguments very subjectively, making it difficult to establish a clear pattern of Baptist thought.[40]

English Christians approached the Bible in a number of different ways. Ideally, all wanted to obey any express commands in worship, although there was some concern if Paul's commands should be followed as closely as Christ's. Some of them felt that a clear example of apostolic practice was also binding. Some felt that way about traditions claimed to go back to the apostles though not recorded in Scripture. But the greatest question was what to do about circumstances not plainly addressed in Scripture. On one side, the Separatist L. F. said that the idea of "indifferent"

---

39. Dickens, *English Reformation*, 180.

40. Gillespie noted that once a thing was imposed by the church, it was no longer indifferent. Gillespie, *Dispute Against the English Popish Ceremonies*, 16ff. His subjective term with respect to the thing indifferent was "significant," as in once a ceremony was significant, it could not be indifferent. He identified "cross, kneeling, surplice, holidays, bishopping, etc." as significant ceremonies but was unable to provide any kind of objective criteria as to what delineated significant from non-significant ceremonies. Ibid., xli. Vavasor Powell similarly argued, "Either such Liturgies or Common-Prayers are indifferent, or not indifferent; if indifferent, then they are not to be imposed upon Christians, but they are to be left to their Liberty, as Christians were left by the Apostles; but if it be not indifferent, then unless a prescript can be shewed from God (it being in his Worship) it is no less than Will-worship, forbidden, *Col.* 2. 23" (Powell, *Common-Prayer-Book no Divine Service*, 6). The primary difference between the two men was Powell believed that nothing indifferent should ever be imposed in worship on anyone, regardless of perceived significance.

was used as a smokescreen to indulge the vanities of the authorities, "For in the worship and service of God, nothing is simply indifferent." He also thought it was a sign of the times that men did not care enough about God's worship to search His Word carefully and exhorted, "therefore not of liberty or indifferencie, but of absolute necessity, for the advancement of Gods glory, if in Gods Worship and service, else it is vanity."[41] On the other side, John Tombes counseled patience in yielding "unto the weak in things indifferent" until "they be more perfectly taught." He even conceded that "in point of Ceremony, and things indifferent, that some things may be unlawfull at one time, which are not unlawfull at another."[42]

The major locus of debate over things indifferent was the established liturgy. Vavasor Powell insisted, "The Scriptures themselves are a sufficient Directory and Rubrick to the Church of God,"[43] but accused the liturgy of supplanting them, defining every action, accounting for every moment of the worship service (unless the bishop gave exception). The liturgy and related injunctions controlled worship, from architecture to attire, in the name of decency and order.[44] London Particular Baptists well-understood the situation:

> They [the defenders of the liturgy] used thus to argue; from, *Matth.* 6. 9. If a set form of prayer be lawfull, then, the Common-prayer-book is lawfull . . . And by this Tenent they brought their people to submit to all their Popish Ceremonies, *viz.* Surplice, Crosse in baptisme, and bowing at the Name of Jesus, &c.
>
> They used thus to argue from, 1 *Cor.* 14. 40. All things in the Church ought to be done decently and in Order: But it is very decent to wear a Surplice, Cope, and Hood, to signe the Infant with the Crosse in Baptisme, and to bow at the naming of Jesus, and to kneel at the receiving of the Sacrament; also the uniformity of Pews in the Church, and the setting of the Table

---

41. L. F., *Speedy Remedie*, 32. For those who followed this line of thought, it is easy to see how austerity would have dominated the circumstances of their worship.

42. Tombes, *Vae Scandalizantum*, 233; Tombes, *Fermentum Pharisaeorum*, 15.

43. Powell, *Common-Prayer-Book no Divine Service*, 2. Benevolent Anglican apologist Bradshaw admitted to Johnson and others, "Though it should bee graunted, that the booke of Common praier in all the parts and percels therof, is not the true worship of God, but containeth in it some devises and inventions of man; yet, the true worship of God (not withstanding) is prescribed in it" (Bradshaw, *Unreasonablenesse of the separation*, n.p.).

44. The outspoken Grantham offered the rhyme, "What if our Lord should come and view these / And hear their Music, and demand of them, / Who 'twas commanded them thus to be drest, / And use those Pipes, when they came to be blest?" (Grantham, *Prisoner against the Prelate*, 76).

True Worship and a New Appreciation of the Scriptures

Altar-wise, and rayling it in; is both very decent and orderly:
Ergo, All these ceremonies ought to be in the Church.[45]

Baptists (and Independents and Presbyterians) despised these particular ceremonies associated with the established church (vestments were addressed in chapter 3; other ceremonies will be addressed in chapter 5).[46] On the one hand, they were not at all convinced that the ceremonies were themselves indifferent; on the other hand, they knew that a commanded ceremony meant a prohibited alternative. Kiffin established the Particular Baptists' priority, "Hence it is, that ye are for a *Church of Christs own Erection*, for a *Ministry of his own Calling*, and for *Ordinances of his own Appointing*." But every invention of man, based on its corrupt source, took them away from and not closer to God's true worship. No man-made form of worship could approach God's own institution in His Word.[47]

It was much easier for Particular Baptists to declare what they were for in general than in specific. The earliest Baptists, like the nonconformists, had worship services that looked very much like prophesyings, being based as directly as they thought possible on 1 Corinthians 14. They did not have a set number or length of prayers or sermons; they felt that the Bible explicitly gave them that flexibility. But Daniel Featley took them all to task for a number of inconsistencies, asking them where the Bible commanded pews, or pulpits, or galleries, or tunes for certain psalms, or

---

45. Cox, Knollys, and Kiffin, *Declaration*, 11–12. Indeed, the Prayer Book itself declared that "without some Ceremonies, it is not possible to kepe any order, or quiete discipline in the churche." *BCP* [1559], "Of Ceremonies."

46. For example, Canne singled out the surplice, the cross in baptism, and kneeling in the Lord's Supper, and cited various nonconformist opinions about them. The surplice was called the popes creature, a lowly rag, Popish apparel, the whore of Babilons smocke, and a filthy Idol. The mark of the cross was the marke of the beast, a jugglers gesture, a magicall instrument, a rite, and badge of the divel. Kneeling at the Supper was Idolatrie, a spawne of the beast, a diabolicall gesture, and a superstition which prophaneth Christs true religion. Canne, *Necessitie of Separation*, 94–97.

47. Norcott, Kiffin, and Claridge, *Baptism Discovered*, Preface (by Kiffin). Knollys observed, "There are divers forms of Religion wherein men worship and serve God according to the different apprehensions and perswasions of persons professing Godliness; whereof some, yea several are of mans devising, *Matth.* 15. 8, 9. compared with *Col.* 2. 20, 22, 23. But, there is a form of Godliness, which is of God's own Institution under the Gospel, wherein Men ought to worship God in Spirit and Truth, *John* 4. 23, 24. according to his own appointments, *Psal.* 3. 3. 16" (Knollys, *Parable of the Kingdom*, 25). The Second London Confession followed Westminster declaring that Jesus "may not be Worshipped according to the imaginations and devices of Men, or the suggestions of Satan, under any visible representations, or any other way, not prescribed in the Holy Scriptures." *London* [1677], Article XXII.

countless other little things that many nonconformists admitted in their worship services.[48] The Baptists certainly cared about such a charge, hence the simplicity of their services, but they were not in a position to answer it. This is where the tension between freedom and uniformity was most evident. If churches were not subject to imposed liturgies, this necessarily implied that every church would have a unique worship service. While that might have sounded fine in theory, the reality was that all Baptists had liturgical limits (infant baptism being an obvious one), and all of their limits were slightly different.[49]

The Regulative Principle versus the Normative Principle

Whereas the regulative principle held that only those things commanded in Scripture were lawful in worship, the normative principle held that any

---

48. His entire tirade is worth noting, "By your favour that is no good inference (*such a thing is not commanded, Ergo it is forbidden by the Law*) for indifferen[t] things are such as neither are commanded, nor forbidden. The standing up at the Gospell, the Nicene creed, and that of Athanasius, the sitting downe in Pewes, or Galleries at Sermon, the preaching in a high Pulpit, with Steps, Mats, Pulpit-cloth, and Cushions, and al house Glasse, are no where commanded; will it therefore follow that they are forbidden? To instance also in the Law of God, though it be true in matter of substance of Religion and points of Faith or manners, and generally in all things necessary to salvation, that what soever is not commanded is forbidden, yet in matter of circumstance, or time, place, habit, or gesture, or something that belongs to the exterior acts of Gods worship onely, that maxime holds not, for example, the setting the Psalmes to be sung to such tunes, and plaid upon such instruments, as are mentioned in the title of the Psalmes, the keeping Fasts on the fift and seventh moneth, celebrating the feasts of dedication, the reading Chapters intermingled with Psalmes, in such or such a number, or order, the lecturing on such or such dayes of the weeke, the receiving the Communion thrice a yeare, or once a moneth, the covering the Communion Table with a linnen cloth, or silke carpet, the standing of Godfathers and Godmothers at the font, nay to have a font in every Church, or to use such formes in christening, marriages, and burials, as now we use, are things not commanded by the law of God, will it follow therefore that they are forbidden?" (Featley, *Gentle Lash*, 5–6). He was mostly concerned about defending his Presbyterian practices, but nonconformists used multiple circumstances he mentioned, and Baptists used other similar circumstances not mentioned here.

49. The Independent and disciple of John Owen, Isaac Chauncy, well grasped the consequences of this freedom. He said of indifferent matters, such as posture and direction, that "every particular church" had the right to determine them, realizing "there will be as many sorts of Ceremonies as there are particular churches." But he was willing to accept that outcome because the alternative, namely Catholic uniformity, never actually achieved complete uniformity or even unity. Chauncy, *Catholick Hierarchie*, 66ff. However, he also spent a great deal of his writing attempting to convince his readers that they should adopt his personal order of ceremonies in worship.

True Worship and a New Appreciation of the Scriptures

action not forbidden by Scripture was lawful. John Owen vilified it quipping, "Teach men to observe whatever I command them; and command you them to observe whatever you think meet, so it be not contrary to my commands."[50] Baptists acknowledged the place of the normative principle, but only in matters of church government or civil law, not worship (a distinction for future study). This is where it became particularly important that baptism be considered an act of worship: it was thus subject to the rules for worship. Few Presbyterians would dare invent a doctrine simply because it wasn't forbidden in Scripture, but they were somehow willing to apply the normative principle to baptism. Barbone used the normative principle specifically to defend the practice of sprinkling. He argued that the purpose of baptism was to hold forth the death and resurrection of Christ, as well as the washing away of sin, which was just as effectively portrayed by sprinkling as total dipping. R. B. and later Spilsbury both countered that Christ's ordinance expressly demanded dipping, which as Kiffin noted earlier expressly forbid any alternative.[51] Other questions involving baptism included whether the example in Acts justified the common practice of private baptism, and whether "in the name of Jesus" or "in the name of the Father, Son, and Holy Spirit" should be used.[52]

The Lord's Supper was probably the most important illustration of this tension, and within that the act of kneeling at the presentation of the host; Westminster Assembly, for example, was asked pointedly to address that matter.[53] William Kiffin warmly remembered "the Old Nonconform-

---

50. Owen, *Discourse Concerning Liturgies*, in *Works*, 15:41–42. He later explained, "It is morally impossible that all instances of men's inventions, all that they can find out to introduce into the worship of God, at any time, in any age, and please themselves therein, should be beforehand enumerated and prohibited in their particular instances" (Owen, *Truth and Innocence Vindicated*, in *Works*, 13:481). His decision to push the argument for the normative principle into the moral realm is very striking.

51. See Barbone, *Reply to R. B.*, 20ff.; and Barbone, *Discourse Tending to Prove*, 7. More generally, Sidenham expressed the consequence of this principle, "Let this be considered, that there is nothing in all the N. T. against the baptizing of Infants, not one hint from any express word dropt from Christ or his Apostles" (Sidenham, *Christian Sober and Plain Exercitation*, 1).

52. Geree, *Vindiciae Paedo-Baptismi*, 59–60; Knollys, *Shining of a Flaming Fire in Zion*, 2. Knollys rejected private baptism and decided that either form of invocation could be used. In the open-communion debate, both Paul and Kiffin used a kind of regulative principle against Bunyan, Paul in saying that baptism was not simply a personal circumstance but an act of the church, and Kiffin in saying that the clear practice of the apostles was binding on the church. Paul, *Some Serious Reflections*, Preface (by Kiffin), 25.

53. The petition also captured the three main positions: "Some at the receiving

ists" who decided that they would rather abstain from the Lord's Supper than kneel at it: "To leave (they say) the Practice of Christ and his Apostles in the manner of Receiving the Sacrament, and to follow the Practice of Men, in a posture Invented by Men is not safe."[54] But he also came of age at a time when the regulative principle was being pushed to extremes. George Gillespie concluded, "That it is not indifferent to sit, stand, pass, or kneel, in the act of receiving the sacramental elements of the Lord's supper, because we are bound to follow the example of Christ and his apostles, who used the gesture of sitting in this holy action." Gillespie went on to add that it was equally not indifferent for the minister to hand the elements to every communicant, for the apostles passed them to one another; it was also not indifferent to repeat the words, "This is my body," or even to use plural pronouns.[55] Even Jeremiah Burroughs counseled that everyone should gather around the table just as the disciples did and follow the specific order of bless, break, pass around.[56]

---

the Elements of the Lords Supper, sayin kneeling is necessary, som warrantable, and some unwarrantable: And some say the same is Idolatrous, who shalbe judges of these differences" (*Humble Remonstrance*, 3).

54. Kiffin, *Sober Discourse*, 121. One of those nonconformists, Johnson, defined in great length the unbiblical elements of the Prayer Book: "The imposing and using of stinted devised Liturgies: The English Portuis, taken out of the Popes latine word for words (save that of a fewe of the grisest things are left out) yet keeping the same frame and order of Collectes, Psalmes, Lessons, Pater nosters, Pistles, Gospels, Versicles, Respondes, &c. Appointing holy dayes to all Sainctes and Angels, to the Virgin Marie, John Baptist, Marke, Luke, and twelve Apostles severallie: togeather with Fastes on the Eaves and on Ember dayes, Fridayes, Satterdayes & Lent: Prescribing the Ministers to pray over the dead, over the Corne and Grasse at some seasons of the yeere, and over Women at their Churching or purification: Joyninge them also to marie with the Ring, which they make a sacramentall signe: And to Baptise likewise with the signe of the Crosse, with Godfathers and Godmothers, with questions demanded of the infant that can not speake nor understande: Giving power, to Women to baptise: And ordeyning that the other Sacraments of the Lords Supper be celebrated kneeling, as when they receyve their maker: and with change of the Words of Christs institution, taking in steed of them, the wordes of the Popes Masse booke, translated into English" (cited in Jacob, *Defence of the Churches and Ministery of England*, 17–18). Johnson went on to declare that when a church commanded an act in worship, it implied to the people that such an act was connected with salvation. Consequently, forcing people to kneel or use the sign of the cross was not indifferent but evil. Cited in Bradshaw, *Unreasonablenesse of the separation*, not paginated. Bradshaw, who did not think it was lawful to impose a ceremony, nonetheless thought that kneeling was an exception because it accurately reflected the appropriate humility and reverence for the moment. Bradshaw, *Several Treatises of Worship and Ceremonies*, not paginated.

55. ". . . as we prove from John 13:12; from Matt. 20:20, with 26; Mark 14:18, with 22" (Gillespie, *Dispute Against the English Popish Ceremonies*, 433, 431, 443ff.).

56. Burroughs, *Gospel-Worship*, 264–65. Barbone followed the same argument to

True Worship and a New Appreciation of the Scriptures

London Particular Baptists acknowledged that certain gestures, offerings, and consecrations were justifiable with respect to worship, and they accepted an explicit command given in the New Testament or a clear example of apostolic practice for their use.[57] But they were unwilling to declare knowledge of the mind of Christ with respect to the biblical example of the Last Supper considering the disagreements floating around London. Consequently, the Particular Baptists as a group did not speak much to the ceremony of the Lord's Supper. The First London Confession did not address it *at all*. They simply could not speak beyond that of which they were certain. Not surprisingly, circumstances of the Lord's Supper would be a factor in later Baptist controversies, and hints of disintegration should already be quite evident. Bunyan could find no command or example of abstaining from the Lord's Supper rather than partake of it in a potentially mixed communion with unbaptized people. Keach even accused such Baptists of slighting the Lord's Supper—itself a clear violation of Scripture.[58] Disagreements over the proper use of Scripture highlighted by its use in worship would become increasingly problematic for these men.

That did not stop the later Baptists from continuing to proclaim a strict interpretation of Scripture in worship. Hercules Collins's imagined

---

its opposite conclusion. He said, "I reason in like case thus, if they eat the Supper in an upper Chamber, or at night, or leaning, the conclusion would be alike to no purpose" (Barbone, *Reply to R. B.*, 27). In other words, that example could never prove that it was meant to be enjoined on all churches.

57. At the end of the century, Cary explicitly noted that "we conceive, that the Example of the Apostles, which hath not a meer temporary Reason, is enough to prove that Institution from God, to which that Practice doth relate." Cary, *Solemn Call*, 72. Tombes, for one, granted the difference between natural worship, which God put into the hearts of all men, and instituted worship, which God expressed in Scripture. He categorized its actions as "inward worship of the soule, as trusting in it, loving it, fearing it, magnifying and extolling of it in their hearts, or outward worship, as by gesture of the body, kneeling, falling downe before it, bowing, lifting up the hands or eyes, kissing, or by offering of gifts, bringing oblation, incense, sacrifice, first fruits, tithes, or by swearing by them, praying to them, making vowes to them, blessing them, singing Hymnes in their praise, consecrating Temples, making Priests, keeping holy dayes to them, (for all these are religious worship)." Tombes, *Jehovah Jireh*, 2–3.

58. See Keach, *Golden Mine Opened*, 24; and Keach, *Laying on of Hands*, 77–78. Kiffin noted that the practice of open-communion accomplished the same with respect to baptism. Kiffin, *Sober Discourse*, 13. More famously, the hymn-singing controversy (see chapter 6) began with Keach leading his church to sing a hymn at the close of the Lord's Supper. "Did not Christ sing an Hymn after the Supper? Would he have left that as a Pattern to us, and annexed it to such a pure Gospel-Ordinance, had it been a Ceremony, and only belonging to the Jewish Worship?" (Keach, *Breach Repaired*, 73).

nonconformist informed a conformist friend that the material difference between them was,

> Christ and his Apostles sate at Supper, you kneel (and impose it) they did it most probably often, yet seldom they did Communicate in the Evening, you at Noon; they break the Bread, you cut it, you License Men to Administer Sacraments, that have no Gift to preach, instead whereof, read only a Homily, we have no Command nor president for such a Practice.[59]

Collins's matter-of-fact tone strongly implies that his church indeed observed those circumstances of sitting and breaking bread in the evening. Keach pointed out that some interpreted Christ's example to mean they should observe the Lord's Supper only in private in families. They also assumed that everyone present would partake of the Supper, though that was nowhere commanded.[60] There was no end to the variations. Jessey's warning resounded, "That if exact Practice be required, and clearness in Gospel-Institution before Communion; who dare be so bold as to say his hands are clean, and that he hath done all the Lord Commands, as to Institutions in his Worship?"[61]

With the passage of time, some Baptists better appreciated the use of Scripture in worship, but with one very important nonnegotiable. While the normative principle might apply to civil government, business, and countless other areas, it could never apply to God's worship in God's church. Powell captured the consequences, "If there be such a latitude granted in things relating to the Worship of God, that any thing that is not forbidden may bee introduced, what can hinder the Papists to bring in their five new Sacraments, Organs, Kneeling at the Sacrament, and a hundred such things, nay a Pope?"[62] Catholics and Anglicans used "Crucifixes, Beads, Altars, Praying to the Saints, Pictures in Churches, Pilgrimages, . . . Bowing at the Name of Jesus; the Cross in Baptism; Surplices in

---

59. Collins, *Some Reasons for Separation*, 13.

60. Keach, *Breach Repaired*, 100–101.

61. Cited in Bunyan, *Differences in Judgment*, 116–17. Williams offered the most interesting consequence of the regulative principle in this matter when he asked, "Since you both seem to magnifie the Seales of Baptisme, and the Lords Supper with a difference and excellency above other Ordinances, We Querie where the Lord Jesus appointed such a difference and distinction?" (Williams, *Queries of highest Consideration*, 11). Early Particular Baptists seemed to agree with him.

62. Powell, *Common-Prayer-Book no Divine Service*, 8, 9. Kiffin commented that Owen made a similar argument at a similar time. Kiffin, *Sober Discourse*, 4.

Preaching; Kneeling at the Sacrament; set forms of Prayer"[63]—nowhere forbidden in Scripture—to an end alien to Particular Baptists. They agreed with Bradshaw that the power to create a form of worship was the power to invent a brand new religion.[64]

A Gradual Discovery: Competing Interpretations of Scripture in Worship[65]

The relationship between worship and hermeneutics proves to be one of the strongest illustrations of the importance of pure worship to the early English Baptists. In brief, these Baptists were willing limit communion or cooperation with one another based on matters of worship, especially when they revolved around a direct interpretation of Scripture. Most in English authority blamed the new sectarianism on the notion that one could interpret God's Rule for himself or herself. Ussher lumped the Baptists in with the Libertines and accused them of rejecting the Word for a supposed word directly from the Spirit; Archbishop George Abbot accused the Baptists of being "unlearned men that seeke to make up a religion out of your owne heads."[66] While some Baptists certainly did so (and eventually became Seekers or Quakers), the rest still drew conclusions from the Bible so at odds with established theology that it must have seemed to authorities as if they were rejecting the Word. Thomas Edwards complained that the sectaries first pulled down images and then spoke ill of Mary, that they removed bishops and then wanted no hierarchy, that they cast out ceremonies and then "cast out the Sacraments," and that they removed the feast days and then ignored the Lord's Day. He actually looked longingly at the days of stricter control when worship was at least predictable.[67]

The Limits of Cooperation

I have already described some of the reasons why Baptists believed they could separate from the established church, focusing on corruptions in

63. Cary, *Solemn Call*, 88.
64. Bradshaw, *Several Treatises of Worship and Ceremonies*, 10.
65. See Keach, *Laying on of Hands*, The Epistle Dedicatory.
66. Ussher, *Body of Divinity*, 361; White, "Samuel Eaton, Particular Baptist Pioneer," 10. Abbot was speaking to Eaton directly.
67. *Gangraena*, The Preface. By 1660, committed Puritans had agreed.

worship. Consequently, the more a church emphasized worship, the more likely it was to isolate itself from other churches. But Grantham also thought those churches that tried to avoid the issue altogether by separating as he would say the husk (the ordinances) from the kernel (the spirit) would inevitably experience their own breach in order as members began to question whether a matter of worship belonged to the husk or the kernel.[68] Owen tried to unite Protestants around a faith based on the revealed truths of the Bible, but every way he described that unity came back to a "desire to know the will of God, and to worship him according to his mind," which was the very source of controversy.[69] Any way they looked outside their own churches, early Baptists had to cooperate with individuals or churches who did not entirely agree with them on matters of worship.

In the beginning, this cooperation was possible. London Particular Baptists shared a common antagonist and had spent time together developing common convictions. This is more evident considering they were not the only baptizers in London. Edward Barber, as has been mentioned, practiced the laying on of hands (and love feasts), a ceremony that hallmarked some General Baptists and provided a visible distinction between them and other Baptists.[70] Particular Baptists achieved their own association by avoiding any more talk of worship than absolutely necessary. Their first confession of faith treated ceremonies, such as the Lord's Supper, very sparsely if at all. But when the time came to write a second confession, a

68. Grantham, *Sigh for Peace,* 88–89. He noted that this approach inevitably led to Quakerism.

69. Owen, *Vindication of the Animadversions on "Fiat Lux,"* in *Works,* 14:278, 257ff. Perhaps the most shocking call to unity came from Isaac Chauncy in 1681. He said that unity should not "trouble and distract their walk, and interrupt their Worship, with the *Newfangled, Multifarious, Brain-sick Laws* of Men, in instituted Worship, nor [place] Uniformity in a heap of *busie, nonsense Ceremonies.*" Instead, unity should be determined thus: "That all Churches *walk by the same rule* of the revealed Will of Christ, and subject themselves to his Laws and Governments, that they be *uniform* in all that he hath made necessary to be *believed* and *practised,* as in all things *necessary to Salvation,* and a *Christians edification* in matters of Communion, as in the word, Sacraments, Prayer, singing Psalms, &c." He admitted that "though there may be some small differences in their Interpretation of those Laws determining thing necessary, and the Exercise of discretion in things *Expedient,* because of dubious and difficult circumstances attending, yet all agree in the *main things* required by Christ, for the way of *Salvation,* and the main *conditions* of Communion." Chauncy, *Catholick Hierarchie,* 73. It is hard to see how Chauncy believed he solved the problem.

70. Edwards noted a meeting at Bishopsgate in 1645 in which Barber laid hands on eighty people, perhaps the first church meeting employing this ceremony. *Gangraena,* 1:45.

generation of worship practices had developed (not to mention the influence of the Westminster Confession and its emphasis on right ceremony), thus they had to be more specific and more cautious.

William Kiffin, reflecting on the open-communion debate, remarked that unity through charity was a blessed thing tending to Christ's glory, "but care must be had in the first place, to observe the Rules given by our great Lord, and to walk according to them, and not for Communion sake to leap over the Order Jesus Christ hath Prescribed in his Word."[71] The perception, probably based on reality, was that the Baptists would not cooperate with anyone who did not agree with them about the ordinances; Jessey had warned, "And that they are weak [the Independent churches], and are more, then there are of those of late baptized; and these are offended at this distance, in denying Communion to such."[72] This made Baptists near-impossible partners for any kind of essential interchurch cooperation. To their credit, Particular Baptists attempted to build some bridges with their confessions, and historians have treated them as more willing partners than other groups of Baptists. Nonetheless, the Independent Isaac Chauncy complained about all Baptists, "But if they make for themselves Rules of Worship which Christ never made, and make their Erring and Sinful Rites (such as are so to us) the standing and unalterable conditions of Communion, we can't communicate with them, by what ever Names such Churches are call'd."[73] Their limit of cooperation was made manifest in worship.

All sides accused the others of false worship based on a false interpretation of the Scriptures. Praisegod Barbone accused the Baptists of turning baptism into an idol and "no Ordinance of *Jesus Christ* at all; [but] error according to their owne ground."[74] Spilsbury countered that the whole point of the New Testament was the administration of the new covenant, and those under its order and ordinances "are the onely true-borne heires of all that is contained in the said new Covenant."[75] Although he was

---

71. Paul, *Some Serious Reflections*, Preface (by Kiffin).

72. Jessey, *Storehouse of Provision*, 102–3.

73. Chauncy, *Theological Dialogue*, 19. That same year, Grantham declared, "But now, for ample or full Communion, I see not how that can be attained and maintained, but where there is antecedent to it, an Union both in Doctrine and Practice, in things necessary to the true Constitution and Government of the Church of Christ" (Grantham, *Loyal Baptist*, 15). Perhaps Chauncy was complaining more about other Baptists than Particular Baptists.

74. Barbone, *Discourse Tending to Prove*, 7.

75. Spilsbury, *Gods Ordinance*, 9.

more concerned about keeping distance from those who refused to give the New Testament sole authority over the ordinances, he also believed that anyone who minimized the ordinances in any way did not truly understand the Gospel, which shared its order and ordinances with the new covenant—this is very important to keep in mind for the next chapter. Jessey believed that infant baptism violated the Second Commandment because it replaced circumcision with a human invention, "making the likeness of things of their own contrivance, of force with Institutions in the Worship of God." But he warned the Baptists that they came dangerously close to the same sin in their emphasis of believers' baptism, not only in rejecting good Christians for want of light in baptism but also in overlooking clear gospel commands for communion in their search for an example of a church that rejected an unbaptized Christian.[76] Not only did Thomas Paul not deny the danger in such handling of the Scriptures, he further lamented that some Baptists had left their churches because they could find no biblical mandate for preaching "by Method, Doctrine, Reason, and Use" or for restricting "the Administration of breaking Bread [to] perticular persons, by Church appointment."[77]

Churches with surviving records verified numerous divisions over matters of worship, especially during the unsettled Interregnum (until persecution began again in 1660). In 1653, the Baptist church at Fenstanton disciplined a couple for having their infant baptized in an established ceremony. The church at Westby accused Fenstanton of hypocrisy for refusing to join them in worship because Westby did not practice the laying on of hands, and yet received individuals in worship sharing Westby's belief. The church at Norborow warned Fenstanton about a man who had left them because they did not practice all six principles of Hebrews 6 in worship.[78] The Western Association, under the influence of Thomas Collier, declared that the laying on of hands was "no ground of the breach of communion amongst or in the churches" and that no individual could leave a church

---

76. Cited in Bunyan, *Differences in Judgment*, 112, 120.

77. Paul, *Some Serious Reflections*, 11–12.

78. *Fenstanton*, 59ff. This was the same year that Jessey wrote to Hexham specifically to counsel them to show charity with respect to the six principles. Not all movement was related to worship, of course. Fenstanton lost members for disagreeing with John Denne, for prioritizing the spiritual meaning of the Scripture, for placing one's personal experience above the text, and for claiming to receive further revelation. Ibid., 341ff., 87ff. The latter were likely related to the Quakers; chapter 6 will explain the relationship between the Baptists, Quakers, and worship.

True Worship and a New Appreciation of the Scriptures

while in agreement over "the essentials of worship."[79] In 1654, the church at Westby split over whether or not there should be a love feast directly before the Lord's Supper. The church at Wisbeach heard instruction from Joseph Wright that those under laying on of hands should separate from those not under it. One-third of the church at Littleport rejected all ordinances and became Quakers. The church at Caxton Pastures nearly split over whether or not they should pray about the unpardonable sin during service. Mistrust was so high that a group of churches near Cambridge decided that their members should only travel carrying a certificate of approval from their home church. In 1656, the church at Wakerly split over the issue of the six principles.[80] The Midlands Association formally declared that their church members could not join in established worship or listen to any unbaptized person preach. In 1657, Tombes' church at Leominster filed a complaint that some members had left to form a new church, likely over closed-communion; the Association concluded those members had liberty so to do.[81]

Hints of Disintegration: The Six Principles

The six principles of Hebrews 6, featured so prominently in the preceding paragraph, deserve special note as an intersection of biblical interpretation, worship, and division. In 1648, Edward Barber wrote against Edmund Calamy that a church was to be gathered "as planted in the primitive times, to wit, by repentance from dead works, faith towards God, the doctrin of dippings, & imposition of hands, as Heb. 6. 1. 2. it being according to the great Charter of the Gospel of Christ and primitive practise."[82] All Baptists

---

79. White, *Association Records*, 54ff. In other words, any individual willing to divide a church over a circumstance such as the laying on of hands was not welcome in their association. In doing so, Collier tried to get in front of the problems facing nearby associations.

80. *Fenstanton*, 136ff., 202ff.

81. White, *Association Records*, 25, 33, 146. Without realizing it, White had elsewhere listed four liturgical factors as the main reasons why churches separated. rebaptism on the grounds of false doctrine, fellowship with Seventh-Day Baptists, mixed communion, and laying on of hands. He argued that only extreme circumstances could overcome the Baptists' need for associations between churches. White, "The Frontiers of Fellowship Between English Baptists," 249–54.

82. Barber, *Declaration and Vindication of the Carriage of Edward Barber*, not paginated. He further cited Acts 2:38–43; Acts 8:12, 36–38; and Acts 10:46–48, each of which only mentioned baptism. The other two principles were the belief in the resurrection of the dead and the eternal judgment. John Bunyan helpfully described what

135

held five of the six; laying hands on all believers at baptism would prove to be the divisive principle. Many General Baptists adopted the practice as normative for all true churches, whereas many Particular Baptists followed Spilsbury in declaring that the laying on of hands was reserved for the apostles.[83] William Kiffin issued a very recognizable argument against the practice: "For any to practise any thing as an Ordinance of God without a command from God, or particular revelation from God, is unlawfull, or Will-worship. But to practice Imposition of hands as an Ordinance of God is unlawful and Wil-worship."[84] His debate against Peter Chamberlain on the subject exposed a number of hermeneutical differences, mainly with respect to Chamberlain's belief that Hebrews 6 did issue such a command. Kiffin argued that Hebrews 6 only established doctrine, not practice; Chamberlain countered that the Bible could not support such a false distinction. Kiffin then surprisingly argued that if the apostles' practices were implicit commands, then all Christians should write Scripture, heal the sick, and raise the dead. Chamberlain quickly reminded him that the same logic was used against baptism, church meetings, and women receiving the Lord's Supper.[85] This issue became a locus for competing interpretations of Scripture in worship.

John Griffith, an important supporter of the practice, clarified it as laying hands upon newly baptized believers to receive the Holy Spirit.[86]

---

was meant by the doctrine of dipping (which he simply called baptism) as "that which by the outward sign is presented to us, or which by the outward circumstance of the act is preached to the believer." Bunyan, *Confession of my Faith*, 97. Note the common assumption of Pauline authorship of Hebrews, as in Grantham, *Paedo-Baptists Apology*, 99.

83. See Spilsbury, *Gods Ordinance*, 11. Collier, also an opposer of the practice, said, "We must distinguish between Precepts, Presidents, and Exhortations given forth to believers upon a common and ordinary account, as to believers, such as may be practised as the effects and fruits of the faith of the Gospel," and concluded that the practice of laying hands was a president [precedent] viable only in the power of the apostles. Collier, *Right Constitution*, 81.

84. *Discourse Between Cap. Kiffin, and Dr. Chamberlain, About Imposition of Hands*, 3–4. Danvers later used a similar argument against laying hands saying, "1. That to every Ordinance of Christ there must be some plain positive word of Institution to Confirm it. 2. To practice any thing in the worship of God, for an Ordinance of his, without an Institution, is Will-worship and Superstition." Thomas Grantham, a General Baptist who supported the practice, easily retorted that the word "plain" was a slippery slope for Danvers to use. See Grantham, *The Fourth Principle of Christs Doctrine Vindicated*, 11.

85. *A Discourse Between Cap. Kiffin, and Dr. Chamberlain*, 10, 18.

86. Griffith, *Gods Oracle & Christs Doctrine*, 37ff.

True Worship and a New Appreciation of the Scriptures

Thomas Grantham stated that its purpose was "to Confirm the Baptized, and orderly to admit into the Church." It was performed between a Christian's baptism and his or her first Lord's Supper by anyone authorized to perform a baptism.[87] By 1680, it had become a distinct ceremony with a liturgy on par with baptism itself:

> Christ's Ministers laying their hands solemnly upon the Head of the Baptised, with Prayer to Almighty God for an increase of the Graces and Gifts of the Holy Ghost, to inable us to hold fast the Faith which we now visibly own, having entred into the Church by Holy Baptism, and also be helped thereby to maintain a constant War against the World, Flesh, and the Devil.[88]

Benjamin Keach ultimately placed the laying on of hands in the category of progressive illumination: "God gradually discovers Himself, and the true Order and Form of his House and Worship."[89] Everyone was bound to walk according to the light he possessed; eventually God would reveal the truth of Hebrews 6 to all sincere Christians, who would be at that time bound to observe them.

The laying on of hands and baptism played parallel roles in church and in worship, especially with respect to church communion (and enjoyed parallel if sometimes contradictory arguments, as for the Baptists who made a biblical argument for closed communion with respect to baptism and an equivalent argument for open communion with respect to laying on of hands). For Grantham, it was a simple matter of interpreting Hebrews 6: either all six principles were essential to a church constitution or none were. Laying on of hands was a universal primitive practice. It could not be a mere figure or type because that argument would invalidate baptism.[90] When Henry Danvers argued that laying on of hands had been corrupted and lacked a plain institution of Christ, Grantham noted that that exact argument had been made against believers' baptism by

---

87. Grantham, *Fourth Principle*, 10. He cited Hebrews 6:2, Acts 8:17, and Acts 19:2.

88. Collins, *Orthodox Catechism*, 34. Collins was one of several Particular Baptists who adopted the practice, perhaps under the influence of his friend Benjamin Keach. It is noteworthy that the Heidelberg Catechism, upon which Collins based this work, said nothing about the laying on of hands.

89. Keach, *Laying on of Hands*, The Epistle Dedicatory. In a fascinating twist, this particular argument echoed an earlier one given in support of the *Book of Common Prayer*, namely that Old Testament worship slowly evolved over the centuries and New Testament worship should be open to the same kind of development. See Canne, *Necessitie of Separation*, 85ff.

90. Grantham, *Sigh for Peace*, 23–29, 83.

immersion. Either the argument was true of both or of neither.[91] Benjamin Keach also responded to Danvers's book by arguing that the examples in Acts 8:17, Acts 19:6, and Hebrews 6:1–2 were as clear as necessary to provide an express command, "For as every Person is actually to repent, believe, and be baptized, so each one ought to come under the practice of Laying on of hands, it being of the same extent, nature and quality with the other, and joined to them."[92]

There should be no confusion why this issue was so explosively disruptive. It followed a nearly identical biblical and liturgical argument as baptism, yet not all Baptists held to it. In *The Searchers for Schism Search'd* (a book Keach believed had not been answered in his lifetime), John Griffith railed that one of the authors of *The Searchers for Schism* had recently undergone the ordinance of hands and soon after repudiated it. Griffith issued the ultimatum that those who fell short of Christ by one principle but still expected to be recognized as a true church should extend the same grace to those churches who fell a different principle short, namely those practicing infant baptism.[93] As further proof of the divisive nature of worship, Griffith said that the burden fell on the one who rejected laying on of hands to initiate reconciliation: "except you repent, and receive the truth candidly in the love of it, until then we have reason to reject you."[94] Just as Particular Baptists could not maintain an essential

91. This is not to mention that the biblical arguments were quite amplified by unbiblical rhetoric. "How hard a thing it is to bring those Sacred Truths of the Gospel to their due Use and Estimation in the Church, which have been abused by the Corruption of the Ages past, those cannot be ignorant, whose Lot it hath been to Labour in that glorious Undertaking, which yet is more particularly made manifest at this time by a late Book Intituled, *Treatise of Laying on of Hands*; wherein the Churches adhearing to that Principle, are not only represented to the World as founded in Sin, Schism, Errour, and Ignorance, By Mr. D. But the Principle it self also rendred Erronious" (Grantham, *Fourth Principle*, 1).

92. Keach, *Laying on of Hands*, 53–54, cf. 39–74. He argued, because Christ instituted the practice, corruptions accumulated over the centuries made no difference, just as with baptism or the Lord's Supper.

93. "Will resolving to do the Will of God when known in a fundamental, give you the esteem of a Church of Christ rightly Constituted? if you, then it will give others we hope in your eyes the like esteem that are short of you in one principle of Christs Doctrine, as you are of us in another; and if so, then ought you to esteem those in the *Presbyterian* and *Independant* way, especially those of them that believe Christ died for all, as you do" (Griffith, *Searchers for Schism Search'd*, 6; cf. ibid, The Epistle; Keach, *Laying on of Hands*, The Epistle Dedicatory).

94. Griffith, *Searchers for Schism Search'd*, 101–2. Just two years later, Grantham wrote, "You see then Brethren, that we lay the ground of our Non-communion with you more upon your *opposing* the truth we hold, than upon your *non-submission* to it" (Grantham, *Sigh for Peace*, 94).

True Worship and a New Appreciation of the Scriptures

unity with the Presbyterians or Independents for their want of believers' baptism by immersion, those under the laying on of hands could not with anyone else for their want of the same. The laying on of hands was just as essential as believers' baptism by immersion to the constitution of a true church.[95]

This is why worship was so disintegrative to the early Baptists. Every practice which they thought had biblical mandate or precedent became a just cause for separation, and those who did not agree with them were accused of harboring "poor conceits and Notions, as if the word of God came out from them"[96] and them only, all the while being open to that same charge potentially on the same practice. Grantham thought Christ's liturgy was so simple in the Jerusalem church, "Christ's own Institution of his Holy Table, and the holy Prayer which he had taught his Disciples, with other Heavenly Rules contained in the Holy Scriptures, was abundantly sufficient, and are so still, to every Faithful Man of God."[97] Yet the "other" heavenly rules proved utterly unstable. He believed that a true church was maintained "according to the pristine Simplicity of the Gospel, without the mixtures of Legal Ceremonies, or humane Innovations"[98] but could not comprehend that the full ceremony of laying on of hands might be such a humane innovation. As for the Particular Baptists, Benjamin Keach brought with him a commitment to the practice from his early days as a General Baptist. While most of his experience will be left for chapter 6, it is germane to note that though the Second London Confession (or for that matter the First) said nothing about laying hands on baptized believers, Keach's revision of the document did. His article XXIII, left for his own church, called the practice "an Ordinance of Christ, and ought to be submitted unto by all such Persons that are admitted to partake of the Lord's Supper."[99] Not surprisingly, a number of London Particular Baptists found Keach's church isolated and uncooperative.

---

95. Grantham, *Sigh for Peace*, 114–16. Ironically, in these pages he listed the reasons why churches should *not* separate from one another.

96. Grantham, *Paedo-Baptists Apology*, 69–70.

97. Grantham, *Hear the Church*, 11–12.

98. Grantham, *Second Part of the Apology*, 13.

99. Keach, *Articles of the Faith of the Church of Christ, Or Congregation meeting at Horsley-down*, 23. He believed strongly that all six principles were fundamental to church communion and foundation. Keach, *Gold Refin'd*, 175.

A Further Reformation from Doctrine to Worship

Keeping in mind the tension between freedom and uniformity, Particular Baptists seemed comfortable with a certain amount of disagreement on biblical matters. They saw themselves, to use Kiffin's term, as "a furtherance rather then a disturbance" of the Reformation.[100] As such, they knew that all parties would not progress at the same rate in their light of the Scriptures, just as they were a step ahead in the process with respect to baptism. However, this claim was made by every group of Baptists holding a variant belief: they were a step ahead on the road to reformation, so to speak, and everyone else needed to accelerate. This image was startlingly effective. Edward Barber used it to justify his earliest steps; he approved of the reforms under Edward VI but claimed the responsibility of continuing it: "we having received more talents, or a greater measure of knowledge, it cannot be but the Lord requires an answerable obedience."[101] Hanserd Knollys sought to encourage his church by interpreting the entire book of Revelation as a description of how the false church persecuted the true church because of their true worship, where "these victors continued in the true and pure Worship of God, according to the Institutions of our Lord Jesus Christ."[102] As the London Particular Baptist association began to disintegrate, Philip Cary called out to them to stay their course, "And therefore so it is, that in these last Ages, when the Reformation first began to be set on foot in the World, the *Doctrinal* part of the Gospel was first notably cleared up, whilst yet there remained a very great Corruption in point of *Discipline*, or in respect of the Primitive Purity of *Gospel-Worship*."[103]

These Baptists saw their task as a furtherance of the great and necessary task of reformation. Just as the continental Reformers endured hardship and division, so would they, but their search for pure worship was no less important than the earlier search for pure doctrine and worth no less sacrifice. Nothing less than the very honor of God and the obedience of all believers were at stake. These Particular Baptists desired to maintain

---

100. Kiffin, *Briefe Remonstrance*, 7. Brooks recognized the role of the idea of ongoing reformation in the hymn-singing controversy, as chapter 6 will explain. He saw that as proof of the importance of worship practices to the disputants but due to his limited scope was not able to connect it with the wider Baptist tradition. See Brooks, "Benjamin Keach and the Baptist Singing Controversy," 27ff.

101. Barber, *Small Treatise of Baptisme*, Preface. He used a similar motivation in *A Declaration and Vindication* that he was called not to follow the Reformers but Christ.

102. Knollys, *Exposition Of the Revelation*, esp. 190. Note the continuity of his emphases expressed in *The World that Now is*.

103. Cary, *Solemn Call*, 73.

True Worship and a New Appreciation of the Scriptures

unity throughout the process of reformation, as much to prove themselves through their love as to protect themselves from heresy, but not at the cost of disobeying the extent of their light.[104] The same Anglicans who had rejected the popish practices of crucifixes, beads, praying to the Saints, icons, and pilgrimages had retained bowing at the name of Jesus, signing the cross in baptism, wearing the surplice in preaching, and kneeling at the Lord's Supper.[105] The same Presbyterians who had rejected those latter practices had retained the church hierarchy, a directory of worship, infant baptism, and compulsory church attendance and tithes. The Baptists saw inconsistency therein and wanted to practice a consistent application of Scripture in their worship because they desired true reverence for God and true humility before Him. Worship was the highest privilege given to man and the ultimate proof of God's goodness that He would reveal true worship. In gratitude and awe, the Baptists resolved that they would "not neglect the good using of that light which God hath already given us, under pretence of waiting for more, 1 *Cor.* 13. 9. *Acts.* 18. 25."[106] William Kiffin drew together all of the Baptists' convictions when he concluded,

> For Gospel Order setled by Apostolical Authority and Direction, as this [believers' baptism by immersion] was, hath not lost

---

104. Surprisingly, Thomas Grantham made the most hospitable claim, "And yet we know, and indeed must confess, that many Things, as to the more convenient performance of Religious Services in a Church-way, are left to the Prudence of the Church, guided therein by the general Rules in the Word of God; and some Things also (which are not of the Essence of Christianity) will seem doubtful to some, and clear to others. And therefore there will be a continual Necessity of brotherly Forbearance one towards another, in some sinless Ceremonies, as many Things may be so esteemed, whilst not made the Boundaries of Communion, and forced upon Christians against their Consciences. For Example: tho Sitting be the most safe Gesture at the Lord's Table, because nearest to Christ's Example; yet if any in Humility, and of Devotion to God, think it their Duty to receive kneeling, this surely cannot justly offend any Christian. And thus also bowing at the Name of Jesus, being left at liberty, when, where, and upon what occasion the Conscience of a Christian may be most pressed to do it, need not offend any, tho it is apparent such bowing is not the meaning of the Text, Phil. 2. 10. And the same may be said of well-composed Prayers; so that still such Forms be used as a matter of Christian Liberty, and not imposed by Law as necessary" (Grantham, *Second Part of the Apology*, 10–11). It is uncertain which is more surprising—that Grantham would be suddenly generous with respect to worship or that he would be specifically generous with respect to those practices most abhorred by Baptists.

105. Cary, *Solemn Call*, 88.

106. Cox, *Appendix to a Confession of Faith*, 11. Kiffin admonished about their light, "there being nothing that intrencheth more upon the Wisdom of God, than that (when he hath prescribed a method in his Word), men should presume to alter or change the same." Kiffin, *Sober Discourse*, 35–36.

any of its native worth and efficacy, or obliging Vertue, by any Disuse or Discontinuance occasioned by any, but ought to be the same to us now, as it was to them in the beginning of such Order; especially considering the day wherein we live, many indeavouring to bring in their own Inventions into the Worship of God, which should make all Christians be more careful and Zealous to Cleave to the Institutions of Jesus Christ, as they were first Delivered by the holy Penmen, and the Practice of the Primitive Christians.[107]

God's Word revealed God's worship to all men. It also revealed God's gospel of salvation. London Particular Baptists realized an intersection and interdependence of the two that for a time set them apart from all other English Christians.

---

107. Kiffin, *Sober Discourse*, 58–59.

five

Gospel Worship and a New Purpose of the Gathering

THE BEAUTY AND SPLENDOR OF GOSPEL WORSHIP: A LITURGICAL THEOLOGY[1]

Perhaps the most significant claim of this book will be that London Particular Baptists used the gospel as a liturgical hermeneutic even if they may not have been fully intentional about (or even aware of) such a practice. They took very seriously the form and presentation of the Gospel in their worship services in more than just their preaching. All of the ecclesiological and hermeneutical considerations heretofore expressed will come into play in this chapter as the Baptists put their own stamp on the basic elements and functions of instituted congregational worship. Their investments in these practices will demonstrate how important pure worship was to them, particularly in their developing theology of gathering, of ceremonies, of spirituality, of preaching, and of too-often-overlooked family worship. This can be seen not only in their writings but also in observations made about them; the indirect evidence offers some very compelling corroboration. In some ways, Baptists were very close to other non-conformists, and yet their trajectory pointed them down a very

---

1. See Tombes, *Fermentum Pharisaeorum*, 6, as opposed to darkened will–worship.

different path; the final chapter will explain why that path never came to full fruition.

Henry Ainsworth summarized all Separatist priorities in worship when he said that "the Sacraments ought to be administred according to the simplicity of the Gospell, without any Popish or other abuses in either Sacrament." Granted, Ainsworth was referring to the entire New Testament rather than the "gospel message" (although he absolutely cared about the church presenting a clear message of salvation),[2] but a number of nonconformists began to make the connection between the pure worship of the primitive church and the saving knowledge of Jesus Christ. While this might seem obvious, note that the establishmentarian mentality came with a heinous side-effect: Thomas Edwards, not alone among Presbyterians or Anglicans, said that he would rather have civil order and uniformity of worship than the guarantee of salvation. Toleration was "the grand designe of the Devil," and England's best hope for peace and success lay in "securing and preserving the Reformed Religion, professed and maintained in the Reformed Churches."[3] Baptists thought exactly the opposite; they would risk or even embrace liturgical chaos for the opportunity to share a pure gospel with an uncoerced heart. Because they lived within the tension between a free church's worship and the apostolic church's worship, they uniquely considered the connection between instituted worship and the message of salvation—even John Owen did not address this subject—because it defined so exceptionally all of their priorities in obedience to God.

2. *Apologie or Defence of Such True Christians as are commonly (but uniustly) called Brownists*, 73. The title page was anonymous, but the preface to the king was written by unnamed leaders of the English church in Amsterdam. Ainsworth later wrote to the Church of England, "For, though I doubt not but the doctrine of your church hath saved many: yet that is Gods extraordinary blessing, not the ordinary effects of your church" (Ainsworth, *Counterpoyson*, 11).

3. *Gangraena*, 1:60/2. Edwards was not being damnably callous about the destiny of his opponents (although he did not care at all for the dissenters); he simply assumed that he taught truth and everyone else taught heresy. He argued that toleration of any man to worship according to novel or non-Christian standards was unheard of in the Old Testament, and it was ridiculous that men had begun to argue contrary allowances in the present, specifically noting Jeremiah Burroughs, the Seeker John Saltmarsh (who influenced a number of Baptists), and Williams's *Bloudy Tenent*. Ibid., 1:59–61/2. Furthermore, both the Anglicans and Presbyterians had an innate universalism in their approach to their churches, that participating in the life of the church was itself the key step toward salvation. In other words, Edwards thought that his prescribed order was part and parcel with salvation. Defending his book, he described it as "a Book of so much truth, that I believe no Book written this hundred years, having so much variety and particularity in it, will be found to have more." Ibid., 1:36.

The Gospel as a Liturgical Hermeneutic

The concept of a liturgical hermeneutic is as ubiquitous as it is elusive. Just as individuals, knowingly or unknowingly, approach their interpretation of Scripture according to a set of rules so also do they approach worship. On the one hand, a liturgical hermeneutic is the principle by which a worshiper understands and shapes worship; on the other hand, it is also a principle by which a worshiper interprets his or her own faith. It can be used to answer two questions: what belief does a church's practice of worship communicate, and what should a church practice in worship in order to communicate its express belief? To call the gospel a liturgical hermeneutic simply means that Baptists considered and intended their worship to communicate and embody the gospel of Jesus Christ.[4] They employed nothing like the sophisticated methods of modern anthropologists and liturgists; they simply were committed both to the New Testament and the basic message and experience of salvation.[5] As has been explained, their freedom was limited by the Lordship of Christ (although they could not agree on everything Christ commanded), and they struggled with the balance between an individual church's authority to establish its own principles of worship and their responsibility to limit their association with potentially false worship. Nonetheless, some of these early Baptists found the answer to all of their questions in the gospel.

John Tombes and John Spilsbury embarked on similar paths in their early publications on worship, and both realized a connection between worship and the gospel in a primitive kind of hermeneutic. Understandably,

---

4. In some ways, this is what Chapell intended to do in his *Christ-Centered Worship*, although he ultimately recapitulated basic Genevan and Westminsterian ideas and thus is not an accurate reference point for what the Baptists attempted. Whereas Chapell started with the human tendency toward ritualism and filled it with historic liturgical resources (which he arbitrarily chose), the Baptists attempted to recapitulate the gospel in its purest simplicity. That the Baptists ultimately failed must receive consideration, but that is beyond the scope of this book.

5. Liturgical theology is a small field, and liturgical hermeneutics is even smaller. It originally focused on underlying structures of worship as proposed by Dix, *Shape of the Liturgy*. More recently it has come to emphasize the rituals themselves as anthropologists have realized how important such behavior is to community and identity; two examples of this method include Moore-Keish, *Do This in Remembrance of Me*; and Anderson, "Worship and Belief: Liturgical Practice as a Contextual Theology," 432–52, both of which investigated how individual church members understood and responded to the ritual of the Eucharist. A third method emerged from the speech-act theory of John Austin and Paul Ricoeur, which accurately argued that the "act" of speech is far more complex than the words spoken.

Tombes was far more analytical, although his conclusions were powerfully simple. In 1641, before he became a baptizer, he preached *Fermentum Pharisaeorum* on Matthew 15:9 ("But in vain they do worship me, teaching for doctrines the commandments of men," AV) before Parliament. He realized that the problem with ceremonial or formal worship was not only its violation of the regulative principle but also its interference with the gospel message. At best, ceremonies or rites did not enhance the possibility of salvation; at worst, they actually distorted the people's view of salvation, "so that by reason of such rites the Gospell is either not considered, or understood carnally."[6] Particular Baptists so carefully considered the outcome of this principle that it will be treated in two separate sections, one dealing with the dichotomy between the carnal and the spiritual and a second dealing with their theology of set forms of worship. Tombes realized that all forms of will-worship tended towards "the Popish conceit of *opus operatum*," that the very act of participating in the ceremony, be it baptism, the Lord's Supper, or a book service, somehow pleased God regardless of the heart's condition.[7] Tombes and Spilsbury connected this with baptism. Believers' baptism not only reinforced one's own assurance of salvation by confirming God's covenant but also communicated that salvation clearly to all present. Infant baptism could do neither; it could not offer any such assurance because it was based entirely on someone else's recollection of the event, and it also tended to harden non-Christians in their lost condition through the sacramental explanation of the rite that all present heard.[8] Both concluded that a worship service should enhance, not distract from, the presentation of the gospel.

The case for a Baptist liturgical hermeneutic can only be constructed piecemeal by the existence of a consistent underlying thought. Hanserd

---

6. Tombes, *Fermentum Pharisaeorum*, 6. He said, "And although I know Ceremonies invented by men are pretended to serve for edification, yet I must professe that I never found in my reading, or experience, that ever any person by such rites, or observances was wonne to the profession of Christ, or brought to any spirituall knowledge of Christ, any true faith or sincere obedience to him" (ibid., 7).

7. Ibid., 10.

8. Spilsbury, *Treatise Concerning Baptisme*, 43, 25. He wrote, "And thus being in covenant with God by faith in Jesus Christ, in which their state consists, and so the agreement made, & the covenant passed between them, now the seale is set to, which is the outward ordinance of Baptisme, to confirme the same; which being done, she is then to enter upon her holy communion in all the rest of Gods holy ordinances thereunto belonging, for her comfort and well-being" (ibid., 43). Tombes expanded, "infant-baptisme is the ground upon which innumerable people ignorant and profane harden themselves as if they were good Christians, regenerate, and should be saved without holiness of life." Tombes, *Apology*, 94; cf. idem, *Short Catechism*, 15.

Gospel Worship and a New Purpose of the Gathering

Knollys hearkened to principles addressed in chapter 3 when he preached to an unruly crowd that the ordinances (in that instance prayer, preaching, and conference) drew their life and power from Christ alone and that the holiness of the church (a regenerate church) was demanded by God for the glory and communion of His Son.[9] His approach, had it been successful, would have associated in his hearers' minds the New Testament ordinances and the experience of salvation in a way unlike Tombes's feared *opus operatum*. This might seem basic, but it was rather foreign in that environment. The fact that Knollys even attempted to encourage his hearers to connect the state of salvation with effective prayer and preaching—every time they heard a prayer they would either ask if they were saved or rejoice in their salvation—showed an awareness of the gospel as more than a condition for but an integral part of the church's worship. Perhaps that is why Spilsbury so emphasized the use of Scripture, because the "Mediatorship of Christ," the only way to bring one into the household of God, was found only in the New Testament.[10] Along those lines, Particular Baptists were very evangelistic in their preaching, a topic that will be the focus of its own section.

Most commonly, Baptists desired to communicate the right use of the ordinances as a consequence of, not a requisite to, salvation (or even proof of salvation[11]). Tombes wrote at great length about Paul's image of "ingraffing;" whereas the paedobaptists considered the engrafting to be baptism, he insisted that Paul was talking about admission to "the saving benefits according to election" and not merely "visible Church-membership by outward ordinance." In so doing, he could connect both the entrance into the assembly and the very act of gathering with salvation such that all present might consider their own condition.[12] Later Particular Baptist thought was clearer. In his recension of the *Heidelberg Catechism*, Collins used the question,

> Q. Do not then both the Word and Sacraments tend to that End, as to lead our Faith unto the Sacrifice of Christ finished on the Cross as to the only grounds of our Salvation?

9. Knollys, *Christ Exalted*, 2, 11, 15.

10. Spilsbury, *Gods Ordinance*, 22. He continued, "This Testament, and Christ the Mediator thereof, and mans salvation, are all so inseparably joyned together by the holy Spirit, that the Gospel holds forth no one of these without the other; so that there is no faith in Christ approved of, apart from the word of the Testament, of which he is the Mediator" (ibid.).

11. See, for example, Collins, *Mountains of Brass*, 1–2.

12. Tombes, *Antipaedobaptism*, 16.

> A. It is even so; for the Holy Ghost teacheth us by the Gospel, and assureth us by the Sacraments, that the Salvation of all of us standeth in the only Sacrifice of Christ offered for us upon the Cross.[13]

Reformers believed that the sacraments (restricted to baptism and the Lord's Supper) were "signs" or "seals" of elements of the covenant, and Particular Baptists largely followed that approach but with two very important differences.[14] Consider that Kiffin echoed Reformed language when he described the significance of baptism, "As the *Supper* is a Spiritual participation of the *Body and Blood* of Christ by Faith, and so (not meerly by the work done) is a means of Salvation; so *Baptism Signs* and *Seals* our Salvation to us, which lies in *Justification* and discharge of sin, &c." The critical difference was that whereas Calvinists jailed Anabaptists for withholding the sacraments from their children, Baptists consistently restricted them to those credibly possessing saving faith—Kiffin called faith and repentance "necessary Antecedents" to baptism—thus making them aspects of their profession.[15] Kiffin partially used that language to convince those Christians who restricted the Lord's Supper to professing Christians that they should treat baptism with the same respect. There can be no doubt that he saw the sacraments as much as an evangelistic tool as a participation in grace, however. For example, Bunyan believed that the

---

13. Collins, *Orthodox Catechism*, 25–26.

14. Compare "A Sacrament is an ordinance of God, wherein by giving and receiving of outward elements, according to his will, the promises of the Covenant of grace, made in the blood of Christ, being represented, exhibited and applyed unto us, are further signed and sealed betwixt God and man" (Ussher, *Body of Divinity*, 365); with "Baptisme is an Ordinance of the Lord annexed to the Word of the Covenant; wherein persons repenting, and believing in Jesus Christ, yielding up themselves to him, in his Name, are solemnly dipt in water, and arise; signifying, representing, and sealing up to them, their Union with Christ . . . The Lords Supper is an Ordinance of the Lord Jesus Christ, left at his departing untill his return, as a Love-Token to his Disciples; who are often to meet together in his Name, as One Body; and sitting down at his Table, and Judging themselves" (Jessey, *Miscellanea Sacra*, 128–29); "baptisme is the Sacrament of our entrance or initiation, the Lords Supper is the Sacrament of our continuance and conversation in the visible body of Christ" (Lambe, *Confutation of Infants Baptisme*, 37); and other definitions of baptism noted in earlier chapters.

15. Kiffin, *Sober Discourse*, 25–26. Richard Allen, not the later Baptist but a Fellow at Oxford, condemned the Baptists for considering the sacraments to be nothing more a profession, thus damning their unbaptized children. Incidentally, he also rejected the Baptists for believing that the church should be pure and that the magistrate should be tolerant of all religions. As further proof of great confusion about the Baptists from the outside, he specifically condemned the Baptists for entertaining further revelation. Allen, *An Antidote Against Heresy*, 2, 107, 115, 123.

Gospel Worship and a New Purpose of the Gathering

sacraments were teaching tools, "both which are of excellent use to the Church, in this world; they being to us representations of the death, and resurrection of Christ, and are as God shall make them, helps to our faith therein." But Kiffin saw in Bunyan's actual practice (which took baptism out of the church) an unacceptable distortion of that message.[16]

The other primary difference was that Particular Baptists equally esteemed all ordinances, which were not restricted to baptism and the Lord's Supper. This even became a problem for them when they could not agree which ordinances could be celebrated in a mixed assembly (for example, the practice of singing, which chapter 6 will address). They saw all ordinances, including preaching, prayer, and reading God's Word, celebrated in congregational worship as the primary if not only means by which evangelism occurred. Knollys combined these streams of thought when he wrote, "Jesus Christ hath instituted and ordained the Ministry of the Gospel, *Eph.* 4. 11, 12, 13. and all Gospel-Ordinances for the salvation of sinners, to the Glory of God the Father." But they never expressed the spiritualism of the ordinances in a way that drifted back to Catholic sacramentalism or forward into Quakerism. Knollys was unequivocal that "The Ordinances of the Gospel give a more clear vision of Christ, than those under the Law."[17] When Benjamin Keach stated that God appointed them "for the begetting of Faith," it was not by causing regeneration, but by putting one's self in a place where God's Spirit was known to work. Keach was not esoterically claiming that God's Spirit moved where God's people celebrated God's ordinances to the potential spiritual benefit of non-Christians present; he was very strict about those who could receive the Lord's Supper at Horsleydown. But God communicated saving truth through the ordinances. Even Baptism was more than a ceremony for the saved but a kind of wordless sermon ("analogical proposition") that presented the facts of the gospel, acknowledging Christ as Messiah and trusting in Him for forgiveness of sin, for all to hear and see.[18] The more

---

16. Bunyan, *Confession of my Faith*, 65, cf. 97. He created the most trouble for himself when the only reason he could give for a believer to be baptized was "That their own Faith by that figure might be strengthened in the death and resurrection of Christ." He had no choice but to conclude that a Christian could decide for himself whether or not he would be baptized. Ibid., 76, 94.

17. Knollys, *World that Now is*, 10; Knollys, *Exposition Of the Revelation*, 190. Importantly, the First London Confession declared preaching as the ordinary means of begetting faith. *London* [1644], Article XXIV.

18. Keach, *Golden Mine Opened*, 448; Tombes, *Vae Scandalizantum*, 416. Keach, whose eucharistic theology has already been described as more Calvinistic than Zwinglian, stated, "We believe that the outward and more ordinary means, whereby

elaborate the setting or ceremony, the more obscured this basic truth became. In their worship, the Baptists wanted to celebrate the purity of the gospel, and they were willing to reevaluate much about their churches in the process.

The Purpose of the Gathering

The initial, oft-overlooked question would be why the church gathered in the first place. For what purpose did God call the local church to assemble? England was a study in contrasts as to this question. Cranmer, through the Prayer Book, turned the gathering into a time of reading the Word and prayer. Laud saw the gathering as a means of bringing people to the sacraments. Puritans, on the other hand, emphasized preaching even to the exclusion of other actions: "the object of worship was to rouse men to think and act about the problems of this world."[19] The early nonconformists had an intentionally simple understanding of their gatherings: they believed that God commanded them to assemble for outward worship.[20] Unfortu-

---

Christ communicates to us the Benefits of Redemption, are his Holy Ordinances, as Prayer, the Word of God, and Preaching, with Baptism, and the Lord's Supper, &c. and yet notwithstanding it is the Spirit of God that maketh Prayer, Reading, &c. and specially the Preaching of the Word, effectual to the convincing, converting, building up, and comforting, through Faith, all the Elect of God unto Salvation" (Keach, *The Articles of the Faith*, 19). Jessey's testimony of Sarah Wight (similar to Katherine Sutton as reported later in this chapter) is an impressive discussion and analysis of a young woman's salvation experience, including her questions about the means of grace (ordinances). Jessey, *The exceeding Riches of Grace Advanced*. Powell printed a compilation of salvation testimonies in 1652 that were very interesting in their strict formula (a Puritan influence?). Consider these lines about the ordinances: "I finde in my heart a very great thirsting after the Ordinances, and a great inlargement of heart, and comfort in the Ordinances, my heart being delighted to be among the people of God, and full of joy in them"; "I finde that I have great comfort, and am much refreshed by Ordinances, a feeling of the Spirit is frequently wrought upon my heart therein"; "I doe desire to follow Gods Ordinances, and finde great inlargements of my heart to God both to, and in the Ordinances"; "My heart is much affected to the Ordinances and Duties"; "I find the want of any of all Gods Ordinances to be grief to me, & that I am at a losse therin"; "I find much comfort from the Word and Ordinances. . . . I find a very great affection in my heart to the people of God, or any that I judge so to bee" (Powell, *Spirituall Experiences, Of sundry Belieevers*, 41, 59, 66, 86, 92–93, 110).

19. Hill, *Century of Revolution*, 82. He said, "Protestant churches were no longer primarily places in which processions were held; they were auditoria for the pulpit" (ibid.). See also Dickens, *English Reformation*, 188; Lake, "Laudian Style," 170, 173; Wright, *Early English Baptists*, 68; and Maltby, "By this Book," 119.

20. Ainsworth combined the outward command of assembly, namely bowing down, praying, preaching, and administering the sacraments, with the inward

nately, as can be seen from the historical context, that had a wide range of possible meanings. L. F. downplayed the civic and ceremonial purposes of the gathering, attacking the false established churches for gathering only at a set place, only at a set time, only with a set schedule, and only according to a set book. He believed that God's worship could not be so restricted.[21] Jeremiah Burroughs downplayed the sacramental and cerebral purposes of the gathering, reminding his hearers that assembly for worship required more than holy living, but specific preparation. In order to draw nigh unto God, the people must have a pure heart; they should meditate on God and His attributes, meditate on the importance of worship, pray and confess their sins, and come to the gathering ready to participate in their duties of worship. He insisted, "If ever we were seriously Intentive or Attentive about any thing, it must be when we are worshiping of the Name of God."[22] There was not much written in answer to this specific question, making it difficult to draw many conclusions.

The fact that some early Baptist worship services resembled "prophesyings" implies that they emphasized edification in their gathering, namely the preaching and teaching of the Word of God. When Kiffin defended his separate congregation, he appealed that they gathered to edify and exhort one another; no one should despise or reproach them that. But he did not mean edification in a reductionistic sense. Later sections will approach these issues in greater detail, but it should be noted that George Gillespie had summarized the Scottish Presbyterian thoughts on this convergence saying that "ceremonies are a great hindrance to edification, because they make much time and pains to be spent about them, which might be and (if they were removed) should be spent more profitably for godly edifying," or preaching and teaching.[23] By all accounts, the Baptists spent a great deal of time and energy in preaching during their worship services, but it would be a mistake to think that they reduced all worship to a weekly Bible conference. The First London Confession did not address the matter of gathering directly (it cited Hebrews 10:25 only tangentially), but it allowed two valuable inferences. In article XLV, the Confession stated that God gave men gifts of preaching and teaching "for the edification, exhortation, and comfort of the Church." And article XXXIII, as noted earlier, identified the visible church "by mutuall agreement, in the practical injoyment

---

rejoinder of fear, faith, hope, and love. Ainsworth, *Arrow Against Idolatrie*, 5–6.

21. L. F., *Speedy Remedie*, 17–27.
22. Burroughs, *Gospel-Worship*, 42–51, 81.
23. Gillespie, *Dispute Against the English Popish Ceremonies*, 85.

of the Ordinances, commanded by Christ their head and King."[24] Both of those intersected in the truly visible manifestation of the church, namely its local assembly. That would mean that Particular Baptists believed they gathered both for edification in preaching and for the enjoyment of the ordinances (granted which could be argued to mean the same thing), and not one purpose at the expense of the other.

This small development indicates that Particular Baptists were responding to various currents of thought in London. They did not ignore the basic consequences, for they resisted tugs toward sacramentalism, Quakerism, and intellectualism. Worship was for God but had benefit for man; worship had a divine structure but a human form; worship was inward and outward, in Spirit and Truth. They did not want to see their worship services reduced to any one side of a number of dichotomies. On the verge of the Glorious Revolution, Hanserd Knollys reminded his readers,

> The end why the Church is so planted, builded and formed, is that they may meet together in *ONE* to *Worship* God *publickly* in Spirit and in Truth in all his *sacred* Gospel Ordinances, to the Glory of God, and for the *mutual* Edification of that *mystical* body of Christ, whose head he is, 1 *Cor.* 14. 23. and *Heb.* 10. 25. *John* 4. 22, 23, 24. 1 *Cor.* 11. 1, 2--11. 2 *Thess.* 1. 12. *and* 1 *Pet.* 4. 10, 11.[25]

Perhaps it could be best summarized that edification was not for mind alone but also body and spirit (if indeed those could be separated). The purpose of the gathering was the orderly celebration of the ordinances, which God gave for His worship and for the building up of the church. The next chapter will introduce a group of Baptists who rejected singing and referred to their gatherings as "lecture-meetings." Among other things, they rejected hymns as set forms of worship, mirroring the question Baptists had had since their beginnings. What was the proper nature of their

---

24. *London* [1644], Article XLV, XXXIII. Grantham was much more explicit to Charles II at the Restoration, "But to avoid Prolixity (O King) be pleased to know, that Your poor Subjects dare not refuse their innocent Meetings, wherein their work is sincerely to Worship God, & pray for Your Majesty, and for all men as in duty they are bound, seeing the Authority by which they are dehorted from the neglect of their Assemblies, *Heb.* 10. 25. is greater than any, whereby Your Majesty can enjoyn the neglect thereof" (Grantham et al., *Second Humble Addresse Of those who are Called Anabaptists in The County of Lincoln*, 1).

25. Knollys, *Exposition Of the Revelation*, 18. This looked very much like a number of other statements Knollys made about the church.

celebration? How should they treat the set forms thereof proposed by the establishment?

A Theology of Ceremonies and Set Forms

Both Laudians and Catholics believed not only in the authority of their liturgies but also the efficacy of their ceremonies, that the common people were more edified by ceremonies than preaching.[26] Dissenters rejected this viewpoint, emphasizing the individual conscience above external ceremonies: "penitence rather than penance."[27] They promoted preaching as God's chosen form of communication and demoted the manmade English liturgies as a substitution for God's own precepts of worship, invoking a number of valuable arguments in addition to the regulative principle. Henry Ainsworth, for example, argued that a church employing an imposed form of prayer implicitly taught the membership that the set prayer should be more likely to be answered than an extemporaneous prayer, but he knew that no human authority could make such a guarantee. Further, and just as heinous, the liturgy took the place of the pastor/shepherd and the Holy Spirit, both of which were appointed by God to guide the church in worship.[28] George Gillespie recognized that a liturgy necessarily emphasized the external because the heart could not be predicted or controlled. How could a liturgical tradition measure the faithful execution of church services if not but by purely objective means? But that meant that men would be measured by their outward gestures and not the devotion of their heart, which would lead to men ultimately resting in the outward even at the expense of the inward. Furthermore, men could inadvertently be confused that they were reverencing the act itself and not God through the act. Most importantly, a concern that affected some more than others,

---

26. One of Mary's Catholic bishops stated that "the observation of ceremonies, for obedyence sake, wyll gyve more light than all the readynge of Scrypture can doe." Duffy, *Stripping of the Altars*, 531. Duffy argued that the Catholics were more in touch with the people than the Puritans.

27. Hill, *Century of Revolution*, 79.

28. *Apologie or Defence*, 66–67. As late as 1684, the Independent Isaac Chauncy's imaginary dialog between John Owen and Richard Baxter contained Owen's argument, "But this is that which the Liturgy takes on it self, namely to supply and determine the matter, to prescribe the manner, and to limit all the concerns of them [prayers and praises], to modes and forms of its own; which is to take the work of Christ out of his hand" (Chauncy, *Theological Dialogue*, 25).

some worried that imposing ceremonies implicitly taught their necessity for salvation.[29]

A common argument raised against the liturgy, especially the Mass, dealt with the affections. On the one hand, the use of ceremonies could create the wrong atmosphere for worship—"a longsome stagelike worship, with organs and musik to make them all merry; as Nebuchadnezar with melodie celebrated the dedication of his golden image."[30] More commonly, the ceremonies were accused of overwhelming the senses, making the person forget what he or she came to do, because "human minds are extraordinarily seized upon and fascinated by the splendor and pomp of ceremonies."[31] The nonconformists also thought about the significance of the rituals themselves. Burroughs made the very astute observation that a sacrament was a sacrament because the outward thing or ritual was made holy for a spiritual end. But Christ instituted the sacraments; if someone else had invented those specific rituals, they should be labeled superstition.[32] Likewise, Owen insisted that the magistrate did not have the power to institute a ceremony because that would imply that the magistrate had authority to give a ceremony significance. But a significant ceremony was by definition a sacrament—"They do not naturally signify the things whereunto they are applied; for if they did there would be no need of their institution"—and the only One who could create a sacrament was Christ.[33] Along these lines, Bunyan argued that the Baptists had given baptism a significance Christ had not and thus had done this very thing Owen warned against. He stated, "It respecteth more a form, then the spirit, and power of Godliness," and accused the Baptists of making baptism effective in itself apart from the faith of the individual.[34]

---

29. Gillespie, *Dispute Against the English Popish Ceremonies*, xxxiv, 216. Gillespie decried, "The Bishop of Winchester exclaims against such as do not kneel, for not regarding the table of the Lord, which has even been thought of all holies the most holy, and for denying reverence to the holy symbols and precious memorials of our greatest delivery, even the reverence which is given to prayer" (ibid.). See also, for example, Clark, *History of English Nonconformity*, 296ff.

30. Ainsworth, *Arrow Against Idolatrie*, 146.

31. Gillespie, *Dispute Against the English Popish Ceremonies*, 82.

32. Burroughs, *Gospel-Worship*, 215. He later noted that the supernatural element of a sacrament existed only because God desired it so. Ibid., 227.

33. Owen, *Truth and Innocence Vindicated*, in *Works*, 13:451.

34. Bunyan, *Confession of my Faith*, 117, 55. He elaborated that Baptists considered a baptism legitimate by virtue of the declaration of faith of the individual and subsequent consent of the church to perform the baptism. Bunyan seemed to believe that such a declaration was often if not usually unaccompanied by true, saving faith.

Gospel Worship and a New Purpose of the Gathering

Importantly, the defenders of the Prayer Book and the *Directory* often responded by pointing out the inconsistencies in the nonconformists' positions. For example, an Anglican argued that a set form of prayer was no different than a hymn or psalm set to meter and even rhyme, "which yet the adversaries of our Common Prayer, practice in their assemblies."[35] Daniel Featley likewise noted that the nonconformists read Scripture, preached, and catechized. Yet the translations of Scripture read in worship, including the chapter and verse divisions, were manmade; the method of preaching by method, doctrine, and use, allowing the preacher to use his own judgment, was manmade; catechizing by question and answer was also a human invention.[36] Most compellingly, Edward Wetenhall thought that the dissenters were just as emotionally attached to "the experience and memory of that Devotion or good affection, which that way of worship has excited, and usually renews in them" as they accused the Anglicans of being to their pomp and ceremony.[37]

The defenders also took up positive arguments, most often with respect to decency (or pomp and grandeur), order, and uniformity. Owen summarized their position, "First, That they tend unto the furtherance of the *devotion* of the worshippers; secondly, That they render the worship itself *comely* and beautiful; thirdly, That they are the great preservers

---

See Bunyan, *Differences in Judgment*, 10–13. As the next section will explain, many Baptists found this division of the inward and outward to be a false dichotomy.

35. BCP [1641], 4. This very effective argument will be taken up in chapter 6; note that John Cotton summarized the common response given in this particular context that God never gave a set form of prayer in either the Old or New Testaments, but did give a set form of psalm in the Old Testament which reasonably applied to the New. See Cotton, *Singing of Psalmes A Gospel-Ordinance*, 30. Interestingly, he also divided the practices of singing and praying; praying by a set form did not require the activity of the Spirit, which broke the second commandment; singing, on the other hand, always manifested such activity. Cuthbert Sidenham echoed Cotton's distinction, noting that singing required a different set of skills. Furthermore, one can "pray along" silently, but one cannot "sing along" silently. Sidenham, *Christian Sober and Plain Exercitation*, 208. Demonstrating his influence on the Baptists, Whinnel followed Cotton's arguments in Whinnel, *Sober Reply*.

36. Featley, *Dippers dipt*, 98–99. Note that when Featley defended the authorized liturgies, he was defending the *Book of Common Prayer*; the *Directory* had not yet been released. Cf. ibid., 86–89. In his debate with the Baptists, Bakewell rightfully clarified that he only needed to prove the lawfulness of using the Lord's Prayer in worship, not its necessity. Bakewell, *Answer, Or Confutation*, 38. Baptists had to contend with a myriad of arguments in this subject, and their burden extended further than that on those in the established churches.

37. Wetenhall, *Of Gifts and Offices*, 2.

of *order* in the celebration thereof."[38] Wetenhall, like many Anglicans, thought that the place of cathedral music was secure "because of the power it hath upon the mind of man, to raise good affections and calm disorderly ones."[39] Much discussion was related to set forms of prayer, often beginning with the question whether the Lord's Prayer was a form or a guide. Featley described the Presbyterian position, "In like manner, prayer is a duty enjoyned by God, & a part of his substantial worship, but the set forms are devised by man, yet according to general rules prescribed in Scripture." He argued that a well-written set form of prayer was far better than a careless extemporaneous prayer, and few men had the gift of effective prayer. He heard many such prayers filled with vain repetition (battologie) and thus sinful in and of themselves.[40] Similarly, Wetenhall noted that the spiritual devotion of the whole church was tied to the man leading in worship; if he were "but a mean Master of speech, memory and invention" in prayer, the church would be "in a miserable condition."[41]

---

38. Owen, *Brief Instruction in the Worship of God*, in *Works*, 15:467. More specifically, some men believed that God required a veneration that far exceeded that for any human, which thus demanded exquisite ceremonies, more exquisite than a coronation or the like. Owen, *Discourse concerning Evangelical Love*, in *Works*, 15:128. He elsewhere noted that benefits such as decency, order, and uniformity had no value apart from edification. Owen, *Discourse Concerning Liturgies*, in *Works*, 15:47.

39. Wetenhall, *Of Gifts and Offices*, 247. Note that Wetenhall still attached informal rules to music. Later in his book, he accused Rome of using too much music and music that was complicated and obscure. He also thought that music being composed in the 1670s was "not grave enough for worship" and that young composers "neglect the matter of what they sing." Ibid., 311, 453–54, 535, 541.

40. Featley, *Dippers dipt*, 98–102. Featley did not argue that extemporaneous prayers were inherently wrong but rather that set forms were necessary, "for there is not one Minister or Curate of a hundred, especially in Country Villages, or parochial Churches, who have any tolerable gift of conceived, as they term them, or *ex tempore* prayers." Ibid. He went on to admit that reading a prayer was not enough for true worship; it must be read with understanding, intention, and affection, even lively faith and fervent affection. Ibid., 107. Earlier, he had written, "I found fault with some carelesse preachers in our dayes, who came into the Pulpit at publike Fasts, and presumed without any premeditation to pray many houres ex tempore, in which they prayers they used much Battologie and vaine repetitions against the expresse commandement of our Saviour, & excluded his prayer, which is the perfect pattern of all prayer" (Featley, *Gentle Lash*, 12). Wetenhall similarly noted that some men simply had a gift of "quickness of thought and readiness of speech" and extensive "abilities [as a] Performer, and as he is Master of phansie and speech." He agreed that men could pray extemporaneously, but very few had that gift. Wetenhall, *Of Gifts and Offices*, 39, 58.

41. Wetenhall, *Of Gifts and Offices*, 65.

Gospel Worship and a New Purpose of the Gathering

John Owen also described a common argument that a specific prayer was only a circumstance of worship and thus lawful for men to impose.[42]

The Baptists were well aware of these intensely debated matters and tried to adopt positions consistent with their principles. John Tombes's early beliefs about forms would help bring him to the Baptist camp. Beginning with a number of established positions, he brought out unique conclusions. For example, he agreed that ceremonies "may beget some kinds of raptures of carnall delight," but noted that they could never "begat sanctifying knowledge [or] sound repentance." In other words, man-made ceremonies could never accomplish the one thing of importance in the church—the salvation and sanctification of a soul—and thus should not take any time from a church's gatherings.[43] Tombes also recognized a subtle consequence of ceremonies: they were on a very slippery slope. The sign of the cross eventually became an object of adoration; praying at catacombs led to invoking martyrs; celebrating the Eucharist became a means of salvation. The slippery slope was not only in the proliferation of ceremonies, as others had noted, but also in the corruption thereof:

> I thinke an instance cannot be given of a device of man pretending to advance piety, and to edifie the Church, when God hath provided other meanes to that end, which hath not in the conclusion hindered piety; and more or lesse, destroyed the purity of Religion. So sottish and blinde is the wisedome of man in appointing and directing the service of God.[44]

Benjamin Cox and other Particular Baptists emphasized the former consequence. They recognized that accepting a set form of prayer eventually led to a Prayer Book, that desiring decency in worship led to vestments

---

42. Owen, *Discourse Concerning Liturgies*, in *Works*, 15:35–36. Owen responded that there was no way to distinguish the substance and accidents of worship; the specific action within the context of worship *was* the worship. This matter will receive subsequent attention.

43. Tombes, *Fermentum Pharisaeorum*, 7. He also noted the similarities to the stage, noting that elaborate ceremonies worked "through melodious soundes or pleasant sights, some kinde of womanish pity, and teares, such as the acting of a stage play will draw from some persons." Ibid.

44. Ibid., 5. Grantham recognized a further consequence. First, "we cannot but think the Church of *England* erred from the Rule of Righteousness, in decreeing Rites and Ceremonies which God has not commanded," then "if it shall be said, That the Ceremonies of the Church of *England* . . . are not sinful; then how shall we be ever able to reprove a Papist?" Grantham, *Second Part of the Apology*, 8, 9.

and genuflections, and that desiring uniformity in worship led to complete external control of a church.⁴⁵

Baptists thought about the relationship between ceremonies and salvation on multiple levels. Charles II promoted the Anglican rituals in part because so much of the population supported them. One group of Baptists implored that such an interest should be a warning *against* the ceremonies, not for them. Their reasoning: the people preferred elaborate rituals precisely because they were not actually Christians. One of the greatest errors of English leadership was their assumption that church attenders were saved in a biblical sense. "The reason why the nations are so generally beguil'd in the concernments of their souls is, because the greatest part being carnal and unregenerate persons, they are naturally inclin'd to such ways of worship, as are accompany'd with external pomp and glory."⁴⁶ Hanserd Knollys, especially in his later years, worried about that a great deal. He thought of the parable of the ten virgins in which the five foolish virgins had every appearance of the form of godliness, right down to their wicks. They had partaken of the ordinances, but had never partaken of the divine nature; they had professed Christ, but did not possess Christ. The form of godliness available in a church's worship could never substitute for the power of the Spirit; "The power of Godliness doth make the Believer fruitful under that form of Godliness which Christ hath Instituted for the Worship of God; and affords him fellowship with the Father, Son and Spirit, 1 Joh. 1. 1, 2, 3."⁴⁷ Knollys enjoyed the emotional benefits of congregational singing in corporate worship; it "makes Melody in our Ears, and stirs up our pure Minds to rejoyce in the Lord," but he asserted that a right heart was sweeter to God than a well-tuned voice. In fact, he thought that "formality," or the worship of God in forms, was one of the manifestations of lukewarmness for which Christ would utterly reject His church.⁴⁸ Even Philip Cary, who strongly desired his readers to keep the purity of divine institutions in their worship, knew that such ceremonial

---

45. Cox, Knollys, and Kiffin, *Declaration*, 11–12. Collins later wrote that the Lord's Prayer was a model, not a form of prayer, emphasizing praise, submission, forgiveness, and protection. Collins, *Orthodox Catechism*, 64–71. Owen most eloquently explained their perspective of Christ's rules for worship: "they were few, and easy to be observed." Owen, *Discourse Concerning Liturgies*, in *Works*, 15:9.

46. Crosby, *History of the English Baptists*, 2:101. Unfortunately, Crosby did not identify the authors or date of this letter.

47. Knollys, *Parable of the Kingdom*, 98, 46.

48. Knollys, *World that Now is*, 77–80. He preferred Scripture songs to humane songs mainly because the latter could potentially contain error. Knollys, *An Exposition Of Revelation*, 58.

Gospel Worship and a New Purpose of the Gathering

purity was not enough by itself to "please our Great Lord and Master" but that they needed to "press through all External Mediums."[49]

Baptists drew other meaningful conclusions with respect to ceremonies. They realized that because Christians were the temple of the Living God, the place of worship was immaterial. This meant they did not have to frequent the Anglican church buildings; it also meant they did not have to worry about the ornamentation of their own such buildings, for "we know the most High dwelleth not in Temples made with hands."[50] Further, they did not gain their boldness to approach the throne of grace by virtue of their ceremonies but by "the Ministry of their merciful and faithful High-priest." Hercules Collins noted that when Paul compared the splendor of God's worship in the Old Testament to the simplicity of that in the New (under Christ), he said God chose the New, preferring "this of the Gospel for the glory, excellency, comeliness of it, unspeakably above the Ministration of the now." He could have retained the outward rites and ceremonies, but chose the simple relationship in Christ.[51] He believed

---

49. Cary, *Solemn Call*, Preface to the Christian Reader.

50. *London* [1646], To the Reader; citing Acts 7:48 (AV).

51. Collins, *Some Reasons for Separation*, 22. Collins said, "'Tis most evident that the Worship of the Old Testament for the beauty and ornament of outward Ceremonies, and the splendor of their observation, far exceeds and excels that Worship which God Commands now." Note that Collins was responding to two common claims, that the ceremonies "tend mightily to the furtherance of the Devotion of the Worshippers [and] render the Worship of God comely and beautiful." Ibid. He went on to repeat the argument against the normative principle first issued by Owen: "the super-added Ceremonies doth not belong to the Institution of Worship nor unto those Circumstances whose disposal falls under the Rule of moral Prudence; therefore they are altogether needless and useless in the Worship of God; it doth not nor cannot add any thing to the due order of Gospel Worship; and albeit they are not particularly and expresly forbidden, for it was simply impossible that all instances [could be listed]." Ibid. Note that this revealed another layer of tension in Particular Baptist perspectives beyond the potential freedom of an individual church to adopt ceremonies or circumstances disagreeable to other churches, namely the freedom of the individual *within* that church to do the same. Those who prioritized the role of the church, such as Kiffin, would never completely leave that determination to the individual but gave the church authority over the individual. Even Richard Allen, who strongly defended the individualistic perspective of hymn-singing, just as strongly argued, "This liberty [of Christian Churches to bring in new *Parts* of Divine Worship], as I conceive, does not authorize a Number of Men in a Christian Church to prescribe RITES or EXTERNAL MODES of Divine Worship, according to our own Judgments, and IMPOSE them upon all other of our Communion. But these things ought to be ordered by mutual agreement of at least the MAJOR PART of the total Members of it" (A[llen], *Brief Vindication of Essay to Prove Singing of Psalms*, 47). Chapter 6 will explore the potential impact of individual worship on these Baptists.

that true worshipers had no need of ornate ceremonies to worship truly; they only needed to follow the simple pattern of Christ. Every individual worshiper could determine the unique circumstances of his or her participation in worship. Collins also realized that coercion in worship proved that the coercers thought the established ceremonies were necessary and not indifferent; he encouraged his church to "hold fast" to "the best of Objects, so of the best of Principles, and pure Spiritual Worship of the Gospel" against all pressure. In other words, a church's worship, namely the absence of man-made ceremonies, was the visible proof of her faithfulness to Christ.[52] Finally, Richard Allen, one of Keach's compatriots during the hymn-singing controversy, argued that the use of ceremonies was far from neutral or indifferent but actually led the soul "rather to the vain and frothy Humour of the *Theatre,* than to the grave and solemn Genius of the *Temple.*" Instead of helping the worshiper engage in spiritual contemplation, it encouraged amusement and sensuality and thus took the people further away from Christ.[53] In every way, Particular Baptists cared about the relationship between worship and the gospel, perhaps more so than their contemporaries.

Worship in Spirit and Truth: Discovering Dichotomies

The argument about set forms of worship drove Baptists to consider the meaning of worship in Spirit and Truth. They recognized the difference between the form and the power of godliness in worship (also termed inward versus outward or moral versus ceremonial). But they were not the first to do so, for this matter was intimately tied up with many others already addressed. When William Bradshaw declared that "the Service and worship of God, standeth not in meats and drinks, nor in any such external Rites having no authority from God," he was arguing that worship not in truth was worship not in Spirit (form without power), or "false worship," "& that form of Gods Service must needs be adulterate, that is made to consist in such things."[54] With respect to inward versus outward, Ainsworth thought that the outward service of worship was meaningless if not joined by inward devotion. In a common example, Gillespie thought that the idolatry of kneeling at the presentation of the element came "not

---

52. Collins, *Voice from the Prison,* 9. Collins applied Christ's appeal to "hold fast" quite frequently to his own church with respect to worship.

53. Allen, *Essay to Prove Singing of Psalms,* xi–xii.

54. Bradshaw, *Several Treatises of Worship and Ceremonies,* 15.

from the nature of the action, but from the opinion of the agent, or rather from his will."⁵⁵ Burroughs insisted that Christians must "stir up the faculties of your souls" in worship and draw nigh unto God with a reverence of attitude because "the Lord doth look more to the principle from whence a thing comes, than at the thing it self."⁵⁶ Edward Wetenhall exhorted that worship not in spirit and truth was "but pageantry, and a more gay affront to God."⁵⁷

As should be expected, Baptists thought about these matters in terms of salvation, or perhaps the regenerate church. Thomas Lambe captured the sentiment when he observed that in allowing all people to participate in the church's ceremonies, "by these meanes have they made the Church very great, though it be not very good."⁵⁸ But John Tombes offered the most critical assessment: participation by the ungodly in church ceremony was not harmless but sinful to them because it made them hypocrites.

> [T]hey thinke they pray well if they be present when the Service booke is read, and say after the Minister, though without knowledge, attention of minde, faith in Gods promises, or fervency of desire: they thinke they receive the Lords supper well, if without

55. Ainsworth, *Arrow Against Idolatrie*, 5–6; Gillespie, *Dispute Against the English Popish Ceremonies*, 171.

56. Burroughs, *Gospel-Worship*, 29, 78ff, 67. While this quote implies that Burroughs treated sincerity as more important than obedience, his larger body of work clearly rejects such a conclusion. Rather, he was exhorting that proper worship required more than right actions but also right intentions. He rhetorically asked what Christians do in worship, knowing that most would answer with actions such as pray, serve, hear the Word, and take communion. He countered that Christians should be more worried about what their souls do in worship: "we must pray with our Souls, we must power [pour] forth our Souls before God, & when we come to hear, our hearts must not go after our Covetousness, we must set our hearts to what we hear, we must hear with our hearts as well as with our ears, our souls must be at work in hearing of the word; when you hear, it is not enough for you to come and sit in a Pew, and have the sound of a mans voyce in your ears, but your Souls must be at work" (ibid., 30, 93, 115). Owen was clear that any notion of worshipping in the heart without regard for action was ridiculous; it was partially on this basis that he established the definition, "That which principally in the Scripture comes under the notion of the worship of God, is the due observance of his outward institutions" (Owen, *Truth and Innocence Vindicated*, in *Works*, 13:447; emphasis added). This was similar to the distinction between the moral and the ceremonial but more related to the difference between natural and instituted worship. For example, Cotton argued that singing psalms was a moral duty and therefore still enjoined on everyone, but singing with instruments was ceremonial under the Old Testament and therefore ceased. Cotton, *Singing of Psalmes a Gospel-Ordinance*, 5.

57. Wetenhall, *Of Gifts and Offices*, 261.

58. Lambe, *Confutation of Infants Baptisme*, The Epistle to the Reader.

> any godly preparation, spirituall meditation, they doe with empty stomacks and faire deportment eate the bread and drinke the wine of solemne seasons: they thinke they use baptisme well, if they get some to stand at the font as sureties, for the Childs faith, (which I thinke to be proper to Christ, *Heb.* 7. 2.) the Childe to be sprinkled with water, & crossed on the fore-head, though there be no sense of the guilt and defilement of sinne, utter ignorance of the excellency and necessity of spirituall mew birth. And the like is their carriage in hearing the word read and preached, in singing of Psalmes, &c.[59]

Without careful explanation on the part of the leader, individuals present would draw their own conclusions as to the value and result of their participation. Furthermore, ceremonies invented by men could only affect the body, being concerned with "washings, gestures, garments, fastings, feastings, processions, buildings, and such like." Men could not create worship in Spirit and Truth because their ceremonies could not "rectifie or amend the Soule: and make it more like to God."[60] Knollys recognized that men could create a form of worship after "the Truth in the Order and Ordinances of the Gospel" (as did the five foolish virgins) but could not worship by the Spirit unless empowered by the Spirit—true worship required both the Word of God and the Gifts of the Spirit.[61]

For Baptists, the intersection of form and power was most visible in baptism. Recalling Bunyan's accusations against them that they made believers' baptism by immersion an idol, or a work worked, they vehemently denied that a proper form singularly made for a proper baptism. John Norcott, in a work reprinted by Kiffin, stated, "So I say of Baptism, it is not Water thrown on the face that makes Baptism; but it is a free consent and subjection to Christ according to the Rule, that makes Baptism."[62]

---

59. Tombes, *Fermentum Pharisaeorum*, 9–10. This particular point led into his memorable argument noted earlier that such devotion to ceremonies was "costly," with the important consequence that greater needs did not receive the proportionate financial support.

60. Ibid., 5. Tombes referred to John 4:23–24 on a number of occasions in his writings, as he did in this particular argument.

61. Knollys, *Parable of the Kingdom*, 15. Owen regularly noted that this explicitly condemned the Prayer Book, which excluded any gifts of the Spirit. See Owen, *Answer unto Two Questions*, in *Works*, 16:245. To be fair, Grantham thought that the established church had lost both the form *and* the power of worship. Grantham, *A Friendly Epistle*, 7. He said, "Where the internal part of God's Worship is wanting, the Externals in Religion avail nothing" (Grantham, *Christianismus Primitivus*, 1:36).

62. Norcott, Kiffin, and Claridge, *Baptism Discovered*, 39. He had given the illustration that a bed could not make a marriage or else all fornication would be marriage.

But this was precisely Bunyan's concern who understood the impossibility of knowing a man's heart, for an unsaved person managing to be baptized would be hardened in his or her apostasy, and an unsaved person observing the baptism might comprehend the entire ceremony "and yet know nothing of what Water-baptism preacheth."[63] However, Kiffin saw Bunyan's cavil as an excuse to avoid conflict; when a church was properly accountable for baptism, the gospel would be clear and salvation surely apparent:

> But in regard we are convinced (1.) That it is the Duty of all Believers to be Baptized in Water upon Confession of their Faith, &c. (2.) That none but such ought to be Baptized. (3.) That such as Practise otherwise deviate from the Rule of the Gospel, and the Precedents Recorded there. (4.) That such a Deviation is in it self disorderly, and in the Consequence dangerous, as bringing many unregenerate Members into the Church, &c.[64]

Christ did not institute ceremonies in worship for any reason short of revealing Himself in His perfect goodness and condescension to men. Philip Cary perhaps said this best, "Moral Laws are good, and therefore commanded: But Positive Worship is commanded, and therefore good."[65] When Baptists spoke of moral laws, they often referred to natural forms of worship, such as praying, or singing, or even the Sabbath. Those simply revealed the presence of God. But instituted forms of worship such as baptism and the Lord's Supper actually revealed Christ's nature and works; alter the form and the power would vanish.

Certainly in the later years, these Baptists recognized that the difference between the form of godliness, or external religious duties, and the power of godliness was the grace of Christ. The power of godliness could easily be counterfeited, especially in the narrow confines of a church service. For Hanserd Knollys, the proof of power in worship was found in the life lived year-round, otherwise the false worshiper deceived his own heart and his religion was in vain.[66] But Benjamin Keach cautioned that

---

63. Bunyan, *Differences in Judgment*, 39.
64. Kiffin, *Sober Discourse*, 6–7.
65. Cary, *Solemn Call*, 70.
66. Knollys, *Parable of the Kingdom*, 34–35. He made the very powerful statement, "Again when Professors and Members of Churches are very frequent and constant in Assembling themselves together to worship God, very zealous and precise in the External part of the Worship of God and seem to be very Conscientious and scrupulous in such things as appertain to the for of Godliness, asserting and contending that all things ought to be exactly done in the Church of God, according to the Rule of the

all such behavior could be fabricated (citing Matthew Mead's *The Almost Christian Discovered*). Because God was Spirit, the difference between carnal and vain repetitions and sanctified worship was "the Spirit of Jesus Christ, flowing from a rectified Nature" or "the indwelling of the quickning Spirit, whereby we have a real participation of Christ."[67] Only God could know the difference, so Keach constantly exhorted his congregation to search their hearts for evidence of such grace. But note a very faint consequence: whereas Knollys remained focused on a corporate approach to Christianity, Keach ever-so-slightly emphasized the individual. It is likely that this important divergence resulted from the subtle distinction in their understandings of Spirit and Truth.

The Purpose and Method of Preaching

The London Particular Baptists lived in a world of diverse attitudes toward preaching. The Marian church revealed the difference between the Puritans and the people: the Puritans preached for knowledge; the people simply wanted to be told how to receive healing in the sacraments.[68] The Laudian church used the Prayer Book to guide the people through a carefully choreographed series of "visible sermons, ideally suited to teach the laity those feelings of reverence, humility and worship appropriate to the meeting between the individual and the divine presence which occurred each time a Christian believer attended divine service," so much so that some Anglicans felt they did not need preachers at all. On the other extreme, some English Protestants emphasized preaching "to the virtual exclusion of all other ministerial functions."[69] The satirized differ-

---

written word of God, and yet walk very disorderly at home, are heady and unruly in their own houses, set no Rules nor Bounds to their obstinate and perverse Wills, to their inordinate and vile affections, to their worldly and covetous hearts, who seem to be Religious yet bridle not their Tongues but deceive their own hearts; *Their Religion is in vain*, James 1. 26. These Professors have a form of Godliness, but they want the power thereof" (ibid.).

67. Keach, *Golden Mine Opened*, 222–23, 326. He said that the consequence of God being Spirit was He "seeks spiritual Worshippers of him, not formal, not external, or carnal Modes, bodily Gestures, consecrated Places, attended with glorious Ceremonies, saying over a few Prayers, in which are many vain Repetitions, not minding whether their matter of Worship be of Divine Institution or not, nor whether they perform their Devotion in the Spirit of Jesus Christ." Keach, *Counterfeit Christian*, 31.

68. Duffy, *Stripping of the Altars*, 530ff.

69. Lake, "Laudian Style," 166, 170, 173. This is not to say that the crown ignored preaching; Charles I said, "People are governed by the pulpit more than the sword in

Gospel Worship and a New Purpose of the Gathering

ence between Puritans and Laudians, preaching versus prayer, was real in many ways. Whereas Stephen Marshall believed that preaching "was the chariot on which salvation came riding into the hearts of men," the Duke of Newcastle believed, "There should be more praying and less preaching, for much preaching breeds faction, but much praying causes devotion."[70] Both Jeremiah Burroughs and the Separatist L. F. blasted the Prayer Book for slighting preaching in its Divine Service, making it "but a circumstantial thing."[71] Conversely, Anglicans excoriated Presbyterians who thought "no reason but Ministers should be engaged to Study for their Prayers as for their Sermons," and "*Hearing* all the *Religion* of the *People*."[72] John Tombes said more judiciously, "They that urge or affect humane religious rites are disaffected and adversaries to Godly Preaching: where the one is set up, the other goes downe."[73]

Baptists held various opinions about preaching related to beliefs previously introduced. Early Baptists had the reputation of being tub-preachers, uncouth and unlearned. John Taylor described Samuel Howe,

> A worthy Brother gave the Text, and then / The Cobler (HOW) his preachment strait began / Extemp'ry without any meditation, / But only by the Spirits revelation, / He went through-stitch, now hither, & now thither, / And tooke great paines to draw both ends together . . . His speech was neither studied, chew'd or champ'd, / Or ruminated, but most neatly vamp'd.[74]

Taylor and Edwards also ridiculed Baptists for receiving instant feedback on their sermons and responding to audience complaints. Far from being unwanted, Edward Barber believed in and encouraged such a model of preaching. On one occasion, he attended Edmund Calamy's sermon and immediately requested the opportunity to respond from Calamy's pulpit (he was chased out of the church building). Later he wondered,

> Whether it be not a Humane Invention, and not Gods Ordinance, for one to go up into a pulpit, and there speake an houre or more, and deliver what he please, without questioning by any

time of peace." Hill, *Century of Revolution*, 77.

70. Hill, *Century of Revolution*, 82–83. Hill found this true even in architecture: "Nonconformist chapels are often indistinguishable from lecture halls" (ibid, 82).

71. Burroughs, *Gospel-Worship*, 164; L. F., *Speedy Remedie*, 29.

72. G. P., *A Word of Exhortation to our Separating Brethren*, 10; Wetenhall, *Of Gifts and Offices*, 578.

73. Tombes, *Fermentum Pharisaeorum*, 8.

74. Taylor, *Swarme of Sectaries*, 8–9.

165

of the Assembly, though never so erronious, or judging by them whose due it is, or adding, if truth, or whether these Scriptures prove not the contrary, *Act.* 13. 16. & 17. 11, 1 *Cor.* 14. 31, 32.[75]

Perhaps out of their desire for respectability, London Particular Baptists early stepped back from the "talkback" sermon, but not the principle behind it. It has already been mentioned that Knollys identified both preaching and conference as ordinances in 1645; Kiffin remembered greatly profiting in his youth from private discussion about the Bible and sermons.[76] Collinson likened the conference to a private theological discussion, whereas the sermon was reserved for public meetings, but apparently some Baptists preferred the empowerment inherent in mixing the two. As late as 1673, Thomas Paul mentioned a Baptist church which split because some members rejected preaching "by Method, Doctrine, Reason, and Use" for the talkback model.[77]

Following Kiffin, London Particular Baptists desired to be reputable preachers and generally followed the Puritan model placed by Stephen Marshall into the *Directory*. But whereas the *Directory* gave edification and *not* salvation as an application of the sermon, the Baptists sought both. Benjamin Cox described their attitude toward preaching, "As the preaching of the Gospel, both for the conversion of sinners, and the edifying of those that are converted; so also the right use of Baptisme, and of the Lords Supper, ought to be till the end of the world, Matt. 28. 19, 20. 1 Cor. 11. 26."[78] Spilsbury believed that it was the duty of the pastor, enlightened by God and enabled by the Spirit, "to preach [the Principles of the Gospel], for the convincing of sinne, and to bring over the heart to believe, and

75. Barber, *Certain Queries*, 6. See also Barber, *Declaration and Vindication*.

76. *Remarkable Passages in the Life of William Kiffin*, 11–12.

77. Paul, *Some Serious Reflections*, 11–12. See also Collinson, *Religion of Protestants*, 267.

78. Cox, *Appendix to a Confession of Faith*, 10; cf. *Directory* [1645], 15–18. The *Directory* offered instruction in the knowledge of truth, confutation of false doctrine, exhortation of duty, public admonition, and applying comfort as the uses of a sermon; it did add "that if any unbeliever or ignorant person be present, he may have the secrets of his heart made manifest, and give glory to God." Ibid., 16–17. Patient observed from Acts 2, "That preaching, and hearing the Gospel preached, is a special means to convert Souls" (Patient, *Doctrine of Baptism*, 4). Burroughs preached that the duties of God's worship were the most precious things, "But none more than the Word, that's the Ordinance to convey the first Grace to those that belong to Gods Election" (Burroughs, *Gospel-Worship*, 195). See also Knollys, *Parable of the Kingdom*, 50–51. London Particular Baptists followed early Separatists in believing that gospel preaching was the proper method of establishing and growing churches. Compare, for example, Ainsworth, *Counterpoyson*, 13; with Knollys, *Moderate Answer*, 19–20.

submit to Christ, and to teach them their dutie to God and man."[79] They felt the tension inherent in this position ("It was a short but momentous step—and to Calvinist ministers a monstrous step—to proclaim that all men were equally eligible to receive divine grace;" the First London confession said a person was "wholly passive" in salvation begat by preaching[80]) but maintained evangelistic sermons. Hanserd Knollys may have found a representative balance when he preached,

> God doth offer Christ to lost sinners without respect to price or person, He invites them, that have no money, to come, and buy Wine, and milk, (that is to say, Christ) without praice, Isa 55. 1. And any one, that will, are invited to take Christ freely: Revel. 22, 17. And whosoever will, let him take the water of life (that is, Christ) freely.[81]

To those who believed they had no power of themselves to come to God, he called,

> It is my duty to preach the Gospel to you, and to exhort you to seek Christ. Act. 17. 22, 27. but it is the meer mercy and free grace of God to drive you to Christ, which nothing but his everlasting love can move him to doe, Jer. 31. 3. You ought to seek, and wait, aske, and have, and use all the meanes which God hath appointed, and afforded you, both secret, private, and publike, Revel. 2. 29. But God must make the meanes effectuall: Acts 16. 14.[82]

This should sound very Puritan, but Particular Baptists consistently made the presentation of salvation one of the "uses" in their sermons; like the other ordinances, the sermon was a means appointed by God unto salvation. Benjamin Keach, a prolific and evangelistic author, believed

---

79. Spilsbury, *Gods Ordinance*, 4.

80. Hill, *Century of Worship*, 170; *London* [1644], Article XXIV. Jessey may have been sensitive to this when he said, "All Gods Institutions and Ordinances [including preaching] are given for good, for profit, for the best edifying, and for most honour to his name" (Jessey, *Storehouse of Provision*, 83). Even Spilsbury thought that pastors somehow restricted their efforts to the elect.

81. Knollys, *Christ Exalted* [sermon on Ephesians 1:4], 12.

82. Ibid., 13. He later said, "The Ministers of Christ must declare the Testimony of God not with excellency of speech, not with enticing words of Mans Wisdom, but their speech and their preaching must be in the Demonstration of the spirit and in power, 1 *Cor.* 2. 1, 2, 4, 5. before the Gospel can come to their hearers hearts in power and in the holy Spirit, and before their hearers can come to Christ, and before they can attain to the power of Godliness" (Knollys, *Parable of the Kingdom Expounded*, 50).

"that plain Way of Preaching used by the Holy Apostles, and our Worthy Modern Divines" meant "to preach Christ!" His friend Thomas Whinnel pointed out that the New Testament left no method of preaching, so there should be no qualms with "the common way" of preaching used by godly Englishmen.[83]

Since the entire worship service was an interactive presentation of the gospel, it should not be surprising that these Baptists were not all afraid of

---

83. Keach, *Display of Glorious Grace*, iii; Keach, *Christ Alone the Way to Heaven*, 46. Keach is a fascinating character worthy of much study, more than chapter 6 will offer. His reference to the Divines here is interesting because he rarely cited them in his sermons (as *The Display* was a collection thereof, containing his most dogmatic proclamation that the "covenant of peace" was the "covenant of grace") and he rarely cited anyone for homiletics. Here are all of the Divines he cited approvingly in *The Display* with page numbers in parentheses: "worthy" Thomas Manton (43); Daniel Williams, a centrist Presbyterian with much sympathy for dissenters (54, 82, 101); John Owen (86, 88, 203); Thomas Goodwin (103); Matthew Poole's famous *Annotations* (110); Presbyterian Stephen Charnock (98, 117, 219, 256); Isaac Chauncy (163, 182–86, 208–11); Westminster's *Larger Catechism* (216); Samuel Petto, the important Independent Puritan and covenantalist (220–21); John Cotton (241); and several of his own works. More generally, with respect to hermeneutics, he regularly cited Joseph Caryl, James Durham, John Cotton, John Owen, and Francis Roberts. Gospel proclamation always created a certain amount of tension for Particular Baptists in their defense of particular atonement, especially for Keach who reacted strongly against his General Baptist past. To him, general atonement meant universalism; he preached in one of *Display*'s sermons, "This Proclamation [of the Covenant of Peace] is not so Universal, but that it wholly dependeth upon God's Sovereign Pleasure, who shall reap the Benefit of it: 'Tis sent to one Nation, and not to another; God is not obliged to send it to all Kingdoms and Nations, nor to all in that Nation whither he is pleased to send it; but if Christ died for all, I mean in the stead of all, to satisfie Divine Justice for every individual Person, then he would be Unjust in not sending the Gospel to them all—But he must Call all, and be sure he would give all the lesser Gifts, as well as the greater, *viz.* the Gospel and Faith, *&c.* to all, as well as his Son to die for then all, and not let them perish in their Sins and Unbelief, for whom Christ died; for without Faith all Adult Persons must perish" (Keach, *Display of Glorious Grace*, 167–68). However, Keach's audience was always under God's pleasure. For example, Keach later preached the use, "And to you, sinners, if you would be found wheat in the day of Christ, then receive Christ's true doctrine, labour to distinguish between truth and error; beware of that strange and new scheme that darkens the free-grace of God, and tends to destroy the covenant of grace; remember to exalt Christ alone in your salvation . . . Be sure to build on Christ alone, and see that that faith thou hast in him, be the faith of God's elect, which sanctifies both heart and life, and is attended with good fruits; you must work from life, and not for life" (Keach, *Exposition of the Parables*, 52). Henry Jacob had also promoted the "plain" and "simple" preaching of Christ and the apostles. See Duesing, "Henry Jacob," 293. Whinnel used the argument cited to defend singing: "Our way of Preaching is never the worse because 'tis the common way that other Churches have among them, and is used by other Ministers, nor no more is our way of Singing" (Whinnel, *Sober Reply*, 6, cf. 38).

the monstrous step of universal proclamation. However, they never took salvation out of God's hands or beyond God's initiative. Saint and sinner alike were exhorted in their sermons, and above all Christ was exalted. But there was one additional way in which Baptists sought the salvation of souls in worship, related very closely to the public preaching of the gospel.

Family Worship

"For Puritans the importance of the Sabbath was its association with preaching, Bible reading, and household prayers."[84] Because Puritans believed that God propagated salvation through families, they highly esteemed the practice of family worship. The Westminster Confession and the *Directory* contained an entire section devoted to it; the head of the household was to prepare everyone for public worship, then account later for what they learned, spending the rest of the day in catechizing and prayer, "that so the profit which they found in the publick ordinances may be cherished and promoted, and they more edified unto eternal life."[85] Baptists were (falsely) accused of putting their children out of the covenant, so they had a vested interest in this practice. By their own principles it would make much sense that they paired public preaching with private teaching of the gospel in families. Unfortunately, London Particular Baptists did not give much attention to this possibility in their early writings. Exceptions include Jessey's gospel-centered *Catechisme for Babes, or, Little Ones*, and a lonely comment about its importance in the Midlands' associational records in 1656.[86] But an episode in 1657 illustrated that they were not oblivious to it.

---

84. Hill, *Century of Revolution,* 85. Payne's assertion, "There can be no doubt that behind the corporate worship of our fathers much family and private devotion was presupposed," may have been more ideal than actual. Payne, "The Free Church Tradition and Worship," 63. Admittedly, that was not his central argument.

85. *Directory* [1645], 58; also *Westminster* [1646], Article XXI, Section VI. Burroughs said that neglecting family worship was "departing from God." Burroughs, *Gospel-Worship*, 33.

86. Jessey, *Catechisme for Babes*; White, *Association Records*, 1:25. A Baptist minister in Bedfordshire, William Wheeler, wrote beautifully in his will, "And one thing more I shall commend / Unto thy trust and tender care; / My Children (Love) whom God did lend / As blessings from his mercy rare, . . . / O pray (Dear Heart) and often pray / Unto thy God, as I have done, / That they may all his Voice obey, / And in his Ways, their Race may run." Clipsham, "William Wheeler's Last Legacy," 34, cited from Wheeler's *Spiritual Portion* published in 1670. He spoke in depth of his responsibility in family worship; at least some Baptists understood this important matter.

Richard Ballamie was a member of the Baptist church in Tiverton when he suddenly joined the Presbyterian church. At the Presbyterians' prompting, he accused the Baptists of slighting the Sabbath and walking loosely. But his harshest accusation was, "I further observed, that their families were without prayer generally; their children without instruction; and surely their constant neglect of duties in their families, made me grow very carelesse of mine in private."[87] Particular Baptists Robert Steed and Abraham Cheare took up Tiverton's cause, saying,

> the Lord knoweth we condemn, abhor, and detest the guilt of this accusation, we faithfully exhort unto these Christian duties, we reprove their neglect; and we are in a readiness to pass publick censures upon the careless and wilfull transgressions of them, as persons offending against plain precepts: The Lord knoweth we long and labour to have our houses as churches of Christ, and our children in submission with all gravity, brought up in the nurture and admonition of the Lord; yet being very jealous that several in Tiverton, and elsewhere, may not have been so careful in the performance of their duty in these things . . .[88]

Steed and Cheare explained in passionate detail that parents and masters should pray for their households for salvation and sanctification, should pray that God reveals to them how best to lead and instruct their household, and should diligently call their families together for prayer and instruction.[89] The ferocity with which they responded to Ballamie's

---

87. Ballamie, *Leper Cleansed*, 5. Much of the book was about infant baptism and covenant theology. However, a close reading reveals that those arguments were planted by the Presbyterians. Ballamie himself had had a personal fallout with the pastor, William Facie. It seems that his actual issues with the church, in addition to his qualm with the pastor, were that the church should obey the magistrate, emphasize family worship, and sing psalms in worship. The "rawest" paragraphs said nothing about infant baptism.

88. Steed and Cheare, *Plain Discovery of The Unrighteous Judge*, 6. After consultation with Tiverton's pastor, they decided that Ballamie's complaint came from a specific situation in which the church allowed a man who had a heathen family not to command them to join him for family prayers. It was not their general rule. Ibid., 43. As a geographical note, Cheare ministered in Plymouth on the southwest coast; Steed ministered in Dartmouth further east on the southern coast; Tiverton was about halfway between Plymouth and Bristol. This controversy was widely known. *History of the Baptist Church, Dartmouth* recorded that Philip Gary succeeded Steed in 1685, the first year Steed's name appeared in London.

89. Ibid., 43. They elaborated, "We do not deny it; but do own, and affirm, That it is the Duty of Parents and Masters fearing God, to be frequent in calling their Families

accusation indicates a near and dear matter to their hearts. Later history would validate this impression, for Cheare was the first man to publish hymns specifically for children, followed closely by Benjamin Keach and John Bunyan.[90]

Keach took particular interest in children, writing multiple pedagogical tools (*The child's instructor*, *The child's delight*, and *Instructions for children*). In his study of Keach's catechisms, Jonathan Arnold found an emphasis on the doctrine of justification and biblical ecclesiology, certainly in line with the regenerate church and the royal priesthood. But Arnold also drew an astounding conclusion about the use of catechisms: "Keach's (and the other Baptists') distinctiveness lay in the exclusive focus on the parent's responsibility rather than the minister's."[91] If Arnold is at all correct, this opens a powerful door into the Baptists' view of worship and the church, raising the profiles both of the pastor and the father. Not yet saved, and thus not church members, children remained the responsibility of the nuclear family head who guided and modeled worship for them until they could participate fully in the church's worship. Children were present but silent observers of corporate worship (as were many of their mothers). Keach compared his church with paedobaptist churches: "our Priviledges not lesser but far greater; our Children have great advantages in having such Parents and Ministers to instruct them, to pray for them, and to set before them a good Example; besides, as soon as capable, they with others have the Gospel preached clearly to them."[92] Thus the connection between family worship and corporate worship was brought together in a full circle of the gospel. Unfortunately, the later history of the Particular Baptists under Charles II was one of unfaithfulness to this great duty. The epistle to the Second London Confession (both 1677 and 1688) declared that neglecting family worship was a chief cause "of the decay of

---

together, instructing them in the Principles of Religion; endeavouring by all means possible, their Conversion and Salvation" (ibid.).

90. Martin, "Baptist Contribution to Early English Hymnody," 195–96.

91 Arnold, "Reformed Theology of Benjamin Keach," 58–60, 66–68. Certainly, Arnold's statement cannot be taken absolutely. For example, Jessey directed *Catechisme for Babes* for use by parents as well as schoolmasters. But Collins focused his *Orthodox Catechism* on families, as did H. P. who compiled Jessey's and Cheare's works in H. P., *Looking-Glass for Children*, whereas Westminster clearly focused its *Longer* and *Shorter Catechisme* on churches. Jessey, with all pastoral concern, heavily emphasized a parent's role in a child's salvation.

92. Keach, *Gold Refin'd*, 121. Walker considered it a "priceless inheritance." Walker, "The Relation of Infants to Church, Baptism, and Gospel in Seventeenth Century Baptist Theology," 262.

Religion in our day."[93] Family worship was a critical matter to the leaders of the London Particular Baptists.

"Some Differences between Many Godly Divines and Us": Perceptions of Baptist Worship[94]

There remains an indirect evaluation of Baptist worship, both through outside descriptions of Baptist practices and roundabout comments by Baptists themselves. Those outsiders did not regularly acquit themselves as objective observers—Richard Baxter once wrote, "where hath there been known a Society of Anabaptists, since the World first knew them, that proved not wicked?"[95]—but even their exaggerations may offer reasonable insight. For example, though John Taylor was intending to ridicule the Brownist sects, he noted that their churches assembled in inconspicuous numbers, and a man opened the worship service with a thirty minute prayer, followed by a sixty minute sermon, followed by another man expanding on the sermon. There would be no reason to fabricate such a description. Furthermore, he noted that these churches welcomed doubters and the curious to their services, implying both that his words could be validated and that at least some Baptist churches knew they worshiped in mixed assemblies.[96]

---

93. *London* [1677], To the Reader. It said, "And verily there is one spring and cause of the decay of Religion in our day, which we cannot but touch upon, and earnestly urge a redresse of; and that is the neglect of the worship of God in Families, by those to whom the charge and conduct of them is committed. May not the grosse ignorance, and instability of many; with the prophaneness of others, be justly charged upon their Parents and Masters, who have not trained them up in the way wherein they ought to walk when they were young? but have neglected those frequent and solemn commands which the Lord hath laid upon them so to catechize, and instruct them, that their tender years might be seasoned with the knowledge of the truth of God as revealed in the Scriptures; and also be their own omission of Prayer, and other duties of Religion in their families, together with the ill example of their loose conversation, have inured them first to a neglect, and them contempt of all Piety and Religion?" (ibid.).

94. Collins, *Orthodox Catechism,* Preface. Collins argued that their differences were marginal enough that they could show charity towards one another.

95. Tombes, *Antidote,* 25–26.

96. Taylor, *Brownists Synagogue,* 5–6.

Gospel Worship and a New Purpose of the Gathering

Observations Related to Prayer and Preparation

Based on this description, at least some Baptist worship was characterized by preaching and prayer. Preaching has already been discussed, but little has been said about prayer. Based on the content of this chapter, it should come as no surprise that London Particular Baptists left no instructions how a minister should pray. To them, prayer was an intensely personal expression. As the Lord left no form or manner of prayer, neither would they. This captured the attention of at least some observers. The description of Barrowist worship in chapter 2 contained the curious phrase, "their kind of prayer," but only noted that it was extemporaneous and the people joined with groans and sighs. Likely, that was enough to identify positively the early separatist manner of prayer. Speaking specifically about a Baptist's prayer, Daniel Featley commented on its extreme length and extemporaneity, noting that the people only altogether said "Amen." He also observed that Baptist prayers lacked the variety of those in the Prayer Book.[97] All of this lined up quite neatly with Baptist priorities in worship already established. However, Baptists were not alone in employing an extensive pre-sermon prayer. The *Directory* outlined a lengthy pastoral prayer with a confession of sin (original sin and particular sins) and guilt, a profession of faith in forgiveness, an invocation of the Holy Spirit, a prayer for sanctification, a prayer for Reformed churches, the king, parliament, cities and seminaries, the Sabbath, the church service, and the preacher. Baptists acknowledged praying for many of those very things, but their separation from the *Directory* clarified that they would not be told anything about which they must pray, and further they would not restrict public prayer to a preacher.[98]

Baptist opinions about the *Directory* established other elements of their worship, as well. For example, Thomas Bakewell complained that though the *Directory* eliminated the sign of the cross in baptism and the use of the surplice, Baptists "stand out as much as ever."[99] On one level this reinforced earlier contentions that Baptists were not satisfied with reforming gestures and vestments; for example, Knollys and Keach demanded that there be absolutely no visual symbols of any kind in a church

---

97. Featley, *Dippers dipt*, 125. Though he threw in his lot with the Presbyterians, Featley was an Anglican at heart.

98. *Directory* [1645], 11–15; note also extensive comments about a pastoral prayer after the sermon; ibid., 17–18.

99. Bakewell, *Justification Of two Points*, 16.

gathering, including a cross.[100] In fact, they would accept no imposed order in worship of any kind (though their own unofficial order may have been just as rigid). But there may have been an additional level of rejection. Presbyterian worship would be termed sober and somber. According to the *Directory*, the people were not to talk at all, not to make any gestures or bows, and not to express any emotion, before or after the service. The service consisted of Scripture reading, psalm, prayer, sermon, prayer, and psalm. It was very orderly, and intended to be efficiently edifying. In *Gangraena*, Edward Barber, Henry Denne, William Kiffin, and Hanserd Knollys each attracted attention for their unsystematic, not-so-solemn manners of preaching (as did Samuel Howe in *A Swarme of Sectaries*). Robert Baillie specifically thought of the Westminster Independents as being "very irreverent" in their celebrations, especially of the Lord's Supper, and there is no reason to believe that the London Particular Baptists would not have emulated their mentors in this manner.[101] To Baillie, this meant "unedifying" in the sense of lacking careful preparation or coherence.

Based on everything said to this point about their emphasis on right, spiritual worship, Baillie's accusation seems out of place for the Baptists

---

100. Knollys believed that all images would turn into idols because Catholics used and worshiped all such images as idols—crosses, crucifixes, altars, paintings, vestments. Knollys, *Exposition Of the Revelation*, 114–15, 171, 244. Keach echoed Knollys's lists but focused on the cross, saying that Catholics "adore it, salute it, pray unto it, and trust therein for Salvation, crying, *Hail, O Cross, our only hope, increase thou to the godly Righteousness, and unto sinners give pardon*; save thou the company gathered together in they praises; yea, the very sign of this Idol made in the Air, upon the forehead, or over any thing is *Sacred* and *Venerable*, and hath force to drive away Devils, and do many like feats: wherefore this abomination hath prevailed above other, and is like *Beelzebub* Prince of the Devils, the Badg of the Beast, and Character of Mystery *Babylon*, Imprinted in Churches, Chappels, Altars, Houses and Highways, in Books, Writings, in Prayers, Sacraments, in Garments, Bodies and Souls of Men, both Quick and Dead; nay, nothing is well hallowed without it, no Sacrament perfect without it." Keach, *Antichrist Stormed*, 84. See also ibid., 56–57, 82–83.

101. In his personal letters about the proceedings of the subcommittee producing the *Directory*, Baillie acknowledged, "We agreed so farr as we went except in a table. Here all of them opposeth us, and we them. They will not, and saith the people will, never yield to alter their practise. They are content of sitting albeit not as of a ryte institute; but to come out of their pews to a table they deny the necessitie of it. We affirme it necessare and will stand to it. The Independents' way of celebration seems to be very irreverent. They have the Communion every Sabbath without any preparation before or thanksgiving after; little examination of people, their very prayers and doctrine before the Sacrament uses not to be directed to the use of the Sacrament. They have, after the blessing, a short discourse and two short graces over the elements, which are distributed and participate in silence without exhortation, reading or singing, and all is ended with a psalm without prayer" (cited in Shaw, *History of English Church*, 342).

(or even the Independents, considering Burroughs). But Baillie was complaining about the internal integrity of the church service; Independents put together their worship services haphazardly, if with much forethought at all, and there is reason to believe the Baptists were liable to this charge as well. Thomas Edwards noted specifically about Baptists that they did not believe they had to meet weekly, for a set length of time, or at a consecrated place, and that a church member could compose his or her own anthem to be sung during worship.[102] Place, time, and duration were and are critical variables for careful planning! To be fair, based on the varying conditions of persecution, Edwards's first three complaints may have been quite misplaced; Kiffin, for one, remembered meeting for all-day worship. However, the question about humane anthems (meaning humanly composed) raises several interesting issues.

Observations Related to Singing

Praising God, under which some included singing, was universally recognized as central to congregational worship. The great and destructive controversy about singing among London Particular Baptists will be covered in the next chapter, but two valuable truths can be learned about Baptist worship based on this observation of their practice of singing: the role of the Spirit in worship, and the limits of active worship. According to those who composed them, many of these humane anthems were spontaneous gifts, as in the case of Katherine Sutton, who was likely a member of Knollys's church. Knollys believed that just as there was a gift of preaching, so also there was of praying and singing: "Singing and Praying are two distinct Ordinances under the Gospel, 1 *Cor.* 14. 14, 15. and two distinct parts of the Worship of God, both which are to be performed by the anointing of the Spirit, *Col.* 3. 16. and *Eph.* 5. 18, 19."[103] This went a step beyond what has already been established in this book, that Baptists believed only true Christians could truly worship. Knollys spoke of a direct intervention of the Spirit in worship: "The Holy Spirit can dictate the Matter, yea and words of praise and singing, as well as the matter and words of prayer." He also believed that Sutton possessed this anointing.[104] According to

---

102. *Gangraena*, 1:23–31.
103. Knollys, *Exposition Of the Revelation*, 76.
104. Sutton, *Christian Womans Experiences*, Preface (by Knollys). See also Spilsbury, *Gods Ordinance*, 4, for an example of another Baptist who believed this principle.

her testimony, after an intense period of doubt and guilt while still in the established church, Sutton was convinced that much of her church's worship was false, including kneeling at Communion, the ceremony of infant baptism, and most importantly the use of formal prayer. She recounted,

> Upon which I even melted in my spirit, and fell into shedding of tears, resolving to separate from, and come no more to joyn in such a way of worship until I had very diligently searched into the true way of Gods worship, as it is written in his blessed word; and in order there unto I made use of all the best books I could get, that were then published to that purpose, and also called in the help of many Godly Ministers of several judgment: but when all this was done I was still unsatisfied in that behalf: And then did I cry unto the Lord to teach mee, and it was by the Lord set upon my heart, that I must not do any thing in the way of his worship but what I had ground for in his holy word; & that Gods Servants were always to observe his pattern in all that they do to him.[105]

After attending to this conviction for a long time, she was baptized and underwent laying on of hands. Receiving the gift of the Holy Spirit, she soon discovered that she had the gift of singing. Over several years, she received prophetic verses—"not stud[i]ed things, but given in immediately"—and apparently sang them soon after reception.[106]

Based on the little that has been published about the Baptist hymn singing controversy, one might get the mistaken impression that the two opposing factions disagreed over whether or not there should be singing in worship. The next chapter will explain the true nature of their disagreement, but suffice it to say at the moment that all sides agreed that there existed a set of conditions under which God should be praised in song. Even Robert Steed, one of the most important voices against Benjamin Keach's manner of singing, agreed in 1658 that proper singing was "the will of Christ."[107] In 1653, Presbyterian Cuthbert Sidenham declared baptizing

---

105. Sutton, *Christian Womans Experiences*, 7.

106. Ibid., 44. Here is an example of a song she received soon after breaking bread: "The Spring is come the dead is gone, Sweet streams of love doth flow: There is a Rock, that you must knock, from whence these stream do go. 2. The Banquets set, the King is come, To entertain his Guest: All that are weary of their sins, He wantes to give them rest. 3. Then come, and take your fill of love, Here's joy enough for all, To see our King so richly clad, And give so loud a call" (ibid., 42).

107. Overlooked by the few historians of the hymn singing controversy, Robert Steed's response to the controversy at Tiverton included, "We do fully and cordially own, speaking to our selves; teaching and admonishing one another in Psalms,

Gospel Worship and a New Purpose of the Gathering

infants and singing psalms the "two grand practical controversies of these times."[108] Sidenham and all others who wrote on the subject of singing (for or against) relied on the structure of the argument established by John Cotton in 1647. Cotton listed four basic questions: whether Old Testament texts could be used in New Testament worship, whether humane songs could be sung, whether the singing should be solo or congregational, and whether setting psalms to meter and rhyme violated the regulative principle.[109] To Sidenham, the primary issue was that some believed only those who possessed the spiritual gift to compose and sing songs should do so, while other believed that group singing according to a psalter was preferrable.[110] He chose the psalter, claiming that the Spirit no longer needed to provide new material for worship.

The early London Particular Baptists spoke very little about the role of the Spirit in worship, which is why such an important topic has been relegated to a section of indirect observation. The matter echoed uncomfortably the doctrines of the Quakers, as the next chapter will explain, and they knew they could not predict the activity of the Spirit. Those in the established church were suspicious of claims of spontaneous revelation, and they strongly discouraged (if not forbade outright) unpredictability

---

Hymns, and spiritual Songs, singing and making Melody with Grace in our heart to the Lord, to be the will of Christ; according to which holy men of God are bound in all generations to sound forth his high Praises in the Church by Jesus Christ: which ought to be performed by them, being merry in the Lord, with Melody in their hearts, and a distinct and chearful voice, expressed either in the Songs of Moses, David; or otherwise, as the Spirit bringeth things to their remembrance, and gives them utterance" (Steed and Cheare, *Plain Discovery*, 42).

108. Sidenham, *Christian Sober and Plain Exercitation*. This book drew the immediate response of William Kaye, *Baptism without Basin*, a book that influenced Benjamin Keach. Interestingly, Keach would cite Sidenham's book to support singing but deny its validity with respect to baptism.

109. Cotton, *Singing of Psalmes*.

110. Sidenham, *Christian Sober and Plain Exercitation*, 189. He believed that the gift of singing (or spiritual poetry) no longer existed. Old Testament psalms were the only inspired texts now available for singing. When Paul spoke of everyone bringing a psalm to worship, he meant a suggestion for one of David's psalms. Ibid., 184, 191. Cotton was much more open-minded, saying, "Neither doe we deny, but that in the publique thanksgivings of the Church, if the Lord should furnish any of the members of the Church with a Spirituall gift to compose a *Psalme* upon any speciall occasion, hee may lawfully be allowed to sing it before the Church, and the rest hearing it, and approving it, may goe along with him in Spirit, and say Amen to it." He clarified, "Though spirituall gifts are necessary to make melody to the Lord in singing; yet spirituall gifts are neither the onely, nor chiefe ground of singing; but the chiefe ground thereof is the moral duty lying upon all men by the Commandment of God" (Cotton, *Singing of Psalmes*, 15, 44).

Pure Worship

in instituted worship. Consequently, they disdained reports of such highly irregular worship practices as allowing someone to stand and sing a song of her own composition. Baptist leaders including Knollys expected and desired the Spirit's activity in their gathering.[111] They may have intentionally rejected the careful worship planning of the Presbyterians because they wanted to leave sufficient space for the Spirit to move. Perhaps they believed that detailed planning belied a lack of faith, or that planning and spirituality were mutually exclusive; autonomy would have hindered but not prevented such planning. London Particular Baptists still carefully planned their sermons and left no indication that they ever failed to preach that sermon in the event of an unforeseen movement of the Spirit, but that does not mean that they did not hope for such a movement.[112] This would also explain why these Baptists eschewed the emotional austerity of established worship, particularly Presbyterian. Worship being personal and corporate, they encouraged fiery preaching and dramatic responses, mental and physical.

This entire matter echoed the dichotomy introduced by John Smyth between book and spirit, as the letter by Hugh and Anne Bromhead in chapter 2 noted. Featley complained about the Baptist belief that "there ought to be no set form of Liturgy or prayer by the Book, but only by the Spirit."[113] Baptists rejected formal worship because the form took the place of the Word and Spirit; Knollys was quite clear that pure worship could only be performed by the Word of God and the Gifts of the Spirit, and he desired pure worship far above respectable worship.[114] But most of the songs in question, including those by Sutton, were written down and brought into the church—an apparent violation of a rejection of book worship or formal worship. Some Baptists worried that "such Forms are

---

111. Knollys wrote, "The holy Spirit is not limited unto the Preaching of the Word; but HE also speaketh and teacheth in the reading of the holy Scriptures. So then, the holy Scriptures ought to be read in the Churches of Saints" (Knollys, *Exposition Of the Revelation*, 25). Morgan used the word "spontaneous" to describe early separatist worship. See Morgan, *Visible Saints*, 27ff. This word connotes a level of human creativity; perhaps "unpredictable" would be more appropriate. As noted earlier, McBeth used both "spontaneous" and "unpredictable" to describe early Baptist worship. McBeth, *Baptist Heritage*, 90.

112. Keach, who diligently wrote out his sermons, said, "He must bring forth and preach it by the help and assistance of the Spirit also, or else it may still be the Human, no Divine Sermon" (Keach, *Breach Repaired*, 136).

113. Featley, *Dippers dipt*, 32; the 1660 edition retained this complaint on page 36.

114. Keach, *Breach Repaired*, 136; Tombes, *Jehovah Jireh*, 5; Knollys, *Parable of the Kingdom*, 15.

Gospel Worship and a New Purpose of the Gathering

not spiritual Worship" but "a bar to the free exercise of the Graces of the Holy Spirit in us."[115] Keach's compromise sparked the controversy of the next chapter: singing did *not* require an extraordinary or miraculous gift of the Spirit because Christ commanded all Christians so to sing; rather, "provided our Hymns are founded directly on God's Word" they could be considered spiritually inspired. London Particular Baptists had long rejected Smyth's absolute putting away of all books in worship. Hercules Collins argued in the *Orthodox Catechism* that "it is as lawful to compose a Hymn, grounded on the Word of God, in a set Form, and deliver it to the People, either by strength of memory, or as written, as [it is to] deliver a Sermon in a set Form, by Notes."[116] Keach and Collins found it a false dichotomy to separate the Spirit from the Form—all true worship was empowered by the indwelling Spirit—but other Baptists warned "if you assert a prescribed Form of Singing, you cannot possibly avoid the bringing in of a Form of Prayer."[117] It can thus be noted that Baptists could not agree on the line between proper preparation for and proper reliance on the Spirit in worship. Because they were willing to divide over this issue, it cannot be denied that they believed pure worship was fundamental to their identity.

Observations Related to Mixed Assemblies

A second truth can be drawn from these observations. Thomas Ford believed that the biggest point of contention with respect to hymn singing was *not* whether humane songs could be used in worship; "The main thing, I conceive, that troubles the most" was how Christians could sing "in a mixt congregation."[118] Church gatherings were mixtures of believers and non-believers. While non-believers could listen to a sermon, they could not truly participate in spiritual worship such as singing. To account for this, some Baptists rejected congregational singing out of hand (though some allowed solo singing) as the only way to prevent non-believers from attempting to participate in active worship.[119] In addition, those Baptists

---

115. Marlow, *Prelimited Forms of Praising God*, Appendix, 43, 48.

116. Collins, *Orthodox Catechism*, 82. Unlike the ability to preach and pray, "God never made any such Promise of giving an extraordinary Gift of Singing" (ibid.).

117. Marlow, *Prelimited Forms*, 31.

118. Ford, *Singing of Psalmes the Duty of Christians*, 34–35.

119. Even Baptists on the same side could not agree about these circumstances. Both Keach and Wright, who promoted singing in church, denied that any could sing a solo, "either by an extraordinary or ordinary Gift." Wright, *Folly Detected*, 55; cf.

noted that gatherings were mixtures of men and women, and Paul also commanded that women keep silence in the churches. Thomas Bakewell complained about the Baptists that they excluded "women and children from having any voice in their Churches."[120] As the hymn-singing controversy illustrated, some Baptist churches took this extremely literally, quarrelling whether women could even say "amen" at the end of a prayer. Knollys's approval of Sutton demonstrated that some Baptists disagreed, but Knollys and Keach both had to write explicit arguments defending the right of women to participate in vocal singing as spiritual Christians (similarly, John Griffith had had to defend his practice of laying hands on baptized women by reminding his detractors that the Spirit was given to all Christians, including women).[121]

Both types of "mixtures" intersected in baptismal practices. Presbyterian John Geree noted the rise of a ceremony called "private baptism" that Baptists had opposed. For convenience, small groups of women were given the authority to conduct infant baptisms in the comfort of a home. According to Geree, Baptists specifically opposed that these baptisms did not take place before the church body and that they were administered by women (Geree agreed with them).[122] But the "public" nature of Baptist baptismal services took a variety of manifestations. For example, the 1641 edition of the Prayer Book noted a great multitude of people going to Hackney Marsh for such, but Nathaniel Homes intimated that at least some of these services were very secretive.[123] On-site baptisteries were a later addition to Baptist churches, so baptismal services would have been separate from the weekly corporate worship service.[124] When conditions

---

Keach, *Breach Repaired*, 145. Both Keach and Allen (following Cotton) argued that singing was a moral duty enjoined on all people. See Keach, *Breach Repaired*, 107; and Allen, *Essay to Prove Singing of Psalms*, 54.

120. Bakewell, *Confutation of the Anabaptists*, n.p.

121. Knollys wrote, "Women have the Essence of Singing (as well as Men) both in their Souls, and with their Voices; and are allowed to speak by all the Churches of Saints" (Knollys, *Answer to a Brief Discourse Concerning Singing*, 11). See also Keach, *Breach Repaired*, 139; Keach, *An Answer to Mr. Marlow's Appendix*, 32–37; and Griffith, *Searchers for Schism Search'd*, 86ff.

122. Geree, *Vindiciae Paedo-Baptismi*, 58ff.

123. BCP [1641], 8. Homes (defending private baptisms) wondered whether a crowd of forty people at a private baptism were not as public as three Baptists at an "uncouth" riverside. Homes, *Vindication of Baptizing Beleevers Infants*, 203.

124. Goadby noted that Horsleydown housed the only baptistery in London for many years into the 1700s. Goadby, *Bye-Paths in Baptist History*, 353; see also White, "Thomas Crosby: Baptist Historian, Part 1," 157.

Gospel Worship and a New Purpose of the Gathering

were calm, Baptists would have encouraged friend and foe to observe their baptisms, taking it as an opportunity to demonstrate and defend their uniqueness. But baptisms were relatively rare, meaning that the most common entry point for a "visitor" would have been the weekly worship service (Broadmead Church, for example, dismissed visitors only when it was time to conduct business).[125]

Based on these observations, it can be concluded that Baptists were keenly aware of participation levels in their worship services, even if they may not have planned them with the same exactitude as Presbyterians or Anglicans. But because they did not enforce uniformity, this awareness took them in different directions. Worship was so important to them that they not only allowed such divergence, they were willing to split over it, they were willing to enjoin absolute silence on the part of their wives, and they were willing to entertain the possibility of a supernatural intrusion of the Holy Spirit. However, not all of them seemed to appreciate the gospel implications of their practices. Both Knollys and Keach encouraged women to participate in their worship services (though they believed women should not administer an ordinance, Knollys indirectly violated this principle by allowing Sutton to offer hymns in worship; Keach refused to allow anyone to sing a solo in his church services), reminding that women were expected to give account of their conversion upon admittance to church membership.[126] Keach even wondered, "You may ask whether they are to praise God as well, and demand a word of Institution for their Breaking of Bread with the Church? for you know some demand a Proof for that."[127] Here an important consequence of gospel worship found its expression: all Christians—men and women, rich and poor—could worship together,

---

125. *Broadmead*, 86. One entry described in great detail a baptism in January 1666/7 on a day the weather turned sharply and unexpectedly cold, so much so that the usual "spectators" stayed inside and thought everyone who participated in the service "mad." The record included a later note that all ten men and four women who were baptized, after ten years, were still in fine health. Ibid., 92ff. With respect to numbers of baptisms, Petty France recorded 108 baptisms between 1675 and 1684. See Dowley, "A London Congregation During the Great Persecution," 233–39. If Petty France followed Broadmead's practice of conducting multiple baptisms at the same time (because they had to travel to water), they averaged no more than a baptismal service per quarter.

126. Knollys, *Answer*, 11; Keach, *Breach Repaired*, 139; Keach, *Answer*, 32–37.

127. Keach, *Breach Repaired*, 142. He thought highly of women: "But if Women may not speak nor teach in no sense in the Church, they must not be admitted to give an account of their Conversion on the Church, or how God was pleased to work upon their Souls: for that Practice is full of Teaching and Instruction, and has been blessed to the Conversion of some other Persons that have been by" (ibid., 139).

regardless of social norms. The fact that some London Particular Baptists would not give a voice to women is a reminder of a rigid regulative principle's hold on them (perhaps driven by a latent chauvinism).

In summary, the commitment to gospel worship took London Particular Baptists in very different directions from other Protestants. They believed that worship was for Christ, to celebrate His salvation and His Lordship over them. That message of salvation, combined with their understanding of election, led to a very intentional and unique (if seemingly haphazard) worship service. Their commitment to the gospel led them to eliminate all ceremonies that detracted from Christ in any way, including infant baptism, sacraments that confused the nature of salvation, and all external forms that distracted the senses. They desired a simple and austere worship that hearkened to some types of Puritan worship, but they used the ordinances to communicate the message of salvation, which was why they believed Christ instituted them in the first place. The purpose of their gatherings was not a base mental edification; worship was for God who communicated spiritual blessings through the encounter. Preaching was not just to teach doctrine but also to stir emotion, to call for a response, and to invite outsiders to Christ. Though Baptists shared many principles with their Protestant brethren, outsiders found their worship services irregular and irreverent; by this they meant that Baptists did not follow a careful liturgy or employ strict ceremony. Baptists believed that the Spirit participated in pure worship, and He was not predictable any more than salvation was predictable. As proof of pure worship's importance to the Baptists, they were willing to let their own disagreements in these matters divide them. It is finally time to evaluate the consequences of the London Particular Baptists' commitment to pure worship.

six

Baptist Worship and a New Identity of the Faithful?

"When First Our Churches Were Planted": A Test of Worship[1]

The title for this chapter comes from a debate leading up to the 1692 meeting of the General Assembly of London Baptists at the Devonshire Square church. The key figures were Hanserd Knollys, William Kiffin, Benjamin Keach, and Isaac Marlow. The subject was instituted worship. While Benjamin Keach has received increased scholarly attention as of late, this debate, known as the hymn-singing controversy, has only received one truly effective analysis.[2] When placed in the unique context

---

1. Whinnel, *Sober Reply*, 14.

2. That would be Brooks, "Benjamin Keach." Since Vaughn, "Public Worship and Practical Theology in the Work of Benjamin Keach," sought to prove that Keach was the most important Baptist theologian of his day (taking grief for labeling him a "practical" theologian, which Keach most certainly was in the non-pejorative sense of the word), a number of valuable works have been published about Keach. Riker, *Catholic Reformed Theologian,* and Arnold, "Reformed Theology of Benjamin Keach," have recently raised Keach's profile with impressive theological treatments, Riker focusing on his doctrines of federalism and baptism, and Arnold on Christology and eschatology. Unfortunately, both avoided the hymn-singing controversy (Arnold deliberately; Riker gave the wrong year of *The Breach Repaired* in his bibliography, indicating

of Baptist priorities, the hymn-singing controversy should be recognized as a key event defining the end of the early Particular Baptist vision and a valuable tool for understanding their opinions on complex theological matters. Benjamin Keach had become a Particular Baptist sometime around 1670, and his church on Horsleydown quickly grew to one of the largest and most influential London Baptist Churches.[3] By 1692, he had a well-established reputation for separating from other Baptists due to worship practices, most immediately congregational singing but mainly laying on hands at baptism, that other Particular Baptists questioned. For that reason, one might wonder why Keach should even be consulted in a book about the early Baptist "tradition" or "identity." The hymn-singing controversy brings my entire argument full-circle, so to speak. The early London Particular Baptists worked hard together to craft a biblical tradition that balanced autonomy and accountability; their driving focus was the pure worship of their Lord Jesus Christ. Two of those leaders, Hanserd Knollys and William Kiffin, were instrumental in bringing in and training a fiery and energetic General Baptist preacher named Benjamin Keach, who in turn became instrumental in guiding and encouraging the next generation of Particular Baptist leaders. All three provided leadership to joint functions of Particular Baptist churches, and all three cared about the thoughts and actions of their fellow Baptists. Both Keach and Kiffin acquiesced to the censure of the General Assembly (as this chapter will explain). Their identity as Particular Baptists meant *something* to them. That "identity" is an overlooked focus in the hymn-singing controversy. One of Keach's opponents defined his practice of hymn-singing as "such a humane Tradition as is utterly inconsistent with their [Baptists'] professed Principles, and to their Practice in other parts of Divine Worship."[4] In oth-

---

non-interest in the matter), even though it overlaps their fields in many ways. Note that Vaughn, Walker, *Excellent Benjamin Keach* (2004), and Copeland, *Benjamin Keach and the Development of Baptist Traditions in Seventeenth-Century England*, all addressed the controversy in their works only to report—not analyze—the issues. Brooks offered a serious and thorough analysis of the hymn-singing controversy. However, none of these works attempted to locate the controversy in the wider Baptist context (which is ironic given Copeland's title). All will receive further attention throughout this chapter.

3. In 1692, a letter was directed to the Baptist churches in London requesting relief for a group of General Baptists enduring persecution. It ended with the specific request, "Pray give the inclosed to Brother Keach; seal it or not, as you see occasion" (*The Lyn Persecution* [1692], 16). Whereas Kiffin once had sufficient political clout to obtain the release of imprisoned Baptists, these General Baptists looked to Keach as the most promising source of assistance in 1692.

4. Marlow, *Prelimited Forms*, 4.

er words, Baptist churches should be marked by Baptist worship. Worship now would uncover the instability of the very identity it helped to create. What was the Particular Baptist tradition? The hymn-singing controversy revealed that they could agree that pure worship was its distinctive, but little else. After the Glorious Revolution, when London Particular Baptists finally had the freedom they had so long sought, corporate worship was the issue they saw both as their redemption and their destruction.

The End of an Era: The Beginning of Disintegration

James II succeeded his older brother Charles in 1685. He was mistrusted for being pro-French (due to his time there in exile) and pro-Catholic, but his eldest daughter and presumptive heir, Mary, was a Protestant married to a Dutch Protestant, William of Orange. However, James produced a son by a Roman Catholic wife in 1688, which pushed the English Protestants over the proverbial edge. During the so-called Glorious Revolution of 1688, Protestants invited William and Mary to force James II from the throne, which he abdicated, and they rallied support of Nonconformists by promising an Act of Toleration. In early 1689, Parliament declared William and Mary joint monarchs; on May 24, they enacted the promised toleration. On July 22, Particular Baptists called for their first official General Assembly, which met September 3–12 that same year. Pastors and messengers from more than one hundred churches gathered in London to celebrate their freedom and ascertain the health of their brethren churches.[5]

The Particular Baptists quickly mourned their lamentable condition. As the messengers looked about themselves, they saw a "want of holy Zeal for God" and they feared "the Power of Godliness being greatly decayed;" most importantly, they grieved "that the Lord's Day is no more religiously and carefully observed."[6] The minutes of this gathering recorded, "And being met together, the first Day was spent in humbling ourselves before the Lord, and to seek of him a right way to direct into the best Means and Method to repair our Breaches, and to recover ourselves into our former Order, Beauty, and Glory."[7] Benjamin Keach, who served as the secretary to the Assembly, believed that this means was proper (pure) corporate worship, leading to the title of his famous treatise, *The Breach Repaired in*

---

5. See Ivimey, *History of the English Baptists*, 1:478–80, for a copy of the summons.
6. *Narrative* (1689), 4, 5.
7. Ibid., 9.

Pure Worship

God's Worship. Baptists withered because they did not worship God properly in the comprehensive sense of the word:

> I am perswaded, for several reasons, since this is so clear an Ordinance in God's Word, that the Baptized Churches, who lie short of the Practice of singing Psalms, *&c.* will never thrive to such a degree as our Souls long to see them, to the Honour of the Holy God, and Credit of our sacred Profession, and Joy and Comfort of those who are truly spiritual among us: for tho many things, as the Causes of our sad witherings, have been inquired into; yet I fear this, and the neglect of the Ministry, are the two chief, which are both holy Ordinances of Jesus Christ; and yet our People, (that is, some of them) do not love to hear of either of them.[8]

Keach began pressing to repair this breach in that first Assembly:

> But though it was thus broached among us, and some Attempts were made to bring it into Use, yet it was little minded till of late the common way of Singing began to be practised at some of our Lecture-Meetings in *London*, and was vehemently pressed forward by Mr. *Keach*, who in the first and greatest Assembly of the Messengers of our Churches, did challenge to dispute the matter; which was there accepted of: but it was not thought convenient by the Assembly to spend so much of their time that way, (and from thence forward Mr. *Keach* and others of his Mind, more strenuously promoted the Practice of this Error;)[9]

---

8. Keach, *Breach Repaired*, 99. Remember that "worship" was used consistently to describe the church's corporate actions. "Worship" should not be reduced to "singing," as it might in modern contexts, elevating the nature of this solution from Keach's perspective. The other matter noted in the quote, the neglect of the ministry, had to do with the maintenance of ministers. This was actually a very important matter to the Baptists; those who were accused of neglecting their pastor's well-being during this hymn-singing debate reacted strongly.

9. "Truth Cleared: Or a brief Narrative of the Rise, Occasion, and Management of the present Controversy concerning Singing in the Worship of God," 4. This brief collection of letters appeared as an anonymous addendum to Marlow, *Truth Soberly Defended*. The most likely editor was Marlow himself. Marlow attended the General Assembly as a messenger from the Mile-End Green church, which had broken away from Horsleydown over hymn-singing and called George Barret as pastor. His use of the term "lecture-meeting" indicates that he had a very different view of the gathering than Keach. Kiffin also remembered this exchange in 1689, and added a similar exchange in 1691: "For he [Keach] was present at the General-Meeting of the Messengers, when he with others of them, were proffer'd a time for a friendly Conference on that Subject whenever they would desire it. Only it was by the unanimous Consent of the whole Assembly agreed, that it was not expedient to have the Controversy argued

Baptist Worship and a New Identity of the Faithful?

Hanserd Knollys and William Kiffin headlined the Assembly as the remaining members of the first generation of Particular Baptists; the thirty-two signers of the Epistle also included the aforementioned Robert Steed, William Collins, George Barret, Benjamin Keach, Thomas Whinnel, and Hercules Collins. With Knollys, Collins, and Keach standing against Kiffin, Steed, and Barret, the question became whether a breach would be repaired or widened. As proof that the matter of pure worship was still their driving principle, these men believed that the breach was not only with one another but also with God Almighty. Both sides believed that the other had abandoned the principles of their proud tradition as well as the blessings of God. Resolution would be hard-fought.[10]

Thomas Whinnel inadvertently explained why this controversy should be held in high consideration with respect to Baptist principles in his entry to the controversy. In 1691, he wrote *Sober Reply to Mr. Robert Steed's Epistle Concerning Singing* (which itself was a response to *The Breach Repaired*) in which he dropped two massive bombshells. First, he accused Robert Steed of being the mastermind behind Isaac Marlow. Not only did Steed preach the sermon that moved Marlow to air his grievances against Horsleydown, a sermon preached soon after the 1689 General Assembly, but also Whinnel believed that Steed helped Marlow write his works.[11] This was particularly grievous because Steed was Knollys's co-pastor at Broken-Wharf church. Whinnel chided "that you were not satisfied to preach down in your Congregation what your Reverend

---

among them at that time, because it would unavoidably obstruct them in the Business they came about, which was for the general Good of all the Churches. Indeed at the last General Meeting [in 1691], Mr. *Whinnel* did craftily and surreptitiously, in Combination with others, on the last Day of that Assembly, when the most part of the Country-Messengers were gone home, and many of the Messengers of the Churches in the City absent, a Time intended only for them that remained, to put in order what had been agreed on in the former days of their Assembling, that it might be presented to the Churches; then did he present something to be debated concerning Persons retaining their Communion with a Church whereof they were Members, though the Practice of common Singing were, contrary to their declared Judgments and Consciences, set up in it; Which being them so unseasonably presented in the Absence of the greater part of the Assembly, it was witnessed against by many then present, as that which was not fit to be debated at that time; it favouring more of a politick Contrivance than of Honesty and Candor" (Kiffin et al., *Serious Answer,* 12).

10. Keach was described as a man "who makes Breaches more than he repairs any." Kiffin et al., *Serious Answer,* 10. The authors would not waste such harsh language on an unimportant topic.

11. Whinnel, *Sober Reply,* 3. This accusation was particularly ironic because Steed counter-accused that Keach was the primary mind behind Whinnel's work. Kiffin et al., *Serious Answer,* 5.

Brother Mr. *Knowles*, your Fellow Elder, who is (as we may say) the Father of the Church, had preached up, but now writ against him also."[12] Second, he turned the debate into a rehearsal of Baptist history and its great and worthy leaders. He cited Tombes ("famous beyond most for the Baptized Way"), Jessey ("pious, prudent, laborious, learned and faithful"), Powell ("learned and godly"), and Knollys ("Reverend, Pious Learned and Laborious") in support of the practice of congregational singing. He concluded, "All the Baptists were not against this way of Singing when first our Churches were planted."[13]

Both at Broken-Wharf and Horsleydown, the debate over hymn-singing became an exercise in Baptist principles, all of which related to worship. Against Keach, who argued that singing was necessary for Baptist churches to regain their former glory, Kiffin (or Steed) countered with the exact opposite:

> And accordingly it was in those Days laid aside by the Baptized Churches, whom the Lord then graciously and eminently owned by many signal Tokens of his Presence among them. But now to our great Grief, some whose Duty and Place it was to have setled, and further to have established the Churches in that Work of Reformation, and declined from it, asserting (with Heat and Confidence) that to sing by a composed Form, with a whole Multitude lifting up their Voices together, the Ignorant and Profane, the Unbelievers or Unconverted with the Church-Members, is an Ordinance of our Lord Jesus.[14]

Marlow, who was married to a member of Keach's church, accused Keach, "And surely if they were truly sensible of the natural Consequences of such a Practice of formal Singing, that the introducing of it into those Churches that have been established on contrary Principles, is the ready way to divide and break them into pieces." The practice of congregational singing would "greatly indanger our reformed Separation, and make it easy for us

---

12. Whinnel, *Sober Reply*, 4. He continued, "One would have thought Modesty, and Respect to his great Age, Learning, and Sincerity, and to prevent reproach, might have stopped your Pen, and unadvised attempt" (ibid.). Steed vehemently denied this charge.

13. Ibid., 13–14. Epithets would be a significant element of the debate.

14. Kiffin et al., *Serious Answer*, 4. Although Kiffin was first listed among the authors, the extremely critical tone of the work indicates that he was not the primary author. The other three authors, Steed, Barret, and Man, had been selected by Isaac Marlow to represent the anti-singing position in a proposed debate with a panel selected by Keach. Not long after that debate fell through, this book appeared.

to glide into the National Way of Worship."[15] To Marlow (and to Keach), this was a controversy over what it meant to be Baptist, and every one of the principles discussed in this book became a forum for fresh debate. Granted, the disputants did not arrange their arguments as such, but I will use the structure of the earlier chapters of this book to organize their primary contentions as clearly as possible. The hymn-singing controversy offers substantial proof that pure worship was the early English Baptist distinctive.

Recapitulating Generations of Debate about Pure Worship

After the first General Assembly declined Keach's request to discuss hymn-singing as a solution to their spiritual malaise and Robert Steed preached against the practice, Keach focused on consolidating his position in his own church. Since the mid-1670s, the church on Horsleydown had sung a hymn after the Lord's Supper and on certain thanksgiving days. But on December 22, 1690, Keach announced a debate and vote for January 1 that the church would begin singing congregational hymns regularly (and soon after published a collection of three hundred hymns called *Spiritual Melody*). Though his opponents accused him of suppressing and bullying them, this proposal passed by a very wide margin.[16] During this buildup, Marlow published *A Brief Discourse concerning Singing in the Publick Worship of God*, which grew into *Prelimited Forms of Praising God, Vocally sung by all the Church together, Proved to be no Gospel-Ordinance*. Hanserd Knollys, Benjamin Keach, and Joseph Wright each responded to Marlow, to which Marlow took great offense, accusing Keach in particular of dealing unfairly with him. Keach and Marlow agreed that there should be a debate in Fall 1691, but it fell through when Keach felt Marlow was being too manipulative with its conditions.[17] Subsequently, Robert Steed published his own thoughts, earning a response by Whinnel and a counter-

---

15. Marlow, *Prelimited Forms*, 11.

16. See Keach, *Breach Repaired*, The Epistle Dedicatory, 4; and "Truth Cleared" in Marlow, *Truth Soberly Defended*, 3–11, 30–43; for two different perspectives on this progression.

17. For this debate, Keach had selected William Collins, Leonard Harrison, Samuel Bagwell, and [Joseph] Masters; Marlow had selected Robert Steed, George Barret, Edward Man, and Richard Hallowell. Three of each four were signees of the 1689 and 1692 Minutes. Of the two exceptions, Bagwell had signed Thomas Whinnel's work and Hallowell was one of the men (including Marlow) chosen to receive contributions to the ministers' fund by the 1689 Assembly.

response headlined by Kiffin. Far from being minor and tangential, this debate was so captivating and disruptive that the 1692 General Assembly had to devote most of its proceedings to the matter, issuing the shocking declaration:

> We have also considered and determined, (that for the prevention of any further Reproach and Dishonor that may come upon the Name of the Lord, and your Holy Profession, that nothing will prove more effectual for this End, than) That all Persons that are concern'd on both Sides in this Controversy, be desired, and we do desire and determine, That they should call in, and bring all their Books hereafter mentioned into this Assembly, or to whom they shall appoint, and leave them to their dispose.[18]

So worried were they about the nature of the debate and its woeful effect on the Particular Baptist tradition that they were willing to attempt full censorship.[19]

The Church

With all of this in mind, this analysis will begin where the book began, with the ecclesiological consideration of a free church for free worship.[20]

---

18. *Narrative* [1692], 12.

19. The Assembly went so far as to say, "That none of the Members of the Churches do buy, give, or disperse any of these Books aforesaid underwrit, nor any other that have those uncharitable Reflections in them against their Brethren; and that no Person do sell them, or give them to others" (ibid., 13). The four books censored were Whinnel's *Sober Reply*, both parts of Marlow's *Truth Soberly Defended*, and Kiffin's *Serious Answer*. That Kiffin bore at least some responsibility for the book is proven by his volunteering to sit under arbitration for his role in the controversy. Wright likely was a General Baptist, else he would have been reprimanded for his hard words against Marlow, "This Man ('tis judged by wise and thinking Men, who are not of our Mind) has done more hurt, and brought more reproach on the holy Name of God, than any one Person for many Years; and a Shame it is to his Abbeters who countenance him in his nonsensical and rediculous way of Scribling, in opposing a precious Ordinance of God" (Wright, *Folly Detected*, 76). The use of "our Mind," meaning Baptist, indicates that the trouble had attracted so much attention that even a General Baptist had to respond. Little else is known about him. He might have been an old leader noted in Whitley, *Minutes of the General Assembly of the General Baptist Churches in England*, 1:xliii.

20. This is one of several areas neglected in the published reports of the hymn-singing controversy, most notably by Copeland who recognized the freedom granted churches with respect to singing in the Second London Confession but missed the larger connection with the "Baptist tradition" he set out to explore. See Copeland, *Benjamin Keach*, 120–40.

Baptist Worship and a New Identity of the Faithful?

When the first General Assembly gathered, they passed seven resolutions governing their role. One was that they would not impose their actions on anyone, "but leave every Church to their own liberty." Another was that "if any particular Offence does arise betwixt one Church and another, or betwixt one particular Person and another, no Offence shall be admitted to be debated among us, till the Rule Christ has given (in that Matter) be first Answered, and the Consent of both Parties had, or sufficiently endeavored."[21] Technically, the 1692 Assembly did not violate the latter resolution; they did not debate the matter on the floor because they did not have a clear Rule of Christ, and censures were given not for the persons' interpretations of Scripture but for their disrespect. But the Assembly did violate the former, realizing that liberty—especially in this all-important matter of worship—could be used to destructive ends, and they *were* willing to restrict that liberty. This was possibly the greatest early test of the tension between freedom and uniformity discussed in chapter 2. Anti-singers argued that the practice of singing was utterly inconsistent with Baptist principles, "the ready way to divide and break [Baptist churches] into pieces," and thus could not be allowed in *any* Baptist church.[22] To them, the limit of Baptist freedom was the limit of Baptist identity, and Baptist identity was tied to Baptist worship. If Baptists had unlimited freedom, they could choose to practice the Anglican Prayer Book service, which would make them Anglicans and not Baptists! But even if they were not so blatant in their trajectory, Marlow feared that the simple step of singing hymns would send unwary Baptists down a slippery slope: "we have reason to believe they have learnt their Notions from the Church of *England*, whereby they are infecting our Churches with such Principles as will naturally lead them to conform at least to their worship."[23] Such conformity was unacceptable within their understanding of Baptist principles.

In this way, the hymn-singing controversy proved that Baptists saw worship as the battleground for ecclesiological freedom. On the one side, Keach cried, "Cannot Christians have the Liberty of their Consciences from their Brethren, to practice a Truth according to their Light, without being charged and censured after this manner, with Carnal Forms, and mischievous Error?"[24] (in a form that soundly echoed Bunyan's indignation in the open-communion debate). And on the other side, Kiffin re-

---

21. *Narrative* [1689], 10.
22. Marlow, *Prelimited Forms*, 11.
23. Marlow, *Clear Confutation*, 22.
24. Keach, *Answer*, 13.

sponded that embracing the principle of hymn-singing would "stigmatize or brand [the Baptized Churches] with the deepest Hypocrisy that depraved Mortals can be guilty of." The glory of the Baptist tradition was its coming out of Roman and Anglican carnal worship, its being "farther delivered" from the anti-Christian apostasy than all other traditions, a new and better Reformation, as it were. If they were to go back to such forms of worship, it would be "the more pernicious to them than others" and "the more grievous and provoking to the Spirit of the Lord."[25] This matter was not a trifle but central to their very identity. Among the General Baptists, Thomas Grantham had established that distinct congregations would stay out of each others' practices, for any deeper kind of unity would demand that they dispense "with most of the principles of our Religion, one by one till indeed we have none left intire."[26] But in the Second London Confession, the Particular Baptists still held out for "the spirit of love and meekness to imbrace and own each other therein; leaving each other at liberty to perform other such services, wherein we cannot concur apart unto God, according to the best of our understanding."[27] In other words, congregational liberty would extend to all practices of which they did not have full and mutual satisfaction of Scriptural certainty, and Particular Baptists would find unity in such charity. Unfortunately, the hymn-singing controversy demonstrated that worship could drive them to opposing claims of certainty (not only about what the Bible did say but perhaps even more so about what the Bible did *not* say), circumventing the very unity to which they aspired. Indeed, Keach lamented that worship

---

25. Kiffin et al., *Serious Answer,* 5, 60, 61. Indeed, it would lead Baptists "even back to lick up the old Vomit." Ibid., 60. This would be another valuable matter for further study illuminated by the hymn-singing controversy. Both Riker and Brooks noted Keach's self-designation as a church reformer much in the same way I noted the Baptists as a "furtherance" of the on-going reformation. But Riker and Brooks emphasized Keach's continuity with the Reformation. Based on the language used in the hymn-singing controversy, one would have to wonder whether these Baptists truly saw themselves as continuing the previous Reformation or taking the next step into something new—a Reformation rooted in worship, not doctrine. See Riker, *Catholic Reformed Theologian,* 127ff; Brooks, "Benjamin Keach," 27ff. Note that Arnold concluded that Keach truly belonged "outside the boundaries of any single confessional group." Arnold, "Reformed Theology of Benjamin Keach," 243.

26. Grantham, *Sigh for Peace,* 119.

27. *London* [1677], 141–42. Kiffin had likewise pled, "we desire to live in Brotherly Love and Christian Society, and if we find our Brethren entertain any unsound Notion with respect to Gospel Truths, we look upon it as our duty to endeavour to inform them of it, in a meek and sober way." Kiffin, *Sober Discourse,* To the Christian Reader.

itself had become viewed as the very source of the trouble and that his view on worship labeled him as anti-Baptist.[28]

This intra- and inter-church persecution did not begin when Keach brought up hymn-singing at the 1689 Assembly. Chapter 2 alluded to a much earlier disintegration. Granted, Keach may have been a part of that trajectory, and if that were true it would have been due to his worship practices. In 1692, William Kiffin complained about "how long he [Keach] hath maintained a Wall of Partition between his and the rest of the Baptized Churches"[29] with respect to laying on of hands, one of the divisive issues covered in chapter 4. Keach had moved to London in 1668 as a General Baptist from Winslow and likely had adopted Particular Baptist beliefs by 1672 when Hanserd Knollys officiated his second wedding. He brought his commitment to the Six Principles with him from his General Baptist heritage, and his church was also singing hymns within two or three years. But his was not the only one. Hercules Collins became pastor of Spilsbury's congregation that then met on Old Gravel Lane in Wapping in 1676 (Keach preached the funeral sermon for the previous pastor, John Norcott), and his *Orthodox Catechism* of 1680 included a significant Appendix defending the ordinance of singing. When he was in prison in 1684, he wrote this powerful appeal:

> [D]o our Enemies deal unmercifully with us? is it not because we have dealt so, one with another? do they deal unjustly with us? is it not for dealing unjustly one with another? do they Persecute us? Alas! Have we not Persecuted each other, because of difference in Opinion, where yet the Image of *God* hath appear'd? for these things, God is Contending with us: Let us all Banish and Expel the *Achan* out of our Hearts, out of our Churches, and shew our selves Zealous against Sin, and exercise Judgment, as *Phineas* of Old did, and it may be the Plague and Judgment may stop; if we cleans our Hearts, our Families, our Churches, then

---

28. Keach, *To All the Baptized Churches*, cited in Brooks, "Benjamin Keach," 133. Brooks deserves credit for transcribing the very rare letters published by Keach and Marlow in response to the 1692 Assembly. Keach also wrote, "I have, dear Brethren, passed under the hardest Dispensation of late, that ever I met withal since I have been in the World; but I hope I can say my Sorrow or Grief is chiefly because the Name of God hereby suffers, and his People are exposed to Reproach. I desire to live no longer than to promote Peace and Union to my Power in all the Churches of the Saints; though I am represented as one that hath not indeavoured after it, because of my Writing in the Defence of Singing the Praises of God" (ibid.).

29. Kiffin et al., *Serious Answer*, 62.

> God may give us our Prophets again, our Sabbaths again, our Ordinances again, our Ministers again:[30]

This would indicate that the Particular Baptists had been harboring dissent long before 1689, and it is not a stretch to deduce worship as the source. Collins's appeal to prophets and Sabbaths and ministers would fall in line with their actual experience of persecution and imprisonment. But he specifically held out ordinances as another desire, which points to some kind of internal dispute or loss with respect to worship.

Hanserd Knollys had also written in favor of hymn-singing in 1681, and he further pointed to lingering discord among Particular Baptists in his exposition of Revelation, published in 1688. He said that Christ walking among the candlesticks represented "His inspection into the Churches Condition, Administrations, Gifts, Operations, and Ordinances." More importantly, it represented "His observation what Disorders, corrupt Opinions, false Doctrines, male-Administrations, and what Formality, Contentions, Divisions, Schisms, or sinful separations are among his Churches."[31] The consummate churchman, Knollys mourned every source of division as a barrier to that unified Baptist church of London he thought Scripture prescribed. In this case, it was the divergent opinions about ordinances (including singing) that concerned him. Specifically, he knew that angry words would lead to closed minds in discussions as sensitive as that over worship. His contribution to the hymn-singing controversy dripped with compassion and concern, crying "No Brother!" and "O my Brother!" even as he prayed for God to speak to hearts so he would not have to argue more harshly.[32]

Chapter 3 also explained the importance of the apostolic church model to the Particular Baptists, and the hymn-singing controversy reinforced this commitment in a bizarre way. Both sides latched on to one statement: "That spiritual and vocal Singing was used in the Primitive and Apostolical Church of Christ, is undeniable."[33] The apostolic pattern was all-important. But the anti-singers highlighted two particular traits of the early church: it was pure, and it was endowed with a special manifestation of the Spirit. Because the current church was neither, the pattern of singing no longer applied. Thomas Ford's observation rang true: some Baptists were greatly concerned that Christians and non-Christians

---

30. Collins, *Voice from the Prison*, 32–33.
31. Knollys, *Exposition Of the Revelation*, 20.
32. Knollys, *Answer*, 3, 5, 12.
33. See, for example, Marlow, *Brief Discourse*, 5; Knollys, *Answer*, 1.

"might have such close and high Communion together, as to unite their Voices in singing the Praises of God;"[34] the *im*purity of the current church with respect to participants not possessing salvation or the full measure of the Spirit disallowed them from attaining or even pursuing the apostolic model. This called into question everything about Particular Baptist primitivism (though eerily similar to Kiffin's argument against the laying on of hands noted in chapter 4), revealing the instability of their so-called regulative principle. And it was ironic because Keach actually saw congregational singing as a unique expression of unity and harmony in a church: "Singing *together* clearly shews, / the *People* should *one* be; / For *Union's* a most lovely thing, / *unite* us *all* to Thee!"[35] He recognized the concern about mixed assemblies but argued, "Unbelievers joyning with them, is one thing, and their joyning with Unbelievers, is another."[36] In other words, these fears must not dissuade Baptists from following a clear apostolic command and practice. Particular Baptists aimed for a pure congregation; if the threat of carnal attendees could prevent a church from attending to this ordinance, those churches should equally abandon hearing prayer and hearing the Word corporately.

In response to this assertion, anti-singers brought back two important trains of thought. On the one hand, some argued that congregational singing was not at all like prayer or preaching because it required an extraordinary gift of the Spirit that one did not need merely to listen and assent. This argument will be taken up below in the discussion of the role of the Spirit in worship. On the other hand, some argued that congregational singing was *not* a clear apostolic command; it was a practice they enjoyed by virtue of their purity and power. But Christ would not command what men could not perform, therefore it was *not* an ordinance.[37] While chapter 4 covered most of the Baptist thoughts about the ordinances, chapter 3 noted the perceived connection between a church and her ordinances: corruption in worship and ordinance was just grounds for separation from a church. In the hymn-singing controversy, Particular Baptists exercised this conclusion one against another. Members of Keach's church, many of

---

34. "Truth Cleared" in Marlow, *Truth Soberly Defended*, 40–41.
35. Keach, *Feast of Fat Things*, 82–83.
36. Keach, *Breach Repaired*, 105. See also Wright, *Folly Detected*, 59.
37. Ironically, both sides used this argument. Keach believed that Christ enjoined all Christians to sing, therefore it could *not* be an extraordinary gift of the Spirit. Marlow believed that singing was an extraordinary gift of the Spirit, therefore it could *not* be enjoined on all Christians.

whom had left it, had this to say about the debate and vote of January 1, 1690/1:

> We say and own, they had the majority, but we also say that we cannot understand that a major Vote is any Proof of Truth; and if the Church of Christ must alter the Worship of God maintained by her, and bring in fresh Pieces of Worship by major Votes, instead of Scripture and sound Arguments from it, then the Church of Christ may in a little time become Antichristian.[38]

Marlow and Steed made similar comments. Note how this stepped away from earlier Baptist beliefs of the mind of Christ inhabiting a true church, as if a church vote were mutually exclusive from truth. But worship was such a powerful matter to them that this disagreement revealed how fragile was their confidence in the true church. Members of Keach's church went on to say that keeping church communion with singers was no different than keeping communion with Anglicans or Catholics! The nature of their communion was tied to their church actions, "especially in the immediate Worship of God."[39] In response, Keach had to argue reminiscent of Barbone, Jessey, and Bunyan: the act of singing was *not* sufficient grounds for church separation, a declaration of no small conceit considering he separated based on the imposition of hands.[40] He went so far as to concede, "We do not look upon Singing, *&c.* an Essential of Communion; 'tis not for the being, but for the comfort and well-being of a Church," and yet he maintained singing as an article of his church's faith and a central element of his church's worship.[41] Both groups forwarded positions ab-

---

38. "Truth Cleared" in Marlow, *Truth Soberly Defended*, 35.

39. Ibid., 37.

40. Keach, *Breach Repaired*, xi–xii, 12. "Reformation," he wrote, "'tis evident, is a hard and difficult Work, and ever was; 'tis no easy thing to restore lost Ordinances." Ibid., 12. Not surprisingly, Whinnel echoed Keach almost verbatim; Whinnel, *Sober Reply*, 64. Keach also noted the hypocrisy in his opponents' position: "I cannot but marvel, that our Brethren should call Laying on of hands, a Doctrine, or Tradition of Men, and render those who plead for it, guilty of adding to the Word of God; and yet receive such into Communion at the Lord's Table" (Keach, *Laying on of Hands*, 92). In other words, if they separated over singing, they should also separate over laying on of hands. Ironically, Keach separated over the latter, yet he argued *against* separating over the former.

41. Keach, *Answer*, 9. This might be a way in which Arnold (and certainly Riker) overestimated Keach's hospitality. Riker, of course, tried to place Keach in a catholic tradition even though catholic truth to Keach was only that truth to which he assented (and therefore by definition not catholic). Arnold would not go so far, but he still insisted that Keach separated the fundamentals of the faith or salvation from the fundamentals of the church, which is why Arnold did not address the hymn-singing

solutely inconsistent not only with the other but even with themselves. The outlook for resolution seemed quite dim. Baptists had once treated every ordinance as a *sine qua non* of fellowship, yet that carriage seemed unsustainable. Just as the Second London Confession avoided the issue of closed-communion, so the 1689 General Assembly avoided singing, neither of which prevented that issue from becoming disruptive. Richard Hubberthorne, a Quaker who was cast out by Baptists for his beliefs about the ordinances, noted this inherent contradiction in their positions on worship: they would not tolerate "those that Worship a false god, or they which Worship the true God in a false way [such as Quakers] . . . But who must be Judge of that Blasphemie, Contempt, or Reproach spoken against the Lord Jesus Christ?"[42] If the Baptists issued proclamations of judgment without recourse to the objective standards they trumpeted, how was that any different let alone greater than the proclamations made by traditions they rejected?

The Scriptures

The hymn-singing controversy reiterated the importance of worship to a right understanding of the Scriptures (and vice versa) and also illustrated the great danger in the Baptists' subjective (or perhaps incoherent) use of the regulative principle. Historians have begun to understand the importance of the regulative principle in this particular debate, but a simplistic or rigid understanding of that principle obscures the tragic and lethal effects of this controversy for the Particular Baptists as a group.[43] Kiffin

---

controversy in his dissertation. But to say that Keach would admit as a Christian someone he would not admit as a member of his church (for disagreeing with him about one of these so-called lesser matters of the church) is a far cry from establishing some kind of formal triage in the contemporary sense. Yes, Keach suggested charity in this matter, but that would not prevent him from insisting that his church practice singing. All of these matters were of critical importance to Keach who, like all of the Particular Baptist leaders in this book, thought that pure worship was their earthly priority. Impure worship might not disqualify someone from entrance into glory, but that was quite beside the point.

42. Hubberthorne, *Answer to Declaration*, 8.

43. One article seemed to imply that Marlow's primary focus in this debate was the regulative principle, glossing over the nuances and implications in that Keach claimed the same ground. Haykin and Robinson, "Particular Baptist Debates about Communion and Hymn-Singing." Both Brooks and Vaughn recognized that Keach and Marlow equally believed the regulative principle supported their argument, which is why they would never be able to resolve their differences. Brooks thought that Marlow applied a rigid, unsophisticated (and hence false) regulative principle whereas

declared, "So we do as boldly, in the fear of the Lord, declare that the Way of common Singing, which they contend for, is after the Rudiments of the World, after the Traditions of Men, but not after Christ."[44] Just as emphatically, Keach countered, "We know no Psalms, but *David's Psalms*, or those called the *Book of Psalms*, and the holy Ghost doth injoin the Gospel-Churches to sing *Psalms*, as well as *Hymns, and spiritual Songs*. Will you take upon you to countermand God's holy Precept?"[45] As Marlow appealed to his audience who had declined from the truth of Gospel-Worship, "I humbly present that which the Lord hath convinced me of through the Light of the Holy Scriptures, to remove the Mistake you are under concerning Singing," so Knollys appealed, "[I] leave you and others of your Perswasion therein, to Consider what I have said, and pray, that GOD will Convince you of your Errour, and make known unto you His Revealed Will in the Holy Scripture of Truth."[46] No Baptist unity could withstand that nature of argument.

Each man absolutely believed that he employed the proper understanding of Scripture with respect to worship; any compromise would of necessity be a step away from pure worship and thus unacceptable. This circumstance becomes clear when the arguments are dissected. Baptists offered their arguments from Scripture in five primary types (with respect to the hymn-singing controversy): an argument from assemblies, an argument from semantics, an argument from the Testaments, an argument from forms, and an argument from silence (the normative principle). The first argument, which said that there was no biblical precedent or command for singing in a mixed assembly, is more appropriately covered under the next subheading. The second argument was lexical. Keach first introduced hymn-singing based on Matthew 26:30 (AV), "And when they had sung an hymn, they went out into the mount of Olives." In the Greek, it read, "Καὶ ὑμνήσαντες ἐξῆλθον εἰς τὸ Ὄρος τῶν Ἐλαιῶν" (NA27, "and after

---

Keach took a broader theological approach. Vaughn tried to paint it as a difference between living in fear (Marlow) and faith (Keach). Both saw the inconsistencies in Keach's positions. See Vaughn, "Public Worship," 83–84, 174–75, 184; and Brooks, "Benjamin Keach," 75–98, 128. Perhaps ironically, Arnold accused Keach of the same "stubborn adherence to a pre-critical reading of Scripture" of which Brooks admonished Marlow (in a different context). Arnold, "Reformed Theology of Benjamin Keach," 240. Frankly, the hermeneutical issues were far more complicated than the "regulative principle" versus the "normative principle," which is why I believe the terms should be abandoned.

44. Kiffin et al., *Serious Answer*, 15.
45. Keach, *Breach Repaired*, 129.
46. Marlow, *Prelimited Forms*, 5; Knollys, *Answer*, 12.

hymning, they went out to the Mount of Olives"). Marlow found three translations of the Bible that rendered the Greek *hymneo* something other than "sing," and concluded, "there is such clear and undeniable Evidence, that the word *Hymnos* a Hymn signifies simply Praise."[47] Hanserd Knollys, for one, quickly and soundly rejected such an idea because it opened a door to Quakerism, a subject of such importance that it will receive its own section.[48] Keach, on the other hand, recognized an even more dangerous consequence to this level of quibbling about words: Marlow's argument undermined the Baptist defense of immersion. He complained that "you make it your Business to trouble our People with the signification of the Greek word *Hymnos*, a *Hymn*, (though you understand not that Language) just after the same manner that the *Pedobaptists* do with the word *Baptizo*; say they, it signified *washing*, as well as *dipping*."[49] In other words, the hymn-singing controversy proved that Baptists were willing to adapt their hermeneutical conventions about the plain senses of words in order to justify their predetermined conclusions—especially in a matter as important as worship—regardless of their stated willingness to submit to biblical truth in all instances. Keach rightly (if hypocritically) noted, "O how hard is it to bring Men off from their own conceited Opinions, or to receive a Truth they either are prejudiced against, or else not willing to have it to be received as an Ordinance of God!"[50]

This controversy also re-opened the debate about the relationship between the Testaments. Chapter 4 noted that the Baptists distinguished themselves by restricting ecclesiology to the New Testament. Hymn-singing forced them to acknowledge that they held very different views about what that meant. In brief, anti-singers promoted what could be termed an antitype/type progression from the Old to New Testament, whereas

---

47. Marlow, *Prelimited Forms*, 8–9, 29–30; *Appendix*, 6–10. He often used Coverdale's Dutch Bible, *Biblia the Bible* (1535), which translated Matthew 26:30 as "and whan they had sayde grace, they wente forth unto mount Olivete." He also appealed to Whitchurch's English translation of Erasmus's New Testament (1540) and Barker's English translation of Beza's Bible (1585), which rendered *hymneo* as "praise" in a few places, declaring, "Our more ancient English Bibles bear a fuller Testimony to the proper Signification of the word *Hymnos* in divers other places, than the later modern Bibles do." Marlow, *Prelimited Forms, Appendix*, 9. Humorously, both of those translations used the word "sung" in Matthew 26:30. To be fair, the Latin Vulgate read, "*et hymno dicto exierunt in montem Oliveti*" ("and having said a hymn, they went out to the Mount of Olives"), which may account for some of the confusion.

48. Knollys, *Answer*, 9.

49. Keach, *Breach Repaired*, 18.

50. Ibid., 89–90.

the pro-singers held a type/fulfillment approach. The former held a more absolute discontinuity between the two. Both sides agreed that anything solely connected with "Levitical, Ceremonial, and external instituted Worship" was abrogated in the new covenant. This included, for example, singing with any kind of instrument.[51] But whereas Marlow read Exodus 15 as proof that singing should be categorized with dancing and instruments as an old form, Keach saw it as prefiguring congregational praise (especially since it came before the Law); the use of instruments was "a Figure of that sweet spiritual Melody the Saints should make from a well-tuned gracious Heart."[52] Anti-singers grouped everything associated with Levitical service as done away with in Christ; the external had been superseded by the internal. Pro-singers believed that its presence in the New Testament, especially the commands in Ephesians 5:19 and Colossians 3:16, proved that singing fulfilled those elements of external worship, doubly so because it was used before the Law.[53] Thus, they felt they could justify continuity between the Testaments in this matter consistently with their other positions. For the purposes of this book, of greatest consequence from this argument, both sides believed they employed the proper Baptist hermeneutic, so to speak, yet came to opposite conclusions and could not come off of their convictions. The controversy paralyzed them.

The fourth argument from Scripture dealt with forms. Keach worried about the confusion surrounding the proper form of singing, not the ceremonial or affective nature of it (which will be covered in the next subsection), but what it meant to speak to one another in psalms and hymns and spiritual songs in worship. He described "one saying 'tis only Heart-Joy; others 'tis no more than to praise or give Thanks to God in Prayer; saith another, 'tis to be performed or done by one single Man alone in the Congregation, tho not one Examples or Precedent in all the Scripture in God's ordinary Worship for any such Practice."[54] This is of particular note because it directly contradicted Knollys's one-time practice in his church; even Marlow acknowledged that an extraordinary movement of the Spirit could result in someone singing an inspired song in a service to the great blessing of all. Keach went so far as to say that he would charge such a sing-

51. See Marlow, *Prelimited Forms*, 12; Keach, *Breach Repaired*, 131.

52. Keach, *Breach Repaired*, 53. See Marlow, *Prelimited Forms*, 9, 12, 13, 24; Keach, *Breach Repaired*, 15, 30, 49, 74, 76, 82, 175. Keach never responded to the comment about dancing.

53. Marlow, *Prelimited Forms*, 14; Kiffin, *Serious Answer*, 58; Keach, *Breach Repaired*, 44, 46, 55, 79, 130, 133; Whinnel, *Sober Reply*, 8.

54. Keach, *Breach Repaired*, 89.

er with will-worship "and no sign of God's Presence at all." Keach believed that the scriptural form of singing was congregational and not individual; his opponents thought that the scriptural form was individual (and rare) and not congregational.[55] But the severe disagreement as to the proper application of the regulative principle went even deeper than this. Robert Steed, before he became Knollys's co-pastor, explained that his church did not sing psalms because the English did not have true psalms but artificial translations given meter and rhyme and set to common tunes.[56] Faithful churches would not employ such human constructs. The pro-singers misunderstood that Steed and others rejected congregational singing outright; they responded that a psalm by definition required such a set form, else how could everyone sing together?[57] Keach, however, recognized a separate threat from Steed's position: the potential deconstruction of all Baptist worship, particularly prayer and preaching. He warned that they had no command or precedent to pray before and after the sermon, nor to preach by method, doctrine, reason, and use—"Must we not use that Practice therefore?" Quite astonishingly, he went on to say that "'tis left to the faithful Servants of God to make use of such a Form or Manner as the Spirit of God may help them to, and the best Form or Method they ought and do make use of, which they judge may most tend to the profit of the People."[58]

If Keach's statement sounds like the normative principle, that is because it is. The final area of debate with respect to Scripture was the argument from silence and the revelation that both sides tacitly employed the normative principle.[59] This blindness supports the claim that these Baptists prioritized pure worship, shaping their principles around it. To be clear, everyone rejected the Anglican use of Scripture in developing worship practices; the dissenting members of Keach's church explicitly de-

55. Marlow, *Prelimited Forms*, 23; Kiffin et al., *Serious Answer*, 4; Steed and Cheare, *Plain Discovery*, 42; Keach, *Breach Repaired*, 145.

56. Steed and Cheare, *Plain Discovery*, 42. See Whitley, *Congregational Hymn-Singing*, 45–87, for a description of popular early English Psalters, especially the editions by Sternhold and Hopkins.

57. Whinnel, *Sober Reply*, 37.

58. Keach, *Breach Repaired*, 178, 173.

59. Haykin and Robinson, Copeland, and Vaughn seemed to downplay this, choosing instead to cast the disputants—primarily Keach for Haykin and Robinson and Marlow for Vaughn—into a role as a strict keeper of a Reformed interpretation of the regulative principle. Brooks, on the other hand, labeled the disagreement about Scripture's silence as the primary disagreement between Keach and Marlow, casting Marlow as the strictarian. Brooks, "Benjamin Keach," 60ff.

clared that the difference between them was not indifferent, "but is about the immediate Worship of God, in which nothing should be indifferent to us." Indeed, Marlow observed that Keach's manner and form of singing, contrary to the command of Christ, confounded his arguments based on a regulative principle in other areas; Whinnel entered (and escalated) the fray precisely because the term "will-worship" was being thrown around.[60] Keach admitted his argument from silence but rightly insisted that every Baptist church did so: "if we do not take our Rule to pray before and after *Sermon from those general Precepts* that injoyn Prayer, then I do declare I know no Rule at all for it in all the New Testament." A rigid interpretation of the regulative principle would result in church members debating whether they should use one loaf or many, whether they should baptized forwards or backwards, quickly or slowly; "Would not these be silly Objections? And yet these appertain to the Form of the Administration of Christ's Ordinance."[61] One might side with Brooks and say that Keach simply better appreciated the true meaning of the regulative principle, that Scripture was never meant to be a rigid liturgy, and in the narrow confines of this debate that might be true.[62] But in the wider context of the Baptist struggle for pure worship, it is evident that Keach had stepped away from a stated principle that he himself claimed. The Bible did not answer every question in the form Englishmen asked. The hymn-singing controversy forced Keach to acknowledge that on behalf of all Baptists, and not all Baptists appreciated the revelation. Needless to say, Marlow accurately cried that the Church of England used that same logic to establish their many forms and accidents of ceremonies. He not so subtly accused the pro-singers that they "do thereby virtually deny that Christ has left his

---

60. "Truth Cleared" in Marlow, *Truth Soberly Defended*, 38; Marlow, *Prelimited Forms*, 9; Whinnel, *Sober Reply*, 1ff. Whinnel spoke on behalf of about thirty singing Baptist churches.

61. Keach, *Breach Repaired*, 102, 181–82.

62. Brooks, "Benjamin Keach," 128. He still found fault with both men, "Keach and Marlow both worked from an assumption that the church had *one* way it could decide important issues, but now they were faced with determining the lines of what was acceptable in order to preserve the community" (ibid., 130). Davies argued that Calvin, who is credited with the quest for a New Testament liturgy, never saw the regulative principle as the rigid rule used by Puritans and reported by historians. Instead, Calvin allowed individual church freedom and even saw nonuniformity of worship as proof that worship was not the essence of Christianity, or at least Christian salvation. See Davies, *Worship of the English Puritans*, 35–41, 244–59. Regardless of the principle's source, Puritans and Baptists both suffered from their inability to understand or label their hermeneutical assumptions.

Baptist Worship and a New Identity of the Faithful?

Gospel-Church compleat Directions in the Holy Scriptures for the Worship of God."[63] That accusation still had great meaning for these Baptists.

In summary, the hymn-singing controversy was absolutely crippling to the Particular Baptists because it exposed the instability of their unique emphasis of worship. In their second confession of faith, they agreed with all "true" Christians that the Word of God was "the foundation and rule of our faith and worship," and further that "All instituted Worship receives its sanction from the precept, and is to be thereby governed in all the necessary circumstances thereof." But in order to acknowledge their camaraderie with "those who do consult the Word of God, cannot yet arrive at a full and mutual satisfaction among themselves, what was the practise of the primitive Christian Church, in some points relating to the *Worship* of God"—points they attempted to restrict to baptism—they conceded that "these things are not of the essence of Christianity."[64] They held out hope, maybe even an unmeasured expectation, that they would agree internally on all fundamental elements of worship and show as much generosity with themselves as with outsiders. But worship was too principled a thing to achieve agreement as to what was or was not "of the essence of Christianity."

THE GATHERING

The hymn-singing controversy reiterated a number of Baptist priorities introduced in chapter 5 addressed under the concept of Gospel Worship. As in the two previous sections, the hymn-singing controversy revealed how seriously Baptists took these principles even as they interpreted them in opposing fashions. Chapter 5 established that many Baptists thought of worship as more than intellectual stimulation but a celebration of Christ and appropriation of salvation in and through His ordinances which included preaching and (for some) singing. The very setup for this

---

63. Marlow, *Clear Confutation*, 23. "[T]herefore must Christians have so great a Liberty to choose and practise what accidental modes and circumstances of Worship they please? If this be granted, then if our Churches please they may practice not only common Singing, but the Common Service of the *Church of England*, Common-Prayer, Common Baptism, or Sprinkling of Infants, Common Gossips to Answer for them, Kneeling at the Altar, and at Confession and Absolution, Bowing to the East and Name of *Jesus*, and may set up Organs for their Publik Worship, and a heap of other Ceremonies that were never appointed by Jesus Christ, but accidentally happened from the Errors and Inventions of Men" (ibid., 22–23).

64. *London* [1677], 109, 115, 141.

controversy reiterated the importance of worship to the Particular Baptists, for they mourned "the Power of Godliness being greatly decayed, and but little more than the Form thereof remaining amongst us" and "that the Lord's Day is no more religiously and carefully observed, both in a constant attendance on the Word of God in that Church to whom Members do belong, and when the publick Worship is over, by a waiting on the Lord in Family-Duties, and private Devotion."[65] But this was not unique. In 1681, Keach lamented a general cooling of zeal, a neglect of prayer, and a neglect of private devotion. In 1684, Collins mourned a neglect of ordinances. In 1688, Knollys warned of the consequences for those who cooled in their spiritual affections for Christ. Even in 1695, Keach cried, "O where is the Life and Power of Religion?"[66] This entire Baptist tradition had recognized a weakness in their gatherings, a weakness that went beyond preaching else Keach would not have suggested its solution lay in congregational singing.

One of the most important contributions Baptists made to the overall understanding of worship was the relationship between worship and the gospel. Chapter 5 explained that Baptists stepped away from Anglican ceremonialism because it had no biblical sanction, and in the process they discovered that ceremonialism obscured the message of the gospel. The hymn-singing controversy both reaffirmed that commitment and revealed a number of proverbial gaps in their armor: arguments once used against formal worship had to be modified to explain how hymn-singing did not violate them. It should not be surprising that Marlow and others felt that congregational hymn-singing contained the essence of formal worship: hymns were human creations (even metrical translations of psalms were), tunes were culturally conditioned (note that both sides agreed that instruments should not be used in corporate worship), and the practice depended on some kind of formal instruction.

Just as Roman and Anglican worship overwhelmed the senses and created a sense of otherworldly presence or ecstasy, so also did singing: "That there may be a natural sensual Joy in the Heart when it is not from the Light and Influence of the Holy Spirit, and therefore we must beware that we make not our Spirits a Standard for the Worship of God, but that we try our Spirits by the Scriptures." To Marlow, singing would be the practice that would desensitize Baptists to their once-strict separation; "it

---

65. *Narrative* [1689], 4, 5.

66. Keach, *Sion in Distress*, 28–31; Collins, *Voice from the Prison*, 20; Knollys, *Exposition Of the Revelation*, 23; Keach, *God Acknowledged*, 38.

would lay such a Foundation for other formal and carnal Worship" that they would slowly but surely drift back into the Anglican mainstream.[67] But his fear was not restricted to the affective nature of singing; he also recognized that singing naturally demanded structure. Lyrics must be authored, tunes must be composed, and voices must be trained. Yes, this created a new clerical class,[68] but more importantly to Marlow this threatened the autonomy of the local church. By definition, lyrics and tunes were accidental modes and circumstances of worship; the Church of England existed by imposing those "indifferent things, upon the Consciences of the Dissenters," and Baptists had without fail sworn never to follow that path.[69] Marlow believed that Keach and his associates violated this foundational Baptist principle by authoring texts and tunes for use in other churches.

Keach could not ignore this charge any more than he could ignore that of will-worship. Christ, who sang after the Last Supper, would not have left a pattern of an invalid ceremony, nor would God have converted a moral duty, such as singing His praise, into a shadow or ceremony. Of greater concern, however, was the extension of Marlow's argument to other elements of worship: "You may as well say Prayer was a Ceremony, because there were divers ceremonial Rites used in the performance of it, particularly that of Incense." In fact, Keach went so far to turn the argument on its head, "I see 'tis time to stand up for the Form of Ordinances, for the Form of Doctrine, and for the Form of sound Words; for if we must part with singing of Psalms, Hymns, &c. from his pretended Arguments about Forms, all external Ordinances must go as well as that of Singing." Keach chose to respond by distinguishing between ceremonies, forms, and formality. Ceremonies were bad, forms were necessary, and

---

67. Marlow, *Prelimited Forms*, 47, 11.

68. Wetenhall described a complicated contemporary hierarchy in the Anglican Church choir of appointed members, instrumentalists, Chanters, and Chancellours, all of which had been in training since boyhood. See Wetenhall, *Of Gifts and Offices*, 428, 523, 528, 532, and 548.

69. Marlow, *Clear Confutation*, 16, 21. "That as the Church of *England* did formerly press their Forms and Ceremonies of Worship, under the Notion of indifferent things, upon the Consciences of the Dissenters, who by no means could be made to swallow them down, tho' gilded over with their Terms; so tho' Mr. *Allen* has declared against imposing of his accidental modes and circumstances of Worship, yet he and his Companions have so far followed the former steps of the Church of *England*, as to press their modes and circumstances, which they own are no essential parts of Gospel-worship, so hard upon our Churches, as to occasion many Troubles and Distractions among us" (ibid., 21).

the attitude of formality separated them: "We are not a pleading for Formal Prayer, nor Formal Singing, nor Formal Preaching neither, nor for any Ceremony of the Mosaic Law, but Spiritual Prayer, Spiritual Singing, and Spiritual Preaching, and only for Spiritual and Gospel-Ordinances."[70] This was terribly important because it was the critical, if fatal, about-face in a long-standing Baptist position. In other words, just as they employed the normative principle, Baptists had always used forms of worship even as they denied doing so. If they embraced it, they could guard against the threat of forms drifting into formality. Anti-singers, who ignored this reality, were *more* susceptible to formality (and equally susceptible to the Quaker heresy as the next section will explain) than the Baptists who knowingly employed forms. Salvation could be communicated in forms; Christ left such forms for the church to employ. Baptists should not be concerned about using Christ's forms, only the forms of men. Keach's position essentially blew the lid off of this explosive issue, and he insisted that it was in line with traditional Baptist priorities. Marlow could not have disagreed more.

Chapter 5 also explored Gospel Worship with respect to the role of the Spirit in congregational worship. Marlow, following similar arguments already noted by Kiffin, thought that singing was a way of having the form of worship without the power therein, "no better than counterfeiting that excellent Gift of the Holy Spirit which was in the Primitive Gospel-Church."[71] As he did with the argument about forms, Keach noted that the same argument could be used about other elements of Baptist worship, in particular preaching. He argued, "But certain it is, they [the apostles] preached by an Immediate and extraordinary Spirit or Inspiration; And so do not we, but by an ordinary Spirit from the mediate Word, and therefore must study, and are left to use what Method we think may be (as I said before) most profitable for the Edification of the People."[72] If hymn-singing

---

70. Keach, *Breach Repaired*, 130; Keach, *Answer*, 6; Keach, *Breach Repaired*, 159. "I find you are so lift up here, as to cry out against Forms that God hath ordained to be used, as there are many Forms of things that are Spiritual, and of Divine Institution. All Spiritual Ordinances have Matter and Form; there is no Prayer, (nor Sermon neither) tho ne'r so Spiritual, but it had its Form. We read of the Form of Doctrine, Form of found Words: Baptism, and Breaking of Bread, have their Forms. And if Men must attend (as helps) upon no Forms of Religion, they must do nothing but mind wholly that which you call the Essence of things within their Spirits. But what is here to gainsay what we say, that this is a Moral Duty?" (Keach, *Breach Repaired*, 155–56).

71. Marlow, *Prelimited Forms*, 15.

72. Keach, *Breach Repaired*, 179. Whinnel noted a contradiction in this anti-singing position. Anti-singers, in this instance Robert Steed, admitted that they did not

Baptist Worship and a New Identity of the Faithful?

counterfeited the movement of the Spirit, then so did preaching from studied notes. Particular Baptists had abandoned Smyth's method decades before, and Keach felt that Marlow did them no favors by dredging it up here. Instead, Keach countered that the Spirit moved in congregational singing by a set form as long as the congregation was regenerate, just as He did in prayer and preaching by those indwelt by Him. For Keach, this fulfilled Baptist principles, not hindered them. The privileges of the Covenant, illumination, grace, the Spirit, spiritual gifts, the fruits of the Spirit, adoption as sons, the righteousness of Christ, were given to individuals, not churches.[73] That understanding had always separated Baptist ecclesiology from other positions. Keach simply pushed this Baptist commitment to its logical end: *individuals* worshiped; churches consisted of individuals who worshiped in congregation, but one man's worship could not credit another man's account. Positively, Keach's commitment led him to emphasize personal devotion to Christ, the individual's attitude of gratitude, so to speak. It also led him to be the first Particular Baptist to write of spiritual warfare in worship; angels and demons were present at a church meeting to help and to hinder the worshipers individually. Each individual was accountable for his or her own focus, attention, behavior, and thoughts; the church did not bear responsibility for the individual to worship.[74] Negatively, it cultivated the seeds of dissolution for London Particular

---

follow the primitive pattern perfectly in every ordinance (prayer, preaching, baptism, the Lord's Supper), so they prayed that the Spirit would help them better discharge those duties; yet they would not sing because they did not fully know the primitive pattern. Whinnel, *Sober Reply*, 56.

73. Keach, *Display of Glorious Grace*, 238–39.

74. Keach, *Christ Alone the way to Heaven*, 84, 105. He wrote, "The Angels take good notice of every person's behaviours in our Assemblies, how they demean themselves with piety, modesty, and sobriety: If any let their Eyes wander or rove about, they observe them. Hence 'tis thought the Women should cover their Faces, especially in Prayer, because of the Observation the Angels make of them and others, whilst in God's holy Worship in his Church: Brethren, like as the Devils attend our Churches, to hinder us in our profiting under the Word; so the good Angels are there also to resist them, and to further our profiting. Satan (as one observes) is first and last at the meetings of God's People, and he hath many ways to obstruct the Souls of Men from hearing with attention; may be lulls them asleep, or fills their minds with prejudice against the Preacher, or against the Word he preaches, or to confuse their thoughts, causing them to think of their worldly Business, perhaps of their Debts, what they owe, or what is owing to them; or of Injuries sustained, and how to seek revenge; or else cause them to fix their Eyes upon one beautiful Object or another, thereby to divert them from what they should mind: But we may conclude the good Angels have as many ways to help us, as the evil have to hinder us" (ibid., 105–6).

Baptists that had been planted by their inability to resolve this particular controversy.[75]

Two more major areas of debate in the hymn-singing controversy, the place of women in worship and the acceptable actions of a mixed assembly, were covered in detail in chapter 5. But the hymn-singing controversy brought their implications to a head. Keach's and Knollys's decidedly pro-women stance earned Marlow's response, "I know not how such Women can satisfie their Consciences in that practice, unless it be through ignorance of the Scriptures."[76] Marlow's supporters declared mixed singing "directly contrary to the Rule of God's Word."[77] There was no possibility of compromise. According to Marlow, this worship practice both threatened the Baptists' continuing reformation and caused Baptists to question their own foundational principle; indeed it was "repugnant to the light of Scripture." Yet according to Keach, this worship practice was the key to restoring Baptist churches to their former favor with God and necessary to fulfill everything they held dear as a tradition.[78] There could be no middle ground in such a debate, especially when the most prominent Particular Baptists opposed one another: Keach and the loud layman, Marlow; Knollys and his co-pastor, Steed; even Kiffin and his co-pastor, Allen. This debate attracted so much negative attention that the 1692 General Assembly had to shut it down unconditionally. A most ominous last word came from Marlow, who violated their moratorium in 1696, "And if any say, that such a strict Discipline as I am for, will hazard the breaking or dividing of many of our Churches about *London*: My Answer is, That if so, 'tis chiefly to be attributed to our singing Elders and Ministers."[79] Peace

---

75. Note that Weaver identified individualism among Baptists long before Keach. Weaver, "Early English Baptists," 141–58.

76. Marlow, *Controversie of Singing Brought to an End*, 13.

77. "But now it is true, through the Grace and Goodness of God we are enlightned into the Erroniousness of the Manner in which it is performed by them, that is, in their using a precomposed and prelimited Form of Words, which they read to the People, and in their uniting their Voices, directly contrary to the Rule of God's Word; therefore we greatly admire Mr. *Keach* should offer to assert so false a thing to the World" ("Truth Cleared," in Marlow, *Truth Soberly Defended*, 41).

78. Marlow, *Prelimited Forms*, 6; Keach, *Breach Repaired*, v–vi. He believed Keach held "such Notions, as are repugnant to the light of Scripture, the known Principles of the body of the Baptized Churches, and that strike at a Foundation principle of Ours [holding the Sacred Scripture to be our only Rule to determine many Modes of Divine Worship], and the Protestants Reformation more in general." Marlow, *Controversie of Singing Brought to an End*, Epistle.

79. Marlow, *Clear Confutation*, 46.

could only be achieved if the Particular Baptists followed the trajectory set by Grantham for the General Baptists—simply ignore the matter—which is exactly what they did.

Of course, by that time it was too late.[80] By 1693, the London churches would lose interest in cooperation. A sparsely attended Assembly spoke harshly of "fears and jealousies one of another on account of our assembling these two or three years last past together, and the methods that have been taken for the promotion of the truths of God professed by us."[81] By 1695, the London churches would cease meeting altogether (which might be why the controversy re-erupted in 1696), according to Ivimey because church members no longer found it important.[82] The appeal of the 1692 Assembly, "We could entreat you, upon our Knees, might we prevail with you in this Matter, that you would join together to keep the Unity of the Spirit, and of our Holy Profession, in the Bond of Peace,"[83] went unheeded. Of all of the challenges the Particular Baptists faced in their early generations, worship was the one they could not overcome. It was too important, too tied to their identity, too personal. Thus not only did the hymn-singing controversy confirm worship as the early English Baptist distinctive but it also explained why Baptists deemphasized it from that time forward.

"Erroneous Principles": Baptists and Quakers[84]

Pure worship was the early English Baptist distinctive. That has been observed in the development of their early thought in three key areas: the church, the Scriptures, and the gathering. It was also observed in the greatest and most debilitating controversy of the early Particular Baptists. But there is one more area of proof that has been mentioned multiple

---

80. MacDonald's thesis that the hymn-singing controversy was a primary cause of London Baptist dissolution has not been refuted. MacDonald, "London Calvinistic Baptists."

81. Cited in Ivimey, *History of the English Baptists*, 1:531. "Dear Brethren, we must say, if this day of liberty be lost with trifling and quarreling amongst ourselves, or from a covetous spirit in us this work of the Lord be hindered, the account will be dreadful, and the next generation may reflect back with grief upon us, that we did not what we could for the service of God and of truth in our generation" (ibid.).

82. Ibid., 547. Whitley recorded that five churches attempted to gather; Whitley, *Baptists of London*, 47.

83. *Narrative* [1692], 12.

84. Knollys, *Answer*, 5.

PURE WORSHIP

times and will serve as the closing "loose end," namely the unique sects connected with the early Baptists. The Six-Principle Baptists earned several prominent mentions in chapter 4. It was a movement that threatened entire Baptist associations and was still being debated in London in the 1690s. Seventh-Day Baptists also drew a rather noticeable following among Baptists; most of the 1689 General Assembly was spent discussing whether to observe the Sabbath or the Lord's Day. John Bunyan, for one, thought that Sabbatarianism threatened instituted worship as much as any position.[85] No other Christian tradition of this era had a sect quite like the Six-Principle or Seventh-Day Baptists. The reason is no other tradition thought about worship quite like the Baptists did. Worship allowed Baptist principles to coalesce into unique, visible expressions, expressions that caused great disruption and angst for the early Particular Baptist leaders.[86] With all that being said, however, the great bogeymen for these Baptists and everyone else were the Quakers, the arch-sectaries.[87]

Not enough has been written about the conflict between the Baptists and the Quakers with most of what has focusing on ecclesiology and Christology.[88] Quaker writings about themselves, however, have empha-

---

85. *Narrative* (1689), 16–17; Greaves, *Glimpses of Glory*, 519–25. Bunyan, Collier, Grantham, Marlow, and others previously mentioned wrote treatises devoted to the proper day of Christian worship. Knollys called the Lord's Day the "Gospel Sabbath." Knollys, *Exposition Of the Revelation*, 7. Sabbatarianism also entered the hymn-singing debate inasmuch as the Jewish Sabbath and its practices (including singing) were argued to be totally incongruent with the Lord's Day. See Keach, *Breach Repaired*, 186, 205, 283–85. Importantly, Keach wrote *The Jewish Sabbath Abrogated* in 1700, and yet asked Joseph Stennett, a Seventh-Day Baptist, to preach his funeral.

86. Bell made a very convincing case that Seventh-Day Baptists were actually rooted in apocalypticism (quite in keeping with his primary thesis). While that does not necessarily dispute my thesis, it is still meaningful that he described their origins stating, "But the debate between Puritans and moderates over the manner of observing the Sabbath caused many to re-examine the practice altogether. Soon the question of the correct time of observation was added to the question of the prescribed manner of observation" (Bell, *Apocalypse How?*, 213). Inasmuch as he drew an indirect relationship between Seventh-Day Baptists and London Particular Baptists by means of Fifth-Monarchy Baptists, this means that even an apocalyptic fire drew fuel from the importance of worship. Politics may have influenced alignments, but this particular issue mattered to Baptists because of its relationship to worship.

87. Goodwin considered the Quakers the "most Diabolical" sect, even above the Baptists. Coffey, *John Goodwin and the Puritan Revolution*, 251. Anglicans thought they were agents of the Jesuits, but the Quakers still headlined Goodwin's and most calls against toleration. See *That Wicked and Blasphemous Petition of Praise-God Barbone*, 12.

88. Greaves, for example, couched Bunyan's arguments against the Quakers entirely in Christological terms. Greaves, *Glimpses of Glory*, 79–87. He even took time

Baptist Worship and a New Identity of the Faithful?

sized the centrality of worship to their entire program, and the Baptist hymn-singing controversy, itself rooted in the Particular Baptist self-identity, provides a unique opportunity to discuss the liturgical side of their contentious relationship.[89] Ted Underwood believed that Baptists and Quakers were so acrimonious because they were so alike (George Fox even formed the first Quaker church out of a Baptist society with which he had fellowship).[90] Just as Baptists, Quakers prioritized primitivism. The Baptist goal was to be like the apostolic church by observing New Testament patterns, but the Quakers actually sought to *become* that church in the power of the Spirit.[91] The Spirit was the ultimate authority for true Christians; everything contained in Scripture was but a shadow of life in the Spirit. Thus partaking of the scriptural ordinances was of little value, there being a strict dichotomy between the spiritual and the physical.[92] Just as Baptists, Quakers prioritized a priesthood of all believers, but the

---

to give a humorous account of their mutual accusations of witchcraft; ibid., 115–21.

89. Quaker Wilson, for example, discovered in Fox's writings an overwhelming desire to rescue people from false worship: "I was to bring them off from all the world's fellowships, and prayings, and singings, which stood in forms without power; that their fellowship might be in the Holy Ghost, and in the Eternal Spirit of God" (Wilson, *Quaker Worship*, 8–9).

90. Underwood, *Primitivism, Radicalism, and the Lamb's War*. But see also Davies, *The English Free Churches*, 62.

91. Underwood captured the difference between the groups in these fundamental issues, "Baptists, on the other hand, refused to enter the primitive time as fully as Quakers and retained a sense of 'difference' between their own age and the extraordinary one of New Testament Christianity. Their authority remained the written Word, which stood between them and the primitive church" (Underwood, *Primitivism*, 21, cf. 84). This is critical to understanding the relationship between Baptists and Quakers. Fox wrote in 1648, "Yet I had no slight esteem of the Holy Scriptures, but they were very precious to me, for I was in that spirit by which they were given forth" (Steere, ed., *Quaker Spirituality*, 69).

92. Underwood, *Primitivism*, 34. Nesti confirmed, "Remaining faithful to the Spirit in worship was the cornerstone of Quaker fellowship and witness to holiness" (Nesti, *Grace and Faith*, 301). Weddle pushed it to its necessary conclusion (following Fox), "Nor was scripture *necessary* for teaching or for salvation, because the nature and authority of the revelations available to the converted were identical to the revelations inspiring the teachings in the Bible" (Weddle, *Walking in the Way of Peace*, 21). As discussed in chapter 4, Baptists struggled with the nature of the dichotomies proposed by the Quakers, ultimately concluding that they were false. Underwood came to a similar conclusion, recognizing that Quakers believed that form and power were mutually exclusive. Baptists, however, kept forms such as baptism because they thought them essential to the primitive pattern. See Underwood, *Primitivism*, 68–75. Copeland thought the authority of Scripture was a main issue between the groups. Copeland, *Benjamin Keach*, 64–65.

Pure Worship

Quaker doctrine looked nothing at all like that of the Baptists. Baptists believed that all Christians had the ability and responsibility for immediate worship of the Father in the Son by the Spirit. But to Quakers, the priesthood had been superseded by a new access to God in the Spirit. It was now meaningless because "each was, alone, to find God."[93] Priests and churches were nothing in these last days.[94] Quakers posed an immense threat to all churches, especially the Baptists by virtue of their similarities. By the late seventeenth century, Baptist leaders had been able to ruminate on this threat (a number of encounters already appearing in this book). When the hymn-singing controversy erupted, they all noted a number of disturbing parallels with their ongoing struggle to keep church members away from the Quaker heresy.[95]

In many ways, Quaker worship was the radical extension of Baptist belief and the realization of many establishment fears. Baptists had the Spirit to interpret Scripture unto pure worship, and they understood that no form of worship would be accepted of God without the power of the Spirit. Consequently, they rejected church tradition and traditional forms of worship. Quakers simply took the next step. Because they had the Spirit,

---

93. Weddle explained this step that so disturbed Baptists, "She [the believer] did not need any priest or minister to interpret God's spirit or to explain the meaning of scripture. Indeed, such intervention was absolutely a bar to the spirit of God, because priests or ministers could transmit only the forms of religion, not the substance" (Weddle, *Walking in the Way of Peace*, 20).

94. Nesti recognized a *de facto* denial of this denial in that Quakers still maintained church assembly and fellowship. Nesti, *Grace and Faith*, 264.

95. If there were any shortcoming of Underwood's work, it would be his neglect of the hymn-singing controversy, which only earned a tangential mention on page 95. This is not to minimize the other (and some would say more important) elements of the wider Baptist-Quaker conflict. Clark argued that the Quakers became the ultimate expression of English nonconformity during this time because the Presbyterians had lost contact with the people they subjected to institutional organization and the Independents and Baptists had become too associated with the government, which certainly would have aroused jealousies. See Clark, *History of English Nonconformity*, 312–13. Horle verified all of these points in Horle, "Quakers and Baptists, 1647–1660," 344–62. Hubberthorne, a Quaker who felt betrayed by Baptists, saw their political pandering to the incoming king as true hypocrisy. He complained, "For you to give up your selves willingly and peaceably unto whatsoever Government is or shall be establid in this Nation, without any limitation, and to submit unto any Power or Magistacy that doth or shall Rule, as the Ordinance of God, without any limitation or qualification, is far below that Spirit which was once in some of you in that Profession" (Hubberthorne, *An Answer to Declaration*, 3). This is particularly important because it drew many people into the orbit of their message of salvation, the "inner light," a matter that cannot be ignored. However, this section does not intend to recapitulate the entire debate, only demonstrate the value of studying its liturgical elements.

Baptist Worship and a New Identity of the Faithful?

they rejected Scripture and *all* forms of outward worship. Gladys Wilson chided, "We are free from the limitations of Calvinistic thought, Puritan outlook, and lack of understanding of human personality."[96] Thomas Morford argued against Baptists, "And for any, as I said before, to take up any Ordinance, (except moved of the Lord) by imitation or tradition, I manifestly affirm, It is absolute Idolatry and Witchcraft, drawing the minds of creatures into outward observations, contrary to the law & Testimony."[97] This meant rejecting all ordinances as shadows. Their services were silent as they quaked in the presence of God. They could sing out loud, but they had no need because the worship of their heart was superior to any outward action. They sang in their heart; they preached in their heart; they took the Lord's Supper in their heart. Prophetic utterances were encouraged, but mostly to the public (women fully participated in this activity, in stark contrast to their position in Baptist churches[98]). Conversely, Particular Baptists gave equal station to the Word of God, the Spirit of God, and the apostolic tradition. Unfortunately, they could not convince every church member of this nuance. To some of their converts out of Anglicanism, emphasizing "pure" worship sounded very much like Quaker "inner" worship, which was little more than denying "outer" worship.[99] This was

---

96. Wilson, *Quaker Worship*, 91. She characterized their worship as mystical and prophetic.

97. Morford, *Baptist and Independent Churches (So called) Set on Fire*, 35. He concluded of the Baptists, "And this hath been the substance of my testimony from the Lord unto you Baptists, That the Lord requires you to wait for the powerings [pourings] forth of his eternall Spirit, and to feel its operation and movings in you; untill then, in the dread, power and authority of the Spirit of the Lord, again I say unto you, Let all flesh keep silence" (ibid., 39).

98. See Mack, *Visionary Women*. Though Mack hinted that Baptist chauvinism was an element in women converts to Quakerism, she only offered a few spectacular examples.

99. The confusion between the radical dissenters (Quakers, Ranters, and Seekers, etc.) on the part of the mainstream nonconformists often came back to worship. Lodowick Muggleton, some kind of Seeker, denounced the Quakers as banal Ranters (and vice versa), yet he shared their views of worship. He argued, "Furthermore, Christ gave her [the church] to understand also, that the worship required by him from his Saints, was an inward stilness by which their souls were made willing to hearken to the voice or motions of his most holy spirit, speaking in them variety of heavenly pleasures concerning the glory of Eternity . . . I have remonstrated to the elect what is the very true God, and his spiritual worship accepted of him; 'tis not outward praying, preaching, fasting, or thanksgiving to be seen of men, but it is an inward, spiritual, solient praying and praising, fasting and feasting upon the glorious things of eternity, which is onely seen by divine eyes . . . All true Christians are now under the Ministry of the holy Spirit, and therefore are no more bound in conscience to Apostolical worship, then the Saints were bound in conscience to Mosaical worship, when they were under

not limited to Baptists, however; many English Protestants saw the falsehood in this Quaker dichotomy between form and power.[100]

Disputants in the hymn-singing controversy covered the same territory, as this chapter has noted. Adding the backdrop of the Quakers brings out some interesting ironies and inconsistencies. Keach thought that the Quaker parallels provided his strongest arguments against the anti-singers: "Thus the *Quakers* have cast off the Holy Ordinances of Baptism, and the Lord's Supper, and have gotten spiritual Ones (in the blind Imaginations of their Hearts) in their room; as you would have a Heart Singing of Psalms without the Voice, so they have got a Heart-baptism without Water, and a Heart-breaking of Bread without Bread or Wine." Keach understood that Quaker "silent meetings" flagrantly rejected the Word of God and the apostolic church—in a word, everything he believed about pure worship.[101] Ironically, in order to defend their rigid regulation of worship practices, anti-singers had to express the same dichotomy of inward versus outward as the Quakers; Keach even recounted that one of his anti-singing church members became a Quaker "and to my Face denied the Resurrection of his Body." Again, both sides believed they correctly interpreted and applied Scripture to worship. Pro-singers believed that the anti-singer hermeneutic stood against the apostolic tradition, resulting in Quaker "heart worship." Anti-singers believed that the pro-singer hermeneutic also stood against the apostolic tradition, mirroring Quaker primitivism in believing they could achieve the purity and power of the apostolic church necessary for such practices as singing. Neither side could admit the danger of their own position.

Hanserd Knollys most clearly expressed the concern:

> I know you [Marlow] are not one of them that approve of silent Meetings, who supposing that they have *a Light* within them, whereby they are capable to worship God *acceptably* without his Gospel-Ordinances of Baptism, the Lord's Supper, and Singing without verbal and vocal Instruments in their *Silent* Meetings. In a word, This *unsound* Opinion of yours, will lead you, and

---

the doctrines of Christ" (Reeve and Muggleton, *Joyful News from Heaven*, 41, 43, 49). Clark argued that Quakers intentionally distanced themselves from Seekers and Ranters. Clark, *History of English Nonconformity*, 361–62.

100. Even the Anglican Thomas Ford took time to note, "[T]hough we must sing with the heart, it will never follow, That therefore we must not sing with the voice, for then it would follow too, that we must not pray with the voice, because we are to pray with the heart" (Ford, *Singing of Psalmes*, 11).

101. Keach, *Breach Repaired*, 123, 14, 146–47; Keach, *Answer*, 12.

others of the same mind, into some Erroneous Principles of them called Seekers, Quakers, and such as are for Non-Churches, if God do not prevent by his Holy Spirit and Grace, or restrain.[102]

Pure worship was paramount. Quaker worship was anathema. Accusing the anti-singers of Quakerism seemed to be almost as devastating as being accused of anti-scripturalism. In this way, the hymn-singing controversy as it involved Quakerism reinforced worship as the distinctive and dissolving focus of Particular Baptists. The radical individualism inherent in Quakerism called out to Baptists, women who felt stifled in Baptist churches (one of Keach's own daughters became a Quaker late in his life), men who felt constricted by the regulative principle, individuals who thought they should be defining their own priesthood. But even those Baptists not drawn away into Quakerism found themselves inexorably pulled by the centrifugal force of their own kind of individualism. Being told that they were priests before God, Particular Baptist church members had to respect none of the restraints imposed in the established churches. In this way, perhaps the Baptists suffered the effects of the Quaker threat despite their deliberate efforts to the contrary. Certainly the hymn-singing controversy heavily damaged the London association, and church members did not particularly care to restore it.

Particular Baptist church leaders understood that charity had to be the dominant attitude in matters of worship, but they were unable to establish the parameters of "indifferent things" within which that charity must extend. Instead, individual Baptists decided those parameters for themselves sometimes with disastrous results. Indeed, Thomas Whinnel mourned that one of the outcomes of the hymn-singing controversy was that outsiders had begun to whisper "that the *Baptists* are turning *Quakers, Enthusiasts*, and what not."[103] The hymn-singing controversy, in addition to the impressive (if underappreciated) litany of claims explained above, also clarified that a major problem Baptists had with Quakers, the great arch-heretics of their day, dealt with worship. Indeed, pure worship was the early English Baptist distinctive.

---

102. Knollys, *Answer*, 5.
103. Whinnel, *Sober Reply*, 63.

seven

Conclusion

The Importance of Pure Worship

Arguing that pure worship was the early English Baptist distinctive, I have focused on Particular Baptists, but based on the primary sources cited herein, future research should uncover a similar conclusion for other early Baptist groups. For the early Particular Baptists, pure worship was their paramount goal, and their quest for such worship shaped them into a unique sect. This book presented a comprehensive case in defense of its thesis, covering social, political, ecclesiological, theological, and historical developments. Seventeenth-century English Christians understood "worship" as the administration of ordinances in a church's corporate services. They understood that the Puritan mark of a true church as the right administration of the ordinances had to do with the church's worship, not simply the proper age for baptism. Early Particular Baptists absorbed that centrality of worship, taking it to new conclusions. Pure worship was their "distinctive" not in the sense of "only" concern but primary or overarching concern.

Worship was thoroughly ingrained in English society and politics. The society that produced the early English Baptists and the institutions that trained some of them centered on the instituted church's worship. To be English was to worship in England's church. The English monarchs understood the power of worship to unite and divide the people. The earliest Baptists had grown up in this model of society; they had attended Anglican churches, and they knew the objective and subjective elements of Anglican ceremonies. They could not have theological or ecclesiological discussions apart from their practical experiences in church worship services. The Baptists knew the scandal they would cause by rejecting *The Book of Common Prayer* and later Westminster's *Directory for Public Worship*, yet their desire for pure worship superseded any such concern. Indeed, worship was a legitimate cause to separate from the established church and form their own churches.

Early Baptist ecclesiology was strongly shaped by their convictions about worship. God demanded worship in Spirit and truth, which meant that only true Christians could truly worship. Churches must be free because true worship could not be coerced any more than salvation, and above all things Baptists did not want to mock God. Similarly, because they believed that worship was the highest function of a church, only Christians could be members of their churches. Their desire to eliminate formalism combined with their conviction of full equality as priests before God led them to eliminate all hierarchy between and within churches. But worship also created the tensions that would dissolve their associational bonds. In their quest for the purest model of worship, that of the apostolic church, these Baptists discovered an intolerable range of interpretations. They appreciated that uniformity brought stability because they believed that a defect in worship was a just cause to separate from a church, and they did not want such separation within their ranks. But the open-communion debate (itself a liturgical debate in many ways) demonstrated that they would not be able to overcome their differences because any disagreement could be cast in terms of worship, elevating it to a debate about the very nature of a church. Pure worship was essential to their understanding of a true church.

Worship also formed the early Baptist doctrine of the Scriptures. Their commitment to the pure worship of Christ and the apostles led them to elevate the New Testament over the Old in all things, considering everything enjoined therein as an ordinance of God. They claimed what is often called the regulative principle, that only biblical ordinances ought to be observed in worship. But their internal disagreements as to its meaning led to their most destructive controversies in that they could not agree how to interpret or apply these ordinances. Furthermore, their rejection of both Anglican and Presbyterian forms of worship as unbiblical (will-worship) led to countless bitter accusations of heresy and

The Importance of Pure Worship

hypocrisy, proving how important worship was to all English Christians at that time. The vagueness with which Baptists approached Scripture and scriptural ordinances in their early confessions demonstrated how carefully they tried to overcome their differences, but pure worship was a goal they would not abandon. Therefore, hermeneutical differences, especially with respect to the laying on of hands at baptism in Hebrews 6, could not be compromised because they drove notions of proper worship. Their "regulative principle" was too unstable. Finally, no loftier claim could be made but that they saw their role as a further Reformation moving beyond the proper interpretation of Scripture to its proper application in worship.

The strongest proof of the centrality of pure worship to the early Baptists was the relationship they drew between pure worship and the pure message of salvation in the gospel of Jesus Christ. They understood the purpose of their gatherings as a presentation of this gospel, not only in mind but also in spirit. Worship was their celebration of this gift from God; the only commensurate activity could be sharing this gift with others. Elaborate ceremonies and rituals obscured the simple beauty of the gospel and must be eliminated; indeed, they believed that God chose the simplicity of New Testament worship over the ornateness of Temple worship. Furthermore, they understood that the corruption in the worship around them was not only in the number of ceremonies but also their nature. Most importantly, they knew that participating in proper worship did not make one holy; if anything it was the other way around, reinforcing their commitment to a regenerate church. They preached for salvation. Parents had responsibility for exposing their children to the gospel in family worship. They desired the unpredictability of the Spirit in their worship. All of these conclusions, many of them at odds with the respectability of established worship, proved the centrality of pure worship to these early Particular Baptists.

Finally, the hymn-singing controversy of the late seventeenth century validates all of the claims made in this book. This was not some quaint dispute about music but a debilitating discourse about the nature of the Baptist identity that would terminate the vision of the early Particular Baptists. The hymn-singing controversy drew lines that longtime associates could not cross, forced the General Assembly to violate its own standards of autonomy, and led to the end of that Assembly in London. It revealed that Baptists did not truly believe in freedom of worship; singing would lead churches back to Anglican oppression as much as non-singing would withhold God's blessings from their churches. Both sides claimed the regulative principle even as they used the normative principle. They fought over the role of women in worship, the Spirit in worship, and set forms in worship. Their inability to squelch the debate proved how important it was to the main disputants.

Pure worship was the early English Baptist distinctive. They heard the charge of Robert Abbot, vicar of Cranbrook, "It is no small change to unchurch a church, to unminister a ministery, and to unworship a worship,"[1] and agreed. Their rallying cry was "the Lord grant that we all may be pressing after more Purity both in the Form and Spirit of Holy-Worship; not declining to any thing that is not of Divine Institution."[2] Hanserd Knollys believed that when Christ came to measure His church, He would inspect them (and their pastors) above all by whether they worshiped Him in Spirit and Truth according to His Word and whether or not they willingly reformed what was remiss in their worship.[3] Benjamin Keach identified God's people saying,

> *God's* Gospel Covenant-People are an United People, being constituted or incorporated into a Church State, according to the Institution of Christ in the New Testament, being separated from the World in *Worship*, and all *Evil Traditions, Customs, &c. Worshiping God in Spirit and in Truth, giving themselves up one to another*; keeping all the Ordinances of Christ *as they were once delivered to the Saints*, owning the Holy Scriptures to be the only *Rule of their Faith and Practice*, having regular and ordained Officers, *viz.* both Pastors and Deacons, and walking in Love, and watching over one another as becometh Saints.[4]

---

1. Collinson, *Religion of Protestants*, 275.
2. Kiffin et al., *Serious Answer to a Late Book*, 63.
3. "The Worshippers of God in his Churches of Saints, ought to be measured by the reed of Gods written Word, as well as the Temple and the Altar of God; that thereby it may appear, they are the true Worshippers of God in his house, and worship him in Spirit and Truth, *John* 24. 23, 24. For the Father seeketh such to Worship him. The Ministers of *Jesus Christ* (who are builders, 1 *Cor.* 3. 9, 10, 11--16. of Gods Gospel Temple) ought to measure the pattern, *Ezek.* 43. 10, 11. of the Churches, Worship, and Worshippers of God in the days of Christ and his Apostles, and to see that the Churches, Worship, and Worshippers of God, now in these latter days, be in all things, as they were then, and to reform those things that are amiss, *Tit.* 1. 5. and 1 *Cor.* 11. 34. 14. 40. *Col.* 2. 5." As for their pastors, "They ought to take care, or heed, that the whole Worship of God, and all the sacred Ordinances of the Lord be Administred according to the Gospel Institutions, Commandments, and Examples of Christ and his holy Apostles" (Knollys, *Exposition Of the Revelation*, 122–23, 123–24).
4. Keach, *Display of Glorious Grace*, 252–53.

The Importance of Pure Worship

Central to all of their thoughts on their purpose and nature was the pure worship of God.

A number of applications can and must be drawn from this claim, many more than would be appropriate to list in this short conclusion. Historians and theologians have overlooked the importance of worship to the Baptist tradition. It might be a simple oversight, or it might be a consequence of a systematic and long-running neglect of a human action relegated to practical (or pragmatic) ministry. Thomas McKibbens insightfully wrote, "It is ironic that the denomination which gives its ministers maximum freedom in liturgical practices is the same denomination which offers minimum training in liturgical principles."[5] Readers may miss the significance of the claims and debates encountered in this book simply because they have never even wondered about them. Baptist churches have borrowed worship practices indiscriminately for multiple generations; their leaders simply do not know what questions to ask. What does God want His children to offer in worship? How do His children know? Do God's children even really care? Certainly, it matters. Thomas Grantham said it as well as possible, "Where the true power of Godliness dwells, there will not be wanting a due zeal for the form of Godliness."[6] But in a tradition that has largely assumed the consequent and emphasized the autonomy of each local congregation, is a solution even possible?

Voices have entered this conversation, though they need to be joined by many more. Christopher Ellis established a meaningful starting point when he insisted that even those traditions that do not acknowledge an explicit theological framework for their corporate worship still employ an *implicit* theology, and that implicit theology desperately needs to be evaluated. Following the Catholic Alexander Schmemann, he recommended a method that even free churches could use: establish the liturgical facts, conduct a theological analysis of those facts, synthesize and engage the broader Christian world in discussion. Note that Ellis attempted to do so with representatives of the entire Free Church tradition (or at least British Baptists), whereas it seems evident that every individual church will need

---

5. McKibbens, "Our Baptist Heritage in Worship," 67. Consequently, many leaders have abdicated their liturgical responsibility. "In the majority of Baptist churches known to me all traces of liturgical discipline have been abandoned under the tyranny of a music group" (Colwell, "Word of His Grace," 208).

6. Grantham, *Christianismus Primitivus*, 2:1. The "form of godliness" in book two dealt exclusively with the public worship of the church. His argument was quite simple: true Christians should desire more than anything to worship God the right way (externally as well as internally).

to open this discussion. But he proposed that the heart of Baptist worship was the Lordship of Jesus; its priorities were attention to Scripture, devotion and openness to the Spirit, concern for the community, and an eschatological orientation; and its central actions were praying, preaching, singing, and sacraments.[7] Those observations line up fairly well with the observations made in this book (begging an excursus into the relationship between the Lordship of Jesus and the gospel of Jesus) and offer hope that a meaningful discussion can take place.

But a larger question remains: how does a church *evaluate* the actions and motivations it observes? Searching for some kind of magical regulative principle proved to be elusive to early Baptists, and this book has demonstrated the hazards of engaging in liturgical debate without a clear awareness of the hermeneutical principles employed. A colloquium of Baptist theologians recently explored the theory and practice of Baptist hermeneutics in hopes of answering that question, discovering promise and peril. Multiple contributors highlighted the importance of primary theology, theology of the community, realizing that a community can encounter and mediate very diverse interpretations of Scripture (the "fray" as one theologian called it) if its bonds are strong enough to prevent "sibling quarrels" from becoming "family-fracturing disagreements." They also trumpeted the role of the Spirit in guiding the community to an authoritative understanding of the text; in its best sense, this process was called "not an interpretative free-for-all, but an exercise in holy listening." Indeed, these attitudes sound very much like those of the early Baptists encountered in this book. Unfortunately, the colloquium could not allay the fears of dissolution caused by hermeneutical dissonance. One contributor thought that the desirable "dynamic, communal submission to the Lordship of Jesus mediated through the word" was achieved when one replaced the question "What does the Bible say?" with "What does Christ say?" Another found the mind of Christ as mediated by the Spirit to mean "The word of God is therefore not to be found within the text, but rather it is spoken afresh to the individual by the Spirit." Only one contributor addressed the idea of hermeneutical principles taught to church groups. But every one of these suggestions have been themselves sources of significant disagreement. What does it say that the very process of determining a hermeneutical structure has already proven to be "family-fracturing"?

---

7. Ellis, *Gathering*, 23–24, 33–34, 101ff, 228ff.

The Importance of Pure Worship

And the proper understanding of the regulative principle has not even been mentioned, let alone addressed.[8]

Certainly this matter is a fray. But it will never be conquered if it is never entered. As Baptist communities begin to take responsibility for their own actions before God, they must pray that the prized mind of Christ overcomes these seemingly insurmountable obstacles. They can learn something very powerful from these early Baptist communities and their insights. Perhaps it is time they reentered this fray from the beginning, discovering for themselves the principles of a Baptist theology of worship. This subject is difficult and dangerous, and many have expressed their unwillingness to engage its theology. But is not God's worship worth this cost?

---

8. Birch, "Baptist and Biblical Interpretation," 166–67; Woodman, "Dissenting Voice," 213, 223, 229.

Bibliography

The Advertisements. In *Documents Illustrative of English Church History*, ed. Henry Gee and William John Hardy, 467–75. New York: Macmillan, 1896. http://history.hanover.edu/texts/ENGref/er81.html.
Ainsworth, Henry. *An Arrow Against Idolatrie*. Amsterdam: n.p., 1611.
———. *Counterpoyson*. n.p., 1608.
———. *A Defence of the Holy Scriptures, Worship, and Ministerie, used in the Christian Churches separated from Antichrist*. Amsterdam: Thorp, 1609.
Ainsworth, Henry, and Francis Johnson. *The Confession of faith of certayn English people, living in exile, in the Low countreyes*. [Amsterdam: Thorp, n.d.]; reprint, 1607.
Allen, Richard. *An Antidote Against Heresy*. London: Macock, 1648.
———. *A Brief Vindication of an Essay to Prove Singing of Psalms*. London: n.p., 1696.
———. *An Essay To prove Singing of Psalms With conjoin'd Voices, A Christian Duty*. London: J. D., 1696.
Ammerman, Nancy Tatum. *Baptist Battles: Social Change and Religious Conflict in the Southern Baptist Convention*. New Brunswick, NJ: Rutgers University Press, 1990.
Anderson, E. Byron. "Worship and Belief: Liturgical Practice as a Contextual Theology." *Worship* 75 (2001) 432–52.
Anderson, Philip J. "A Fifth Monarchist Appeal and the Response of an Independent Church at Canterbury, 1653." *BQ* 33 (1989) 72–80.
———. "Letters of Henry Jessey and John Tombes to the Churches of New England, 1645." *BQ* 28 (1979) 30–40.
An Apologie or Defence of Such True Christians as are commonly (but uniustly) called Brownists. N.p., 1604.
Arnold, Jonathan W. "The Reformed Theology of Benjamin Keach (1640–1704)." DPhil thesis, Oxford University, 2010.
Articles agreed on by the Archbyshoppes. London: Richard Jugge and John Cawood, 1571. http://www.reformed.org/documents/index.html?mainframe=http://www.reformed.org/documents/articles_39_1572.html.
Baillie, Robert. *The Disswasive From The Errors of the Time*. London: Tyler, 1654.
Bakewell, Thomas. *An answer, or confutation of divers errors broached, and multiulned by the seven churches of Anabaptists*. London: n.p, 1646.
———. *A Confutation of the Anabaptists, And All others who affect not Civill Government*. London: M. O., 1644.
———. *A Justification Of two Points now in Controversie with the Anabaptists Concerning Baptisme*. London: n.p., 1645.
Ballamie, Richard. *The Leper Cleansed, or the Reduction Of an Erring Christian*. London: Eglesfield, 1657.

Bibliography

Baptist Faith and Message 2000: Critical Issues in America's Largest Protestant Denomination. Ed. Douglas K. Blount and Joseph D. Wooddell. New York: Rowman & Littlefield, 2007.

Barber, Edward. *Certain Queries, Propounded To the Churches of Christ.* N.p., n.d.

———. *A Declaration and Vindication of the carriage of Edward Barber.* London: n.p., 1648.

———. *A Small Treatise of Baptisme, or, Dipping.* n.p., 1641.

Barbone, Praisegod. *A Defence of the Lawfulnesse of Baptizing Infants.* London: Bell, 1644.

———. *A Discourse Tending to prove the Baptisme in, Or under the defection of Antichrist, to be the Ordinance of Jesus Christ.* London: Allen, 1643.

———. *A Reply to the Frivolous and impertinent Answer of R. B. to the discourse of P. B.* London: n.p., 1643.

Baxter, Richard. *Plain Scripture proof of infants church-membership and baptism.* London: n.p., 1653.

Bell, Mark R. *Apocalypse How? Baptist Movements during the English Revolution.* Macon, GA: Mercer University Press, 2000.

Betteridge, Alan. "Early Baptists in Leicestershire and Rutland, Part 1." *BQ* 25 (1974) 204–11.

———. "Early Baptists in Leicestershire and Rutland, Part 3." *BQ* 25 (1974) 354–78.

B[ewick], I[ohn]. *An Antidote Against Lay-Preaching.* London: n.p., 1642.

Birch, Ian. "Baptists and Biblical Interpretation: Reading the Bible with Christ." In *The "Plainly Revealed" Word of God? Baptist Hermeneutics in Theory and Practice*, ed. Helen Dare and Simon Woodman, 153–70. Macon, GA: Mercer University Press, 2011.

Bishop, George. *An Illumination to Open the Eyes of the Papists (so called) and of All other Sects.* London: n.p., 1661.

The Boke of Common Praier, and Administration of the Sacramentes, and other Rites and Ceremonies in the Churche of Englande. London: Grafton, 1559.

The Booke of Common Prayer, now used in the Church of England, Vindicated. London: n.p., 1641.

Bowls, Edward. *The Mysterie of Iniquitie, Yet Working In the Kingdomes of England, Scotland, and Ireland, for the destruction of Religion truly Protestant.* Edinborough: n.p., 1643.

Brachlow, Stephen. *The Communion of Saints: Radical Puritans and Separatist Ecclesiology 1570–1625.* New York: Oxford University Press, 1988.

Brackney, William H. *A Genetic History of Baptist Thought.* Macon, GA: Mercer University Press, 2004.

Bradshaw, William. *Several Treatises of Worship and Ceremonies.* London: n.p., 1660.

———. *The Unreasonablenesse of the separation.* Dort: Waters, 1614.

Brewer, Paul D. "Embracing God's Word in Worship." *BHH* 27 (1992) 13–22.

A Brief Confession or Declaration of Faith. London: G. D., 1659.

Briggs, John. "The Influence of Calvinism on Seventeenth-Century English Baptists." *BHH* 39 (2004) 8–25.

Brightmann, Frank Edward, and Kenneth Donald Mackenzie. "The History of the Book of Common Prayer down to 1662." In *Liturgy and Worship: A Companion to the Prayer Books of the Anglican Communion*, ed. W. K. Lowther Clarke, 130–97. New York: Macmillan, 1932.

Bibliography

Brooks, James C. "Benjamin Keach and the Baptist Singing Controversy: Mediating Scripture, Confessional Heritage, and Christian Unity." PhD diss., Florida State University, 2006.

Bunyan, John. *A Confession of my Faith, And A Reason of my Practice*. London: n.p., 1672.

———. *Differences in Judgment about Water-Baptism, No Bar to Communion*. London: n.p., 1673.

Burrage, Champlin. *The Early English Dissenters*. Cambridge: University Press, 1912.

Burroughs, Jeremiah. *Gospel-Worship, or, The Right Manner of Sanctifying the Name of God in General*. London: Cole, 1658.

Burrows, J. L. *What Baptists Believe*. Baltimore: Wharton, 1887.

Busher, Mark Leonard. *An Exhortation Unto the Learned Divines assembled At Westminster*. Amsterdam: n.p., 1643.

Canne, John. *A Necessitie of Separation From the Church of England*. London: n.p., 1634.

Cardwell, Edward. *A History of Conferences and Other Proceedings connected with the Revision of the Book of Common Prayer*. Oxford: University Press, 1849.

Carroll, B. H. *Baptists and Their Doctrines*. New York: Revell, 1913.

Carruthers, S. W. *The Everyday Work of the Westminster Assembly*. Philadelphia: Presbyterian Historical Society, 1943.

Cartwright, Thomas. *A replye to an answere made of M. Doctor Whitgifte*. n.p., 1573.

Cary, Philip. *A Solemn Call Unto all that would be owned as* Christ's *Faithful Witnesses*. London: n.p., 1690.

Caryl, Joseph. *The Moderator: Endeavouring A full Composure and quiet Settlement of those many Differences*. London: n.p., 1652.

Chapell, Bryan. *Christ-Centered Worship: Letting the Gospel Shape Our Practice*. Grand Rapids: Baker Academic, 2009.

Chauncy, Isaac. *The Catholick Hierarchie: Or, The Divine Right of a Sacred Dominion in Church and Conscience*. London: n.p., 1681.

———. *Ecclesiasticum: Or A Plan and Familiar Christian Conference, concerning Gospel Churches, and Order*. London: T. S., 1690.

———. *A Theological Dialogue: Containing the Defence and Justification of Dr.* John Owen *from the Forty Two Errors Charged upon him by Mr. Richard Baxter*. London: n.p., 1684.

Clapham, Henoch. *Theological Axioms*. Amsterdam: n.p., 1597.

Clark, Henry W. *History of English Nonconformity*. Vol. 1. London: Chapman & Hall, 1911.

Clements, K. W. "The Significance of 1679." *BQ* 28 (1979) 2–6.

Clipsham, E. F. "William Wheeler's Last Legacy." *BQ* 22 (1967) 30–40.

Coffey, John. *John Goodwin and the Puritan Revolution*. New York: Boydell, 2006.

Collier, Thomas. *Certaine Queries; Or, Points now in Controvercy Examined*. n.p., 1645.

———. *The Right Constitution and True Subjects of the Visible Church of Christ*. London: Hills, 1654.

Collins, Hercules. *The Antidote Proved A Counterfeit*. London: n.p., 1693.

———. *Believers Baptism from Heaven, and of Divine Institution. Infants Baptist from Earth, and Human Invention*. London: Hancock, 1691.

———. *The Marrow of Gospel-History*. London: n.p., 1696.

———. *Mountains of Brass: Or, A Discourse upon the Decrees of God*. London: Harris, 1690.

Bibliography

———. *An Orthodox Catechism: Being the Sum of Christian Religion Contained in the Law and Gospel.* London: n.p., 1680.

———. *Some Reasons for Separation From the Communion of the Church of England.* London: How, 1682.

———. *A Voice from the Prison, or, Meditations on* Revelations III. XI. *Tending To the Establishment of Gods Little Flock.* London: Larkin, 1684.

Collinson, Patrick. *The Religion of Protestants: The Church in English Society 1559-1625.* Oxford: Clarendon, 1982.

Colwell, John E. "The Word of His Grace: What's So Distinctive about Scripture?" In *The "Plainly Revealed" Word of God? Baptist Hermeneutics in Theory and Practice,* ed. Helen Dare and Simon Woodman, 191–209. Macon, GA: Mercer University Press, 2011.

A Confession of Faith Of seven Congregations or Churches of Christ in London, which are commonly (but uniustly) called Anabaptists. London: Simmons, 1646.

A Confession of Faith, Of the several Congregations or Churches of Christ in London, which are commonly (though unjustly) called Anabaptists. London: M[atthew] S[immons], 1651.

The Confession of Faith, Of those Churches which are commonly (though falsly) called Anabaptists. London: n.p., 1644.

A Confession of Faith, Put forth by the Elders and Brethren Of many Congregations of Christians, (Baptized upon Profession of their Faith) in London and the Country. London: n.p., 1688.

A Confession of Faith. Put forth by the Elders and Brethren Of many Congregations of Christians (baptized upon Profession of their Faith) in London and the Country. London: Harris, 1677.

Cook, Edward. *Some Considerations Proposed to all you that sing Davids Sundry.* n.p., 1670.

Copeland, David A. *Benjamin Keach and the Development of Baptist Traditions in Seventeenth-Century England.* Lewiston, NY: Mellen, 2001.

Cotton, John. *Singing of Psalmes a Gospel-Ordinance.* London: n.p., 1650.

Cox, Benjamin, Hanserd Knollys, and William Kiffin. *A Declaration Concerning The Publike Dispute Which Should have been in the Publike Meetinghouse of Alderman-Bury.* London: n.p., 1645.

Cox, Benjamin. *An Appendix to a Confession of Faith.* London: n.p., 1646.

Crosby, Thomas. *The History of the English Baptists.* 4 Vols. London: Robinson, 1739–1740.

Dargan, E. C. *The Doctrines of Our Faith.* Nashville: Sunday School Board, 1905.

Davies, Horton. *The English Free Churches.* London: Oxford University Press, 1952.

———. *The Worship of the English Puritans.* Westminster: Dacre, 1948.

De Laune, Thomas, and Benjamin Keach. *Tropologia: A Key to Open Scripture Metaphors.* London: J. R. & J. D., 1682.

Dickens, A. G. *The English Reformation.* New York: Schocken, 1964.

A Directory for the publick Worship of God. London: n.p., 1645. Reprint, Halifax: Munro, 1828.

A Discourse Between Cap. Kiffin, and Dr. Chamberlain, About Imposition of Hands. London: n.p., 1654.

Dix, Gregory. *The Shape of the Liturgy.* Westminster: Dacre, 1945.

Bibliography

Dockery, David S. "The Church, Worship, and the Lord's Supper." In *The Mission of Today's Church: Baptist Leaders Look at Modern Faith Issues*, ed. R. Stanton Norman, 37–50. Nashville: B.& H., 2007.

———. *The Doctrine of the Bible*. Nashville: Convention Press, 1991.

Dowley, T. E. "Baptists and Discipline in the 17th Century." *BQ* 24 (1971) 157–66.

———. "A London Congregation During the Great Persecution: Petty France Particular Baptist Church, 1641–1688." *BQ* 27 (1978) 233–39.

Duesing, Jason G. "Counted Worthy: The Life and Thought of Henry Jessey, 1601–1663, Puritan Chaplain, Independent and Baptist Pastor, Millenarian Politician and Prophet." PhD diss., Southwestern Baptist Theological Seminary, 2008.

———. "Henry Jacob (1563–1624): Pastoral Theology and Congregational Ecclesiology." *BQ* 43 (2010) 284–301.

Duffy, Eamon. *The Stripping of the Altars: Traditional Religion in England, c. 1400–c. 1580*. New Haven: Yale University Press, 1992.

Edwards, Thomas. *Antapologia, or, A full answer to the Apologeticall narration of Mr Goodwin, Mr Nye, Mr Sympson, Mr Burroughs, Mr Bridge, members of the Assembly of Divines*. London: G. M., 1644.

———. *The First and Second Part of* Gangraena: *or A Catalogue and Discovery of many of the Errors, Heresies, Blasphemies and pernacious Practices of the Sectaries of this time*. London: T. R. & E. M., 1646.

———. *Reasons Against the Independent Government of Particular Congregations*. London: Cotes, 1641.

Elliot, Ralph H. *The "Genesis Controversy" and Continuity in Southern Baptist Chaos: A Eulogy for a Great Tradition*. Macon, GA: Mercer University Press, 1992.

Ellis, Christopher J. *Gathering: A Theology and Spirituality of Worship in Free Church Tradition*. London: SCM, 2004.

———. "Gathering around the Word: Baptists, Scripture, and Worship." In *The "Plainly Revealed" Word of God? Baptist Hermeneutics in Theory and Practice*, ed. Helen Dare and Simon Woodman, 101–20. Macon, GA: Mercer University Press, 2011.

The English Spira: Being A Fearful Example of an Apostate. London: n.p., 1693.

F., L. *A Speedy Remedie against Spirituall Incontinencie*. n.p., 1640.

Featley, Daniel. *The Dippers dipt. Or, The Anabaptists Duck'd and Plung'd Over Head and Eares, at a Disputation in* Southwark. London: n.p., 1645.

———. *The Gentle Lash, Or the Vindication Of Dr Featley, a knowne Champion Of The Protestant Religion*. n.p., 1643.

Fiddes, Paul S. *Tracks and Traces: Baptist Identity in Church and Theology*. Waynesboro, GA: Paternoster, 2003.

Fincham, Kenneth, editor. *The Early Stuart Church, 1603–1642*. Stanford: Stanford University Press, 1993.

Folk, Edgar Estes. *Baptist Principles*. Nashville: Sunday School Board, 1909.

Ford, Thomas. *Singing of Psalmes The Duty of Christians*. London: W. B., 1659.

Garrett, James Leo, Jr. *Baptist Theology: A Four-Century Study*. Macon, GA: Mercer University Press, 2009.

———. "Restitution and Dissent Among Early English Baptists: Part I." *BHH* 12 (1977) 198–210.

Geree, John. *Vindiciae Paedo-Baptismi: or, A Vindication of Infant Baptism*. London: Field, 1645.

Bibliography

Gillespie, George. *A Dispute Against the English Popish Ceremonies Obtruded on the Church of Scotland.* n.p.: S. I., 1637; reprint, Dallas: Naphtali, 1993.

Goadby, J. Jackson. *Bye-Paths in Baptist History: A Collection of Interesting, Instructive, and Curious Information, not Generally Known, Concerning the Baptist Denomination.* London: Stock, 1871.

Goodwin, John. *A Quaere, Concerning the Church-Covenant, Practised in the Separate Congregations.* London: Cranford, 1643.

Goodwin, Thomas. *A Glimpse of Sions Glory: Or, The Churches Beautie specified.* London, Larner, 1641.

Grantham, Thomas. *The Baptist against the Papist: Or, The Scripture and Rome in Contention about the Supream Seat of Judgment, in Controversies of Religion.* London: n.p., 1663.

———. *Christianismus Primitivus: Or, the Ancient Christian Religion.* London: n.p., 1678.

———. *The Fourth Principle of Christs Doctrine Vindicated.* London: n.p., 1674.

———. *A Friendly Epistle to the Bishops and Ministers of the Church of England.* London: n.p., 1680.

———. *Hear the Church: or, an Appeal to the Mother of us All.* London: n.p., 1687.

———. *The Loyal Baptist: Or An Apology for the Baptized Believers.* London: n.p., 1684.

———. *The Paedo-Baptists Apology for the Baptized Churches.* n.p., 1671.

———. *The Prisoner against the Prelate: or, A Dialogue between the Common Goal and Cathedral of Lincoln.* n.p., 1662.

———. *The Quaeries Examined, Or, Fifty Anti-Quaeries Seriously Propounded to the People called Presbyterians.* London: n.p., 1676.

———. *St. Paul's Catechism: Or, A brief and plain Explication of the Six Principles of the Christian Religion, as recorded Heb. 6. 1, 2.* London: n.p., 1687.

———. *The Second Part of the Apology for the Baptized Believers.* London, n.p., 1684.

———. *The Seventh-day-Sabbath Ceased as Ceremonial.* London, n.p., 1667.

———. *A Sigh for Peace; or The Cause of Division Discovered.* n.p., 1671.

Grantham, Thomas, et al. *The Second Humble Addresse Of those who are Called Anabaptists in The County of Lincoln.* London: Dover, 1660.

Greaves, Richard. *Glimpses of Glory: John Bunyan and English Dissent.* Stanford, CA: Stanford University Press, 2002.

Griffith, John. *Gods Oracle & Christs Doctrine, or, The six Principles of Christian Religion.* London: Moon, 1655.

———. *The Searchers for Schism Search'd.* London: n.p., 1669.

Haigh, Christopher, ed. *The English Reformation Revised.* Cambridge: Cambridge University Press, 1987.

Hall, Thomas. *The Font Guarded With XX Arguments.* London: R. W., 1652.

Hammett, John S. *Biblical Foundations for Baptist Churches: A Contemporary Ecclesiology.* Grand Rapids: Kregel Academic, 2005.

Hammond, Henry. *The Baptizing of Infants Reviewed and Defended from the Exceptions of Mr. Tombes.* London: Flesher, 1655.

Hankins, Barry. *Uneasy in Babylon: Southern Baptist Conservatives and American Culture.* Tuscaloosa: University of Alabama Press, 2002.

Hart, D. G. *Deconstructing Evangelicalism: Conservative Protestantism in the Age of Billy Graham.* Grand Rapids: Baker Academic, 2004.

Hayden, Roger. "Broadmead, Bristol in the Seventeenth Century." *BQ* 23 (1970) 348–59.
Haykin, Michael A. G., and C. Jeffrey Robinson. "Particular Baptist Debates about Communion and Hymn-Singing." In *Drawn into Controversie: Reformed Theological Diversity and Debates Within Seventeenth-Century British Puritanism*, ed. Michael A. G. Haykin and Mark Jones, 284–307. Oakville, CO: Vandenhoeck & Ruprecht, 2011.
Hetherington, W. M. *History of the Westminster Assembly of Divines.* New York: Robert Carter & Brothers, 1859.
Hill, Christopher. *The Century of Revolution 1603–1714.* London: Nelson, 1961.
The History of the Baptist Church, Dartmouth. Dartmouth: Tozer, 1950.
A History of the Westminster Assembly of Divines. Philadelphia: Presbyterian Board of Publication, 1841.
Homes, Nathanael. *A Vindication of Baptizing Beleevers Infants.* London: Simmons, 1645.
Horle, Craig W. "Quakers and Baptists, 1647–1660." *BQ* 26 (1976) 344–62.
Howe, Samuel. *The Sufficiencie of the Spirits Teaching, without Humane-Learning.* [Amsterdam]: n.p., 1640.
———. *A Vindication of the Cobler.* n.p., 1640.
Hubberthorne, Richard. *An Answer to a Declaration Put forth by the general Consent of the People called Anabaptists.* London: n.p., 1659.
The humble Advice of the Assembly of Divines, Now by Authority of Parliament sitting at Westminster. London: n.p., 1646.
An Humble Remonstrance In The Behalfe of the Protestants of this Kingdome. London: n.p., 1643.
Hussey, Maurice. "Christian Conduct in Bunyan and Baxter." *BQ* 14 (1951) 75–83.
Hussey, William. *An Answer To Mr. Tombes his Scepticall Examination of Infants-Baptisme.* London: n.p., 1646.
Hustad, Donald P. "Baptist Worship Forms: Uniting the Charleston and Sandy Creek Traditions." *RE* 85 (1988) 31–42.
Hutton, William Holden. *The English Church (1625–1714).* New York: AMS, 1903.
Ivimey, Joseph. *A History of the English Baptists.* 4 vols. London: n.p., 1811.
Jacob, Henry. *A Defence of the Churches and Ministery of Englande.* Middelburgh: Schilders, 1599.
———. *The Divine Beginning and Institution of Christs true Visible or Ministeriall Church.* Leiden: Hastings, 1610.
Jenkens, Charles A., editor. *Baptist Doctrines.* St. Louis: Barns, 1881.
Jessey, Henry. *A Catechisme for Babes, or, Little Ones.* London: Hills, 1652.
———. *The exceeding Riches of Grace Advanced.* London: Simmons, 1647.
———. *Miscellanea Sacra; or, Diverse Necessary Truths.* London: T. M., 1665.
———. *A Storehouse of Provision to further Resolution in severall cases of Conscience.* London: Sumptner, 1650.
Jeter, Jeremiah B. *Baptist Principles Reset.* Ed. R. H. Pitt. Richmond: Religious Herald, 1902.
Jones, Philip. *A Restatement of Baptist Principles.* Philadelphia: American Baptist Publication Society, 1909.
Keach, Benjamin. *An Answer to Mr. Marlow's Appendix.* London: Hancock, 1691.

Bibliography

———. *Antichrist Stormed: Or, Mystery* Babylon *the great Whore, and great City, proved to be the present Church of* Rome. London: n.p., 1689.
———. *The Articles of the Faith of the Church of Christ, Or Congregation meeting at* Horsley-down. London: n.p., 1697.
———. *The Breach Repaired in God's Worship*. London: Hancock, 1691.
———. *Christ Alone the way to Heaven: or,* Jacob's *Ladder Improved*. London: Harris, 1698.
———. *The Counterfeit Christian; Or, The Danger of Hypocrisy*. London: Pike, 1691.
———. *The Display of Glorious Grace: Or, the Covenant of Peace, Opened*. London: Bridge, 1698 or 1689.
———. *Exposition of the Parables in the Bible*. Reprint, Grand Rapids: Kregel, 1974.
———. *A Feast of Fat Things Full of Marrow*. London: B[enjamin] H[arris], 1696.
———. *God Acknowledged: Or the True Interest of the Nation*. London: n.p., 1695.
———. *Gold Refin'd; Or, Baptism in its Primitive Purity*. London: n.p., 1689.
———. *A Golden Mine Opened: Or, The Glory of God's Rich Grace Displayed in the Mediator to Believers*. London: n.p., 1694.
———. *Laying On of Hands Upon Baptized Believers, As such, Proved an Ordinance of* Jesus Christ. London: Benj[amin] Harris, 1698.
———. *Sion in Distress or the Groans of the Protestant Church*. Boston: S. G., 1683.
Kiffin, William. *A Briefe Remonstrance of The Reasons and Grounds of those People commonly Called Anabaptists, for their Seperation*. London: n.p., 1645.
———. *A Sober Discourse of Right to Church-Communion*. London: Larkin, 1681.
Kiffin, William, et al. *A Serious Answer to a Late Book, Stiled A Reply to Mr. Robert Steed's Epistle*. London: n.p., 1692.
Kiffin, William, et al. *The Humble Apology Of some commonly called Anabaptists*. London: Hills, 1660.
Kilcop, Thomas. *A short Treatise of Baptisme*. n.p., n.d..
Kingsley, J. Gordon, Jr. "Opposition to Early Baptists." *BHH* 4 (1969) 18–30.
Kirtley, James. *The Baptist Distinctive and Objective*. Philadelphia: Judson, 1926.
Klaiber, Ashley J. "Baptists at Bewdly: 1649–1949." *BQ* 13 (1949) 116–124.
———. *The Story of the Suffolk Baptists*. London: Kingsgate, 1931.
Knollys, Hanserd. *An Answer to A Brief Discourse Concerning Singing*. London: n.p., 1691.
———. *Apocalyptical Mysteries, Expounded*. London: n.p., 1667.
———. *Christ Exalted: in a Sermon*. London: n.p., 1645
———. *An Exposition Of the whole Book of the* Revelation. London: n.p., 1688.
———. *A Moderate Answer unto Dr. Bastwicks Book*. London: Coe, 1645.
———. *The Parable of the Kingdom of Heaven Expounded*. London: n.p., 1674.
———. *The Shining of a Flaming fire in Zion*. London: Coe, 1645.
———. *The World that Now is; and the World that is to Come: Or the First and Second Coming of* Jesus Christ. London: Snowden, 1681.
Knutton, Immanuel. *Seven Questions about the Controviersie betweene the Church of England, and the Separatists and Anabaptists*. London: Tho[mas] Paine, 1644.
Lake, Peter. "The Laudian Style: Order, Uniformity and the Pursuit of the Beauty of Holiness in the 1630s." In *The Early Stuart Church, 1603–1642*, ed. Kenneth Fincham, 161–86. Stanford: Stanford University Press, 1993.
Lambe, Thomas. *A Confutation of Infants Baptisme*. London: n.p., 1643.
[Lawrence, Henry]. *Of Baptisme*. Rotterdam: n.p., 1646.

Leonard, Bill J. *Baptist Questions, Baptist Answers: Exploring Christian Faith*. Louisville: Westminster John Knox, 2009.

———. *Baptists in America*. New York: Columbia University Press, 2005.

———. *The Challenge of Being Baptist: Owning a Scandalous Past and an Uncertain Future*. Waco: Baylor University Press, 2010.

A Letter of the Ministers of the City of London. London: n.p., 1645.

Leuenberger, Samuel. *Archbishop Cranmer's Immortal Bequest: The Book of Common Prayer of the Church of England*. Trans. Lewis J. Gorin. Grand Rapids: Eerdmans, 1990.

Liberty of Conscience: or the Sole means to obtain Peace and Truth. n.p., 1643.

The Lyn Persecution. n.p., 1692.

MacCulloch, Diarmaid. *The Later Reformation in England 1547-1603*. New York: St. Martin's, 1990.

———. *Thomas Cranmer*. New Haven: Yale University Press, 1996.

MacDonald, Murdina. "London Calvinistic Baptists, 1689–1727: Tensions Within a Dissenting Community under Toleration." DPhil thesis, University of Oxford, 1983.

Mack, Phyllis. *Visionary Women: Ecstatic Prophecy in Seventeenth-Century England*. Berkeley: University of California Press, 1992.

Maltby, Judith. "'By the Book': Parishoners, the Prayer Book and the Established Church." In *The Early Stuart Church, 1603-1642*, ed. Kenneth Fincham, 115–138. Stanford: Stanford University Press, 1993.

———. *Prayer Book and People in Elizabethan and Early Stuart England*. Cambridge: Cambridge University Press, 1998.

Marlow, Isaac. *A Brief Discourse concerning Singing in the Publick Worship of GOD in the Gospel-Church*. London: J. M., 1690.

———. *A Clear Confutation of Mr. Richard Allen*. London, n.p., 1696.

———. *The Controversie of Singing Brought to an End*. London: n.p., 1696.

———. *Prelimited Forms of Praising God, Vocally sung by all the Church together, Proved to be no Gospel-Ordinance, In a Sober Discourse concerning Singing*. London: n.p. 1691.

———. *Truth Soberly Defended in a Serious Reply to Mr. Benjamin Keach's Book*. London: n.p., 1692.

Marshall, Steven. *A Defence of Infant-Baptism: In Answer to two Treatises, and an Appendix to them concerning it*. London: Ric[hard] Cotes, 1646.

Martin, Hugh. "The Baptist Contribution to Early English Hymnody." *BQ* 19 (1962) 195–208.

Matthews, A. G. *Introduction to Calamy Revised*. London: Independent, 1959.

McBeth, H. Leon. "Baptist Beginnings." *BHH* 15 (1980) 36–41.

———. *The Baptist Heritage: Four Centuries of Baptist Witness*. Nashville: Broadman, 1987.

———. *Early English Literature on Religious Liberty to 1689*. New York: Arno, 1980.

McKibbens, Thomas R. "Our Baptist Heritage in Worship." *RE* 80 (1983) 53–69.

Middleditch, Robert T. *A Baptist Church, the Christian's Home*. Charleston: Southern Baptist Publication Society, 1854.

Mitchell, Alexander F. *The Westminster Assembly: Its History and Standards*. London: Nisbet, 1883.

Bibliography

Monck, Thomas, et al. *An Orthodox Creed: Or, A Protestant Confession of Faith*. London: n.p, 1679. In W. Madison Grace, "An Orthodox Creed." *Southwestern Journal of Theology* 48, no. 2 (2006) 127–82.

Moore-Keish, Martha L. *Do This in Remembrance of Me: A Ritual Approach to Reformed Eucharistic Theology*. Grand Rapids: Eerdmans, 2008.

Morford, Thomas. *The Baptist and Independent Churches (So called) Set on Fire*. London: n.p., 1660.

Morgan, Edmund S. *Visible Saints: The History of a Puritan Idea*. New York: New York University Press, 1963.

Muller, Richard A., and Rowland S. Ward. *Scripture and Worship: Biblical Interpretation and the Directory for Public Worship*. Phillipsburg: P. & R., 2007.

Mullins, E. Y. *The Axioms of Religion: A New Interpretation of the Baptist Faith*. Philadelphia: Griffith & Rowland, 1908.

A Narrative of the Proceedings of the General Assembly Of divers Pastors, Messengers and Ministering-Brethren of the Baptized Churches, met together in London. London: n.p., 1689.

A Narrative of the Proceedings of the General Assembly Of the Elders and Messengers of the Baptized Churches sent from divers parts of England *and* Wales. London: n.p., 1691.

A Narrative of the Proceedings of the General Assembly, Consisting Of Elders, Ministers and Messengers, met together in London, from several Parts of England *and* Wales. London: n.p., 1692.

Nelson, Stanley A. "Reflecting on Baptist Origins: The London Confession of Faith of 1644." *BHH* 29 (1994) 33–46.

Nesti, Donald S. *Grace and Faith: An Analysis of Early Quaker Soteriology and Sacramentality*. Pittsburgh: n.p., 1975.

Nicholson, J. F. V. "The Office of 'Messenger' amongst British Baptists in the Seventeenth and Eighteenth Centuries." *BQ* 17 (1958) 206–25.

Norcott, John, William Kiffin, and Richard Claridge. *Baptism Discovered Plainly & Faithfully, According to the Word of God*. London: n.p., 1694.

Norman, R. Stanton. *The Baptist Way: Distinctives of a Baptist Church*. Nashville: Broadman & Holman, 2005.

———. *More Than Just a Name: Preserving Our Baptist Identity*. Nashville: Broadman & Holman, 2001.

Nowlin, William Dudley. *What Baptists Stand For*. Louisville: Baptist Book Concern, 1922.

Nuttall, Geoffrey F. "Church Life in Bunyan's Bedfordshire." *BQ* 26 (1976) 305–13.

Nutter, Bernard. *The Story of the Cambridge Baptists*. Cambridge: Heffer & Sons, 1912.

Owen, J. M. Gwynne. *Records of an Old Association Being A Memorial Volume of the 250th Anniversary of the Midland, Now the West Midland, Baptist Association*. Birmingham: AllDay, 1905.

Owen, John. *The Works of John Owen*. Ed. William H. Goold. 18 vols. London: Johnstone & Hunter, 1850–1855; reprint, Carlisle, PA: Banner of Truth Trust, 1965–1968.

P., G. *A Word of Exhortation to our Separating Brethren of whatever Denomination, especially those commonly called Anabaptist*. Oxford: Hall, 1663.

P., H. *A Looking-Glass for Children*. London: n.p., 1673.

Patient, Thomas. *The Doctrine of Baptism, And the Distinction of the Covenants*. London: Hills, 1654.

Patterson, Paige. *Anatomy of a Reformation: The Southern Baptist Convention, 1978–2004*. Fort Worth: Seminary Hill Press, 2005.
Paul, Thomas. *Some Serious Reflections On that Part of M. Bunions Confession of Faith Touching Church Communion with Unbaptized Persons*. London: Smith, 1673.
Payne, Earnest A. "Baptists and the Laying on of Hands." *BQ* 15 (1954) 203–15.
———. "The Free Church Tradition and Worship." *BQ* 21 (1965) 51–63.
Pendleton, J. M. *Three Reasons Why I Am a Baptist*. Nashville: Graves, Mark, 1857.
Phillips, C. S. *The Background of the Prayer Book*. London: SPCK, 1938.
Pitts, Bill. "Arguing Regenerate Church Membership: Baptist Identity during Its First Decade, 1610–1620." *BHH* 44 (2009) 20–39.
Poe, Harry L. "John Bunyan's Controversy with the Baptists." *BHH* 23 (1988) 25–35.
Powell, Vavasor. *Common-Prayer-Book No Divine Service*. London: Livewell Chapman, 1660.
———. *Spirituall Experiences, Of sundry Belieevers*. London: n.p., 1652.
A Publick Dispute Betwixt John Tombs, John Cragge, Henry Vaughan, *Touching Infant-Baptism*. London: n.p., 1654.
Puritanism and Liberty, Being the Army Debates (1647–9). Ed. A. S. P. Woodhouse. Chicago: University of Chicago Press, 1951.
Remarkable Passages in the Life of William Kiffin. Ed. William Orme. London: n.p., 1823.
Renihan, James M. "'Truly Reformed in a Great Measure': A Brief Defense of the English Separatist Origins of Modern Baptists." *The Journal of Baptist Studies* 3 (2009) 24–32
Rich, Antony D. "Thomas Helwys' First Confession of Faith, 1610." *BQ* 43 (2009) 235–41.
Riker, D. B. *A Catholic Reformed Theologian: Federalism and Baptism in the Thought of Benjamin Keach, 1640–1704*. Eugene, OR: Wipf & Stock, 2010.
Rust, Paul R. *The First of The Puritans and the Book of Common Prayer*. Milwaukee: Bruce, 1949.
Shaw, William A. *A History of the English Church During the Civil Wars*. London: Longmans, Green, 1900.
Sidenham, Cuthbert. *A Christian Sober and Plain Exercitation of The two grand practical Controversies of these Time; Infant-Baptism and Singing of Psalms*. London: Mabb, 1657.
Smectymnuus. *An Answer to a Booke Entituled, An Humble Remonstrance*. London: n.p., 1641.
Smith, M. T. "1677/89 BCF Assistant." http://www.reformedontheweb.com/1677-89LondonBaptistConfessionofFaith.pdf.
Smyth, C. H. *Cranmer & the Reformation under Edward VI*. Westport, CT: Greenwood, 1926.
Smyth, John. *The Differences of the Churches of the Seperation*. n.p., 1608.
———. *Paralleles, Censures, Observations*. n.p, 1609.
Some, Robert. *A Godly Treatise containing and deciding certaine questions, mooved of late in London and other places, touching the Ministerie, Sacraments, and Church*. London: Barker, 1588.
Spilsbury, John. *Gods Ordinance, The Saints Priviledge*. London: Simmons, 1646.
———. *A Treatise Concerning the Lawfull Subject of Baptisme*. London: n.p., 1643.
Spurr, John. *English Puritanism 1603–1689*. NY: St. Martin's, 1998.

Bibliography

Steed, Robert, and Abraham Cheare. *A Plain Discovery of The Unrighteous Judge and False Accuser.* n.p., 1658.

Steere, Douglas V., editor. *Quaker Spirituality: Selected Writing.* New York: Paulist, 1984.

Sturgion, John. *A Plea for Tolleration of Opinions and Perswasions in Matters of Religion, Differing from the Church of England.* London: Dover, 1661.

Sutton, Katherine. *A Christian Womans Experiences of the glorious workings of Gods free grace.* Rotterdam: Goddaeus, 1663.

Taylor, John. *The Brownists Synagogue, or a late Discovery Of their Conventicles, Assemblies, and places of meeting.* n.p., 1641.

———. *Religions Enemies: with a brief and ingenious relation as by Anabaptists, Brownists, Papists, Familists, Atheists and Foolists sawcily presuming to tosse religion in a blanquet.* London: n.p., 1641.

———. *A Swarme of Sectaries, and Schismatiques: Wherein is discovered the strange preaching (or prating) of such as are by their trades Coblers, Tinkers, Pedlers, Weavers, Sowgelders, and Chymney Sweepers.* n.p., 1641.

That Wicked and Blasphemous Petition of Praise-God Barbone, and his Sectarian Crew. London: n.p., 1660.

Tolmie, Murray. *The Triumph of the Saints: The Separate Churches of London 1616–1649.* Cambridge: Cambridge University Press, 1977.

Tombes, John. *An Addition to the Apology For the two Treatises concerning Infant-baptisme.* London: Hills, 1652.

———. *An Antidote Against the Venome of a Passage, in the 5th direction of the Epistle Dedicatory to the whole Book of Mr. Richard Baxter.* London: Sumptner, 1650.

———. *Antipaedobaptism, Or No plain nor obscure Scripture-proof of Infants Baptism, or Church-Membership.* London: Hil[l]s, 1652.

———. *An Apology or Plea for the Two Treatises, and Appendix to them concerning Infant-baptisme.* London: n.p., 1646.

———. *An Examen of the Sermon Of Mr. Stephen Marshall, About Infant-Baptisme, in a Letter sent to him.* London: R. W., 1645.

———. *Felo de Se. Or, Mr. Richard Baxters Self-destroying.* London: Hills, 1659.

———. *Fermentum Pharisaeorum, or, The Leaven of Pharisaicall Wil-Worship.* London: Cotes, 1643.

———. *Jehovah Jireh: or, Gods Providence in Delivering the Godly.* London: Cotes, 1643.

———. *A Plea for Anti-Paedobaptists, Against the Vanity and Falshood of Scribled Papers, Entituled, The Anabaptists Anatomiz'd.* London: Hills, 1654.

———. *A Serious Consideration of the Oath of the Kings Supremacy.* London: Hills, 1660.

———. *A Short Catechism About Baptism.* London: Hills, 1659.

———. *A Supplement to the Serious consideration of the Oath of the Kings Supremacy.* London: Hills, 1660.

Torbet, Robert G. *A History of the Baptists.* Rev. ed. Valley Forge, PA: Judson, 1963.

A True Confession of the Faith, and Humble Acknowledgment of the Alegeance, which wee hir Mastesties Subjects, falsely called Brownists, doo hould towards God. n.p., 1596.

Twisse, William, et al. *Certaine Considerations to Disswade Men from Further Gathering of Churches in this present juncture of Time.* London: White, 1643.

Tyacke, Nicholas. "Archbishop Laud." In *The Early Stuart Church, 1603–1642,* ed. Kenneth Fincham, 51–70. Stanford: Stanford University Press, 1993.

Underhill, Edward Bean, editor. *The Records of a Church of Christ, Meeting at Broadmead, Bristol, 1640-1687*. London: Haddon, 1847.

———. *Records of the Churches of Christ, Gathered at Fenstanton, Warboys, and Hexham. 1644-1720*. London: Haddon Brothers. 1854.

———. *Tracts on Liberty of Conscience*. London: Haddon, 1846.

Underwood, Ted LeRoy. *Primitivism, Radicalism, and the Lamb's War: The Baptist-Quaker Conflict in Seventeenth-Century England*. Oxford: Oxford University Press, 1997.

Ussher, James. *A Body of Divinity: Or the Sum and Substance of Christian Religion*. London: R. J., 1702.

Vaughn, James Barry. "Benjamin Keach." In *Baptist Theologians*, ed. Timothy George and David S. Dockery. Nashville: Broadman & Holman, 2000.

———. "Public Worship and Practical Theology in the Work of Benjamin Keach (1640-1704)." PhD thesis, St. Andrews, 1989.

Walker, M. J. "The Relation of Infants to Church, Baptism, and Gospel in Seventeenth Century Baptist Theology." *BQ* 21 (1966) 242-62.

Walwyn, William. *The Compassionate Samaritane*. [London]: n.p., 1644.

Wamble, Hugh. "Early English Baptist Sectarianism." *RE* 55 (1958) 59-69.

Ward, Wayne. "The Worship of the Church." In *The People of God: Essays on the Believers' Church*, ed. Paul Basden and David S. Dockery, 63-73. Nashville: Broadman, 1991.

Weaver, C. Douglas. "Early English Baptists: Individual Conscience and Eschatological Ecclesiology." *Perspectives in Religious Studies* 38 (2011) 141-58.

———. *In Search of the New Testament Church: The Baptist Story*. Macon, GA: Mercer University Press, 2008.

Weddle, Meredith Baldwin. *Walking in the Way of Peace: Quaker Pacifism in the Seventeenth Century*. New York: Oxford University Press, 2001.

Wetenhall, Edward. *Of Gifts and Offices in the Publick Worship of God*. Dublin: n.p., 1678.

Whinnel, Thomas. *A Sober Reply to Mr. Robert Steed's Epistle Concerning Singing*. London: n.p., 1691.

White, B. E. "The English Particular Baptists and the Great Rebellion, 1640-1660." *BHH* 9 (1974) 16-29.

White, B. R. "Baptist Beginnings and the Kiffin Manuscript." *BHH* 2 (1967) 27-37.

———. *The English Separatist Tradition from the Marian Martyrs to the Pilgrim Fathers*. London: Oxford University Press, 1971.

———. "The Frontiers of Fellowship Between English Baptists, 1609-1660." *Foundations* 11 (1968) 244-56.

———. "Henry Jessey: A Pastor in Politics." *BQ* 25 (1973) 98-110.

———. "The Organisation of the Particular Baptists, 1644-1660." *JEH* 17 (1966) 209-16.

———. "Samuel Eaton, Particular Baptist Pioneer." *BQ* 24 (1971) 10-21.

———. "Thomas Collier and Gangraena Edwards." *BQ* 24 (1971) 99-110.

———. "Thomas Crosby: Baptist Historian, Part 1." *BQ* 21 (1968) 154-68.

———. "Who Really Wrote the 'Kiffin Manuscript'?" *BHH* 1 (1966) 3-10.

———. "William Kiffin—Baptist Pioneer and Citizen of London." *BHH* 2 (1967) 91-103.

White, B. R., ed. *Association Records of the Particular Baptists of England, Wales and Ireland to 1660*. London: Baptist Historical Society, 1971.

Bibliography

Whitley, W. T. *The Baptists of London: 1612–1928*. London: Kingsgate, 1928.

———. *Congregational Hymn-Singing*. London: Dent & Sons, 1933.

———. *Minutes of the General Assembly of the General Baptist Churches in England, with Kindred Records*. 2 vols. London: Kingsgate, 1909.

———. *The Witness of History to Baptist Principles*. London: Alexander & Shepheard, 1897.

Whosoever Will: A Biblical-Theological Critique of Five-Point Calvinism. Nashville: B. & H. Academic, 2010.

Williams, Roger. *Queries of highest Consideration*. London: n.p., 1643.

Wilson, Gladys. *Quaker Worship*. London: Bannisdale, 1952.

Winter, E. P. "Calvinist and Zwinglian Views of the Lord's Supper among the Baptists of the 17th Century." *BQ* 15 (1954) 323–29.

———. "The Lord's Supper: Admission and Exclusion among the Baptists of the Seventeenth Century." *BQ* 17 (1958) 267–81.

Woodhouse, H. F. *The Doctrine of the Church in Anglican Theology, 1547–1603*. London: SPCK, 1954.

Woodman, Simon. "The Dissenting Voice: Journeying Together toward a Baptist Hermeneutic." In *The "Plainly Revealed" Word of God? Baptist Hermeneutics in Theory and Practice*, ed. Helen Dare and Simon Woodman, 213–28. Macon, GA: Mercer University Press, 2011.

Woolley, Davis C. "Editorial." *BHH* 1 (1966) 2.

Wright, Joseph. *Folly Detected: Or, Some Animadversions on a Book called, A Brief Discourse Concerning Singing*. London: n.p., 1691.

Wright, Stephen. "Baptist Alignments and the Restoration of Immersion, 1638–44 Part 1." *BQ* 40 (2004) 261–80.

———. "Baptist Alignments and the Restoration of Immersion, 1638–44 Part 2." *BQ* 40 (2004) 346–69.

———. *The Early English Baptists, 1603–1649*. Rochester: Boydell, 2006.

———. "Edward Barber (c. 1595–1663) and His Friends Part 1." *BQ* 41 (2006) 355–70.

Wrightson, Keither. *English Society 1580–1680*. New Brunswick: Rutgers University Press, 1982; reprint, 2003.

Yarbrough, Slayden A. "The English Separatist Influence on the Baptist Tradition of Church–State Issues." *BHH* 20 (1985) 14–23.

Yarnell, Malcolm B., III. "Neither Calvinists nor Arminians but Baptists." White Paper 36. http://www.baptisttheology.org/documents/NeitherCalvinistsNorArminiansButBaptists.pdf.

———. *Royal Priesthood in the English Reformation*. Oxford: Oxford University Press, forthcoming.

Index

Adams, Richard, 19, 23, 55
Adiaphora, 39, 123
Ainsworth, Henry, 14, 34, 36, 38, 53, 88, 111, 144, 153, 160
Allen, Richard, 159–60, 180, 204
Ames, William, 44, 55
Amsterdam, 10, 34, 144
Arminianism, 8, 40–41, 47
Army, New Model. *See* New Model Army

Baillie, Robert, 44, 46, 96, 174
Bakewell, Thomas, 45, 47, 67, 77, 155, 173
Baptism, 5–6, 8–10, 20, 39, 55–59, 61–62, 81, 92, 95–114, 117–18, 127, 136–38, 146–49, 154, 162–63, 180–81
Baptism, believers', 5–6, 56, 95, 97, 99, 134, 139, 146, 162
Baptism, infant, 19, 56, 81, 104, 108, 121, 146, 180
Barber, Edward, 21, 46, 56–57, 74–75, 81, 132, 135, 140, 165
Barbone, Praisegod, 9, 20, 56–59, 84, 96–101, 107–8, 113–14, 117, 133
Barrow, Henry, 32, 34, 36, 57
Baxter, Richard, 49–50, 77, 92, 122, 153, 172
Bedfordshire, 100–101, 169
Book of Common Prayer, 14, 27–30, 34–35, 38, 41, 44, 50, 56, 66, 76, 91, 101, 109, 125, 150, 162, 164–65

Bradshaw, William, 13, 30, 88, 111–12, 119, 124, 160
Broadmead, 10, 21, 62, 75, 181
Bromhead, Hugh and Ann, 36–37
Brownists, 45–46, 53, 172
Burroughs, Jeremiah, 9, 12, 14–15, 20, 45, 54, 92, 119–20, 128, 144, 151, 154, 161, 165–66, 169
Busher, Leonard, 66

Calamy, Edmund, 42, 45, 81, 121, 135, 165
Calvinism, 3, 8, 12, 40–41, 64, 80, 116, 148, 167, 202
Cambridge, 20, 32, 74
Canne, John, 9–10, 34, 62, 125
Cartwright, Thomas, 32, 62, 111
Chamberlain, Peter, 136
Charles I, 40–42, 49, 164
Charles II, 49–50, 152, 158, 171
Chauncy, Isaac, 106, 126, 132–33
Cheare, Abraham, 50, 170–71
Clapham, Henoch, 14
Coleman Street, 21–22, 74
Collier, Thomas, 21, 47, 80, 117, 134
Collins, Hercules, 23, 71, 76, 95, 103, 109, 129, 137, 147, 159–60, 171, 179
Collins, William, 23, 187, 189
Confession, First London (1644), 19, 47, 60, 72, 73, 77, 99–100, 103, 106, 115, 117, 149, 152, 167

239

Index

Confession, First London (1646), 47, 114, 159
Confession, First London (1651), 47, 115
Confession, Second London (1677), 64–65, 90, 93, 116, 171–72, 192, 203
Confession, True (1596), 38, 60, 89
Confession, Westminster (1646), 64, 68, 117, 125, 133, 169
Cotton, John, 155, 161, 168, 177
Covenant, 54, 59, 79–82, 94–96, 114, 148, 168–70, 220
Cox, Benjamin, 20–23, 47, 66, 81, 83, 115, 117, 121–22, 157, 164
Cox, Nehemiah, 23, 100
Cranmer, Thomas, 9, 27–29, 34, 38–39, 89, 111, 150
Cromwell, Oliver, 49
Cromwell, Thomas, 27

Danvers, Henry, 136–38
Denne, Henry, 18, 20, 22, 75, 174
Denne, John, 37, 58, 99, 134
Devonshire Square, 23, 104, 183
Directory for Public Worship, 13, 43–44, 69, 91, 107, 166, 169, 173–74
Discipline, Church, 9, 11, 61–62, 85, 106, 117

Eaton, Samuel, 76, 131
Edward VI, 28–29, 140
Edwards, Thomas, 47, 60, 67, 69, 74, 131, 144, 165, 175
Elizabeth I, 29–34, 39

Family Worship, 169–72, 204, 219
Featley, Daniel, 42, 49, 53, 61, 68–69, 72, 114, 120, 125, 155–56, 173, 168
Ford, Thomas, 179, 194, 214
Fox, George, 211

Geree, John, 97, 114, 118, 180
Gifford, John, 100
Gillespie, George, 21, 43–44, 67, 112, 123, 128, 151, 153–54, 160
Glorious Revolution, the, 50, 152, 185
Goodwin, John, 22, 45, 91, 96, 210
Goodwin, Thomas, 9, 20, 43–44, 55, 87
Grantham, Thomas, 15, 50, 61, 67, 78, 86–87, 92, 98, 115–16, 124, 132, 136–39, 141, 162, 192, 209, 221
Griffith, John, 22, 50, 136, 138, 180
Grindal, Edmund, 31

Hall, Thomas, 80, 122
Hardcastle, Thomas, 23, 75
Helwys, Thomas, 8, 34, 37, 66, 105
Henry VIII, 26–29
Hermeneutic, 9, 17, 131, 136, 145–46, 198–200, 214, 222
Howe, Samuel, 45–46, 76, 83, 113, 165, 174

Independents, 4, 8, 19, 31, 46–49, 54, 66, 72, 79, 106, 174–75, 202

Jacob, Henry, 19, 34, 37, 54, 168
James I, 39–41
James II, 50, 185
Jessey, Henry, 15–16, 19–21, 56, 58, 87, 92, 95, 97–101, 104, 106–7, 116, 118, 130, 133–34, 150, 167, 171, 188
Johnson, Francis, 20, 34–35 37, 53, 120, 128

Keach, Benjamin, 14, 22–23, 63–64, 71, 79, 84–89, 90, 117, 129–30, 137–39, 149, 164, 168, 171, 173, 179–81,

Index

Keach, Benjamin (*cont.*) 183–93, 195–202, 204–8, 214, 220
Kiffin, William, 1, 5, 10, 15, 17–21, 23, 31, 45, 48, 55, 58–64, 71, 75, 82, 85, 87, 90, 94–96, 98–99, 102, 103, 106, 108, 113, 119, 125, 127, 129, 133, 136, 140–41, 148–49, 151, 159, 163, 166, 175, 184, 186–88, 190–93
Knollys, Hanserd, 15, 17, 20–21, 23, 50, 60, 63, 69–71, 73, 75, 78, 85–87, 117, 121, 140, 147, 149, 152, 158, 162–64, 166–67, 173–75, 178, 180–81, 187–89, 194, 198–201, 204, 210, 214, 220

Lambe, Thomas, 21, 74–75, 95–96, 161
Lathrop, John, 19–20
Laud, William, 40–41, 152, 164
Laying on of hands, 14, 22, 75, 118, 134–39, 180, 184, 196, 219
Levellers, 49, 66, 74
Lilburne, John, 49, 75
Liturgy, 18, 28, 37, 116, 124, 153–54, 202
Lord's Supper, 14, 41, 64, 77, 100–102, 117, 119, 125, 127–30, 148, 163, 189

Marlow, Isaac, 183, 186–91, 197–202, 205–8
Marshall, Stephen, 24, 44–45, 56, 72, 80, 93, 97, 165–66
Mary I, 29, 39

New Model Army, 49, 74
Norcott, John, 23, 71, 162, 193
Normative Principle, 35, 103, 111–12, 126–27, 130, 159, 201, 206

Nye, Philip, 20, 43

Oates, Samuel, 22
Ordinance, definition of, 15–16, 117–18
Owen, John, 4, 62, 68, 71–73, 76, 127, 132, 152–53, 161
Oxford, 20, 22, 56, 74

Patient, Thomas, 10, 75, 108, 117, 176
Paul, Thomas, 23, 61, 101–2, 127, 134
Powell, Vavasor, 14, 50, 66, 76, 123–24, 130, 150
Preaching, 18, 30–31, 34, 36, 44, 49, 60, 64, 117, 134, 150–53, 164–69, 201, 206–7
Presbyterians, 13, 19, 31, 39–49, 56, 64, 66–73, 76–79, 122, 127, 141, 144, 156, 174, 178, 212
Priesthood of Believers, 4, 28, 52, 54, 61–62, 71–76, 109, 211–12
Prophesyings, 31, 35–36, 125, 152
Psalms in Worship, 117, 155, 161, 176–77, 186, 198, 201
Puritans, 12, 30–34, 37, 39–43, 62, 77, 88, 102, 109, 150, 164–65, 169, 202

Quakers, 131–35, 197, 209–15

Regulative Principle, 12, 35, 53, 102, 111, 120, 126, 130, 182, 197, 201–2, 214, 218
Restoration, the, 13, 44, 66, 152

Separatists, 9–12, 19–20, 25, 30–39, 46, 53–54, 66, 83, 94, 105–6, 116
Sheppard, Thomas, 20
Sidenham, Cuthbert, 127, 176–77

Index

Singing, 107, 117–18, 129, 152, 155, 158, 161, 168, 175–80, 186, 188, 191, 193–209
Smectymnuus, 44, 101
Smyth, John, 11, 34, 36–38, 57, 178
Spilsbury, John, 17–21, 56–59, 79–80, 82–84, 95–96, 106–18, 113–14, 133, 136, 146–47
Steed, Robert, 1, 23, 100, 160, 176–77, 187–89, 201
Sutton, Katherine, 150, 175–76

Terrill, Edward, 3, 10, 74, 99
Tillam, Thomas, 21
Tiverton, 170
Tombes, John, 15–16, 21–23, 47, 56, 61, 67, 72, 77, 80–81, 96–98, 104–5, 118, 120, 122, 124, 146–47, 157, 188
Twisse, William, 71

Walwyn, William, 66
Westminster Assembly, 22, 43–45, 47, 66–68, 71, 89, 94, 112, 127, 171
Wetenhall, Edward, 44, 49, 74, 155–56, 161
Whinnel, Thomas, 63, 155, 168, 187, 202, 215
Whitechapel, 22
Whitgift, John, 32, 111
Williams, Roger, 47, 54–55, 130

www.ingramcontent.com/pod-product-compliance
Lightning Source LLC
Chambersburg PA
CBHW050848230426
43667CB00012B/2204